Southwest Colorado
High Country Day Hikes

Ouray, Silverton & Lake City

by Anne and Mike Poe

Take a Hike Guidebooks®

Cover photo by Anne Poe
Ice Lake near Silverton, Colorado

Southwest Colorado
High Country Day Hikes

Ouray, Silverton & Lake City

by Anne and Mike Poe

Published by Take A Hike Guidebooks
848 N Rainbow Blvd. #1804
Las Vegas, NV 89107

To order books, email: takeahikeguidebooks@gmail.com

Trail conditions change frequently in the backcountry due to many factors. We appreciate hiker's comments and feedback. For trail updates, corrections, feedback or comments, go to: facebook.com/takeahikeguidebooks.

If you are unhappy in any way with this book, please contact us at takeahikeguidebooks@gmail.com and we will do our best to meet your needs.

ISBN 978-0-9829766-5-4

Book Layout & Cover Design	Kelly Jo Tullberg, KJ Graphic Design
Maps	Created with Garmin Basecamp
Map Design	Anne Poe
Photography	Anne and Mike Poe
Contributing Photographers	Sigrid Werbitsch Vienna, Austria Rozanne Evans Ridgway, Colorado
Contributing Researchers	Sigrid & Andy Werbitsch Vienna, Austria Rozanne Evans and Al Lowande Ridgway, Colorado Warren Wieboldt Silverton, Colorado Jen and Randy Parker Ridgway, Colorado

Other books by Anne and Mike Poe

- Crested Butte Colorado 65 Scenic Day Hikes 2012
- Southwest Colorado High Country Day Hikes Telluride 2013
- Utah National Parks Arches & Canyonlands Day Hikes 2013
- On Our Own: A Bicycling Adventure in Southeast Asia 2011

Printed in Korea

Dedication

To Betsy & Bill, Molly & John
For always believing in us

Hike	Name	Circuit	Difficulty	Stars	Miles	Gain	Aspen	Flowers	Vehicles	Page
Ouray Town Hikes 1-7						**TH Map pg. 24**				
1	Ouray Perimeter Trail Loop	Loop		3	4.14	+1529	Y		CAR	26
2	Upper Cascade Falls & Chief Ouray Mine	RT		3	4.46	+2290	Y		CAR	32
3	Portland Mine Loop	Loop		3	3.48	+1223	Y		CAR	36
4	Baby Bathtubs Loop	Loop		2	0.73	+284	Y		CAR	40
5	Oak Creek to Silvershield	Shuttle		2	4.12	+1273			CAR	42
6	Ice Park Loop	Loop		2	1.98	+523			CAR	46
7a	Sutton Mine Trail to Ouray Overlook/ Return 1	RT		2	0.98	+600			CAR	48
7b	Sutton Mine Trail to Bear Creek Overlook/ Return 2	RT		4	3.20	+1305		Y	CAR	
7C	Sutton Mine Trail to Mine/ Return 3	RT		4	4.12	+1579		Y	CAR	
Ouray Environs Hikes 8-15						**TH Map pg. 52**				
8a	Yankee Boy Basin Start 8a to Pass	RT		5/6	5.14	+1941		Y	SUV	54
8b	Yankee Boy Basin Start 8b to Pass	RT		6	3.02	+1234		Y	4X4	
8c	Yankee Boy Basin Start 8c to Pass	RT		6	2.00	+597		Y	4X4	
8d	Yankee Boy Basin Start 8d to Blue Lakes North Access Trailhead	Shuttle		6/3	7.69	+1042		Y	4X4	
9a	Yankee Boy Basin Loop/ Start 9a	Loop		5/6	3.95	+1336		Y	CAR	60
9b	Yankee Boy Basin Loop/ Start 9b	Loop		6	1.90	+688		Y	4X4	
10a	Blue Lakes Trail to Lower Lakes/ Return 1	RT		3/6	6.68	+2226		Y	CAR	66
10b	Blue Lakes Trail to Upper Lakes/ Return 2	RT		3/6	8.68	+3111		Y	CAR	
10c	Blue Lakes Trail to Blue Lakes Pass/ Return 3	RT		3/6	11.38	+4471		Y	CAR	
10d	Blue Lakes Trail to Yankee Boy Basin	Shuttle		3/6	7.69	+4045		Y	CAR 4X4	
11a	Blaine Basin to Waterfall Viewpoint/ Return 1	RT		3	4.32	+1017		Y	CAR	70
11b	Blaine Basin to Lower Basin/ Return 2	RT		3/5	6.26	+1925		Y	CAR	
11c	Blaine Basin to Upper Basin/ Return 3	RT		3/5	7.26	+2250		Y	CAR	
12	West Dallas Creek Trail	RT		4	3.78	+921	Y	Y	SUV	74
13	Baldy Peak via Storm's Gulch Loop	Loop		3/6	6.84	+2692	Y	Y	CAR 4X4	78
14a	Bear Creek Trail to Overlook/ Return 1	RT		5	2.42	+1289			CAR	82
14b	Bear Creek Trail to Grizzly Bear Mine/ Return 2	RT		5	4.92	+2614			CAR	
14c	Bear Creek Trail to Yellow Jacket Mine/ Return 3	RT		5	8.42	+3884			CAR	
15a	Spirit Gulch to Basin/ Return 1	RT		3/5	3.18	+924	Y	Y	CAR	86
15b	Spirit Gulch to Highest Point/ Return 2	RT		6	5.06	+1575	Y	Y	CAR	
15c	Spirit Gulch to Shuttle	Shuttle		6	6.56	+1653	Y	Y	CAR	

Hike	Name	Circuit	Difficulty	Stars	Miles	Gain	Aspen	Flowers	Vehicles	Page
Silverton North Hikes 16-25						**TH Map pg. 94**				
16a	Black Bear Pass Start 16a to Pass	RT		5	6.32	+1991		Y	CAR	96
16b	Black Bear Pass Start 16b to Pass	RT		5	4.32	+1493		Y	SUV	
17	Grand Traverse	Shuttle		6	8.06	+1353		Y	C/S	100
18a	Porphyry Basin Loop/ Start 18a	Loop		6	5.44	+1562		Y	SUV	106
18b	Porphyry Basin Loop/ Start 18b	Loop		6	3.32	+903		Y	4X4	
19a	Porphyry Basin to Columbine Pass/ Start 19a	RT		6	6.94	+2244		Y	SUV	112
19b	Porphyry Basin to Columbine Pass/ Start 19b	RT		6	4.74	+1578		Y	4X4	
20a	Columbine TH to Saddle/ Return 1	RT		2/6	4.12	+2305		Y	SUV	118
20b	Columbine TH to Lake/ Return 2	RT		2/6	6.42	+2779		Y	SUV	
20c	Columbine TH to Pass/ Return 3	RT		2/6	7.96	+3233		Y	SUV	
21a	US Basin to McMillan Peak	RT		6	3.86	+1541		Y	SUV	122
21b	US Basin to Shuttle	Shuttle		6	3.77	+1263		Y	SUV	
22	Ohio Peak	RT		6	2.00	+738		Y	SUV	128
23	Nancy's Grassy Peak	RT		6	4.00	+1271		Y	SUV	132
24	Silver Cloud Mine	RT		3	2.34	+995			CAR	136
25	Paradise Basin	RT		4	2.76	+1042		Y	CAR	138
Silverton West & South Hikes 26-34						**TH Map pg. 146**				
26a	Clear Lake Trail/ Start 26a	RT		6	3.80	+1603		Y	SUV	148
26b	Clear Lake Trail/ Start 26b	RT		6	2.60	+1166		Y	SUV	
27a	Ice Lake Trail Start 27a to Ice Lake	RT		3/6	6.40	+2635		Y	CAR	152
27b	Ice Lake Trail Start 27b to Ice Lake	RT		3/6	5.32	+2129		Y	CAR	
27c	Add Fuller Lake	RT		6	+1.60	+307		Y	CAR	
27d	Add Island Lake	RT		6	+1.10	+228		Y	CAR	
28	Hope Lake Pass	RT		3/5	4.88	+1866		Y	SUV	160
29a	Rico-Silo Trail to Rolling Pass/ Return 1	RT		3/6	4.86	+1886		Y	SUV	162
29b	Rico-Silo Trail to Jura Knob/ Return 2	RT		6	8.12	+2749		Y	SUV	
30a	Pass Creek Trail to Engineer Basin/ Return 1	RT		3/6	5.20	+1201		Y	CAR	168
30b	Pass Creek Trail to Jura Knob/ Return 2	RT		6	10.08	+2685		Y	CAR	
30c	Pass Creek Trail to Little Molas Lake	Shuttle		6	14.66	+3566		Y	CAR	
31	Little Molas Colorado Trail North	RT		5	5.00	+947		Y	CAR	172
32	Little Molas Colorado Trail South/ Go any distance	Shuttle		4	2.38	+272		Y	CAR	174
33	Spencer Saddle	RT		6	5.48	+1883		Y	CAR	176
34	West Lime Creek	RT		3	5.70	+1273			CAR	182

Hike	Name	Circuit	Difficulty	Stars	Miles	Gain	Aspen	Flowers	Vehicles	Page
Silverton East Hikes 35-48						**TH Map pg. 184**				
35a	Whitehead Trail to Pond Overlook/ Return 1	RT		6	5.02	+1411		Y	SUV	186
35b	Whitehead Trail to Peak & Loop	Loop		6	6.18	+2241		Y	SUV	
36	Kansas City Mine	RT		4	4.00	+1795		Y	CAR	192
37a	Velocity Basin to Saddle/ Return 1	RT		6	1.94	+1330		Y	CAR	194
37b	Velocity Basin to Peak/ Return 2	RT		6	2.74	+1910		Y	CAR	
38a	Little Giant Basin Start 38a to Ridge	RT		6	3.44	+1740		Y	SUV	200
38b	Little Giant Basin Start 38b to Ridge	RT		6	1.94	+1081		Y	SUV	
38c	Add to Promontory	RT		6	+0.36	+218		Y	SUV	
38d	Add to Peak	RT		6	+1.00	+492		Y	SUV	
39a	Silver Lake Trail Start 39a to Lake	RT		6	3.22	+1708		Y	SUV	206
39b	Silver Lake Trail Start 39b to Lake	RT		6	2.22	+1102		Y	4X4	
40	Boarding House	RT		6	3.50	+1824			4X4	210
41	Stony Pass CDT South/Any Distance	RT		6	8.20	+2007		Y	SUV	216
42	Canby Mountain Loop & Options	Loop		6	3.20	+1021		Y	SUV	220
43	Cunningham Gulch to CDT	RT		5	3.70	+1490		Y	SUV	226
44a	Highland Mary Lakes Trail to HM Lakes/ Return 1	RT		6	3.50	+1393		Y	SUV	230
44b	Highland Mary Lakes Trail to Verde Lakes/ Return 2	RT		6	6.00	+1806		Y	SUV	
44c	Highland Mary Lakes Trail to Continental Divide Loop	Loop		6	7.36	+2341		Y	SUV	
45a	Spencer Basin Trail to Spenser Basin/ Return 1	RT		6	3.52	+1526		Y	SUV	236
45b	Spencer Basin Trail to Sugarloaf Peak/ Return 2	RT		6	5.80	+2316		Y	SUV	
45c	Spencer Basin Trail to Highland Mary Lakes Loop	Loop		6	6.56	+2388		Y	SUV	
46	Maggie Gulch to CDT	Loop		6	3.32	+1145		Y	SUV	242
47a	Maggie Gulch to Crystal Lake Start 47a	RT		4	3.20	+1407		Y	SUV	246
47b	Maggie Gulch to Crystal Lake Start 47b	RT		4	1.64	+736		Y	SUV	
48	Minnie Gulch to CDT & Ridge	RT		6	9.50	+2332		Y	SUV	250
Lake City Hikes 49-67						**TH Map pg. 258**				
49a	Tumble Creek to Creek Crossing/ Return 1	RT		3	3.96	+785			CAR	260
49b	Tumble Creek To View Meadows/ Return 2	RT		4	6.44	+1590		Y	CAR	
49c	Tumble Creek to Saddle/ Return 3	RT		5	8.40	+2007		Y	CAR	
50a	CT East from Spring Creek Pass to Mesa/ Return 1	RT		3/5	3.80	+1370			CAR	264
50b	CT East from Spring Creek Pass to Ponds/ Return 2	RT		3/5	9.60	+1978		Y	CAR	
50c	CT East from Spring Creek Pass to Miner's Creek/ Return 3	RT		3/5	11.80	+2752		Y	CAR	
50d	CT East from Spring Creek Pass to Baldy Cinco Peak	RT		3/5	5.83	+2510		Y	CAR	

The Grenadiers: Hike 44

Hike	Name	Circuit	Difficulty	Stars	Miles	Gain	Aspen	Flowers	Vehicles	Page
Lake City Hikes continued										
51	CT West from Spring Creek Pass	RT		4/6	8.80	+1424			CAR	270
52a	473 to Rambouillet Park/ Go any distance	RT		5	8.92	+1106		Y	CAR	274
52b	473 to Slumgullion Peak	RT		6	7.00	+1374		Y	CAR	
53a	CT East from Wager Road to Return 1	RT		6	5.44	+1446		Y	4X4	278
53b	CT East from Wager Road to Return 2	RT		6	7.40	+1740		Y	4X4	
53c	CT East from Wager Road to Shuttle 1	Shuttle		6	8.25	+1610		Y	4X4	
53d	CT East from Wager Road to Shuttle 2	Shuttle		6	11.30	+2158		Y	4X4	
53e	CT East from Wager Road to Shuttle 3	Shuttle		6/3	12.20	+1660		Y	4X4	
54a	CT West from Wager Road to Saddle/ Return1	RT		6	7.56	+1461		Y	4X4	286
54b	CT West from Wager Road to Cataract TH	Shuttle		6/3	10.50	+2047		Y	4X4	
55a	Cataract Gulch Trail to Waterfall/ Return 1	RT		3	4.00	+2184		Y	CAR	292
55b	Cataract Gulch Trail to Lake Viewpoint/ Return 2	RT		3/5	9.80	+3731		Y	CAR	
55c	Cataract Gulch Trail to CDT/ Return 3	RT		3/6	11.00	+4073		Y	CAR	

Cooper Creek Upper Basin from notch: Hike 59

Hike	Name	Circuit	Difficulty	Stars	Miles	Gain	Aspen	Flowers	Vehicles	Page
Lake City Hikes continued										
56a	Cuba Gulch to CT/ Return 1	RT		3/6	6.16	+1889		Y	SUV	298
56b	Cuba Gulch to High Point/ Return 2	RT		3/6	7.72	+2308		Y	SUV	
56c	Cuba Gulch to Return 3	RT		3/6	8.96	+2547		Y	SUV	
57a	Snare Basin Trail to Lower Basin/ Return 1	RT		5	5.10	+1647	Y	Y	SUV	304
57b	Snare Basin Trail to Snare Basin/ Return 2	RT		5	8.00	+2500	Y	Y	SUV	
58a	Silver Creek Trail to Redcloud Peak/ Return 1	RT		6	9.26	+3994		Y	SUV	310
58b	Silver Creek Trail to Sunshine Peak/ Return 2	RT		6	12.00	+5287		Y	SUV	
59a	Cooper Creek to 2nd Creek Crossing/ Return 1	RT		5	4.94	+1407		Y	SUV	314
59b	Cooper Creek to High Basin/ Return 2	RT		5	6.52	+2104		Y	SUV	
59c	Cooper Creek to Lake/ Return 3	RT		5	7.58	+2648		Y	SUV	
60	American Basin	RT		6	1.80	+424		Y	SUV	320
61a	Handies Trail to Grouse Gulch Saddle	RT		6	3.54	+1935		Y	SUV	324
61b	Handies Trail to Sloan Lake/ Return 1	RT		6	3.06	+1334		Y	SUV	
61c	Handies Trail to Handies Peak/ Return 2	RT		6	5.40	+2498		Y	SUV	
61d	Handies Trail to Grizzly Gulch TH	Shuttle		6	6.62	+2498		Y	SUV	
62a	Uncompahgre Trail to Viewpoint/ Return 1	RT		6	4.74	+1545		Y	4X4	330
62b	Uncompahgre Trail to Rock Climb/ Return 2	RT		6	6.60	+2378		Y	4X4	
62c	Uncompahgre Trail to Peak/ Return 3	RT		6	7.30	+2988		Y	4X4	
63a	Ridge Stock Driveway to Ridge/ Return 1	RT		6	5.70	+1472		Y	4X4	336
63b	Ridge Stock Driveway to Peak/ Return 2	RT		6	6.70	+1806		Y	4X4	
63c	Ridge Stock Driveway to Ridge walk/ Return 3	RT		6	11.76	+2171		Y	4X4	
63d	Ridge Stock Driveway to Shuttle	Shuttle		6/3	13.00	+1836		Y	4X4	
64a	Matterhorn Basin to High Saddle	RT		6	4.96	+1723		Y	4X4	342
64b	Matterhorn Basin to Matterhorn Peak	RT		6	6.40	+2844		Y	4X4	
64c	Matterhorn Basin to Wetterhorn Peak	RT		6	7.20	+2836		Y	4X4	
65a	Matterhorn Cutoff to Alice Creek Loop	Loop		6/3	6.07	+2119		Y	SUV	348
65b	Matterhorn Cutoff to Waterfall/ Return 1	RT		6	3.00	+1315		Y	4X4	
66a	High Country Traverse to American Lake/ Return 1	RT		6	6.46	+815		Y	4X4	354
66b	High Country Traverse to Boundary/ Return 2	RT		6	10.12	+1397		Y	4X4	
66c	High Country Traverse to N Henson Creek Road/ Option 3	Shuttle		6	7.44	+479		Y	4X4	
66d	High Country Traverse to Mary Alice TH/ Option 4	Shuttle		6/3	9.48	+1314		Y	4X4	
66e	High Country Traverse to Matterhorn TH/ Option 5	Shuttle		6	10.39	+1615		Y	4X4	
67	American Flats to Engineer Pass	Shuttle		5	6.93	+2163		Y	4X4	364

Table of Contents

Spencer Saddle: Hike 33

Introduction

Why Hike Southwest Colorado

There is a special aura about Southwest Colorado. The region has an astounding array of geologic formations, including hot springs, Anasazi cliff dwellings in Mesa Verde, the highest mountain top mesa in the world at Grand Mesa, the majestic Black Canyon of the Gunnison River and most of the highest peaks on the northern continent situated in its five national parks and five wilderness areas. It has more Victorian buildings, mining history, ghost towns, wild flowers, magnificent aspen forests, picturesque auto tours and 4-wheel drive high mountain exploration roads than any other geographic area in the north continent, and perhaps all the world. This is of course not to mention some of Colorado's best snow skiing. Along with all of this is some of the most memorable high country hiking imaginable.

This volume features three historic Victorian towns as the hubs for 67 scenic trails: Ouray, Silverton and Lake City. We include early season trails that have lower elevations, but most of the hikes are above timberline with trailheads starting over 9,000 feet and climbing to over 14,000 feet. Hiking above timberline is extremely gratifying; it evokes a sense of grandeur not found in the forests or lower elevations. Numerous hikes follow parts of the spectacular Continental Divide Trail and the Colorado Trail. Many hikes are cross country following intermittent animal and old pack trails. We included some of the most popular 14ers as well as some of the easier peaks to introduce this type of environment to some that might not otherwise experience the opportunity.

This is Colorado high country hiking at its best. We enjoyed the months on the trails and hope you enjoy this book.

Why this Guidebook is Different

This book is exclusively day hikes, written for you, the day hiker. You love to hike, but you don't have any interest in shuttling a heavy pack on your back, or sleeping on the ground. You prefer to hike light and return to your camper or hotel for a good meal and a comfortable sleep. All the hikes in this book can be walked in a day. There are long ones, short ones, easy ones, and difficult ones, but after each hike you can sleep in a bed.

As avid day hikers ourselves, we have found over the years that our time has become more precious. When we go to a new area, it takes effort to research what hikes are right for us. Often, we are visiting the area for just a weekend, or a week, and wish to find the best hike we can for the time we have. We are very particular about the kind of hikes we are looking for. We have also discovered, in conversation with many day hikers we met along the trail, that they too have specific parameters in mind when selecting a hike. Our values are incredibly similar.

When we hike, we want to be wowed. We want to be thrilled along the way with views of looming peaks and cascading rivers plunging into profound chasms. We like vistas that stretch from horizon to horizon. We like precipitous cliffs and trails that cling to them. We like to descend into massive river canyons. We like intriguing twists and turns that hide, then reveal their secrets as we round each corner. We want to surround ourselves with fields of bright and cheery wildflowers spilling across acres of colorful meadows, the horizon exploding with peaks and valleys demanding exploration. We like color: wildflowers, aspens, oak, red rocks, turquoise lakes, big skies. We want killer photo opportunities.

We don't like to hike for miles in thick, viewless forests. We are not fond of scrub and brush that stands taller than our five foot, five inch frames. We are quickly irritated by cantankerous boulder strewn trails that force our eyes downward. We dislike hiking an uninspired trail all day for the sake of one final viewpoint.

When we go purposely to a wilderness area to hike, we are looking for more than just exercise. We want the remaining wilderness pieces of our world to awaken our primordial senses and unleash our civilized constraints. We want to feel the pulse of wild nature course through our veins as it energizes and quickens our step.

Yankee Boy Basin: Hike 9

We want to be overwhelmed by so much splendor that it spills over in enthusiasm for days thereafter. We seek the superlatives Mother Nature created.

Many hiking guides leave us guessing as to what the trail really has to offer. How many times have you read a trail description that tells you where to start and end, but offers no clues as to what might excite you along the way? How do you really know if you want to spend your precious time on this hike? Like us, many hikers are engaged in the art of guessing when it comes to choosing a satisfactory trail.

A guidebook should guide. Its purpose is to provide a variety of information and detail so the reader can decide which hikes are personally most suitable. In addition to important information such as distance, difficulty, and other basics, we think there should be a rating system for scenic value. Of course, like difficulty ratings, scenic ratings are subjective. This system developed around our personal preferences, and from around preferences other hikers have shared with us. We have rated these hikes using criteria that are essential to us when choosing to do a particular hike. We hope our system helps you find the trails that are worth your precious time.

Scenic Rating System

- **Six Stars:** These are often hikes that go up peaks or to high passes where expansive vistas evoke the feeling of Rocky Mountain grandeur.
- **Five Stars:** You may not ascend a peak or hike to a pass. The scenic splendor of the trail may be manifested in following a rushing stream, or winding through a grove of stately aspens. Dramatic vistas are frequent, becoming consistent. There are beaver ponds, lakes, wildflowers, expansive meadows, peaks, gorges. Many views encompass a staggering 180 degrees.
- **Four Stars:** The scenery is grand along the way, but it is less consistent. There may be some short sections hiking through dense forest. The high adrenaline experience is not as sustained as a six or five star hike, but the experience is exhilarating, and you will look forward to repeating this hike.
- **Three Stars:** These hikes are very worthwhile, as there are vistas along the way. More time may be spent hiking through forests, but the forests are mature and healthy and create an overall feeling of beauty and tranquility. There may be other items of interest along the trail; a creek, ponds, small waterfalls. It is a very satisfying hike.
- **Two Stars:** These trails, for much of the total distance, may pass through thick forest with only occasional views. They may impart less a feeling of wilderness; there may be roads or houses nearby.
- **One Star:** These hikes travel mostly through forest that may have more deadfall. The trees are not as stately. There are fewer vistas. The area feels overused. The destination is not really special compared to other choices.
- **A Range of Stars:** Example 2&6: This is a hike where the end portion of the trail is very scenic, but hikers must spend time along a less interesting approach. Hikers can decide if the destination is worth the effort. Example: 5&2: The beginning portion of the trail is more scenically rich than the ending section.

Summary Section

In addition to the star ratings, there is a summary box near the beginning of every hike. This is your instant reference to what you will see on this hike. You do not need to read the Trail Description to know if you want to do this hike.

How To Use This Guide

Maps

Maps are the essence of a guidebook. The book is divided into six sections. Each section begins with a Trail Locator Map, a map of the area with the trails numbered. The primary purpose of these maps is to help you find the trailhead easily. We have designated the roads you need to take to get there as paved, gravel, and 4WD. In many guide books, finding the trailhead becomes a source for complaint. We agree; locating a TH should not be challenging!

Following the Trails Locator Maps are the individual trails, each with their own map detailing the route. Use the GPS numbers to see the route and check out the corresponding GPS chart for mileage, elevation and important directions along the way.

Find the Hikes You Want

The Hikes Chart is innovative. It is a complete chart that, at a glance, provides you with information to help you search for a particular hike: star rating, difficulty level, distance, shuttle, loop, or round trip hike, elevation gain, the best wildflower and aspen hikes, and vehicle access.

CDT Trail: Hike 41

Difficulty

Like scenic ratings, difficulty is subjective. We use six categories to help you define for yourself how difficult the hike would be for you: total distance, difficulty rating, surface, gradient, highest elevation, and elevation gain and/or loss.

TOTAL DISTANCE is expressed as the total mileage it takes to complete the round trip, the loop, or to arrive at the shuttle point.

DIFFICULTY RATING is a summary assessment of the total hike that takes into consideration distance, surface conditions, gradient, highest elevation, and elevation gain or loss. The categories are represented by colors and words as follows: Easy (green), Moderate (cyan), Moderately Strenuous (blue), Strenuous (orange), Very Strenuous (red).

SURFACE: Are you walking on packed dirt or stumbling over and around rocks and roots? Is the trail slick, is there loose talus that requires extra caution, or can you watch the scenery go by? Since no trail has the same surface conditions from start to finish, we have written a brief description of the various conditions encountered.

GRADIENT affects most hikers more than distance. We divide gradient into the following categories and use colors on the trails for visual aid: Easy, Moderate, Moderately Steep, Steep, and Very Steep.

- **Easy Gradient:** Trail climbs between 0 to 400 feet per mile (green).
- **Moderate gradient:** Trail climbs between 400 to 600feet per mile (cyan).
- **Moderately Steep:** Trail climbs between 600 to 800 feet per mile (blue).
- **Steep gradient:** Trail climbs between 800 to 1,000 feet per mile (orange).
- **Very Steep gradient:** Trail climbs over 1,000 feet per mile (red).

Yellow: Represents connecting and other trails. It does not symbolize any gradient.

HIGHEST ELEVATION: Many of the hikes in this book start above 9,000 feet. If you come from lower elevations and wish to hike for a few days, most likely you will not be acclimatized. Researchers suggest that one adjust to higher elevations by sleeping at least one night at 8,000 feet or two nights at 7,000 feet before the hike. If you know elevation affects you, you might consider starting with easier hikes while you acclimate.

ELEVATION GAIN: The figure proceeded by a plus sign. It is the sum of all the uphill segments along the route. This figure is the total amount of elevation gained from the start to the return point and back to the start on a round trip hike, and from the start to the end on a loop or shuttle hike.

ELEVATION LOSS: The figure proceeded by a minus sign. It is the sum of all the downhill segments along the route. This figure is the total amount of elevation lost from the start to the return point and back to the start on a round trip hike, and from the start to the end on a loop or shuttle hike. We show the loss figure only when the amount is significant, or the hike is more downhill than uphill.

Hiking Times

Assessing hiking times is even more personal than difficulty ratings. Some folks have long strides, others like to keep a slower pace. On average, we hike 2.0 mph on easy hikes, 1.5 mph on moderate, and 1.0 on strenuous. We don't stop for lunch or rests other than a quick snack or a photo opportunity. Times stated are for the complete hike. We were in our late 60s at the time we hiked these trails.

Recommended Vehicle to Trailheads

Many of the access roads are dirt and gravel roads or rocky 4x4 roads. Such roads are graded infrequently. Conditions vary by amount of usage and weather. Rough washboard, drainage ditches cutting across the roadbed, loose rock, very steep sections, and one lane roads with few pullovers are the major considerations. The Hikes Chart lists the preferred vehicle.

- **CAR** designates that any low clearance vehicle can drive the road.
- **SUV** designates that any high clearance vehicle or pick-up truck, short or long wheel base, can negotiate the road. Cars may scrape the under carriage.
- **4X4** designates that only a 4-wheel drive vehicle, ATV, or motorcycle can negotiate the access road.

Time & Mileage to Trailheads

We tell you the estimated time and the mileage to get to the TH. Some roads require slower driving than others because they are rough, narrow, or steep. We describe the road; we want to be sure you know what's there.

Hike Options

Depending on the type of vehicle needed to get to a trailhead, we have detailed information for different start options. Or, perhaps a hike is longer than you wish to do; look for shorter option return points. We have detailed the difficulty level and scenic value for such options in the Hikes Chart as well as in the hike explanation. You don't have to dismiss a long hike because it is too far.

GPS Charts

Instead of long descriptions, the GPS chart puts important data in one quick and easy reference.

The GPS number, the first column in the chart, corresponds to the number in the circle on the map. The chart then lists the mileage covered to each point, the co-ordinates, elevation, and special considerations.

How We Obtain Trail Data

We have hiked every trail in this book. We do not take data from pre-existing maps or other guide books as some of these sources may be outdated. Nor do we rely on the posted signs along some trails. The distance and elevation data we offer is extracted from the Garmin E-Trex Venture HC series GPS. No consumer GPS is totally accurate. In addition, no two people can hike in the same steps. Even following cairns and other markers, our routes will be slightly different. Therefore, our mileages for a hike may disagree with pre-existing maps and books.

Map Legend

- Paved Roads
- Gravel Roads
- Suv/4wd Roads
- 70 Interstate
- 191 US Highway
- 145 Colorado State Highway
- 14 County Roads
- 645 Forest Service Roads
- N Map Orientation
- Buildings
- Public Toilet
- Picnic Area
- Scenic Overlook
- P Parking Area
- 24 Start Hike 24 here
- Easy Trail Gradient 0 to 400 ft gain
- Moderate Trail Gradient 400 to 600 ft gain
- Moderately Strenuous 600 to 800 ft gain
- Strenuous Trail Gradient 800 to 1000 ft gain
- Very Strenuous Gradient 1000+ ft gain
- Other Hiking Trails
- Motorized Hiking Trails
- Campsite
- Mountain Peak
- Airport

Glossary of Terms

- **OVC:** Ouray Visitor Center
- **SVC:** Silverton Visitor Center
- **LCVC:** Lake City Visitor Center
- **RT:** Round trip
- **TH:** Trailhead
- **CDT:** Continental Divide Trail
- **CT:** Colorado Trail
- **CG:** Campground
- **Junction:** We use the words "unmarked junction", and "marked or signed junction" in the text and GPS charts. We use both to mean: a place where things join. We want the words to send up a red flag when you read them: look for a connecting trail. It may be very faint. Many "junctions" are not signed. Some are signed, but may not match the maps you purchased. A lot of very exciting trails in this book follow an unsigned trail.

Carry This Guide

There is a lot of information in this guidebook. It is meant to be carried with you when you hike. The most important reason for doing so is that many "junctions" are unmarked; there may be too many to memorize. Additionally, when you hike one trail, you may pass the routes to other hikes. We show the connecting hikes in yellow along with their hike numbers. This makes it easy to see how they interconnect. Your understanding and appreciation of the area will grow exponentially. It allows you to see the terrain for a future hike or change your mind and hike a different trail on the spur of the moment. You will know where that intriguing trail goes. Other hikers may inspire you to go on their favorite trail. The information you need is in your hands.

When you carry the book, you can consult the GPS charts to know how far you have gone and how much time you may linger before turning back. You will know what to expect ahead, what is yet to see and experience.

The color coded maps give information about changing levels of difficulty along the trail. Gage your fitness and assess how far you might go. Some of the long, difficult hikes have scenic beginnings that are not difficult. Consult the maps and look for green or cyan colored trails near the beginning of six star hikes and go only that far.

Some of the photos have routes drawn on them to aid in finding your way. Other photos may inspire you to create your own memorable photography.

Uncompahgre Peak from Hike 63

Other Considerations

Weather

Weather must be considered when hiking in the Colorado mountains. The prime high altitude hiking season is also the prime monsoon season. There are frequent afternoon thunderstorms. Be prepared for strong winds, dropping temperatures, sudden heavy rainfall, and lightning. Take warning from approaching dark clouds and plan ahead to hike down off exposed ridges. Do not take cover from lightning under lone trees, in shallow caves, or against cliff edges. If necessary, squat down and hide in brush or grass away from such objects. A safe rule of thumb is to plan arriving at your highest elevation point by noon or 1:00 P.M. at the latest so you can get to lower elevation before the thunderstorms arrive.

Water

Water is essential for hikers to maintain good condition, even more so at high elevations. Too many day hikers convince themselves they can drink when they get back because they don't want to carry the extra weight. On a cool or cloudy day, the signs of thirst are reduced, which tempts day hikers to drink even less. Don't make these mistakes. The muscles need to flush out lactic acid while you are hiking to maintain fitness.

We recommend using a bladder system as opposed to a water bottle hidden in your pack. A bladder makes it convenient to take sips every fifteen minutes whether you feel thirsty or not. For best results, drink about 16 ounces for every hour of exercise. If you are hoping to obtain water along the route from one of many streams or creeks, carry a proper filter or treat the water with iodine solution. Both products are available at most outdoor stores. Cattle and sheep, as well as wildlife, roam freely

San Juan Range: Hike 21

throughout this area. All water should be considered infected. On longer hikes, we also take several small bottles of water with a sports drink mixed in. It re-hydrates, replenishes, and refuels better than water alone.

High Altitude

Common signs of unhealthy reaction to elevation are headache, nausea, stumbling, and shortness of breath. There are products sold in high elevation communities to help with altitude adjustment, or you can try aspirin, but the best remedy for altitude sickness is to hike down.

Hypothermia

Hypothermia is a condition in which the internal body temperature is at least 3.6° F below the normal 98.6°. The body functions begin to slow down and deteriorate. Early symptoms are excessive shivering and slurred speech. Wearing soaked clothing in prolonged cold temperatures can precipitate the condition. Hypothermia is serious and can lead to death. Layered synthetic clothing and fleece outerwear and raingear for emergency use is prudent. Hikers should also be prepared to spend a night in the wilderness.

Prevention

Prevention is better than rescue. Regardless of the length or difficulty of hike, a prudent hiker will always follow certain rules and carry specific safety items.

- Hike with a partner, rather than alone.
- Sign in at the trailhead register if there is one. That makes it easier for rescue parties to find you.
- Tell someone where you are going and when you expect to return. Give them the license plate number of your car or the phone number of a family member or friend.
- Wear layered clothing designed to wick away sweat. Cotton is not recommended.
- Wear ankle supporting boots with good tread as opposed to sandals or sneakers.
- In addition to food and water, always carry the following items: rain gear, flashlight, basic first aid kit, matches or lighter, pocket knife, sunglasses, sunscreen, sunhat, extra clothing, map and compass, emergency shelter or space blanket, insect repellent.

Colorado Rescue

A Colorado Outdoor Recreation Search and Rescue card (CORSAR) can be purchased at all Forest Service locations and most outdoor stores throughout Colorado for $3.00 per person per year or $12.00 for 5 years. When you purchase a card, two thirds of the money goes into a fund to reimburse search and rescue teams for actual expenses. Rescue services in Colorado are free of charge. They operate on donations such as come from this card to provide the public this amazing service.

Ouray, Colorado

Known as the Little Switzerland of America, Ouray is an historic town nestled at the end of a box canyon surrounded by the majestic mountains of the San Juan Range in Southwest Colorado. Settled in the 1880's and 1890's by a growing mining population, most of the existing roads and pack trails were built by these hearty folk and have been reborn as current day recreational trails. The trails here are steep as the mountains rise straight up from the valley floor. Evidence of mining activity flourishes; it is incomprehensible how the miners got equipment to such difficult locations but hikers will see evidence of their efforts everywhere.

Ouray was originally inhabited seasonally by Ute Indians that spent the summers hunting in the area and bathing in the sacred mineral waters near the end of the box canyon town site. The pools

View of Ouray from Perimeter Trail

Ouray has many historic buildings

were known by the Indians to be therapeutic and were named Uncompahgre, the Ute word for hot mineral springs. The Utes served as mountain guides for Spanish explorers in the 1700's but were coerced in the 1870's into ceding the land of the San Juan Mountains to the mining of gold and silver. Some of the larger mines in Colorado were developed near Ouray. By 1888 there were over 2,600 inhabitants and the Denver RR arrived.

We have chosen 7 trails easily accessible from the town center. The newest and perhaps most popular may be the Perimeter Trail that surrounds the town and offers many different vistas. Due to the lower elevation starting about 8000 feet these trails are suitable for early season hiking. The remaining 8 hikes take you into the heart of the San Juan Mountains. Snows may linger longer; the highest elevation is 13000 feet. Vistas are thrilling. Enjoy!

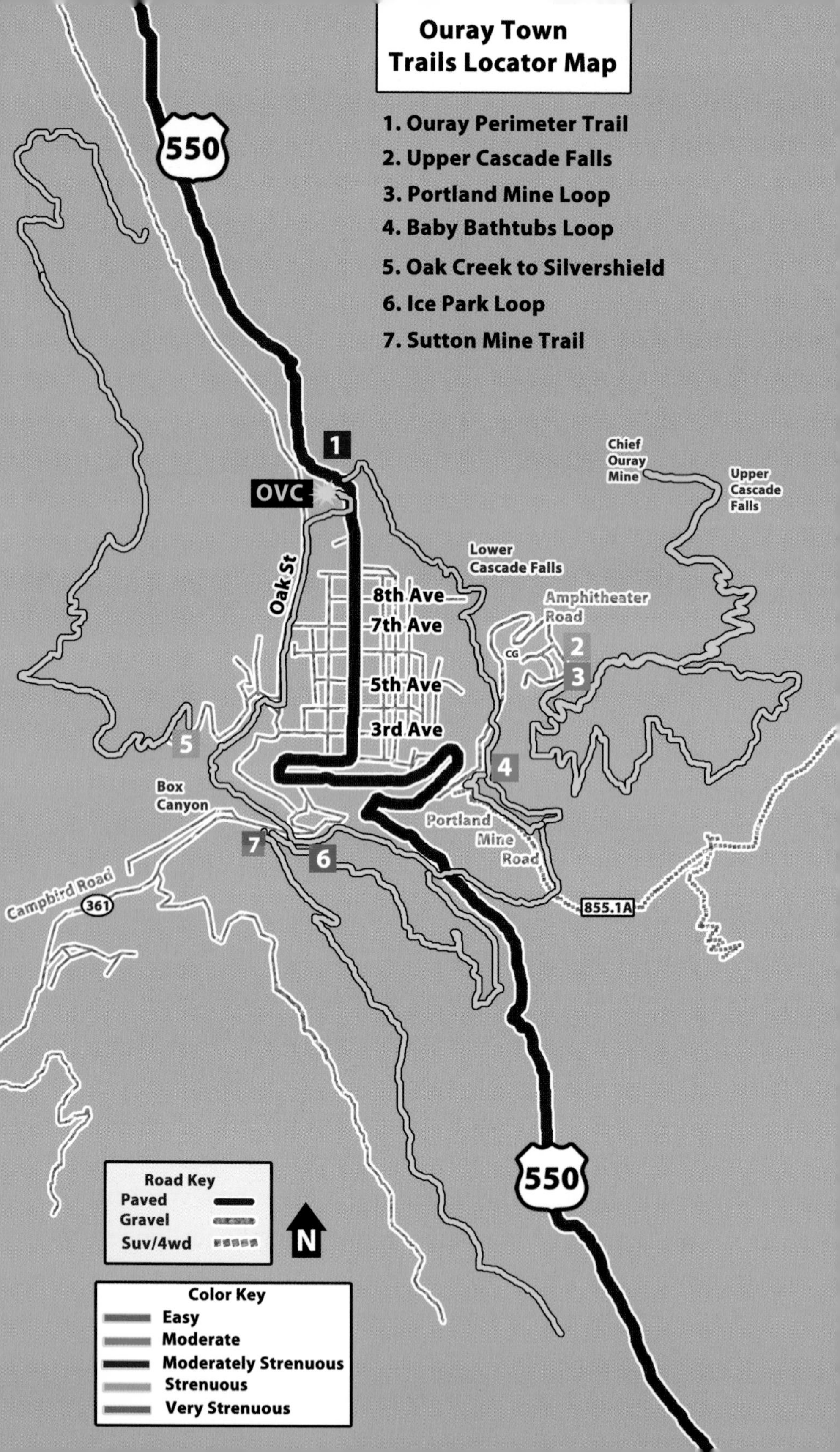
Ouray Town
Trails Locator Map
1. Ouray Perimeter Trail
2. Upper Cascade Falls
3. Portland Mine Loop
4. Baby Bathtubs Loop
5. Oak Creek to Silvershield
6. Ice Park Loop
7. Sutton Mine Trail
550
1
OVC
Oak St
8th Ave
7th Ave
5th Ave
3rd Ave
Chief Ouray Mine
Upper Cascade Falls
Lower Cascade Falls
Amphitheater Road
CG
2
3
4
5
Box Canyon
Portland Mine Road
7
6
Campbird Road
361
855.1A
550
Road Key
Paved
Gravel
Suv/4wd
N
Color Key
Easy
Moderate
Moderately Strenuous
Strenuous
Very Strenuous

Ouray Perimeter Trail

Star Rating

☆☆☆

Highest point on trail

Total Distance	4.14 mile loop
Difficulty Rating	Moderately Strenuous
Surface	Mostly small gravel and packed dirt
Gradient	Varies from very steep to easy
Average Time	4 hours
Elevations	TH: 7,708; Highest: 8,438; Gain: +1,529
Maps	Ouray Trail Group: Hiking Trails of Ouray County

Summary

Kudos to Ouray Trail Group for building this exciting, scenic loop around the perimeter of Ouray. Though it is not a wilderness hike, it offers a tremendous variety of stunning views of the Uncompahgre Basin, and the massive peaks that form it. The trail incorporates sheer cliffs, flowered meadows, healthy mixed forests, waterfalls, deep gorges, explosive vistas, and some 4x4 roads. There are numerous access points so shorter sections can be done separately. A spectacular section above Oak Street that will finish the loop is planned for the future. This is a must hike for visitors to Ouray.

Directions to Trailhead

There are 7 access points:

- OVC: East side of Hwy 550 TH sign ❶. Recommended Vehicle: Car
- Lower Cascade Falls: East end of 8th Ave ❷. Recommended Vehicle: Car
- East end of 5th Ave ❸. Recommended Vehicle: Car
- Baby Bathtubs TH: From OVC, drive south on Hwy 550 for 1.7 miles to Amphitheater Campground sign. Turn left. Follow paved road 0.11 miles to TH on other side of bridge. Several small parking areas ❺. Recommended Vehicle: Car
- Portland Mine Road: From OVC, drive south on Hwy 550 for 1.7 miles to Amphitheater Campground sign. Turn left. Follow paved road 0.10 miles and turn right on steep gravel road just before bridge. Drive 0.25 miles to Perimeter Trail sign. Small parking area across road. No more parking beyond. Walk 0.15 miles up this steep, narrow, rocky road past a second Perimeter sign ❾ to a third Perimeter Trail sign on south side of road ❿. Recommended Vehicle: SUVs
- Hwy 550: From OVC, drive 2.1 miles south on Hwy 550 to small signed parking area on right (W) and Perimeter Trail sign ⓫. Recommended Vehicle: Car
- Camp Bird Road. From OVC, drive 1.0 miles south on Hwy 550. Turn right on Camp Bird Road and drive 0.30 miles to Perimeter TH sign on right ⓮. Across from Sutton Mine TH sign. Park on roadside. Recommended Vehicle: Car

Descent after Box Canyon

Trail Description

Do the entire trail, or walk a smaller section based on the information below.

GPS 1-2 Visitor Center to Lower Cascade Falls: Very Strenuous

This is a spectacular cliff hugging trail with very steep ascents and descents and views to kill for. It climbs 560 feet in less than 0.60 miles. We spent two hours photographing and enjoying the spectacular vistas. Close up views of Lower Cascade Falls. You can exit this portion of the trail at 8th Ave ❷. Walk back on Main St. to the Visitor Center.

GPS 3-4 Lower Cascade Falls to Baby Bathtubs TH: Moderately Strenuous

This 0.74 mile portion starts with a short steep ascent that becomes moderate to easy as the trail winds through mixed forest. There are occasional partial views of Lower Cascade Falls behind you as you climb. There are two exceptional views of the Canyon Creek Gorge, 13,452 foot Whitehouse Mountain, and Twin Peaks across the basin about halfway along the trail. If walking just this section, return the way you came or leave a shuttle vehicle at the Baby Bathtubs TH parking area on Amphitheater Campground Road.

View of Ouray near start of trail

GPS 5-11 Baby Bathtubs to Hwy 550: Moderately Strenuous.

This 0.92 mile section offers a variety of terrain and scenery. The trail starts up moderately steeply following along Little Portland Creek through mixed forest and oak brush. There are numerous places to peer down into the deep canyon this small volume of water has carved. Further up, smooth glacial carved rock form little bathtubs when the water is low. Follow the Perimeter Trail signs to a bridge and cross the creek ❼. The trail remains in the woods. Take the signed left fork ❽, passing Three Pines Day use area, and then intersecting with Portland Mine 4x4 Road ❾. Go left up the road about 300' to another Perimeter Sign ❿. From here the trail enters spectacular open areas and climbs to the highest point with marvelous 180 degree views. What a spot! Descend moderately steeply to Hwy 550 ⓫, where, if you did only this section, you would have to leave a shuttle vehicle in the small parking area ⓬ or walk Hwy 550 about 0.60 miles back to your car at Baby Bathtub TH.

GPS 12-13 Hwy 550 to Camp Bird Road: Moderate.

This is a very short section of 0.35 miles between Hwy 550 and Camp Bird Road. It is a moderate downhill that begins in the open then soon enters mixed forest before the short steep descent to Camp Bird Road. There are some nice views.

GPS	Mile	Latitude	Longitude	Elevation	Comment
Visitor Center to Lower Cascade Falls					
1	0.0	38,01.789N	107,40.348W	7,708′	Start Perimeter Trail east side of Hwy 550 across from Visitor Center.
2	0.73	38,01.504N	107,39.928W	8,027′	Signed junction: Cascade Falls Trail and Perimeter Trail
Lower Cascade Falls to Baby Bathtubs TH					
3	1.02	38,01.445N	107,39.951W	8,191′	5th Ave access to Perimeter Trail
4	1.37	38,01.170N	107,39.896W	8,123′	Meet Amphitheater Road. Walk down 0.1 miles to Baby Bathtub TH.
Baby Bathtubs to Hwy 550					
5	1.47	38,01.077N	107,39.915W	8,113′	Baby Bathtubs TH sign. Follow this trail.
6	1.69	38,00.982N	107,39.717W	8,324′	Signed junction: Left to Portland Mine. Go straight.
7	1.75	38,00.986N	107,39.673W	8,360′	Signed junction: To Portland Mine Trail. Straight ahead dead end. Go right over bridge.
8	1.82	38,00.965N	107,39.747W	8,287′	Signed junction: Go left on Perimeter Trail.
9	1.88	38,00.859N	107,39.720W	8,343′	Junction: Portland Mine Road; turn left and go up road for 300 feet.
10	2.0	38,00.808N	107,39.699W	8,438′	Signed junction: Leave Portland Mine Road. Start on trail again.
11	2.39	38,00.838N	107,39.999W	8,189′	Hwy 550. Cross to west side. Resume trail.
Hwy 550 to Camp Bird Road					
12	2.44	38,00.835N	107,40.056W	8,233′	Signed junction: Left for Ice Park Trail; right for Perimeter Trail
13	2.79	38,00.959N	107,40.361W	7,994′	Junction: Camp Bird Rd. Go left and follow road 500 feet uphill to Perimeter Trail sign.
Camp Bird Road to Visitor Center or go out and back to tunnel					
14	2.95	38,00.937N	107,40.512W	8,060′	Junction: Leave Camp Bird Road and follow trail.
15	3.20	38,01.056N	107,40.731W	7,987′	Canyon Bridge Gorge and tunnel
16	3.35	38,01.146N	107,40.723W	8,010′	Temporary end of trail. Walk 0.94 mile via Queen St and Oak St to Visitor Center. Well signed
1	4.14	38,01.789N	107,40.348W	7,708′	Finish loop

GPS 14-16,1 Camp Bird Road to Visitor Center or go out and back to tunnel: Easy to Tunnel; moderately steep downhill with cliffs and cables after tunnel.

The trail is not yet completed all the way to the Visitor Center. There is about 1.0 miles of walking on town roads at the end. If you have started at the Visitor Center, it makes sense to go all the way through to the finish. Otherwise, you can just walk this section out and back to the other side of the tunnel and see the best scenery. The trail is mostly flat to the Canyon Creek suspension bridge where you can peer straight down into this amazing gorge ⓯. Walk through the old water tunnel. There is a donation box at the end to help the Ouray Trail group complete the trail. Descend the cliff edged steps guarded by cables and ropes if you are continuing to the Visitor Center. Once at the bottom and on city streets, signs direct you to the finish. What a hike!

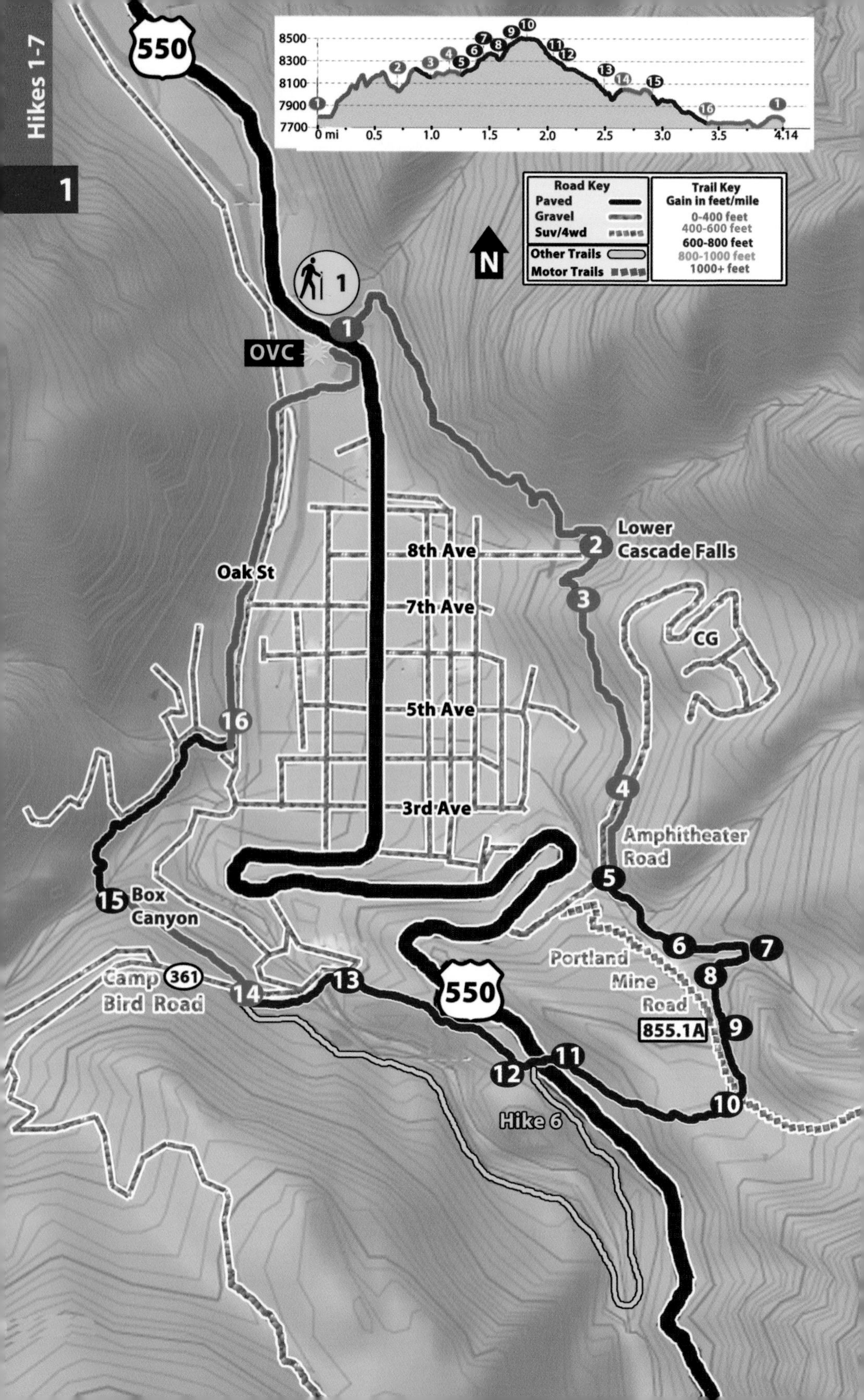
550
8500
8300
8100
7900
7700
0 mi
0.5
1.0
1.5
2.0
2.5
3.0
3.5
4.14
Road Key
Paved
Gravel
Suv/4wd
Other Trails
Motor Trails
Trail Key
Gain in feet/mile
0-400 feet
400-600 feet
600-800 feet
800-1000 feet
1000+ feet
N
OVC
Lower Cascade Falls
8th Ave
7th Ave
5th Ave
3rd Ave
Oak St
CG
Amphitheater Road
Box Canyon
Camp Bird Road
361
Portland Mine Road
855.1A
550
Hike 6

Lower Cascade Falls from the trail

2

Upper Cascade Falls & Chief Ouray Mine

Star Rating

☆☆☆

Hayden Mountain dominates view

Total Distance	4.46 miles RT
Difficulty Rating	Strenuous
Surface	Packed dirt with loose rock that tends to slide underfoot especially on steep sections
Gradient	1.5 miles of steep uphill
Average Time	4 hours
Elevations	TH: 8,399; Highest: 10,116; Gain: +2,290
Maps	Ouray Trail Group: Hiking Trails of Ouray County
Directions to TH	From OVC, drive south on Hwy 550 for 1.7 miles to the signed junction for Amphitheater Campground. Drive 1.0 miles on the campground road to the end. Ample parking and a TH sign with a very good map mark the start of the hike.
Time & Distance to TH	10 minutes; 2.7 miles
Recommended Vehicle	Car

Upper Cascade Canyon

Upper Cascade Falls

Oak trees on lower trail

Summary

Hike through mature mixed forest with plenty of views of Canyon Creek, Hayden Mountain, Twin Peaks and the Sneffels Range as well as close ups of the Amphitheater wall. About halfway to the top, the views expand to include Red Mountain and a bird's eye view of Yankee Boy Basin. Capture a photo of Ouray 2500 feet below with Whitehouse Mountain for a dramatic backdrop. The falls plunge over a precipice and carve a deep picturesque gorge.

Trail Description

Signage at all the junctions on this trail is very good. The trail starts off level through open forest that displays an amazing variety of vegetation from old growth Douglas Firs to a rich and colorful understory of oak brush and seasonal flowers. Photographic views of the surrounding peaks are frequent. The trail turns to steep after the junction to Lower Cascade Falls ❸ and continues as such through the forest to ❺. Here the trail begins a steeper series of switchbacks that ascend 990 feet in 0.75 miles. Views become increasingly more spectacular.

By the time the high point is reached at ⑥ you are high above the valley floor looking across at Twin Peaks and Red Mountain. The trail levels out as it clings to the cliff edge and leads around to the falls. Soon, the mine buildings come into view. How on earth did the early miners find such a spot! You may not be able to continue to the mine depending on the falls volume of water.

GPS	Mile	Latitude	Longitude	Elevation	Comment
1	0.0	38,01.317N	107,39.624W	8,399′	Start Upper Cascade Falls Trail.
2	0.18	38,01.217N	107,39.695W	8,407′	Signed junction: Go left (E) to Upper Cascade Falls. Portland Trail to right (S)
3	0.53	38,01.351N	107,39.514W	8,645′	Signed junction: Go straight (E) to Upper Cascade Falls. Lower Cascade Falls to left (W)
4	0.76	38,01.351N	107,39.300W	8,932′	Signed junction: Go straight (NE) to Upper Cascade Falls. Portland Trail (SE) to right
5	0.87	38,01.374N	107,39.198W	9,139′	Start series of switchbacks. Trail gradient becomes steep.
6	1.62	38,01.589N	107,39.200W	10,113′	Top of climb. Trail levels off.
7	2.0	38,01.760N	107,39.187W	10,056′	Upper Cascade Falls
8	2.23	38,01.808N	107,39.416W	10,116′	Chief Ouray Mine buildings. Return

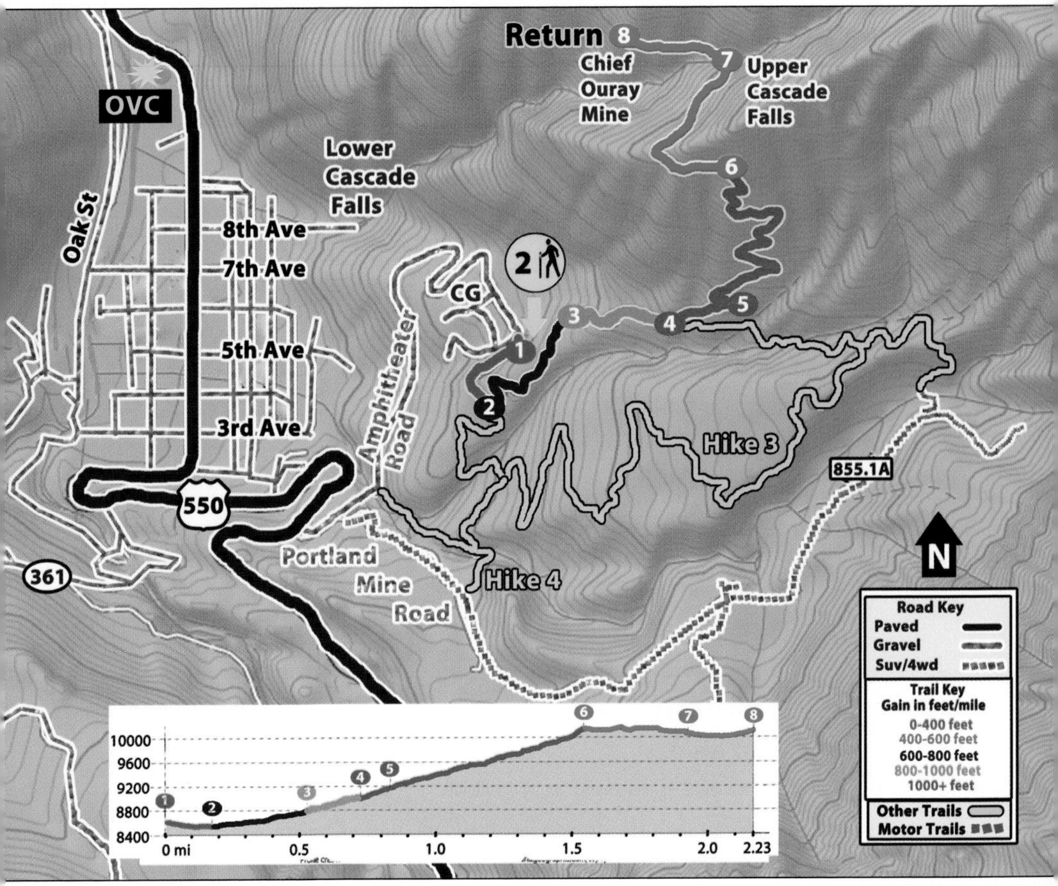

Portland Mine Loop

Star Rating

☆☆☆

Total Distance	3.48 mile loop
Difficulty Rating	Moderate
Surface	A mixture of packed dirt and some sections with loose rock
Gradient	Moderate
Average Time	2.5 hours
Elevations	TH: 8,399; Highest: 9,229; Gain: +1,223
Maps	Ouray Trail Group: Hiking Trails of Ouray County

Signed viewpoint

Directions to TH	From OVC, drive south on Hwy 550 for 1.7 miles to the signed junction for Amphitheater Campground. Drive 1.0 miles on the campground road to the end. Ample parking and a TH sign with a very good map mark the start of the hike.
Time & Distance to TH	10 minutes; 2.7 miles
Recommended Vehicle	Car

Summary

This is a forest hike but for every ten minutes in the woods, there are amazing views of various peaks and the amphitheater wall to stimulate your interest. Relatively low elevation and early season access makes this a great conditioning hike. Good outing for children. The oak brush turns bronze in fall.

Trail Description

Hike this trail counterclockwise for easy elevation gain. All the junctions are signed. The trail starts out downhill, crosses a major drainage, and then begins a long, but moderate switchback ascent to a fabulous overlook ❺. There are many various views along the route. Instead of looping back via the 4x4 Portland Road (which is an option you can take at ❻), we prefer staying on the hiking trail through the woods to ❼. Then, it is a steeper descent with lots of views back to the start.

Many vistas across valley

GPS	Mile	Latitude	Longitude	Elevation	Comment
1	0.0	38,01.317N	107,39.624W	8,399′	Start Portland Mine Loop from Amphitheater CG end of road.
2	0.18	38,01.217N	107,39.695W	8,407′	Signed junction: Go right (SE) for this loop. Left (E) goes to Upper Cascade Falls.
3	0.30	38,01.188N	107,39.745W	8,392′	Signed junction: Go left (E). Straight goes to 5th Ave & Town.
4	0.50	38,01.101N	107,39.659W	8,344′	Signed junction: Go left (NE) uphill. Right (S) downhill goes to Baby Bathtubs.
5	2.11	38,01.238N	107,38.977W	9,197′	Signed Scenic Overlook
6	2.21	38,01.294N	107,38.927W	9,229′	Signed junction: Highest point; go left (NW) downhill for loop. Right (NE) goes to Portland Mine Road.
7	2.62	38,01.351N	107,39.300W	8,932′	Signed junction: Go left (W) downhill for loop. Right to Upper Cascade Falls.
8	2.92	38,01.351N	107,39.514W	8,645′	Signed junction: Go left (SW) for loop. Right (W) goes to Lower Cascade Falls.
2	3.32	38,01.217N	107,39.695W	8,407′	Signed junction: Go straight for loop.
1	3.48	38,01.317N	107,39.624W	8,399′	Finish loop.

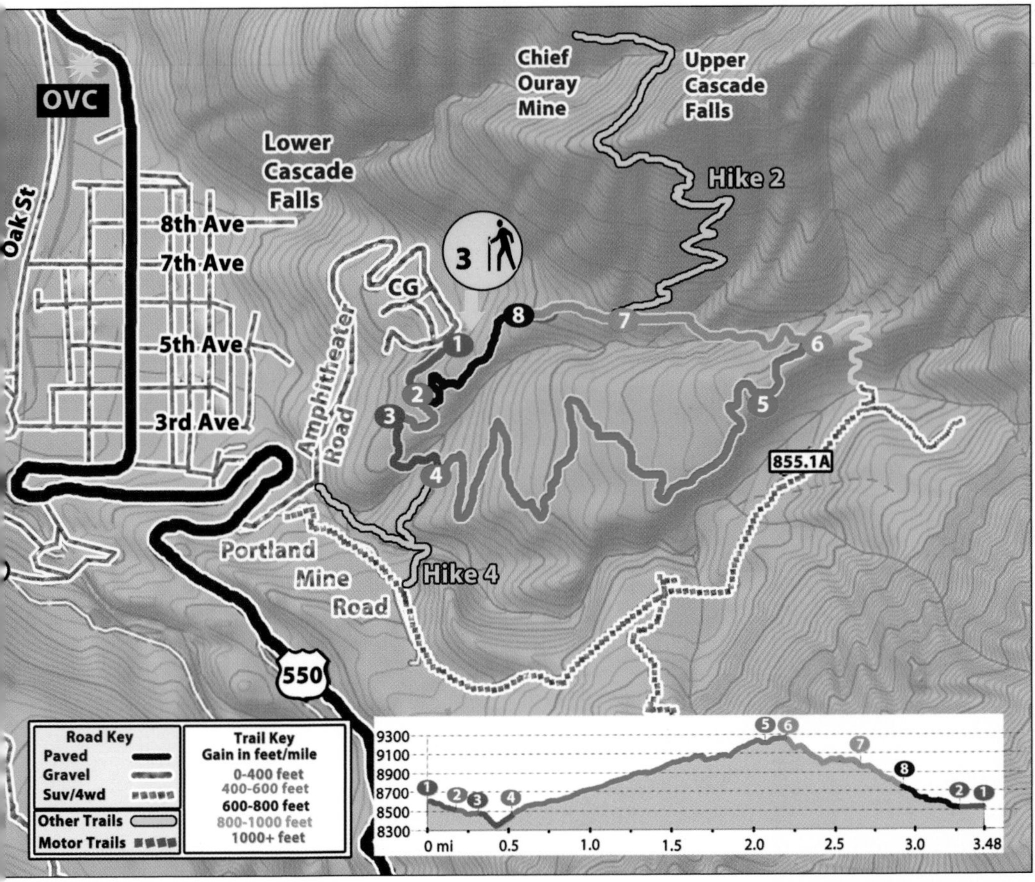

4

Baby Bathtubs Loop

Star Rating

☆☆

Directions to TH

From Ouray Visitor Center, drive south on Hwy 550 for 1.7 miles to Amphitheater Campground sign. Turn left. Follow paved road 0.11 miles to TH on other side of bridge. There are 4 parking areas along the roadside before the bridge. Trailers not recommended.

Time & Mileage to TH

5 minutes; 1.81 miles

Recommended Vehicle

Car

Pictured: View upstream from Trailhead

Total Distance	0.73 Loop
Difficulty Rating	Moderate
Surface	Packed dirt and 4x4 road
Gradient	Moderately Steep to creek crossing
Average Time	1 hour
Elevations	TH: 8,113; Highest: 8,360; Gain: +284
Maps	Ouray Trail Group: Hiking Trails of Ouray County

Summary

A short walk along a forested creek with wonderful swimming holes in summer. Aspens and oak brush offer great fall color. Early season access and conditioning. Good for children.

Trail Description

The trail climbs along the banks of a pretty creek. There are numerous spots where hikers can peer over the edge of the deep, narrow canyon to the creek far below. As you ascend, the gradient eases and bathtubs carved into the smooth rock invite swimming and exploring. Continue to a bridge ❸ that crosses the creek. The trail straight ahead is no longer used. The trail left goes to Portland Mine. We like to make a loop out of this hike by crossing the bridge and returning via Portland Mine Road. This route offers wonderful views of the Amphitheater, and the town of Ouray nestled between the massive peaks.

GPS	Mile	Latitude	Longitude	Elevation	Comment
1	0.0	38,01.077N	107,39.915W	8,113′	Start Baby Bathtub Loop at bridge.
2	0.22	38,00.982N	107,39.717W	8,324′	Junction: Left to Portland Mine Trail. Go straight.
3	0.28	38,00.986N	107,39.673W	8,360′	Junction: Left to Portland Mine Trail. Straight ahead dead end. Go right over bridge for loop or return from here.
4	0.35	38,00.965N	107,39.747W	8,287′	Junction: Left to Perimeter Trail. Go straight ahead.
5	0.41	38,00.950N	107,39.793W	8,303′	Trail meets Portland Mine Road. Go down road.
6	0.65	38,01.043N	107,39.995W	8,132′	Portland Road meets Amphitheater Road; go right.
1	0.73	38,01.077N	107,39.915W	8,113′	End baby Bathtubs hike at parking areas.

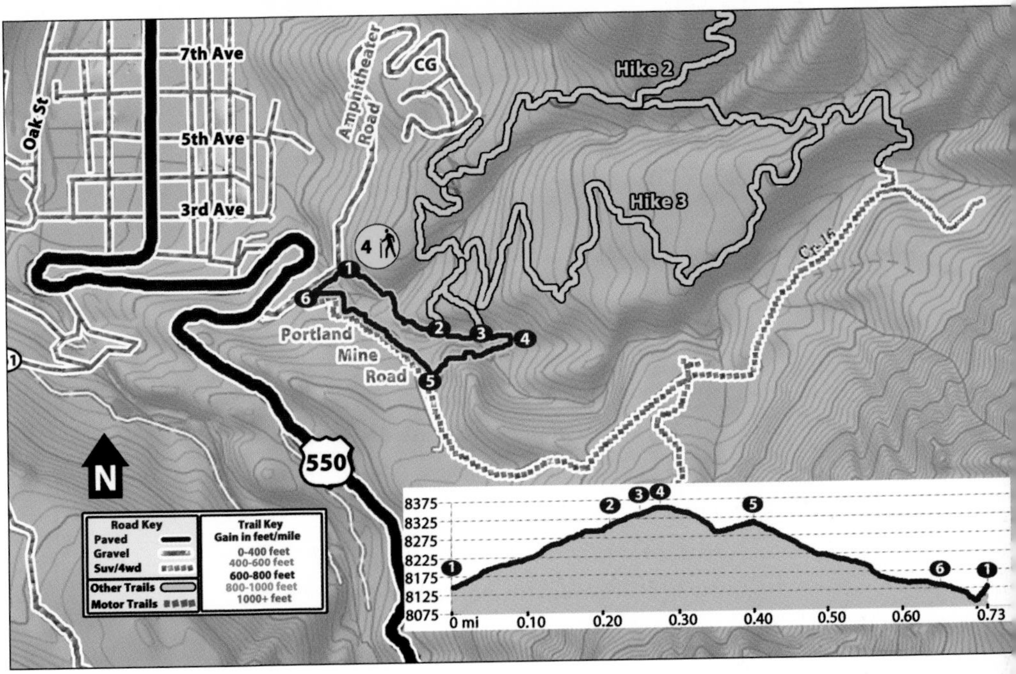

Oak Creek to Silvershield

Star Rating

☆☆

View from Calhoun Memorial Overlook

Total Distance	4.12 miles from start to shuttle point
Difficulty Rating	Strenuous
Surface	Dirt packed to high point; loose gravel to bottom at Silvershield
Gradient	Steep at beginning and end; moderate through middle section
Average Time	4 hours
Elevations	TH: 8,135; Highest: 9,335; Gain: +1,273
Maps	Ouray Trail Group: Hiking Trails of Ouray County

Directions To Trailhead
From OVC, drive 0.04 miles south on Hwy 550 to 7th Ave. Turn Right (W). Drive to Oak Street 0.10 mile and turn left (S). The roads are all gravel from here. Another 0.20 miles and turn right (W) on Queen Street. There is a large pull off area on the left at this junction; this is the only place to park if the TH parking is full. (There are only two spaces and limited turn around at the TH.) If you park on Queen Street, add 0.50 miles gain to walk to the TH. Alternatively, from Queen Street, drive another 0.10 mile to Pine Crest Street. Turn left (S) Continue up two switchbacks. After Mother Lode Lane, the road gets rockier and narrow. There is a TH sign.

Time & Mileage to TH
5 minutes; 1.2 miles

Recommended Vehicle
Car

Shuttle
From the OVC, drive 0.04 miles south on Hwy 550 to 7th Ave. Turn right (W). Drive to Oak Street 0.10 mile and turn right (N). Drive another 1.1 mile to Silvershield Road. Turn left (W) and park in the small meadow at the end. Signed TH.

Summary

Low elevation and early season access make this a great conditioning hike. Most of the views are in the first half of the trail to the high point. It travels primarily through old growth spruce forest. There are many optional routes to expand this hike. They are all through dense forest and steep.

Trail Description

We prefer to hike this trail clockwise as the elevation gain is 400 feet less. An old, overgrown trail takes off just 0.10 mile from the start ❷. Go straight ahead. From the TH to ❸, gain 775 feet in 1.0 mile. A short easy section follows before another big climb of 472 feet in 0.6 mile to ❺. This is steep stuff! There are a few viewpoints looking out through the forest. Now start downhill which gets steeper as you descend. Signed junctions guide the way.

GPS	Mile	Latitude	Longitude	Elevation	Comment
1	0.0	38,01.151N	107,40.778W	8,135′	Start Oak Creek to Silver Shield Trail.
2	0.10	38,01.182N	107,40.792W	8,159′	Unsigned junction: go straight ahead.
3	0.91	38,01.271N	107,41.125W	8,903′	Signed Junction: Go straight ahead (W). Left (S) goes to Oak Creek Trail.
4	1.11	38,01.309N	107,41.308W	8,761′	Stream crossing
5	1.82	38,01.628N	107,41.040W	9,335′	Highest elevation. Signed junction; Go right (E). Straight ahead (N) goes to Twin Peaks.
6	3.03	38,02.398N	107,41.291W	8,646′	Signed junction: Go right (W). Straight ahead goes to Corbett Canyon.
7	3.82	38,02.543N	107,41.079W	7,864′	Calhoun Memorial Overlook
8	4.12	38,02.354N	107,40.954W	7,550′	Finish at Silver Shield Road.

A moderate stretch along a bench

View up valley

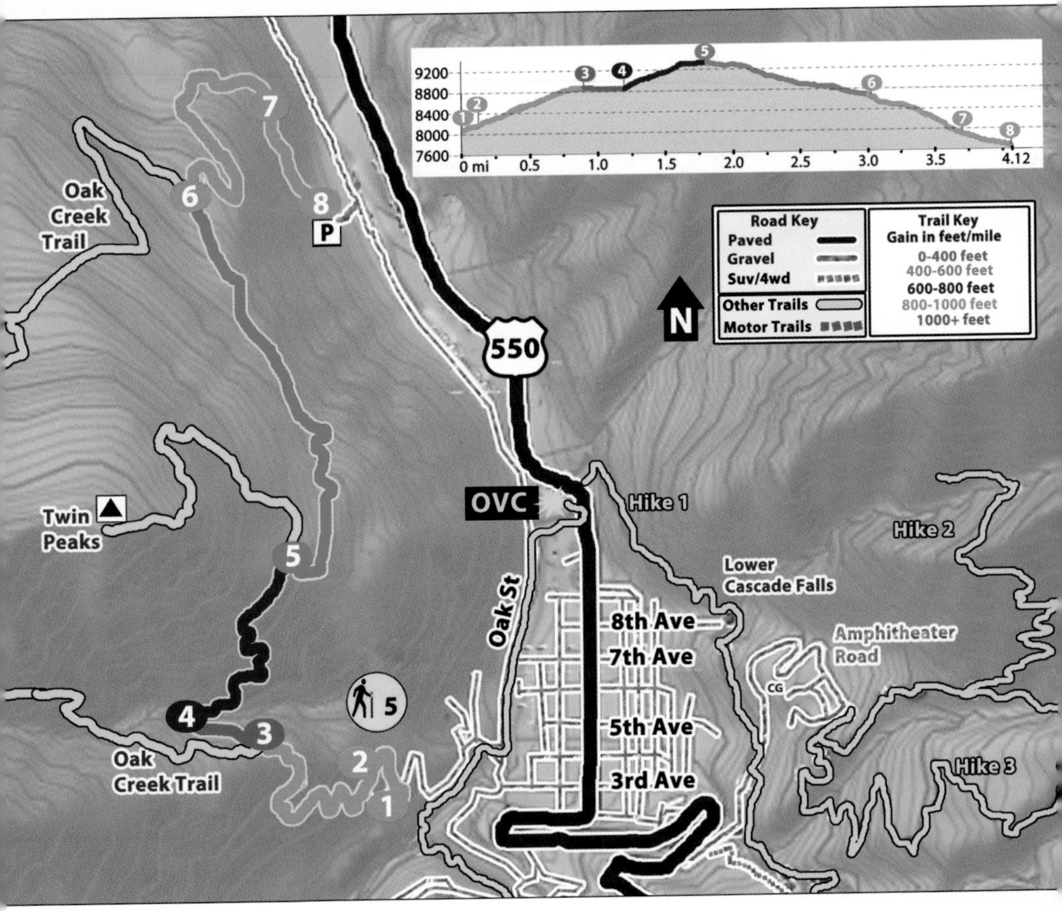

Ice Park Loop Trail

6

Star Rating

☆☆

View of Abrams midway along trail

Total Distance	1.98 mile loop
Difficulty Rating	Easy
Surface	A mixture of packed dirt and some sections with loose rock
Gradient	Easy
Average Time	1.5 hours
Elevations	TH: 8,104; Highest: 8,233; Gain: +523
Maps	Ouray Trail Group: Hiking Trails of Ouray County
Directions to TH	From OVC, drive south on Hwy 550 for 1.0 miles to Camp Bird Road. Turn right and drive 0.40 miles to second TH sign on left which is past the Ice Park Entrance. (The first TH sign is just before the bridge. That is where you will finish the loop.) Do not be confused and take the Sutton Mine Trail (hike 7) which is a narrow trail and goes straight uphill. Ice Park Loop starts on the wider track. They are next to each other.
Time & Distance to TH	5 minutes; 1.4 miles
Recommended Vehicle	Car

Summary

This is a very easy trail with little climbing if hiked counter-clockwise. Passes primarily through spruce forest. It opens early season and is relatively low elevation. There are some views of Abrams and Hayden Mt. The west leg follows the old water pipe line and has some views of the Uncompahgre Canyon.

Trail Description

We hike this loop counter-clockwise to take advantage of the gentler gain in elevation. The trail is primarily through spruce forest; there are several access points to view the canyon and river, especially at ❷ and ❸. There are a few more openings after ❹ as you descend to Camp Bird Road ❺. Walk up the road back to your vehicle.

GPS	Mile	Latitude	Longitude	Elevation	Comment
1	0.0	38,00.934N	107,40.561W	8,104′	Start Ice Park Loop.
2	0.70	38,00.692N	107,39.984W	8,103′	Viewpoint of river canyon
3	0.95	38,00.528N	107,39.889W	8,089′	Bridge across canyon; great canyon views
4	1.43	38,00.835N	107,40.056W	8,233′	Signed junction: Go straight (NW). Right goes to Hwy 550.
5	1.81	38,00.959N	107,40.361W	7,994′	Camp Bird Rd. Go left up road to start.
1	1.98	38,00.934N	107,40.561W	8,104′	Finish Ice Park Loop.

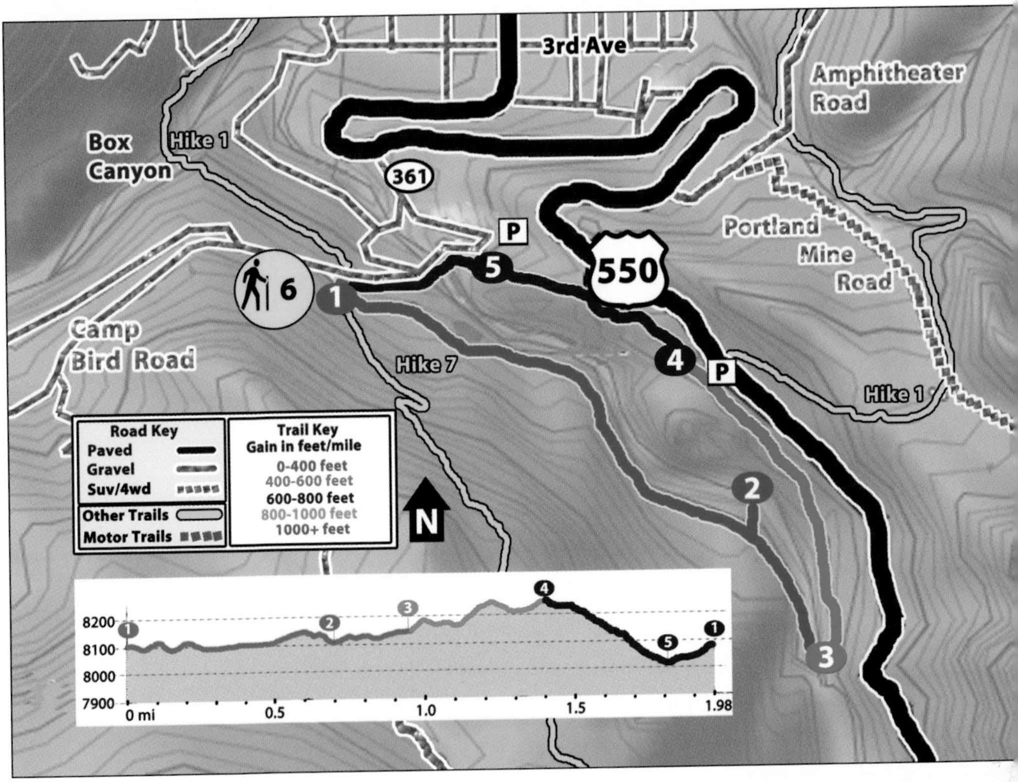

Sutton Mine Trail Options

Star Rating

☆☆

☆☆☆☆

7a: To Ouray Overlook/ Return 1

Total Distance	0.98 miles RT
Difficulty Rating	Very Strenuous
Surface	Packed dirt with loose rock
Gradient	Very Steep
Average Time	1.5 hours
Elevations	TH: 8,109; Highest: 8,684; Gain: +600

7b: To Bear Creek Overlook/ Return 2

Total Distance	3.20 miles RT
Difficulty Rating	Moderate with very strenuous climb from start
Gradient	Very Steep first 0.49 miles; Moderate after
Average Time	2.5 hours
Elevations	Highest: 8,994 ; Gain: +1,305

Summary

A very steep climb through dense spruce forest to the Ouray Overlook. From there to the Bear Creek Overlook, the trail offers spectacular vistas of Ouray, the Amphitheater, the Uncompahgre Gorge, and Mt Abram. Spring wildflowers, and fall aspens add variety and color. Re-enter forest for the final stretch to the mine.

View from second overlook

	7c: To Mine/ Return 3
Total Distance	4.12 miles RT
Difficulty Rating	Moderately Strenuous
Gradient	Very Steep first 0.49 miles. Moderate to Moderately Steep after
Average Time	3.5 hours
Elevations	Highest: 8,994; Gain: +1,579
Maps	Ouray Trail Group: Hiking Trails of Ouray County

Directions to TH	From OVC, drive 1.0 miles south on Hwy 550. Turn right (W) on Camp Bird Road. Drive 0.40 miles to the TH sign on the left. Take the narrow trail going uphill. The wide track adjacent is Ice Park Loop TH. Park on the road.
Time & Distance to TH	5 minutes; 1.4 miles
Recommended Vehicle	Car

Trail Description

The first 0.75 miles of this hike climbs 982 feet in elevation. The trail is narrow in parts and good footing can be an issue because of the steepness. There are some narrow rock outcrops to negotiate. There are no views until the Ouray Overlook.

From the first Ouray Overlook ❷ to the Bear Creek Overlook ❺, the climb becomes moderate and the vistas expand in every direction. This is the most beautiful section of the trail. Grassy meadows, aspens, spring yellow Aster flowers, even desert Clarets add astounding variety and color. Photo opportunities of the surrounding peaks abound. There is a clear view of the Bear Creek Trail carved out of the cliffs on the east side of the gorge.

From Bear Creek Overlook ❺ the trail meanders through forest and meadow and begins its descent to the old mines. Cross two creeks. Again the trail is steep and slippery and thick brush hampers progress. Not far before the mine buildings there is a marvelous view of Bear Creek waterfall ❻. It is now an easy walk to the end of the trail. The Neosho mine entrance is blocked, but an old ore cart, tracks, cables and other remains tell of a difficult life on the edge of a cliff. One hundred yards beyond the Antique Store ❼ stands the original bunkhouse.

View from Ouray Overlook

GPS	Mile	Latitude	Longitude	Elevation	Comment
1	0.0	38,00.940N	107,40.563W	8,109′	Start Sutton Mine Trail.
2	0.49	38,00.727N	107,40.415W	8,684′	First Ouray Overlook/ Return 1
3	0.85	38,00.505N	107,40.184W	8,947′	Second Ouray Overlook
4	1.25	38,00.196N	107,40.120W	8,947′	Start a series of small ponds.
5	1.60	37,59.998N	107,39.960W	8,994′	Bear Creek Overlook/ Return 2
6	1.91	37,59.847N	107,39.758W	8,776′	View of Bear Creek waterfall
7	2.06	37,59.742N	107,39.666W	8,772′	Antique store and other mine buildings/ Return 3

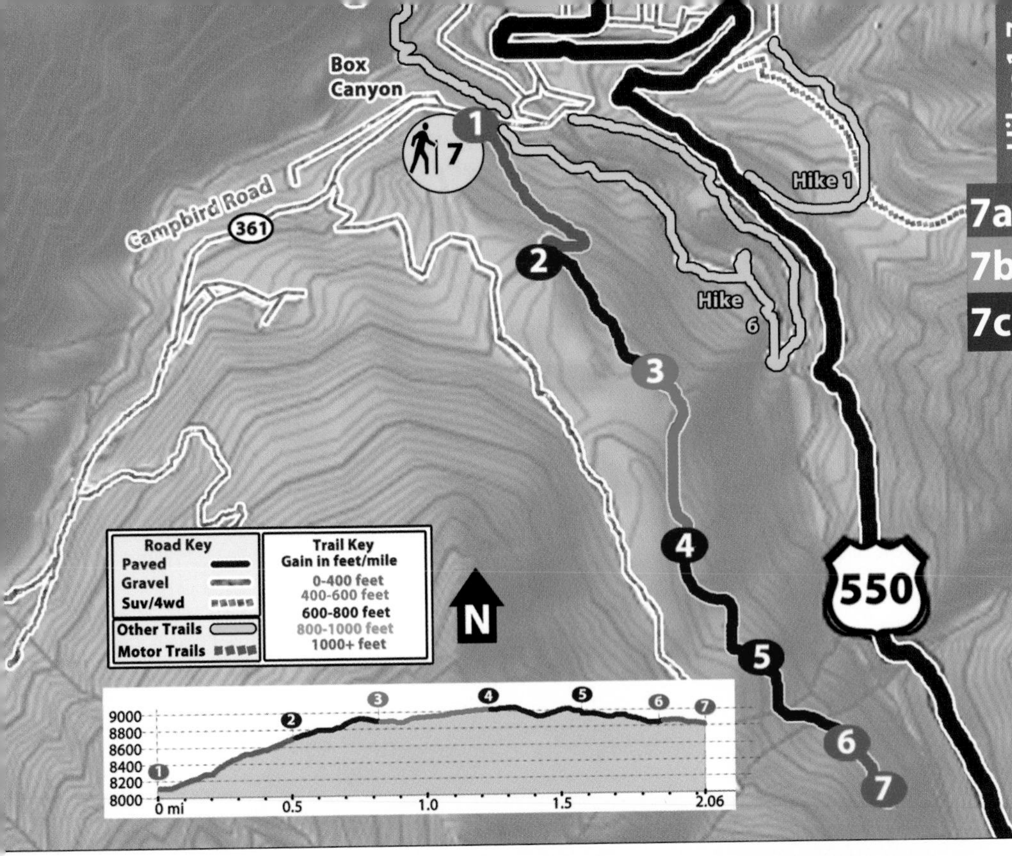

Antique House at mine site

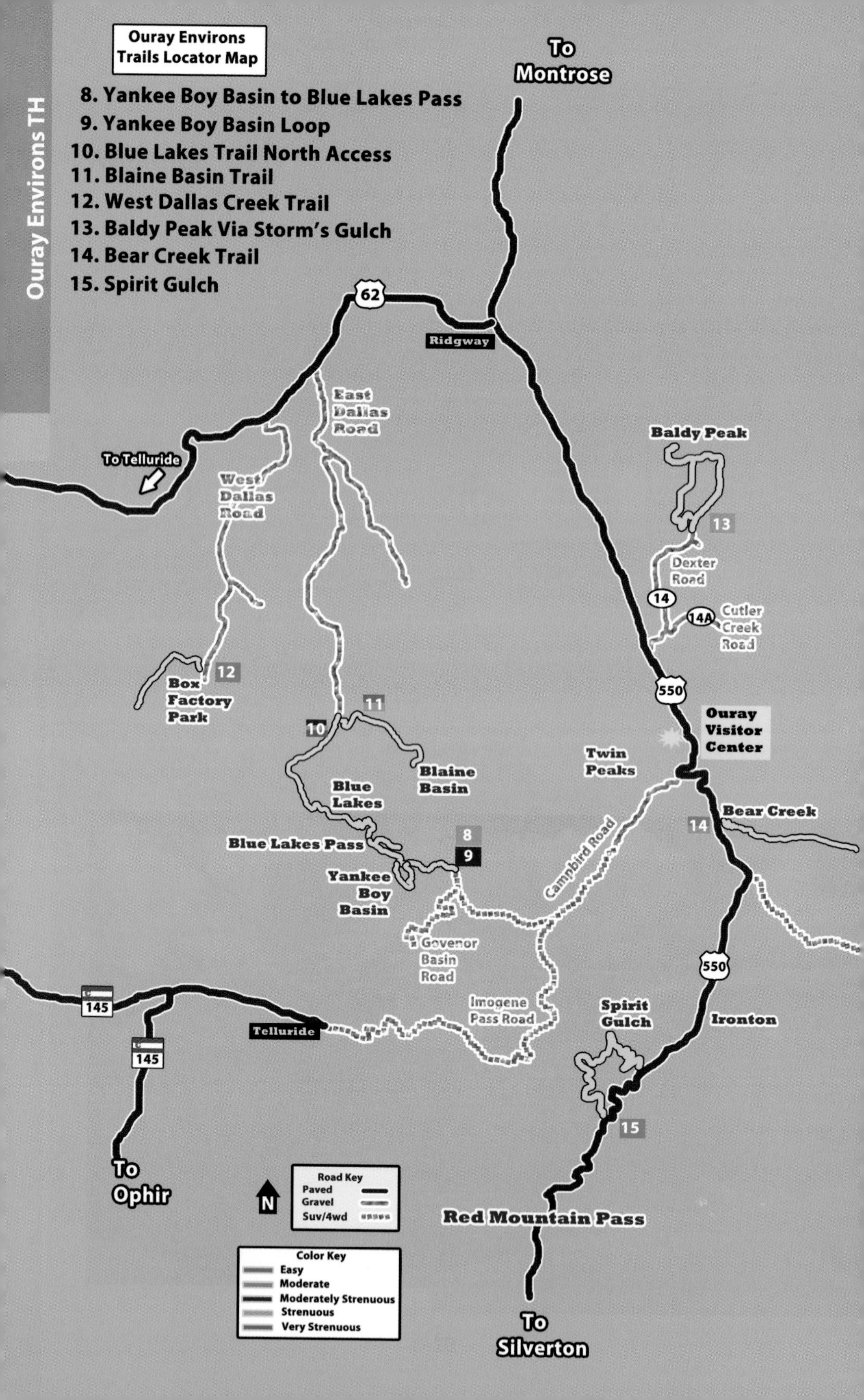
Ouray Environs
Trails Locator Map
8. Yankee Boy Basin to Blue Lakes Pass
9. Yankee Boy Basin Loop
10. Blue Lakes Trail North Access
11. Blaine Basin Trail
12. West Dallas Creek Trail
13. Baldy Peak Via Storm's Gulch
14. Bear Creek Trail
15. Spirit Gulch
To Montrose
62
Ridgway
To Telluride
East Dallas Road
West Dallas Road
Baldy Peak
13
Dexter Road
14
14A
Cutler Creek Road
12
Box Factory Park
550
Ouray Visitor Center
11
10
Twin Peaks
Blaine Basin
Blue Lakes
Bear Creek
14
8
9
Blue Lakes Pass
Campbird Road
Yankee Boy Basin
Govenor Basin Road
550
145
Imogene Pass Road
Spirit Gulch
Ironton
Telluride
145
15
To Ophir
N
Road Key
Paved
Gravel
Suv/4wd
Red Mountain Pass
Color Key
Easy
Moderate
Moderately Strenuous
Strenuous
Very Strenuous
To Silverton

Yankee Boy Basin to Blue Lake Pass Options

Star Rating ☆☆☆☆☆

Blue Lakes from pass

8a: Start 8a to Pass

Total Distance	5.14 miles RT
Difficulty Rating	Strenuous
Surface	Main road is difficult loose rock; secondary roads are dirt packed
Gradient	Easy for first 0.80 miles than strenuous
Average Time	5 hours
Elevations	TH: 11,333; Highest: 12,961; Gain: +1,941

8b: Start 8b to Pass

Total Distance	3.02 miles RT
Difficulty Rating	Strenuous
Surface	Mostly dirt packed to ⑨. Slippery side hill to summit
Gradient	Strenuous
Average Time	4 hours
Elevations	TH: 11,780; Gain: + 1,234

8c: Start 8c to Pass

Total Distance	2.0 miles RT
Difficulty Rating	Moderate
Surface	Extremely rocky to ⑨. Slippery side hill to summit
Gradient	Easy to moderate for first 0.68 miles than strenuous
Average Time	2 hours
Elevations	TH: 12,418; Gain: +597

8d: Start 8c to Blue Lakes North Access TH

Total Distance	7.69 miles to shuttle point
Difficulty Rating	Moderate; most of the hike is seriously downhill
Surface	Extremely rocky to ⑨. Slippery side hill to pass and down other side to Upper Lakes
Gradient	Steep ascent to Pass; very steep descent to Lakes. Mostly moderate below lower lake
Average Time	4.5 hours
Elevations	TH: 12,418; Highest; 12,961; Gain: +1,042; Loss: -4,045
Maps	Ouray Trail Group: Hiking Trails of Ouray County

Directions to TH	From OVC, drive 0.8 miles south on Hwy 550. Turn right at the signed Junction Camp Bird Road. Set odometer to zero here. Bear left at the first junction (Box Canyon Falls). Stay right at the second junction (mile 4.6, Camp Bird Mine). Bear right at the third junction (mile 6.1, Imogene Pass). Bear right at mile 7.0 where sign says Ruby Mine Site. The left fork goes to Governor Basin. SUV vehicles should park at the outhouse which is mile 7.8 (Start 8a). 4x4 SWB vehicles can continue. Stay right at all junctions, following the main track. Parking spot for several vehicles at mile 8.5. There is only room for two cars at the actual TH (Start 8b) at mile 8.7. If you drive to the end of the road at mile 9.6, you will be hiking on a different but much shorter and easier route to the pass (Start 8c-d).
Time & Distance to TH	45 minutes; 8.6 to 9.7 depending on the start point
Recommended Vehicle	To Start 8a at outhouse: SUVs. This is a heavily used gravel road especially on weekends. The upper portion is rough and narrow with steep cliffs. To Start 8b and 8c-d after outhouse 4x4 SWB recommended as the road deteriorates to very rocky, steep and narrow.

Summary

Yankee Boy Basin is a bit of a tourist Mecca with commercial jeep tours and lots of private vehicles on the various 4x4 roads. This being said, once on the actual hiking trail to Blue Lake Pass, the hiker enters a quiet world of alpine splendor. A wonderful variety of terrain, peaks, creeks, waterfalls and expansive vistas unfold as you ascend. The view of Blue Lakes down the other side of the pass is breathtaking. Sneffels looms above your right shoulder. The entire hike is above tree line.

Trail Description

This description for hikers starts at the outhouse. If you are able to drive further, find your start point in the text below and read on. From the outhouse, hikers can proceed up the main jeep road for 0.85 miles to ❼ where the real hiker trail starts, or, take lesser jeep roads with less traffic and more interest for 1.06 miles to ❼. The description below follows the latter route.

At the first junction past the outhouse ❷, go left. The road is easier dirt packed walking compared to the very rocky main road. It crosses some overflow streams and makes a short loop through old campsites back to the main road at ❸. Follow the main road a short distance to the next fork (Private Land sign ❹). Go left down the lesser road which again is easier walking on dirt. The road leads to the edge of Canyon Creek. Follow this road to its end at a small turnaround ❺. A narrow, steep trail leaves the turnaround heading directly back to the main road. There are many flowers in this short climb up the hill. Arrive back on the main road at ❻ and a large parking spot where the sign says "Short wheel base vehicles proceed". It is now just 0.18 miles to the hiking trail and Start 8b at ❼.

View back down valley after Start 8b

Wright's Lake

Looking back from above Wright's Lake

As you ascend from ❼, views of peaks and valleys expand dramatically. There are more waterfalls along Canyon Creek. The trail reaches Wright's Lake and follows and old road around the east side to ❽ where the trail picks up again. Now climb beside another creek in a narrower canyon with amazing vistas all around until reaching a bench at ❾. You are standing right below Sneffels and can clearly see the trail scaling up to Blue Lake Pass. Climb this last pitch which is slippery side hill and very steep. The view of Blue Lakes from the pass is outstanding.

If you drove to Start 8c-d, the shorter route is extremely rocky walking through big, angular rocks all the way to ❾ but the gradient is moderate. It is the shortest and easiest route all the way through to Blue Lakes Trailhead on the other side of the pass. For a description of that part of the trail, read hike 10.

GPS	Mile	Latitude	Longitude	Elevation	Comment
Start 8a					
1	0.0	37,59.293N	107,45.917W	11,333′	Start 8a: Blue Lakes Pass from outhouse
2	0.15	37,59.374N	107,46.036W	11,417′	Unsigned Junction: hikers go left (S); 4x4 go straight (W).
3	0.38	37,59.408N	107,46.179W	11,433′	Unsigned Junction: hiker route joins 4x4 road.
4	0.50	37,59.383N	107,46.311W	11,400′	Signed Junction: Private Land; Hikers go left (SW); 4x4 vehicles go straight (NW).
5	0.81	37,59.288N	107,46.535W	11,538′	Road ends at turnaround. Hikers go up hill (NW) to find little trail.
6	0.91	37,59.341N	107,46.619W	11,660′	Junction with main jeep road. Sign says only short wheel base vehicles from here.
Start 8b					
7	1.06 / 0.0	37,59.374N	107,46.775W	11,780′	Start 8b: Hiking trail begins.
8	1.54 / 0.48	37,59.473N	107,47.074W	12,198′	Signed Junction: Leave jeep road and turn left (NE) on trail around Wright's Lake.
9	2.23 / 1.17	37,59.759N	107,47.571W	12,657′	Signed Junction: Blue Lakes Pass straight ahead (NW); Sneffels Trail and Start 8c-d to the right
10	2.57 / 1.51	37,59.878N	107,47.713W	12,961′	Blue Lake Pass. Return.
Start 8c-d					
11	0.0	37,59.694N	107,47.089W	12,418′	Start 8c-d; Upper parking, 4x4 access only
12	0.53	37,59.840N	107,47.418W	12,623′	Signed Junction: Blue Lake Pass straight; Sneffels to the right
13	0.56	37,59.791N	107,47.543W	12,665′	Signed Junction: Blue Lake Pass straight ahead (SW); Sneffels to the right (NW)
9	0.68	37,59.759N	107,47.571W	12,657′	Junction: Right to Blue Lake Pass; left to Start 8b
10	1.0	37,59.878N	107,47.713W	12,961′	Blue Lake Pass. Return or continue to Blue Lake Trailhead on the other side of the pass.

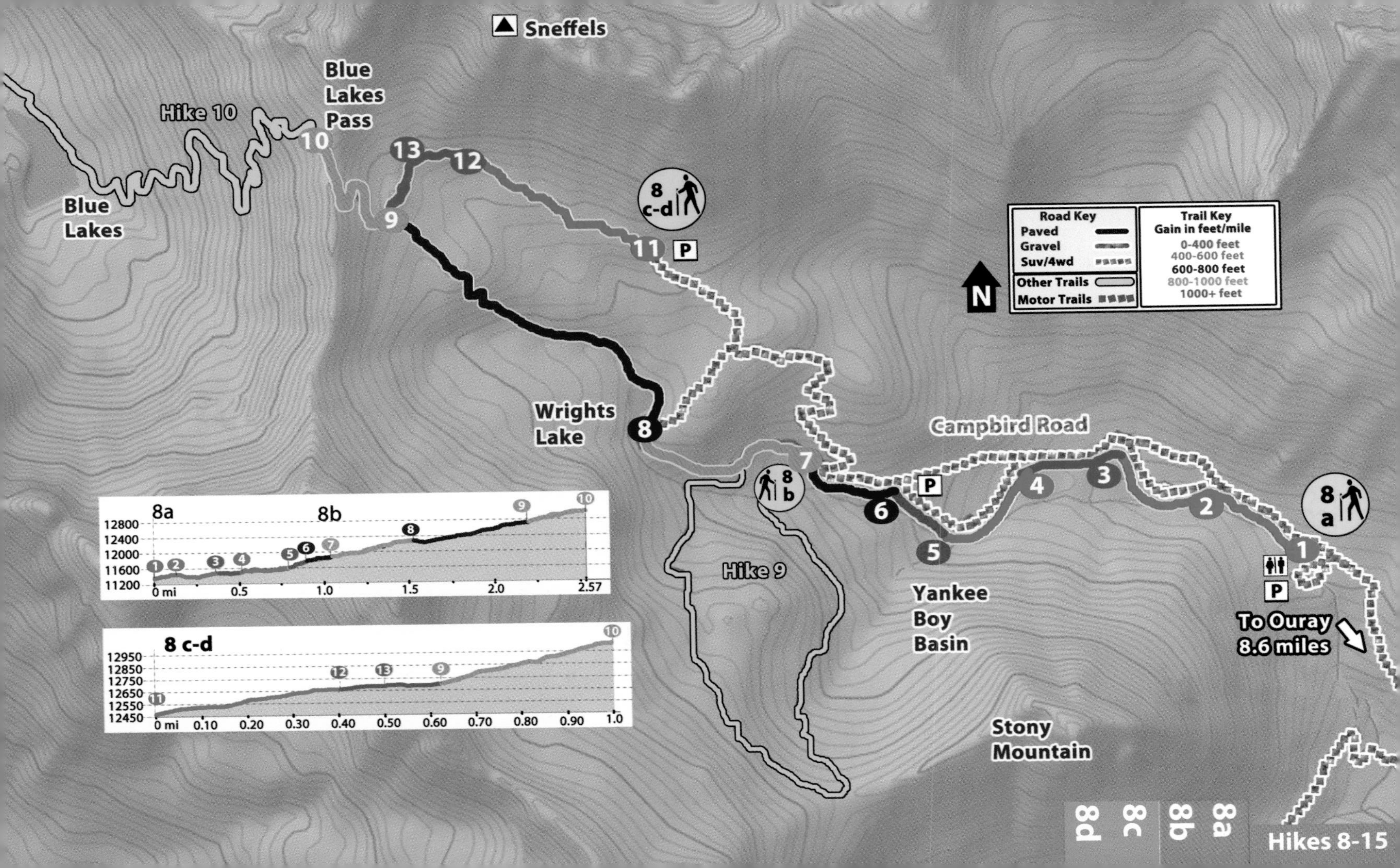
Sneffels
Blue Lakes Pass
Hike 10
Blue Lakes
8 c-d
P
Road Key
Paved
Gravel
Suv/4wd
Other Trails
Motor Trails
Trail Key
Gain in feet/mile
0-400 feet
400-600 feet
600-800 feet
800-1000 feet
1000+ feet
N
Wrights Lake
Campbird Road
8 b
Hike 9
8 a
Yankee Boy Basin
To Ouray 8.6 miles
Stony Mountain
8a
8b
12800
12400
12000
11600
11200
0 mi
0.5
1.0
1.5
2.0
2.57
8 c-d
12950
12850
12750
12650
12550
12450
0 mi
0.10
0.20
0.30
0.40
0.50
0.60
0.70
0.80
0.90
1.0
8a
8b
8c
8d
Hikes 8-15

9a
9b

Yankee Boy Basin Loop

Star Rating
☆☆☆☆☆
☆☆☆☆☆

9a: Start 9a for Loop

Total Distance	3.95 mile loop
Difficulty Rating	Moderately Strenuous due to 0.40 mile of Very Strenuous ascent
Surface	4x4 road and cross country over tundra. Intermittent trails
Gradient	Mostly Moderate but with 0.40 miles very steep climb
Average Time	3.5 hours
Elevations	TH: 11,333; Highest: 12,316; Gain: +1,336

View of Governor Basin from saddle

Directions to TH

From OVC, drive 0.8 miles south on Hwy 550. Turn right at the signed Junction Camp Bird Road. Set odometer to zero here. Bear left at the first junction (Box Canyon Falls). Stay right at the second junction (mile 4.6, Camp Bird Mine). Bear right at the third junction (mile 6.1, Imogene Pass). Bear right at mile 7.0 where sign says Ruby Mine Site. The left fork goes to Governor Basin. SUV vehicles should park at the outhouse which is mile 7.8 (Start 9a). 4x4 SWB vehicles can continue. Stay right at all junctions, following the main track. Parking spot for several vehicles at mile 8.5. There is only room for two cars at the actual TH (Start 9b) at mile 8.7.

Time & Mileage to TH

45 minutes; 8.6 to 9.5 depending on start point

Recommended Vehicle

To Start 9a at outhouse: SUVs. This is a heavily used gravel road especially on weekends. The upper portion is rough and narrow with steep cliffs. To Start 9b after outhouse 4x4 SWB recommended as the road deteriorates to very rocky, steep and narrow.

	9b: Start 9b for Loop
Total Distance	1.90 mile loop
Surface	Mostly cross country over tundra. Intermittent trails
Average Time	2.5 hours
Elevations	TH: 11,780; Gain: +688
Map	Not on any map

Leave trail at Start 9b and hike to creek

Summary

Spectacular. If you do not wish to climb the steep ascent to the Governor Basin Overlook, at least walk into the basin as far as 8. It offers a quiet and adventurous alternative to the Yankee Boy Basin experience. If you go all the way around, you will be thrilled by the expansive vistas, waterfalls, seasonal meadows of wildflowers, and above tree line walking. The basin overlook at 11 is a rare treat few people see. This is a route finding hike that does not require a high level of experience. Use our photos as guidance.

Route to saddle

Trail Description

This description for hikers starts at the outhouse. If you are able to drive further, find your start point in the text below and read on. From the outhouse, hikers can proceed up the main jeep road for 0.85 miles to 7 where the real hiker trail starts, or, take lesser jeep roads with less traffic

Route from saddle

and more interest for 1.06 miles to ❼. The description below follows the latter route.

At the first junction past the outhouse ❷, go left. The road is easier dirt packed walking compared to the very rocky main road. It crosses some overflow streams and makes a short loop through old campsites back to the main road at ❸. Follow the main road a short distance to the next fork (Private Land sign ❹). Go left down the lesser road which again is easier walking on dirt. The road leads to the edge of Canyon Creek. Follow this road to its end at a small turnaround ❺. A narrow, steep trail leaves the turnaround heading directly back to the main road. There are many flowers in this short climb up the hill. Arrive back on the main road at ❻ and a large parking spot where the sign says "Short wheel base vehicles proceed". It is now just 0.18 miles to the hiking trail and Start 9b at ❼.

Standing at the trailhead sign, look left (S) across Canyon Creek up the wide drainage basin that flows into Yankee Boy Basin. Spot the long, flat ridgeline at the far south end of that drainage. That is your goal: Governor Basin Overlook. Leave the trail at the TH and hike towards Canyon Creek on a faint trail aiming for a spot above the small waterfall. Cross where you can. After ascending the bank, do not climb the hill in front of you, but contour southeasterly around it, staying as level as you can. You should connect with an animal trail that takes you around the corner into the aforementioned basin. Walk to the convergence of the two streams ❽ in this basin. For those who do not wish to climb, this is a good return point. The wildflowers and views will have been plenty reward. To continue, walk straight uphill (W) between the two streams on the grassy rise. You will encounter a dry

View of creek basin from overlook

Route from basin back to main trail

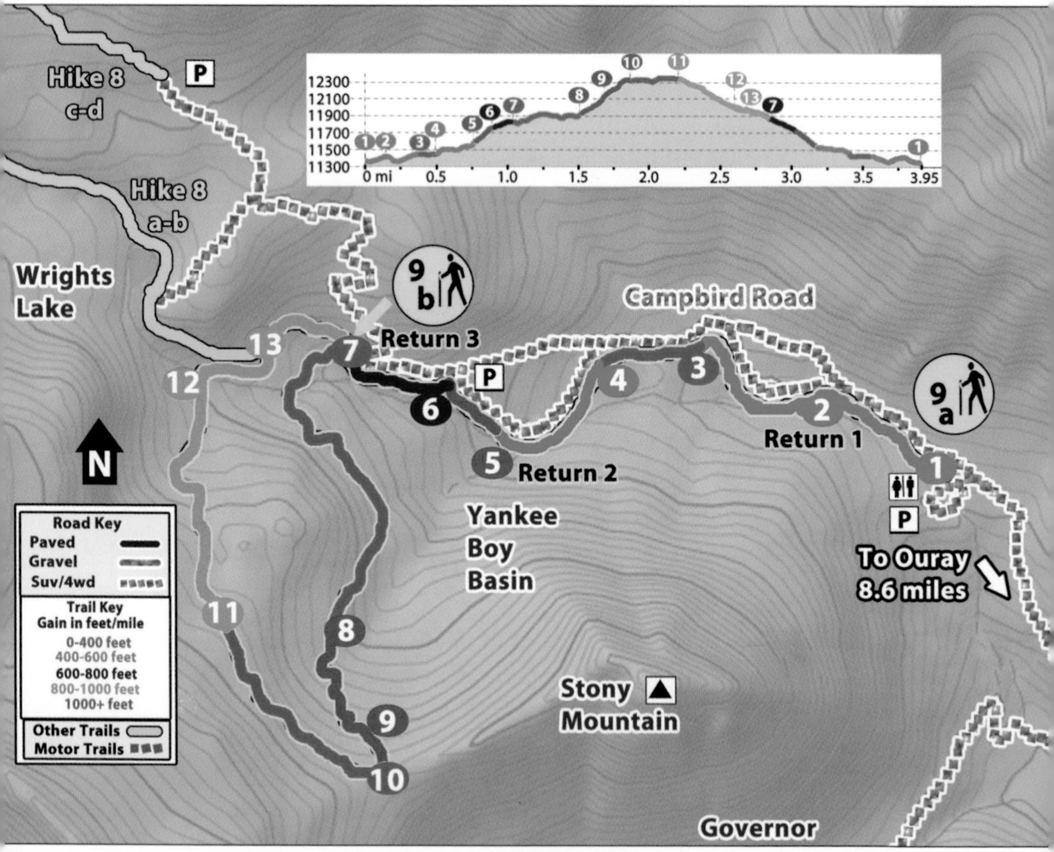

streambed that goes straight uphill like a stairway. This provides good footing and direction to ❾, a broad bench. From here, pick your own route to the wide and obvious saddle to the south ❿. Wow, you did it. Enjoy the views of Governor Basin. Stony Mountain is the pyramid-like pinnacle to the east. You are face to face with Sneffels to the north and can see the Blue Lake trail. Looking north, spot the massive, grey glacial moraine coming down from the left. At the bottom is Wright's Lake, which you cannot see yet. Your goal is to contour towards that moraine. In about 0.60 miles of wonderful, easy, scenic walking, you will come to a precipice and overlook the most beautiful basin with two major merging creeks ⓫. This is our favorite spot; a relatively undiscovered alpine beauty. Pick your descent to the basin. Climb the small grassy knoll on the other side and you will clearly see the Blue Lake Trail below. Take the line of least resistance, exploring the abundant creeks and waterfalls. Cross Canyon Creek where you can. A flat bench leads easily east to intersect the trail near the pile of yellowish mine tailings ⓭. Return down the trail to your vehicle.

GPS	Mile	Latitude	Longitude	Elevation	Comment
Start 9a					
1	0.0	37,59.293N	107,45.917W	11,333'	Start 9a: Yankee Boy Loop from outhouse
2	0.15	37,59.374N	107,46.036W	11,417'	Unsigned Junction: hikers go left (S); 4x4 go straight (W).
3	0.38	37,59.408N	107,46.179W	11,433'	Unsigned Junction: hiker route joins 4x4 road.
4	0.50	37,59.383N	107,46.311W	11,400'	Signed Junction: Private Land; Hikers go left (SW); 4x4 vehicles go straight (NW).
5	0.81	37,59.288N	107,46.535W	11,538'	Road ends at turnaround. Hikers go up hill (NW) to find little trail.
6	0.91	37,59.341N	107,46.619W	11,660'	Junction with main jeep road. Sign says only short wheel base vehicles from here. Parking

GPS	Mile	Latitude	Longitude	Elevation	Comment
Start 9b					
7	1.06 / 0.0	37,59.374N	107,46.775W	11,780'	Start 9b: Blue Lakes Pass TH. Leave main trail and hike towards Canyon Creek. Cross above little waterfalls.
8	1.56 / 0.50	37,59.062N	107,46.717W	11,917'	Streams converge in basin. Hike up between them in a dry streambed and climb straight up it like a staircase.
9	1.76 / 0.70	37,58.967N	107,46.801W	12,079'	Top of climb up dry stream bed to bench
10	1.96 / 0.90	37,58.831N	107,46.745W	12,296'	Overlook Governor Basin
11	2.26 / 1.20	37,59.038N	107,46.995W	12,316'	Overlook stream basin
12	2.66 / 1.62	37,59.339N	107,47.016W	11,977'	Cross creek. Look for safe spot.
13	2.78 / 1.72	37,59.378N	107,46.926W	11,937'	Meet Blue Lake Trail. Go downhill.
7	2.96 / 1.90	37,59.374N	107,46.775W	11,780'	TH sign on 4x4 road. Meet vehicle here or walk down road to your start point.
1	3.95	37,59.293N	107,45.917W	11,333'	Start 9a Outhouse parking lot

Blue Lakes Trail North
Access to Lakes & Pass

10a
10b
10c
10d

Star Rating
☆☆☆
☆☆☆☆☆

Lower Blue Lake

10a: To Lower Lake/ Return 1

Total Distance	6.68 miles RT
Difficulty Rating	Moderately Strenuous
Surface	Mostly packed dirt but with loose rocky sections interspersed
Gradient	Moderately steep
Average Time	4.5 hours
Elevations	TH: 9,438; Highest:10,972; Gain: +2,226

10b: To Upper Lake/ Return 2

Total Distance	8.68 miles RT
Difficulty Rating	Strenuous
Surface	Dirt packed, rocky sections and scree
Gradient	Steep
Average Time	5.5 hours
Elevations	TH: 9,438; Highest:11,721; Gain: +3,111

Summary

Hike through dense forest, with a wonderful understory of many different wildflowers, to a classic glacial basin at Lower Blue Lake. The south wall of the lake's basin is a giant waterfall in spring. Seasonal wildflowers carpet the basin floor. It is magical. Optional extensions continue to the grand vistas around the upper lakes and Pass. This is the more difficult route to the Pass than Hike 8, and a more strenuous way to hike the entire trail with a shuttle.

	10c: To Pass/ Return 3
Total Distance	11.38 miles RT
Difficulty Rating	Very Strenuous
Surface	Dirt packed, rocky sections and scree, slippery side hill to pass
Gradient	Very Steep
Average Time	7 hours
Elevations	TH: 9,438; Highest:12,961; Gain: +4,471
	10d: To Yankee Boy Basin
Total Distance	7.69 miles from start to shuttle point
Difficulty Rating	Very Strenuous
Surface	Dirt packed, rocky sections and scree, slippery side hill to pass
Gradient	Very Steep
Average Time	6 hours
Elevations	TH: 9,438; Highest:12,961; Gain: +4,045; Loss: -568
Maps	Ouray Trail Group: Hiking Trails of Ouray County
Directions to TH	From OVC, drive 10 miles north on Hwy 550 to Ridgway. Turn left (W) at the traffic light towards Telluride on Hwy 62. Drive 5 miles to National Forest Access East Dallas Creek Road CR 7 sign. Turn left (S) and stay on the main gravel road. At the third cattle guard, take the right fork. It is 9 miles from the highway to the signed TH. There is camping and an outhouse one mile below the TH parking lot.
Time & Distance to TH	50 minutes; 19 miles
Recommended Vehicle	Car; although East Dallas Creek Road is gravel, it is generally a good road.
Shuttle	See Hike 8 if hiking through to Yankee Boy Basin

Trail Description

This trail is deceptive when rating difficulty. The average gradient mathematically to the lower lake works out to be moderate at 492 feet per mile, but it climbs in steep sections and flattens out for stretches. In our opinion this steep and flat configuration can be more tiring than a consistent gradient.

Most of the trail climbs through spruce forest with limited views. The forest however, has a beautiful understory of wildflowers and lush greenery that makes it a pleasurable experience. After crossing the creek at mile 1.85 ❸,views of the surrounding peaks open up. By ❹, the views become more consistent and rewarding. At ❺, the trail comes back to the stream and at ❻ there are marvelous views of waterfalls. When you get to the lake, be sure to walk along the south shore, crossing several streams, to see the wall of waterfalls at the far end.

Final approach to lake basin

A sign ❼ marks the turnoff to the upper lakes and pass. If continuing to the upper lakes; return to ❼ and go right. Notice the log bridge across the outlet stream requires gumption to cross! There is little alternative during higher flows.

The trail to the upper lakes is steep and thickly overgrown in sections before coming to a beautiful waterfall. Then enter more open terrain and rocky slabs. There are beautiful vistas of lower lake from this section. Although the upper lakes are not as dramatic as the lower, there are far fewer hikers and the views of the cirque are wonderful. Another 1.35 miles of very steep climbing gets you to the pass and panoramic vistas off both sides. This is a much more difficult route to Blue Lakes Pass than Hike 8. It is also the more strenuous way to hike the entire trail. It is much easier starting from Yankee Boy Basin side.

GPS	Mile	Latitude	Longitude	Elevation	Comment
1	0.0	38,02.062N	107,48.440W	9,438′	Start Lower Blue Lakes Trail.
2	1.45	38,01.255N	107,49.254W	10,249′	Mt Sneffels Wilderness sign
3	1.85	38,01.052N	107,49.533W	10,311′	Cross creek. Wet shoes in early season
4	2.52	38,00.626N	107,49.227W	10,687′	Views begin opening up more frequently.
5	3.0	38,00.324N	107,49.111W	10,758′	Trail comes to streamside.
6	3.06	38,00.275N	107,49.106W	10,874′	Views of waterfall
7	3.34	38,00.122N	107,48.991W	10,972′	Lower Blue Lake/ Return 1
8	3.65	38,00.194N	107,48.836W	11,249′	Cross waterfall.
9	3.93	38,00.118N	107,48.651W	11,558′	Middle Lake
10	4.34	37,59.970N	107,48.327W	11,721′	Upper Lake outlet stream/ Return 2
11	5.69	37,59.878N	107,47.713W	12,961′	Blue Lakes Pass/ Return 3

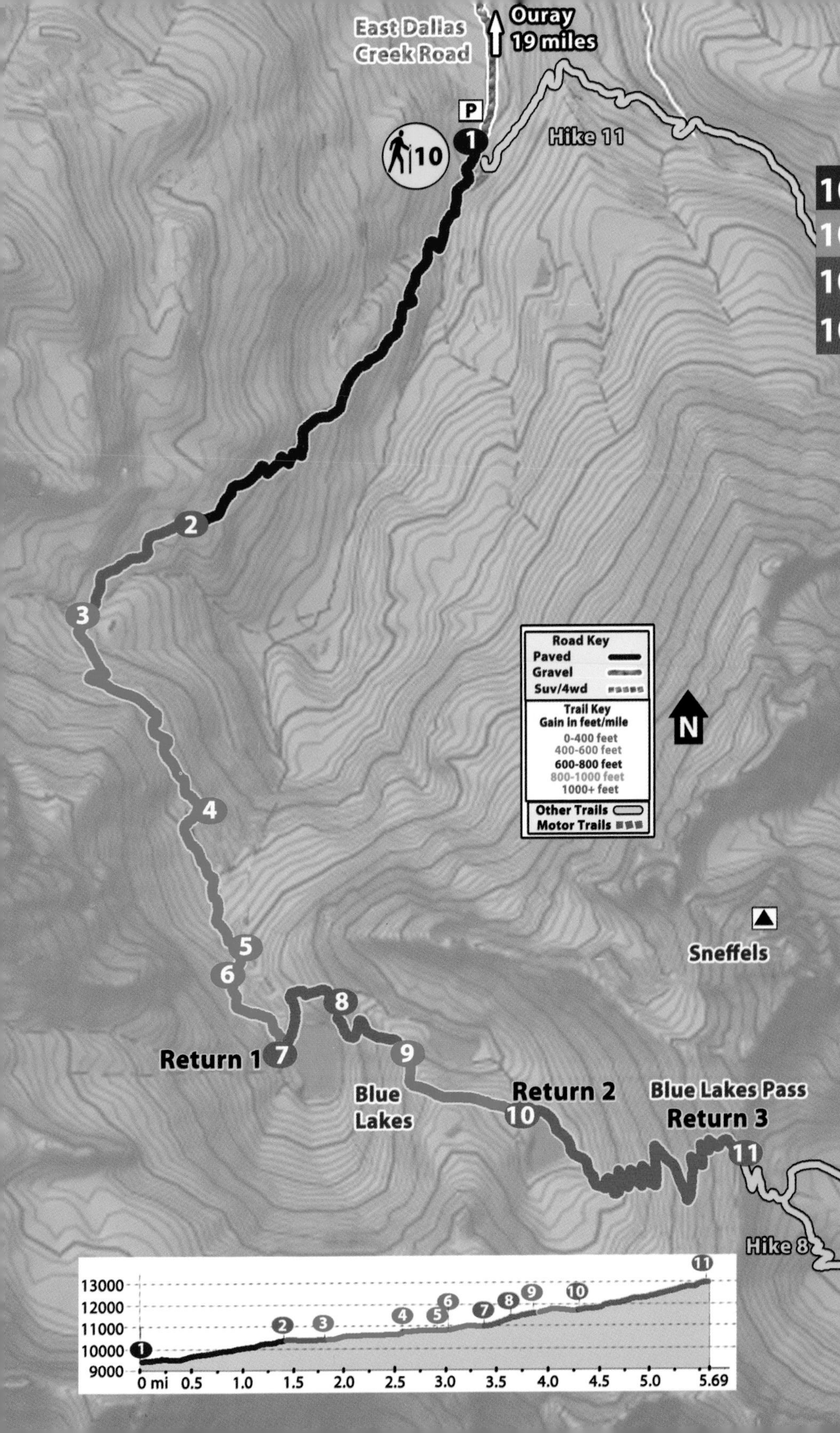
East Dallas
Creek Road
Ouray
19 miles
P
1
10
Hike 11
2
3
Road Key
Paved
Gravel
Suv/4wd
Trail Key
Gain in feet/mile
0-400 feet
400-600 feet
600-800 feet
800-1000 feet
1000+ feet
Other Trails
Motor Trails
N
4
5
6
Sneffels
7
8
9
Return 1
Blue
Lakes
Return 2
10
Blue Lakes Pass
Return 3
11
Hike 8
13000
12000
11000
10000
9000
0 mi
0.5
1.0
1.5
2.0
2.5
3.0
3.5
4.0
4.5
5.0
5.69

Blaine Basin Options

Star Rating
☆☆☆
☆☆☆☆☆

11a
11b
11c

Lower Blaine Basin

11a: To Waterfall Viewpoint/ Return 1

Total Distance	4.32 miles RT
Difficulty Rating	Easy
Surface	Packed dirt and some rocky sections
Gradient	Easy
Average Time	2 hours
Elevations	TH 9,438; Highest; 9,871; Gain: +1.017

11b: To Lower Blaine Basin/ Return 2

Total Distance	6.26 miles RT
Difficulty Rating	Strenuous
Surface	Much of the trail is rocky, especially the steep section
Gradient	To mile 2.16 is easy; from 2.16 to the end is strenuous
Average Time	4.5 hours
Elevations	TH: 9,438; Highest: 10,715; Gain: +1,925

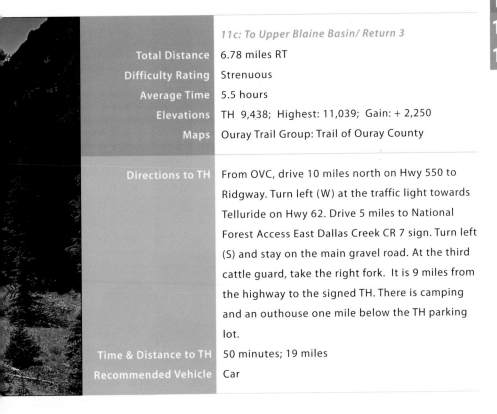

	11c: To Upper Blaine Basin/ Return 3
Total Distance	6.78 miles RT
Difficulty Rating	Strenuous
Average Time	5.5 hours
Elevations	TH 9,438; Highest: 11,039; Gain: + 2,250
Maps	Ouray Trail Group: Trail of Ouray County
Directions to TH	From OVC, drive 10 miles north on Hwy 550 to Ridgway. Turn left (W) at the traffic light towards Telluride on Hwy 62. Drive 5 miles to National Forest Access East Dallas Creek CR 7 sign. Turn left (S) and stay on the main gravel road. At the third cattle guard, take the right fork. It is 9 miles from the highway to the signed TH. There is camping and an outhouse one mile below the TH parking lot.
Time & Distance to TH	50 minutes; 19 miles
Recommended Vehicle	Car

Summary

This is an easy hike for 2.4 miles through open forest with a variety of interesting sections including intermittent peak views, small wildflower meadows blooming in season, a roaring creek and two magnificent waterfalls. The last mile to the basin is very steep and rocky but offers great views near the top. Blaine Basin brings you right up against the base of Mt.Sneffels. Three waterfalls cascade down the walls. It is not as dramatic a basin as Blue Lake but gets a lot less hiker traffic.

Trail Description

The first section of the trail from ❶ to ❷ gently ascends an old road lined with wildflowers. There are wonderful views of the Blue Lake Peaks behind you as you climb, and some small open meadows. The trail can be very wet in many places all the way to ❺. The trail come to a creek crossing that requires wet shoes ❷ at mile 1.16. If you walk back down the trail 30 feet, you will see a narrow trail heading upstream. Follow it about 100 yards to a log bridge crossing and save changing into wet shoes. This next section, between ❷ and ❹ passes through some lovely flowered meadows and mixed aspen/spruce forest with lots of wildflowers. There are no views out, but it is a peaceful and lovely part of the trail. From the log crossing at 4 to another at 5 the trail follows the roaring stream more closely. Cross the logs at 5 and look up immediately to see a magnificent waterfall. This is a good short option return point. Once you move on, you will not see it again and the trail soon begins a steep ascent. A second waterfall appears in another hundred yards through an opening to the right, but you will only see it at that spot. Come to a signed junction 6 and the trail now enters thick forest and leaves the creek to start the climb to the basin. There are no more views until near the top of the climb which is very steep (700 feet) and rocky. Once in the basin, you are surrounded by high peaks including 14,150 foot Mt Sneffels. Return from here or continue another 0.26 miles and 325 feet higher to the upper basin where you feel very close to the sheer walls of the cirque.

Only view of this waterfall after crossing creek at return 1

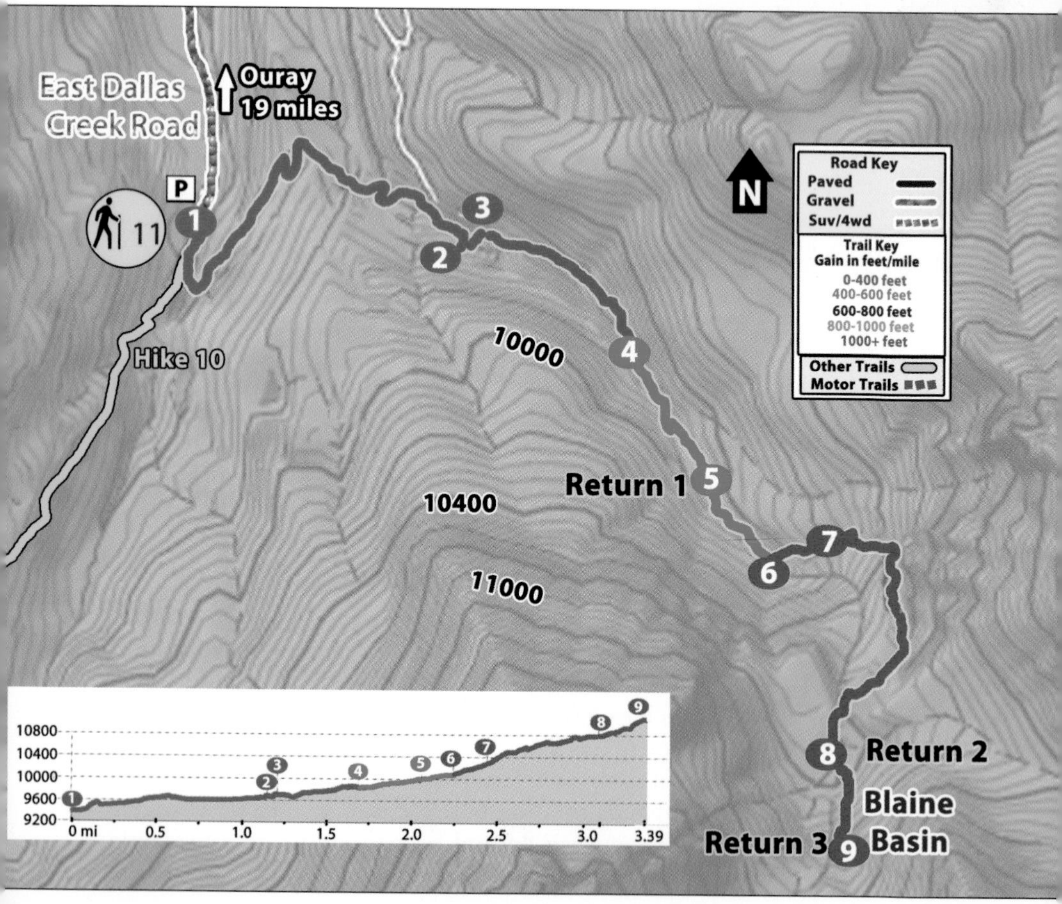

GPS	Mile	Latitude	Longitude	Elevation	Comment
1	0.0	38,02.062N	107,48.440W	9,438′	Start Blaine Trail.
2	1.16	38,02.038N	107,47.808W	9,639′	Cross stream or go back 30 feet. Take small trail going upstream to log bridge and cross there.
3	1.28	38,02.078N	107,47.766W	9,628′	Signed Junction: Go right (SE).
4	1.76	38,01.861N	107,47.407W	9,697′	Cross creek over log bridge.
5	2.16	38,01.619N	107,47.236W	9,871′	Cross Creek over log bridge. Waterfall views/ Return 1
6	2.39	38,01.483N	107,47.089W	9,954′	Signed junction: Go left uphill.
7	2.54	38,01.519N	107,46.960W	10,093′	Signed junction: Wilson Creek. Take right fork.
8	3.13	38,01.146N	107,46.938W	10,715′	Lower Blaine Basin/ Return 2
9	3.39	38,00.954N	107,46.924W	11,039′	Upper Blaine Basin/ Return 3

Return point 1 before steep climb begins

West Dallas Creek Trail

Star Rating

☆☆☆☆

View of San Juan Range from return 1

Total Distance	3.78 RT to cabin site
Difficulty Rating	Moderate
Surface	Packed dirt
Gradient	Easy & moderate with very short strenuous section
Average Time	2.5 hours
Elevations	TH: 9,231; Highest: 9,827; Gain: +921
Maps	Latitude 40: Telluride, Silverton, Ouray

Directions to TH

The drive to this trailhead is a 5 star scenic drive! From the OVC, drive 10 miles north on Hwy 550 to Ridgway. Turn left (W) on Hwy 62 towards Telluride. Drive 6.7 miles to the signed turnoff to West Dallas Creek Rd. Zero your odometer here. This is a good gravel road. There are many spur roads to private property; follow the obvious main road. Drive 6 miles to the National Forest Sign. At mile 6.6, there is a Dallas Creek TH sign. Ignore it and continue driving to mile 6.7 and drive across the creek. Stay to the right at the Y for 100 yards more. The TH starts at the orange gate. It is in a beautiful meadow called Box Factory Park with stunning views of the San Juan Range.

Time & Mileage to TH

1 hour; 23.5 miles

Recommended Vehicle

SUVs. The last 0.8 miles to the trailhead are very rough.

Summary

A very short easy hike with aspens and wildflower meadows. Stunning close up views of the San Juan Range and distant views of the Cimarron Range. This is a relatively unknown trail and not detailed in any books.

Trail Description

The trail starts moderately uphill through a beautiful aspen forest with a colorful under story of various wildflowers. Soon, it descends easily and you enter a big meadow with Lupine and close up views of the San Juan Range. Cross the creek ❸; in spring you might have to go upstream a 100 feet so you can jump

Aspens and flowers at beginning of trail

across it. Ascend the short but strenuous hill to the obvious top 4 enjoying the colorful wildflowers and aspens in season. You are very close to the San Juan Range. In the distance, you can see the Cimarron Range as well. This makes a good short option return point. If you continue from 4 the trail is an old road that enters aspen and spruce forest and there are only a couple more views of the mountains. It is a pleasant walk to an old cabin site, but in spring, the trail has become the creek course and is very muddy and wet. Follow this road. At a junction 5 stay on the jeep road straight ahead. The trail to the right is actually the Dallas Trail and is marked with a blue cross country ski sign, but we find the route less attractive as it enters thick forest with a lot of blow down. At another unmarked junction 6 cross the water canal and take the road uphill to the right. Stay to the right as it enters a meadow 7 and in 100 yards you will see the old cabin site 8. There is no more trail from here.

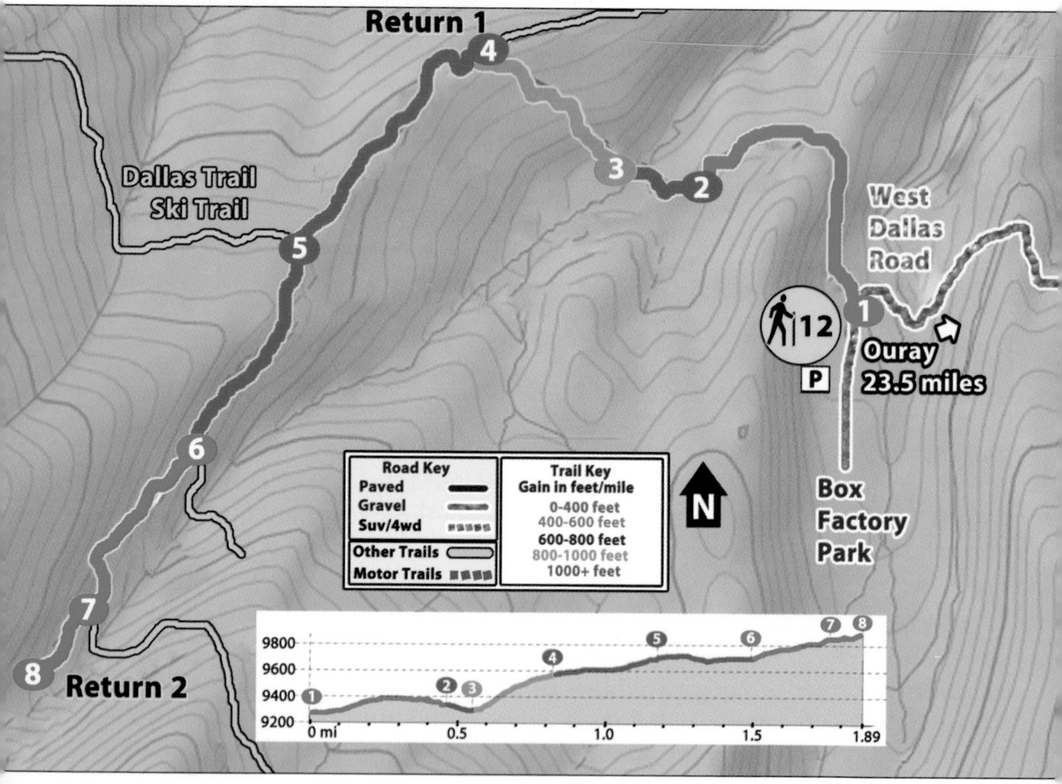

Halfway up to top

GPS	Mile	Latitude	Longitude	Elevation	Comment
1	0.0	38,02.902N	107,51.659W	9,231′	Start West Dallas Creek Trail.
2	0.40	38,03.048N	107,51.900W	9,265′	Enter big meadow with views and flowers.
3	0.50	38,03.060N	107,51.993W	9,283′	Cross Creek. Go upstream 50′ to jump it.
4	0.81	38,03.189N	107,52.242W	9,575′	Top of meadow. Good return point
5	1.21	38,02.979N	107,52.489W	9,641′	Junction: Marked ski trail goes right. Better hiking with views straight ahead.
6	1.51	38,02.737N	107,52.656W	9,691′	Cross water canal and go uphill to right for old cabin site.
7	1.81	38,02.551N	107,52.815W	9,695′	Unmarked junction: go right uphill to old cabin site. Lower trail crosses stream and stays in the trees for a long distance.
8	1.89	38,02.488N	107,52.872W	9,827′	Old Cabin site. No more trail. Return.

13

Baldy Peak via Storm's Gulch Loop

Star Rating

☆☆☆

☆☆☆☆☆

View from Baldy Peak

Total Distance	6.84 mile loop from 13a to Peak
Difficulty Rating	Strenuous
Surface	Much of the surface is rough and rocky. The lower portion of Baldy Trail is heavily overgrown with brush and very rough and rocky. This adds difficulty to the hike overall
Gradient	There are very steep sections alternating with more restful moderate sections
Average Time	6 to 8 hours
Elevations	TH: 8,476; Highest: 10,603; Gain: +2,692
Maps	Ouray Trail Group: Hiking Trails of Ouray County
Directions to TH	From OVC, drive 1.7 miles north to Dexter Creek Road (CR 14). Turn right and drive on good gravel road for 0.95 miles. Turn left on Cutler Creek Road 14A and cross the bridge. Drive 2.58 miles to Start 13a to an open field that leads to the Cutler Creek TH. Park here and walk 0.32 miles to the signed Baldy TH unless you have a 4x4 short wheel base vehicle. Go down the steep, rocky road to the left of the field, cross two streams (wet shoes recommended for walkers) and arrive at the Baldy trailhead which is Start 13b
Time & Distance to TH	30 minutes; 5.55 to Start 13b
Recommended Vehicle	Car to Start 13a; 4x4 to Start 13b

Hike aspen forest up Storm Gulch

Summary

Superb views of the San Juan, and Cimarron Ranges, the Uncompahgre Plateau, Red Mountain, Abram, even on a clear day, the La Sal Range near Moab. The mountains and peaks stack one behind the other in 3D. In season wildflowers cover the meadows and brilliant fall color from golden aspen to red oak paint the hillsides. By doing the loop, experience two totally different environments: Storm's Gulch trail is intimate as it climbs through fir and aspen forests; Baldy Trail is mostly wide open with far reaching vistas.

Trail Description

Baldy trail is south facing and is clear of snow early season. For this reason, on a hot day, it can also be a very hot climb. We recommend climbing in the cool shade of the forest, and descending in the heat. Within a hundred yards of

Return leg of route. Beautiful vistas!

the Baldy TH sign is the junction for Storm's Gulch Trail ❸. Take the right fork following the creek. Cross it at the next junction ❹ with Shortcut Trail. Continue straight (NE) at this junction and ascend through fir and aspen forest all the way to the junction with the Baldy Trail ❻. This is an arduous climb of 1,308 feet in 1.29 miles. The forest shade keeps the climb cool and comfortable. There are incredible vistas of Sneffels and Hayden on this part of the climb. From the junction with Baldy Trail ❻, the trail turns moderate and offers fabulous views of the Cimarron Range all the way to the junction to Baldy Peak ❼. From this latter junction, there are views of the Cimarron and San Juan Ranges. It is a 180 degree panorama of mountain peaks, and valleys blessed with wildflowers, aspens, oaks and spruce. If you go the additional 1.66 miles RT to Baldy Peak ❽, you will gain additional views of the Uncompahgre Plateau, the Uncompahgre River valley, Ouray, the Dallas Divide, and even the La Sal Range near Moab, Utah.

Returning to ❼, take the trail SW down Baldy Ridge. Most of the route is open (and exposed) to continuous mountain vistas. Wildflowers bloom along the trail, beautiful aspen and spruce forests dot the valley hillsides. It is what landscape painters paint! Eventually the trail descends into oak brush ❾ which has overcome the trail so completely as to hide your footing. About 1.0 miles of loose rocks, deep horse cuts, and very narrow path all contribute to the price paid for the splendid day of hiking.

GPS	Mile	Latitude	Longitude	Elevation	Comment
1	0.0	38,05.198N	107,40.356W	8,476′	Start 13a: Park here unless driving 4x4 SWB vehicle.
2	0.32	38,05.450N	107,40.319W	8,603′	Start 13b: Baldy TH. Need 4x4 SWB to drive here.
3	0.38	38,05.475N	107,40.316W	8,440′	Signed junction: Go right (N) for Storm's Gulch Trail, left (W) to Baldy if not making a loop.
4	0.78	38,05.791N	107,40.138W	8,885′	Signed junction: Go straight ahead (NE) for Storm's Gulch Trail. Shortcut Trail is to the right (E).
5	1.37	38,06.224N	107,39.745W	9,435′	Cross Creek again.
6	2.07	38,06.707N	107,39.710W	10.127′	Unmarked junction: Baldy Trail. Go left (W) to Baldy Peak. Right (E) makes a loop with shortcut trail.
7	2.83	38,06.649N	107,40.315W	10,493′	Signed junction: West to Baldy Peak or South on Baldy Trail back to vehicle.
8	3.66	38,06.630N	107,40.873W	10,603′	Baldy Peak.
7	4.49	38,06.649N	107,40.315W	10,493′	Signed junction: Go south on Baldy Trail.
9	5.82	38,05.698N	107,40.747W	9,574′	Trail deteriorates and is fiercely overgrown from here to finish.
2	6.54	38,05.450N	107,40.319W	8,603′	Baldy TH sign; Start 13b
1	6.84	38,05.198N	107,40.356W	8,476′	Finish Baldy Trail at Start 13a

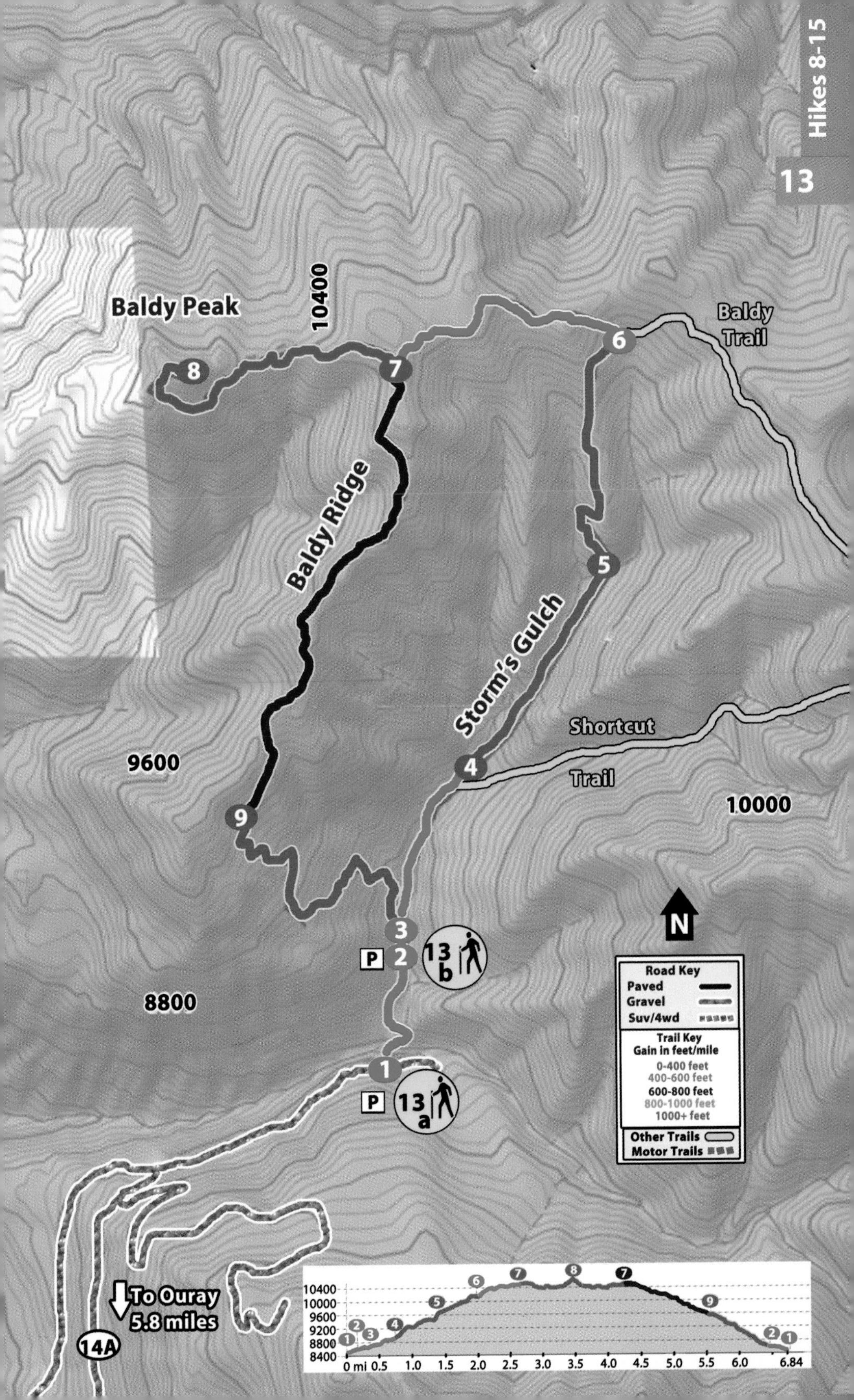
Baldy Peak
10400
Baldy Trail
Baldy Ridge
Storm's Gulch
Shortcut Trail
9600
10000
8800
13 a
13 b
N
Road Key
Paved
Gravel
Suv/4wd
Trail Key
Gain in feet/mile
0-400 feet
400-600 feet
600-800 feet
800-1000 feet
1000+ feet
Other Trails
Motor Trails
To Ouray 5.8 miles
14A
10400
10000
9600
9200
8800
8400
0 mi 0.5 1.0 1.5 2.0 2.5 3.0 3.5 4.0 4.5 5.0 5.5 6.0 6.84

Bear Creek Trail Options

14a
14b
14c

Star Rating

☆☆☆☆☆

View of Ouray ascending switchbacks

14a: To Overlook/ Return 1

Total Distance	2.42 miles RT
Difficulty Rating	Moderately Strenuous
Surface	First mile is broken slate; remainder is packed dirt with loose rock
Gradient	1.0 mile of Steep from TH to top of switchbacks
Average Time	2 hours
Elevations	TH: 8,439; Highest: 9,432; Gain: +1,289

14b: To Grizzly Bear Mine/ Return 2

Total Distance	4.92 miles RT
Difficulty Rating	Moderately Strenuous
Surface	First mile is broken slate; remainder is packed dirt with loose rock
Gradient	1.0 mile of Steep from TH to top of switchbacks; Moderate to mine
Average Time	4 hours
Elevations	TH: 8,439; Highest; 9,957; Gain: +2,614

	14c: To Yellow Jacket Mine
Total Distance	8.42 miles RT
Difficulty Rating	Strenuous
Surface	First mile is broken slate; remainder is packed dirt with loose rock
Gradient	1.0 mile of Steep from TH to top of switchbacks; 2.4 miles Moderate; 0.7 Steep to mine
Average Time	6 hours
Elevations	TH: 8,439; Highest: 11,183; Gain: +3884
Maps	Ouray Trail Group: Hiking Trails of Ouray County
Directions to TH	From OVC, drive south on US Hwy 550 for 3.0 miles. As soon as you pass through the tunnel, there is a small parking area on the right (W) side of the highway. A sign marks the TH.
Time & Distance to TH	10 minutes; 3.0 miles
Recommended Vehicle	Car

Summary

This trail is an old mining route that is carved into the sheer cliffs high above Bear Creek and the Uncompahgre Gorge. The trail is a fascinating engineering accomplishment and offers a unique hiking experience. It is part of the Colorado Hard Rock 100 foot race that goes from Silverton to Lake City, Ouray, Telluride and back to Silverton. As you hike farther, spectacular vistas of Whitehouse Mountain, Hayden Mountain, Red Mountain, Mt Abram, Potosi Peak and finally even Engineer Pass can be viewed from the trail.

Mid section along cliffs

Trail Description

This trail is not recommended for hikers who do not like narrow trails on cliff edges.

That said, because much of the trail is south facing, it can be hiked by mid-June most years. We divide the trail into three parts because each offers a very different experience. From the TH to the top of the switchbacks (❷ overlook), the climb is steep, the trail cuts through broken slate, and passes from forest to thrilling vistas of the Uncompahgre Gorge and the town of Ouray. The second part from the top to Grizzly Bear Mine ❸ contours high above Bear Creek on a very narrow trail cut out from the cliffs with views straight down and straight up. There is a gradual ascent through lovely aspen forest just before reaching the old boiler site. The mine shaft itself is across the river gorge. The third part from Grizzly Bear Mine to Yellow Jacket Mine drops down to Bear Creek ❹, undulates through forest and meadow, crosses the creek ❺(wet shoes recommended during snow melt season) and then climbs relentlessly to the Yellow Jacket Mine ❻. Amazing views of the entire Whitehouse Massive framed by the Bear Creek Gorge can keep photographers very busy on this section.

Near top of switchbacks: Photo by Rozanne Evans

GPS	Mile	Latitude	Longitude	Elevation	Comment
1	0.0	38,00.311N	107,39.715W	8,439′	Start Bear Creek Trail.
2	1.21	38,00.193N	107,39.351W	9,432′	Top of switchbacks. Return 1
3	2.46	37,59.926N	107,38.315W	9,957′	Grizzly Bear Mine; Return 2
4	3.39	37,59.923N	107,37.447W	10,532′	Trail meets creek level.
5	3.57	37,59.874N	107,37.286W	10,597′	Cross creek. Wet shoes through snow melt
6	4.21	37,59.746N	107,36.669W	11,183′	Yellow Jacket Mine. Return 3

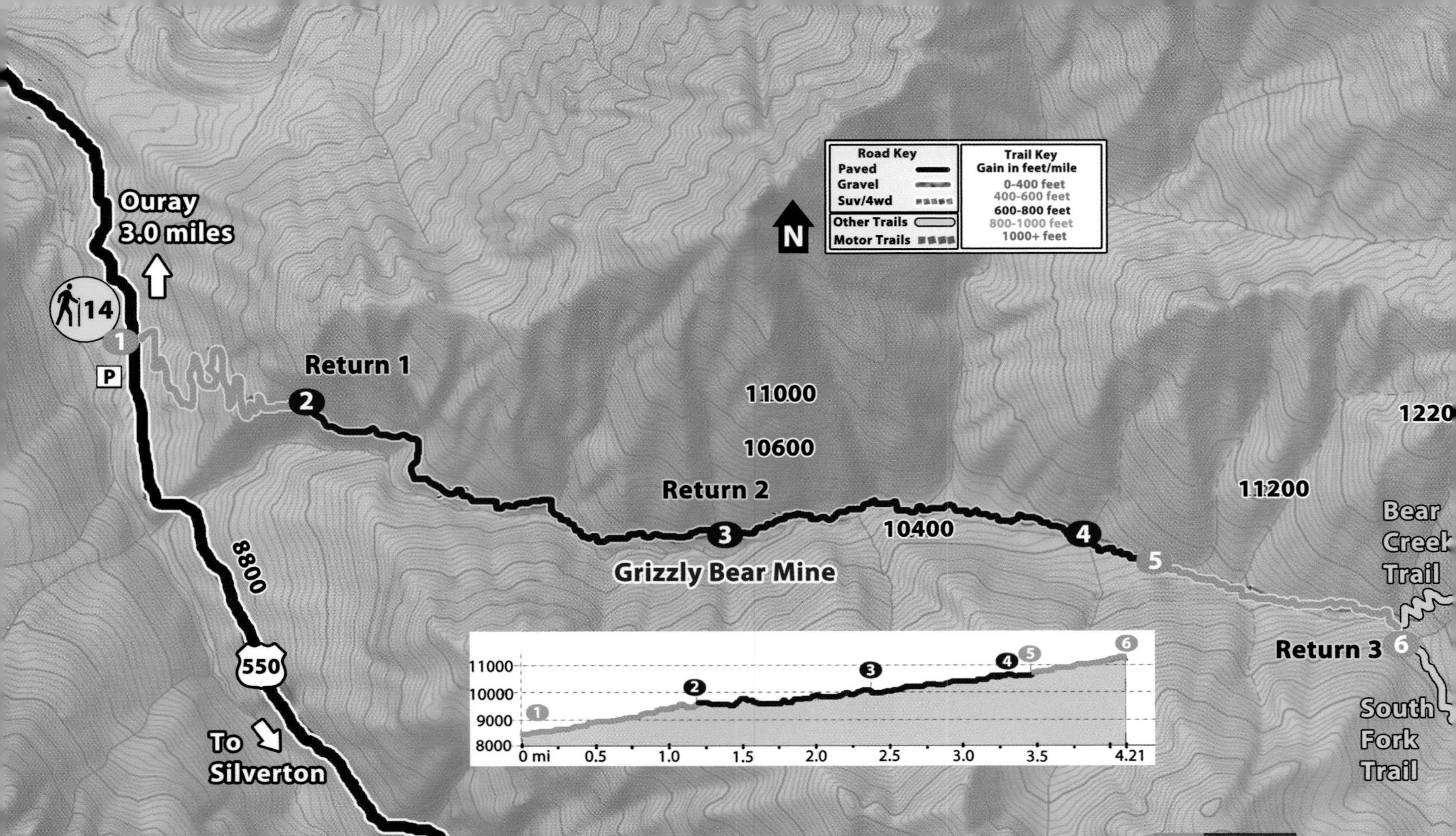

Ouray
3.0 miles
14
P
Return 1
Return 2
Return 3
Grizzly Bear Mine
11000
10600
10400
11200
1220
8800
550
To Silverton
Bear Creek Trail
South Fork Trail
N
Road Key
Paved
Gravel
Suv/4wd
Other Trails
Motor Trails
Trail Key
Gain in feet/mile
0-400 feet
400-600 feet
600-800 feet
800-1000 feet
1000+ feet
11000
10000
9000
8000
0 mi
0.5
1.0
1.5
2.0
2.5
3.0
3.5
4.21

Spirit Gulch Options

15a
15b
15c

Star Rating
☆☆☆
☆☆☆☆☆☆

15a: To Basin/ Return 1

Total Distance	3.18 miles RT
Difficulty Rating	Moderate
Surface	Old road surface is mostly loose rock entire hike
Gradient	Moderate
Average Time	2 hours
Elevations	TH: 10,668; Highest; 11,425; Gain: +924

15b: To Highest Point/ Return 2

Total Distance	5.06 RT
Difficulty Rating	Moderate

Entering Spirit Basin

Directions to TH

From the OVC, drive 11.7 miles south on Hwy 550 to the first switchback above the Red Mountain Mining Overlook (south of milepost 82). There is a locked gate with a no parking sign at the switchback, but parking is okay as long as you do not block the gate. Otherwise, park in the overlook and walk to the gate. There is no TH sign. You will be walking the no longer used mining track.

Time & Mileage to TH

35 minutes; 11.7 miles

Recommended Vehicle

Car

Gradient	Moderate with 0.94 miles moderately strenuous from basin to high point
Average Time	3.5 hours
Elevations	TH: 10,668; Highest; 12,054; Gain: +1,575

15c: Shuttle

Total Distance	6.56 miles from start to shuttle
Difficulty Rating	Moderate
Gradient	Moderate with 0.94 miles moderately strenuous from basin to high point
Average Time	4.5 hours
Elevations	TH: 10,668; Highest: 12,054; Gain: +1,653; Loss: -2,324
Maps	Ouray Trail Group: Hiking Trails of Ouray County

Summary

Go out and back any distance you like, or hike the route with shuttle for more time and views above tree line. This track goes to a beautiful basin with amazing seasonal wildflowers, creeks, waterfalls, and views of the three Red Mountains. If continuing, climb above the basin and contour around for completely different perspectives of the surrounding peaks. Wet shoes recommended for 3 creek crossings through mid-July.

Several creeks to cross

Trail Description

Miners carved roads into much of Colorado's scenic backcountry. This trail is a gem, reaching a high alpine basin quickly and continuing on to contour high above Red Mountain Pass. The road winds up through old mine sites with lots of relics. Though at first you hike in spruce forest, it is open to many wonderful vistas of the three Red Mountains and beyond. Cross three creeks early on at ❷, ❸, and ❹. Reach the old Barstow Mine site at ❺ in Commodore Gulch surrounded by 13,000 foot peaks. Wildflowers grow along the roadside and there are plentiful views of the Red Mountains. After an especially nice viewpoint at ❻, it's only 0.23 more miles to Spirit Basin ❼ where seasonal wildflowers flourish on the hillsides against a backdrop of towering peaks. Explore the basin and return from here for a short outing if

Views of Red Mountain from trail

First viewpoint

Looking back down valley from road above basin

Descending road to shuttle. WOW!

you wish. Looking north, see the track where it climbs the flower filled hillside and continue to the high point ⑧ for a wonderful added excursion. Once at the top, the road diverges. Take the lower, wider track that goes straight ahead (N). Now, it is a long, gentle contour with wonderful views all the way to ⑩ where you finally enter lovely aspen trees to the trails end.

GPS	Mile	Latitude	Longitude	Elevation	Comment
1	0.0	37,54.947N	107,42.208W	10,668′	Start Spirit Gulch Trail at gate.
2	0.33	37,55.142N	107,42.365W	10,610′	Cross first stream.
3	0.45	37,55.267N	107,42.369W	10,719′	Cross second stream.
4	0.55	37,55.298N	107,42.437W	10,783′	Cross third stream.
5	0.81	37,55.217N	107,42.635W	10,930′	Old Barstow mine site
6	1.36	37,55.470N	107,42.524N	11,254′	Viewpoint
7	1.59	37,55.579N	107,42.615W	11,425′	Cross creek into Spirit Basin. Return 1
8	2.53	37,55.816N	107,42.568W	12,054′	Top of climb: unmarked fork. Return 2; or take lower old grassy covered track straight ahead.
9	3.53	37,56.358N	107,42.113W	11,732′	Old Greyhound Mine site
10	5.10	37,55.957N	107,41.684W	10,877′	Enter aspen trees to end of trail.
11	6.56	37,55.738N	107,41.406W	10,021′	Trail meets Hwy 550.

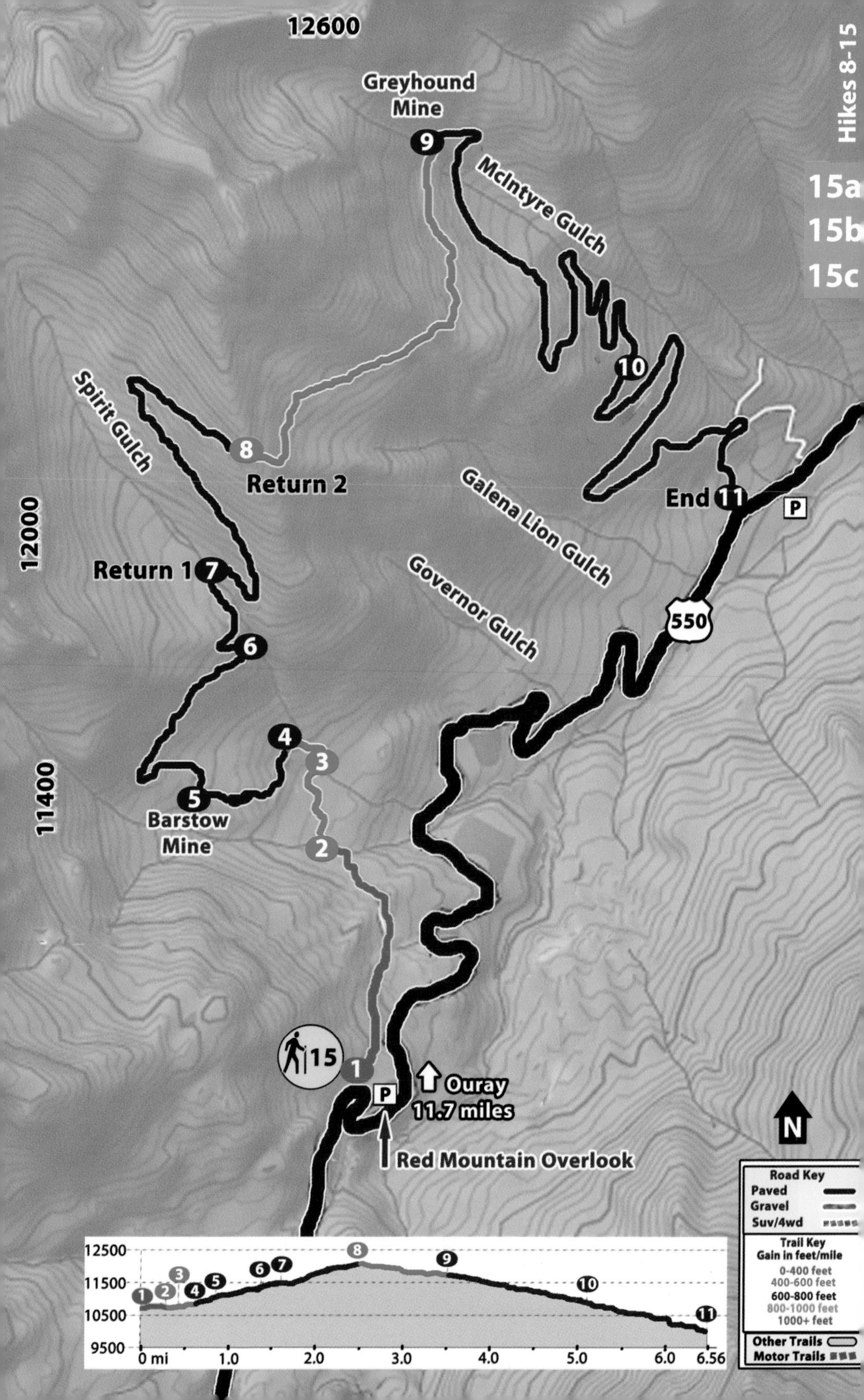
12600
Greyhound Mine
9
McIntyre Gulch
10
Spirit Gulch
8
Return 2
Galena Lion Gulch
End 11
P
12000
Return 1 7
Governor Gulch
550
6
4
3
11400
5
Barstow Mine
2
15
1
P
Ouray 11.7 miles
Red Mountain Overlook
N
Road Key
Paved
Gravel
Suv/4wd
Trail Key
Gain in feet/mile
0-400 feet
400-600 feet
600-800 feet
800-1000 feet
1000+ feet
Other Trails
Motor Trails
12500
11500
10500
9500
0 mi
1.0
2.0
3.0
4.0
5.0
6.0
6.56

Silverton: Silver hauled out by the ton

In the 1880's large numbers of settlers from Europe were encouraged to migrate to Silverton with the promise of free land. Most were men of lower economic means who worked in the mines and on the railroads. The historical society describes the developing town as rough violent and turbulent. Casualties in the mines, bars and on the streets were common. Aided by the influence of gambling, prostitution and liquor, lynchings and suicides were frequent events. Evidence of much of the early rugged history of the town remains today in the restored older buildings and the original buildings situated on the back gravel streets. Many of the structures are still saloons today, somewhat as they were in the early history.

Silverton's draw is its authentic historical charm and friendly populace that makes visitors feel so welcome. There are pleasant

Silverton

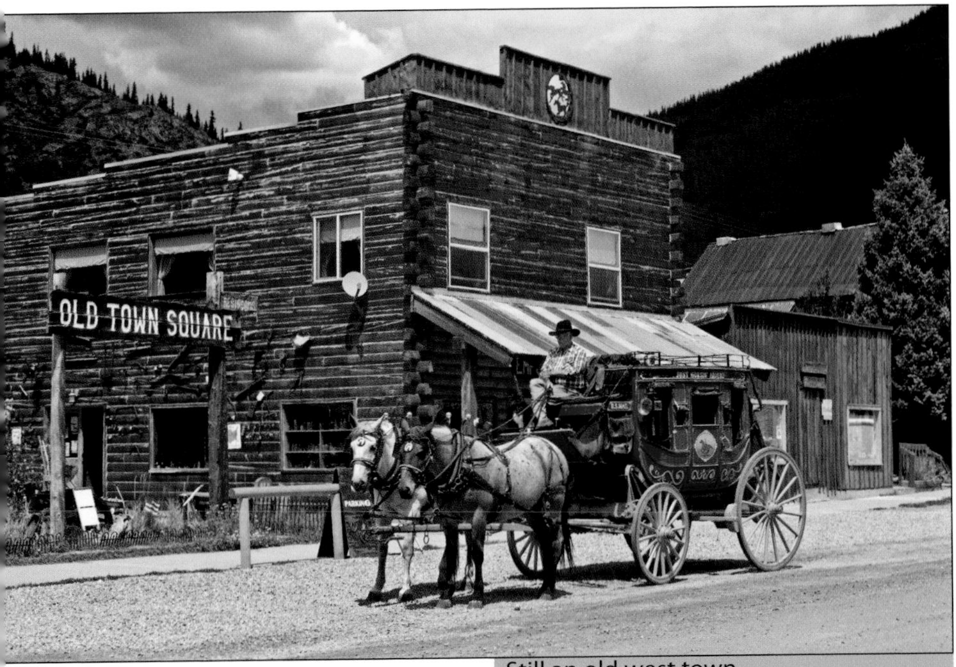

Still an old west town

RV parks, historic hotels, and plenty of free dispersed camping. San Juan Backcountry Tours and Rentals offers trailhead drop-off and shuttle service The famous Durango-Silverton narrow gage train arrives every summer day bringing world travelers into its embrace. Be sure to stop in at the Silverton Visitor Center; it is an excellent resource and the staff are delighted to share their knowledge of the area.

The area is saturated with old mining roads that give access to many of the hikes. The miners also built hundreds of pack trails to their private holdings; these amazing trails provide the bulk of the hiking routes in this section. Some trails are steep and rugged; many trails are across open tundra with explosive vistas. The Silverton area will expose hikers to some of the most dramatic and rugged high country hiking in the state, including parts of the Continental Divide Trail and the Colorado Trail. This is special stuff. Enjoy!

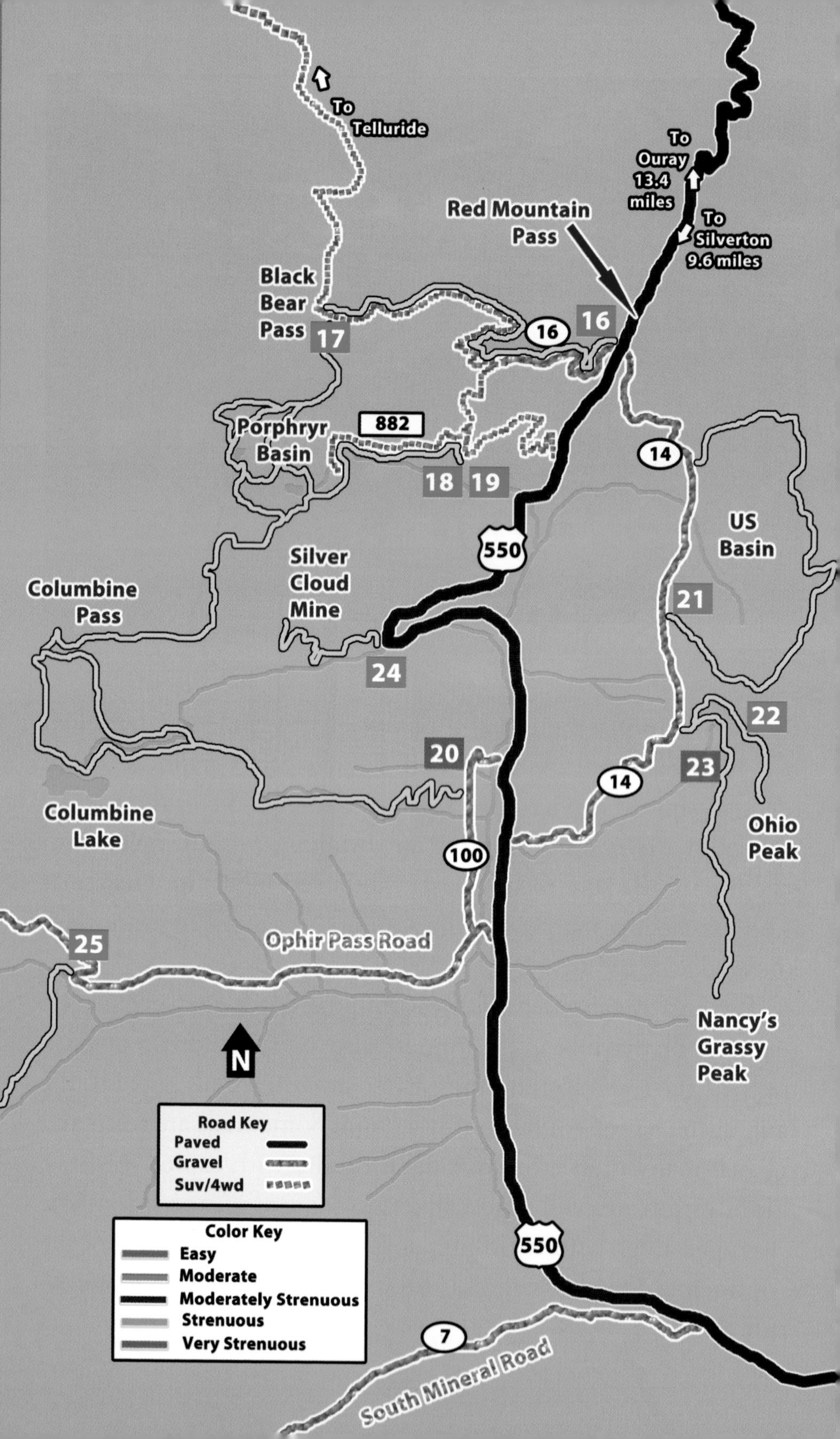
To Telluride
To Ouray 13.4 miles
To Silverton 9.6 miles
Red Mountain Pass
Black Bear Pass
17
16
16
882
Porphryr Basin
18
19
14
US Basin
550
Silver Cloud Mine
Columbine Pass
21
24
22
20
23
14
Ohio Peak
Columbine Lake
100
Ophir Pass Road
25
Nancy's Grassy Peak
N
Road Key
Paved
Gravel
Suv/4wd
Color Key
Easy
Moderate
Moderately Strenuous
Strenuous
Very Strenuous
550
7
South Mineral Road

Silverton North Trails Locator Map

16. Black Bear Pass
17. Grand Traverse
18. Porphyry Basin Loop
19. Porphyry Basin To Columbine Pass
20. Columbine TH to Columbine Pass
21. US Basin to McMillan Peak
22. Ohio Peak
23. Nancy's Grassy Peak
24. Silver Cloud Mine
25. Paradise Basin

16a
16b

Black Bear Pass via Road

Star Rating

☆☆☆☆☆

16a to Pass

Total Distance	6.32 miles RT
Difficulty Rating	Moderate
Surface	This is an active 4x4 road with good dirt pack and tight gravel surface
Gradient	Moderate
Average Time	4.5 hours
Elevations	TH: 11,084; Highest: 12,841; Gain: +1,991

16b to Pass

Total Distance	4.32 miles RT
Average Time	3.5 hours
Elevations	TH: 11,516; Gain: +1,493
Map	Trails Illustrated #141: Silverton, Ouray

High Viewpoint

Directions to TH	From SVC, drive 9.6 miles north on Hwy 550 to the signed Black Bear Road (County Rd 16 near milepost 80). This is a popular jeep road and is busy on weekends. Ample parking at highway junction for Start 16a. Or, drive 1.0 miles to unsigned Porphyry Basin Junction and park there for Start 16b.
Time & Distance to TH	30 to 40 minutes; 9.6 to 10.6 miles
Recommended Vehicle	Car to Start 16a; SUVs to Start 16b at Porphyry Basin junction

Summary

Entirely open to wide vistas right from the start, this hike features magnificent waterfalls, carpets of seasonal wildflowers, amazing views of peaks and valleys that get bigger as you ascend. It may be a favorite 4x4 road for vehicles, but it is worth every walking second. Traffic is minimal mid-week. This is high alpine scenery at its best; we give it a 5 star rating instead of 6 only because it is on an active road. If you want easy car access, easy walking, and stunning vistas, hike this trail!

Trail Description

This side of Black Bear Pass is a very good jeep road that ascends moderately. It is very pleasant walking. The first mile ascends just 486 feet and winds through a wide alpine basin. Come to a junction ❷ to Porphyry Gulch. Seasonal wildflowers can be very thick by this point. Two magnificent waterfalls plummet down the sheer rock walls. Continue straight uphill for Black Bear Pass. The second 1.5 miles climbs 692 feet. Reach a switchback and now there are added vistas of the three Red Mountains and down valley to Ouray. It gets more amazing as you climb. The pass is more barren but the views are 180 degrees. What a hike!

GPS	Mile	Latitude	Longitude	Elevation	Comment
1	0.0	37,53.807N	107,42.801W	11,084′	Start 16a at Hwy 550 & Black Bear Pass Road.
2	1.0 / 0.0	37,53.718N	107,43.555W	11,516′	Start 16b at unsigned junction to Porphyry Gulch; go straight uphill.
3	2.42 / 1.42	37,54.051N	107,43.821W	12,444′	Ponds. Gradient becomes moderate again.
4	3.16 / 2.16	37,53.960N	107,44.585W	12,841′	Summit Black Bear Pass.

Hiking the lower road

Waterfalls are visible throughout the hike

One of many waterfalls

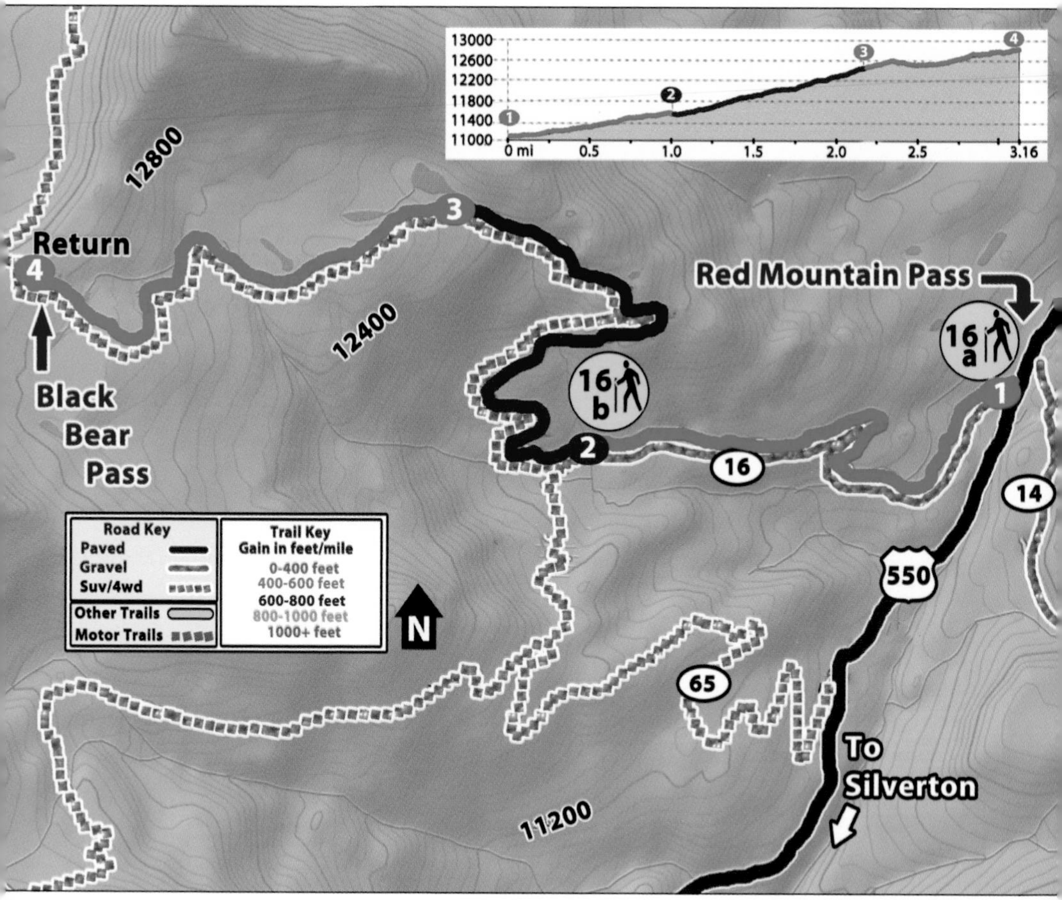

Grand Traverse

Star Rating

☆☆☆☆☆

On route to Columbine Pass; Photo by Rozanne Evans

Total Distance	8.06 miles from start to shuttle point
Difficulty Rating	Moderate
Surface	Animal trails, cross country tundra, 1.5 miles of loose gravel that slides on steep descent
Gradient	Mostly moderate. Last mile is very steep downhill
Average Time	6 to 8 hours
Elevations	TH: 12,840; Highest: 13,100; Gain: +1,353; Loss: -3,872
Map	Latitude 40: Telluride, Silverton, Ouray. San Juan Mountain Maps 2010: Telluride, Silverton, Ouray. Only some trails are on maps
Directions to TH	From SVC, drive 9.6 miles north on Hwy 550 to the signed Black Bear Road (County Rd 16 near milepost 80). Drive 3.16 miles on CR 16 to Black Bear Pass. This is a popular jeep road and is busy on weekends. Park at the pass.
Time & Distance to TH	1 hour; 12.8 miles
Recommended Vehicle	SUV

Descending to Columbine Lake from Pass; Photo by Sigrid Werbitsch

Shuttle From SVC, drive 5.5 miles north on Hwy 550 and turn left onto signed Ophir Pass Road, CR 8 (just south of milepost 76). Cross the bridge and drive about another 200 yards to a sharp right turn onto CR 100. Drive up the hill 0.7 miles to an unmarked steep path on the left side. A wide spot in the road can park 3 small cars. For more parking, drive uphill another 300 yards to the old Imogene Mine tailings. If you continue this road, it meets US 550 but there is a creek crossing that may be deep in the spring.

Time & Mileage to Shuttle 25 minutes, 6.2 miles

Recommended Vehicle SUV

Last basin to descend

Summary

This is a traverse we put together that encompasses 5 spectacular basins, 5 passes, lakes, waterfalls, wildflowers and so much more. Though the hike is 8 miles long, most of it is moderate; elevation gain is 1353 feet. It starts at 12,841 feet and stays high until the final 2.0 miles when you finish at 10,325 feet. Trails are intermittent, but the route is easy to see as you progress. Our photos will give you guidance as well. This is Colorado high country at its finest!

Trail Description

Black Bear Pass to first saddle

There is no trail to the saddle separating Black Bear Basin and Porphyry Basin. Look due south from Black Bear Pass for an obvious saddle. It is a moderate contour of 0.50 miles to get there 2. Once on this saddle, you can see your entire route around Porphyry Basin to the saddle on its southern side 5. From 2 you have two route options. Start your descent and continue south to 2a which takes you across the Porphyry Basin floor to Porphyry Lake. We prefer leaving this trail about a third of the way down and keeping a contour due west just below the rock fall areas to reach 3, a saddle that overlooks beautiful Mud Lake Basin. From there, it is an easy descent to Porphyry Lake 4. Before descending, look south over Porphyry Lake to the saddle at 5. There is a long, grassy slope leading to that saddle. After passing Porphyry Lake, climb just a bit, pass an un-named lake on your left and climb that grassy slope to 5. Look back for splendid views of Bullion King Lake.

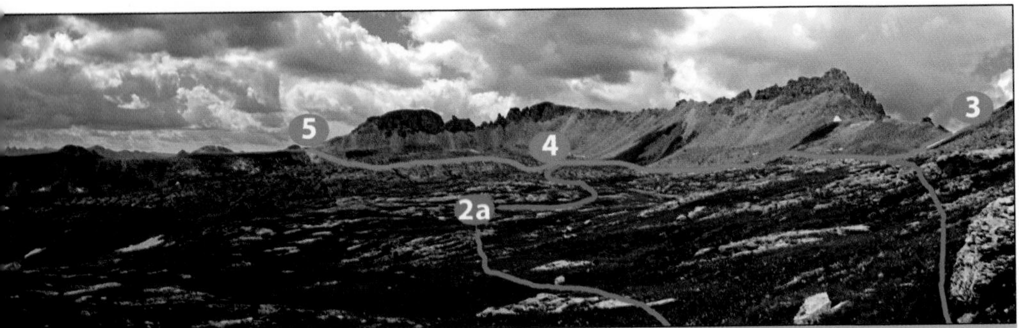

View from first saddle overlooking Porphyry Basin

Now you are overlooking Silver Cloud Mine Basin. Your route is to head west and south, around the daunting rock barriers to your right. Keep as high a contour as you can. There are numerous game trails to choose from. You will have to descend into a very wide gully 6 to get around the rock walls. Once you have ascended and are around the rock promontory, you can see Columbine Basin and Columbine

Pass ❼. This section might take 2 hours from ❻ to ❼. Stay on the pass to ❽ admiring the views down to Lewis Lake. It is an easy contour to Columbine Lake ❾ from the pass. The turquoise color is amazing. From the lake, take the trail that follows the right bank of the outlet creek down a steep section to an obvious flat area ❿. Do not cross the creek; head due east and pick up a really good trail all the way to the finish. You will climb a little bit to ⓫, entering the last basin along a cliff edge. Start the long descent through this beautiful basin, into the trees, and down the very steep trail to the finish.

Route through wide gully

GPS	Mile	Latitude	Longitude	Elevation	Comment
1	0.00	37,53.960N	107,44.585W	12,841′	Black Bear Pass. Start Grand Traverse.
2	0.50	37,53.600N	107,44.523W	12,860′	Saddle: Views into Porphyry Basin
2a	N/A	37,53.399N	107,44.852W	12,734′	Small waterfall & cairn mark alternate route through Porphyry Basin.
3	1.06	37,53.526N	107,45.080W	12,936′	Saddle: Views of Mud Lake Basin
4	1.41	37,53.241N	107,45.139W	12,805′	Porphyry Lake. Continue south towards ❺.
5	1.96	37,52.954N	107,44.812W	12,835′	Saddle from Porphyry Basin
6	2.64	37,52.646N	107,45.238W	12,554′	Bottom of wide gully
7	3.80	37,52.418N	107,46.204W	13,100′	Columbine Pass
8	4.00	37,52.290N	107,46.318W	13,044′	Columbine Pass
9	4.80	37,51.740N	107,45.999W	12,706′	Columbine Lake
10	5.04	37,51.898N	107,45.900W	12,538′	Outlet creek from Lake. Do not cross.
11	6.02	37,51.755N	107,44.954W	12,535′	Cross saddle into next basin.
12	7.00	37,51.590N	107,44.240W	11,471′	Enter trees from here to finish.
13	8.06	37,51.618N	107,43.684W	10,325′	Finish Grand Traverse at Columbine Trailhead.

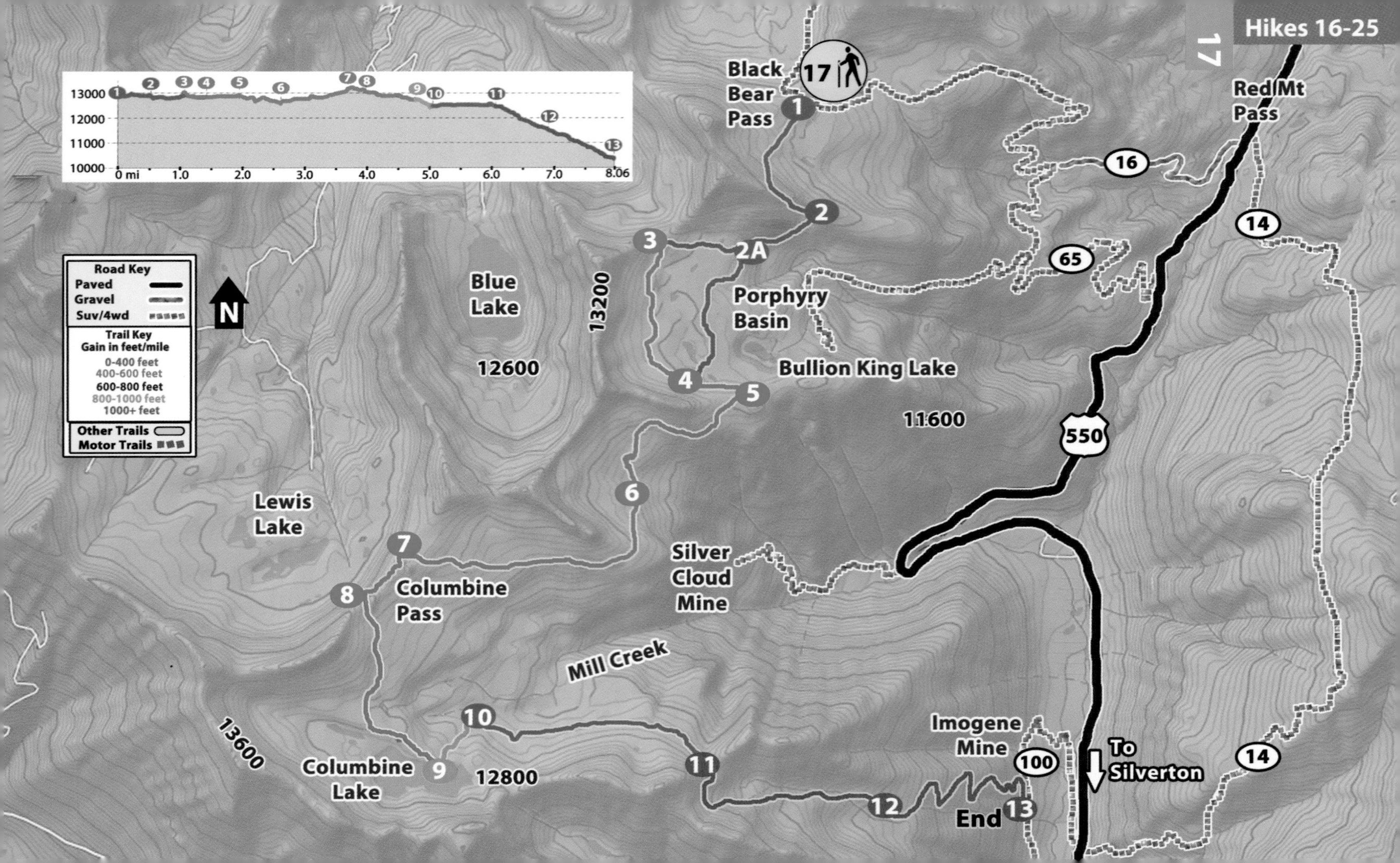
13000
12000
11000
10000
0 mi
1.0
2.0
3.0
4.0
5.0
6.0
7.0
8.06
Road Key
Paved
Gravel
Suv/4wd
Trail Key
Gain in feet/mile
0-400 feet
400-600 feet
600-800 feet
800-1000 feet
1000+ feet
Other Trails
Motor Trails
N
Black Bear Pass
17
Red Mt Pass
16
14
65
Porphyry Basin
Bullion King Lake
11600
550
Blue Lake
13200
12600
Lewis Lake
Columbine Pass
Silver Cloud Mine
Mill Creek
13600
Columbine Lake
12800
Imogene Mine
100
End
To Silverton

Lewis Lake from Columbine Pass

Descending Columbine Creek

18a
18b

Porphyry Basin Loop

Star Rating

☆☆☆☆☆

Bullion King Lake

18a for Loop

Total Distance	5.44 miles RT
Difficulty Rating	Moderate
Surface	Jeep road, grassy tundra, packed trails
Gradient	Mostly moderate with steep option to ❾
Average Time	3.5 hours
Elevations	TH: 11,813; Highest: 13,062 at ❾; Gain: +1,562

18b for Loop

Total Distance	3.32 miles RT
Average Time	2.5 hours
Elevations	TH: 12,388; Gain: +903
Map	Latitude 40: Telluride, Silverton, Ouray. Only parts of the routes are mapped

Directions to TH	From SVC, drive 9.1 miles north on Hwy 550. (That is 0.7 miles south of Red Mountain Pass & milepost 80). The tiny, unmarked road to Porphyry Basin is on the left and is very easy to miss. There is a big yellow road sign that says, "Falling Rock", where you turnoff, but you see only the back of this sign coming from Silverton. Once on Porphyry Road, drive 1.64 miles to Start 18a. Park in the wide grassy area just before a switch back to the right. If you have a jeep type vehicle, drive another 1.06 miles to Start 18b. Be aware of extremely narrow sections and very steep drop offs. If you do not have a jeep type vehicle, you can walk the road from Start 18a to Start 18b almost as fast as vehicles can drive it. It is a beautiful section with great views of waterfalls, deep chasms, rock walls and wildflowers.
Time & Distance to TH	Start 18a: 45 minutes; 10.74 miles. Start 18b: 1 hour; 11.8 miles
Recommended Vehicle	SUV to Start 18a; Jeep from Start 18a to Start 18b. The entire road is only one vehicle wide. Switchbacks are extremely tight even for SWB vehicles. After Start 18a, a danger sign warns of very narrow sections even for jeeps. Steep drop offs.

View of Red Mountains from basin

Summary

Porphyry Basin is a glacial basin with small lakes, sharp, dramatic peaks, waterfalls, creeks, marshes and prolific wildflowers. It is a gem! Wander about anywhere in the basin or follow our loop route which takes you up to various saddles with wonderful views into other basins and brings you back through the heart of the basin floor. Trails are intermittent but it is easy to see where you are going. Use our photos for directional aids.

Trail Description

No matter your start point, this is a beautiful basin to explore about freely. You can see most destination points as you proceed. Routes are obvious even though trails are intermittent. There are three saddles shown on the map by 9, 10 and 11. Saddle 9 is the steepest to ascend. Climb the obvious grassy area to get to it. The views of Mud Lake Basin are superb but they are the same from Saddle 10 which is must easier to ascend. It is possible to walk the ridge between 9 and 10 but it is extremely difficult; huge boulders and rocks jumbled precariously together shift underfoot. There is risk of injury. From 10, it is an easy contour to 11. Just stay below the scree fields in the grass for an easy route across. As you approach 11, you will likely find the good trail that ascends the final stretch to the pass. This is beautiful walking, with wonderful views of the entire Porphyry Basin and across the other side to Black Bear Pass. From

Route from Porphyry Lake to saddles

⑪, as you descend back into Porphyry Basin, take the good path south towards ⑫, a little waterfall. A single stone marker leads you from there towards a deep red colored notch in the rocks. Do not ascend that notch but walk left (SE) around a pretty marshy area with wildflowers. Soon you will be back at ⑥ and can return to your vehicle by the route you came.

Loop route

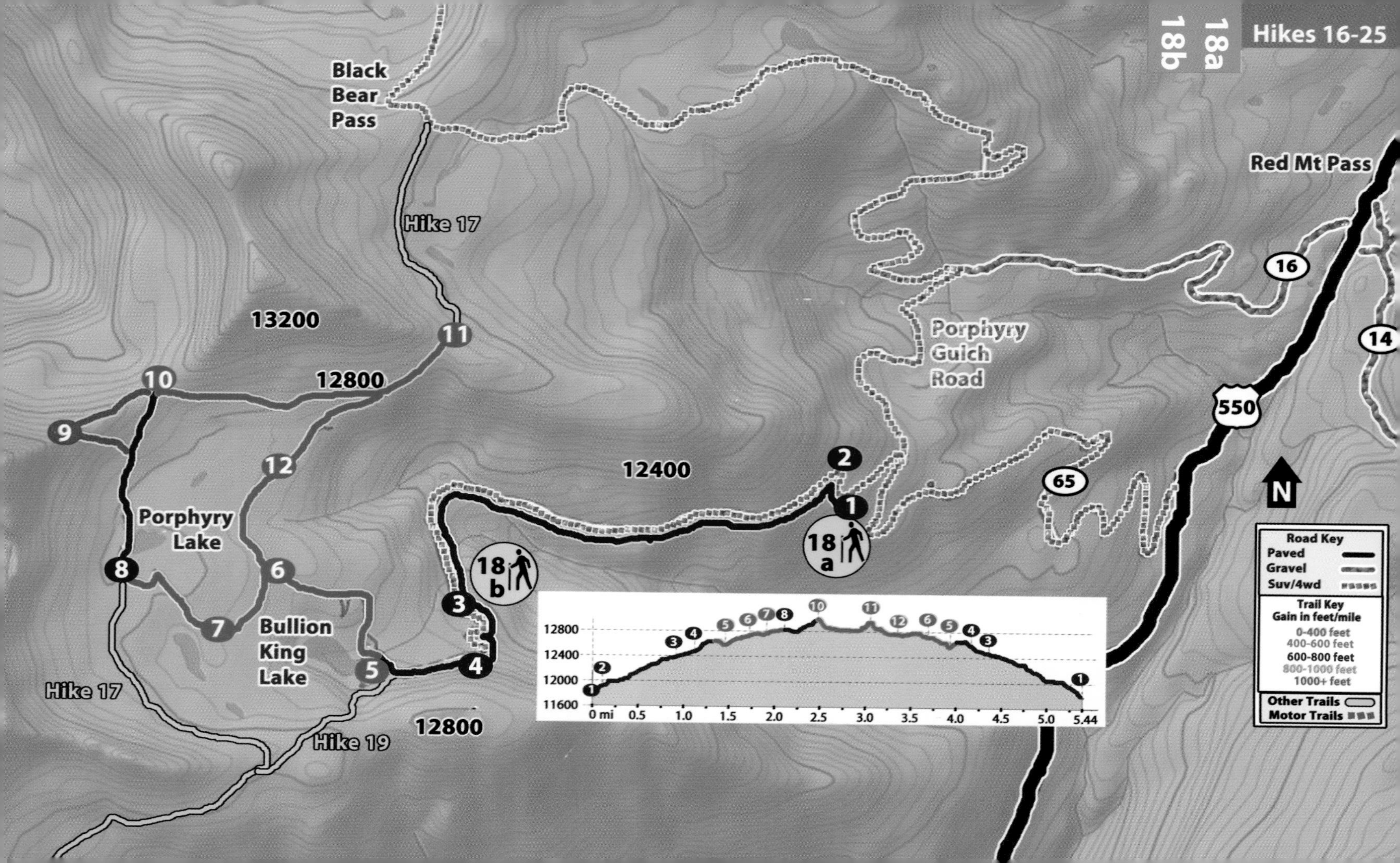
Black Bear Pass
Red Mt Pass
Hike 17
13200
12800
12400
12800
Porphyry Gulch Road
Porphyry Lake
Bullion King Lake
Hike 17
Hike 19
550
16
14
65
18a
18b
N
Road Key
Paved
Gravel
Suv/4wd
Trail Key
Gain in feet/mile
0-400 feet
400-600 feet
600-800 feet
800-1000 feet
1000+ feet
Other Trails
Motor Trails
12800
12400
12000
11600
0 mi
0.5
1.0
1.5
2.0
2.5
3.0
3.5
4.0
4.5
5.0
5.44

GPS	Mile	Latitude	Longitude	Elevation	Comment
1	0.00	37,53.362N	107,43.765W	11,813′	Start 18a; park in grassy area below danger sign.
2	0.05	37,53.387N	107,43.785W	11,871′	Danger sign. Jeep type vehicles only beyond here
3	1.06 / 0.00	37,53.174N	107,44.490W	12,388′	Start 18b: Upper parking in grassy area has room for several vehicles.
4	1.18 / 0.12	37,53.114N	107,44.457W	12,458′	End of road. Minimal turnaround space. Boulders block progress.
5	1.42 / 0.36	37,53.068N	107,44.675W	12,540′	Bullion King Lake. Look north to see old road and follow it uphill.
6	1.74 / 0.68	37,53.233N	107,44.864W	12,709′	Main track goes left; notice return route comes thru small gully and is not on a trail.
7	1.89 / 0.83	37,53.155N	107,44.964W	12,740′	Old mine site. Track ends. Go straight west toward rock wall. See un-named lake below and to your left. Follow the dry stream bed as it goes uphill to your right. Do not climb the knoll to your right.
8	2.12 / 1.06	37,53.241N	107,45.139W	12,805′	Porphyry Lake. For loop, go around left shore and start gaining elevation slowly. Go to ⑨ or ⑩.
9	NA	37,53.453N	107,45.248W	13,062′	Add 0.30 miles up and back down and 223 feet gain. Possible to follow ridge to ⑩ but boulders are unstable and risk of injury exists. Same views as from ⑩.
10	2.47 / 1.41	37,53.526N	107,45.080W	12,936′	Views of Mud Lake Basin
11	3.03 / 1.97	37,53.600N	107,44.523W	12,860′	Views to Black Bear Pass
12	3.43 / 2.37	37,53.399N	107,44.852W	12,734′	Small waterfall & cairn mark return point. Head south towards red cut in cliff but do not ascend it. Contour left of it around marshy area. Go through small notch to ⑥.
6	3.66 / 2.60	37,53.233N	107,44.864W	12,709′	Meet old track again. Return to Bullion King Lake and your vehicle the way you came.
5	3.96 / 2.90	37,53.068N	107,44.675W	12,540′	Bullion King Lake
4	4.21 / 3.15	37,53.114N	107,44.457W	12,458′	Boulders blocking jeep road
3	4.34 / 3.32	37,53.174N	107,44.490W	12,388′	Start 18b
1	5.44	37,53.362N	107,43.765W	11,813′	Start 18a

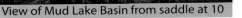

View of Mud Lake Basin from saddle at 10

Waterfall at 12

19a
19b

Porphyry Basin to Columbine Pass

Star Rating

☆☆☆☆☆

19a to Pass

Total Distance	6.94 miles RT
Difficulty Rating	Moderate
Surface	Jeep road & animal trails
Gradient	Moderate
Average Time	5 hours
Elevations	TH: 11,813; Highest: 13,100; Gain: +2,244

19b to Pass

Total Distance	4.74 miles RT
Surface	Mostly animal trails
Average Time	4 hours
Elevations	TH: 12,388; Gain: +1,578
Map	No trails marked on any maps

Columbine Lake from Pass

Directions to TH From SVC, drive 9.1 miles north on Hwy 550. (That is 0.7 miles south of Red Mountain Pass & milepost 80). The tiny, unmarked road to Porphyry Basin is on the left and is very easy to miss. There is a big yellow road sign that says, "Falling Rock", where you turnoff, but you see only the back of this sign coming from Silverton. Once on Porphyry Road, drive 1.64 miles to Start 19a. Park in the wide grassy area just before a switch back to the right. If you have a jeep type vehicle, drive another 1.06 miles to Start 19b. Be aware of extremely narrow sections and very steep drop offs. If you do not have a jeep type vehicle, you can walk the road from Start 19a to Start 19b almost as fast as vehicles can drive it. It is a beautiful section with great views of waterfalls, deep chasms, rock walls and wildflowers.

Time & Distance to TH 45 min. & 10.74 miles to Start 19a; 1 hour & 11.8 miles to Start 19b

Recommended Vehicle SUV to Start 19a; Jeep from Start 19a to Start 19b. The entire road is only one vehicle wide. Switch backs are extremely tight even for SWB vehicles. After Start 19a, a danger sign warns of very narrow sections even for jeeps. Steep drop offs.

Summary

This hike takes you into two beautiful basins and summits two moderate passes for superb views and variety. It is all above tree line; it is mostly cross country using animal trails. Destinations are easy to see from afar; use our photos as guides. If you want to see Columbine Lake, and its scenic basin, this is a much less strenuous route than hike 20.

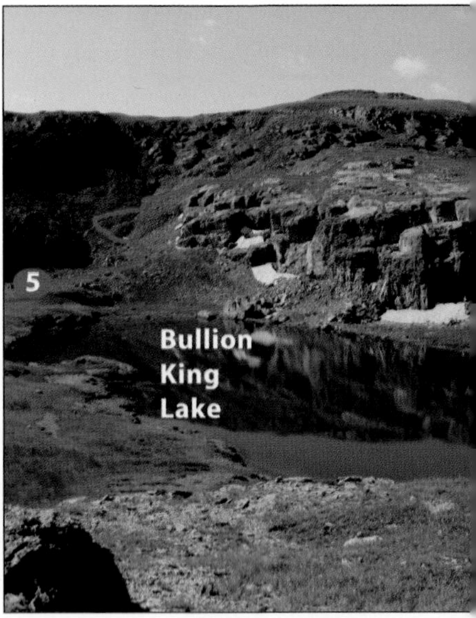

Trail Description

If you are hiking from Start1, you will be viewing waterfalls and prolific wildflowers in the dramatic lower basin. Stay on the main jeep road, avoiding turning off on minor roads to mines. The road ends at ❹ where boulders block vehicle progress. Follow on up to the picturesque Bullion King Lake ❺. From the lake shore, look south and you will see a trail cutting up through steep scree and cliffs to a saddle. The saddle is your first destination. From there, you overlook the Silver Cloud Mine Basin and see parts of Hwy 550 far below. Your route is to head west and south, around the daunting rock barriers to your right. Keep as high a contour as you can. There are numerous game trails to choose from. You will have to descend into a very wide gully ❻ to get around the rock walls. Once you have ascended and are around the rock

Route through wide gully

Route from Bullion King Lake to first saddle

promontory, you can see Columbine Basin and Columbine Pass ❼. This section might take 2 hours from ❻ to ❼. It is an easy contour to the lake shore from the pass, if you wish to continue. Hike 17, The Grand Traverse, describes how to go all the way past Columbine Lake, into another basin, and down the steep descent to Columbine Trailhead near Hwy 550 for a shuttle route.

Lewis Lake from Columbine Pass

GPS	Mile	Latitude	Longitude	Elevation	Comment
1	0.00	37,53.362N	107,43.765W	11,813′	Start 19a: Park in grassy area below danger sign.
2	0.05	37,53.387N	107,43.785W	11,871′	Danger sign. Jeep type vehicles only beyond here
3	1.06 / 0.00	37,53.174N	107,44.490W	12,388′	Start 19b: Upper parking in grassy area has room for several vehicles.
4	1.18 / 0.12	37,53.114N	107,44.457W	12,458′	End of road. Minimal turnaround space. Boulders block progress.
5	1.42 / 0.36	37,53.068N	107,44.675W	12,540′	Bullion King Lake. Look south to see trail going up steep hill to saddle.
6	2.33 / 1.27	37,52.646N	107,45.238W	12,554′	Bottom of wide gully
7	3.47 / 2.37	37,52.418N	107,46.204W	13,100′	Columbine Pass

Looking back towards deep gully

Route out of deep gully.

Approaching Columbine Pass

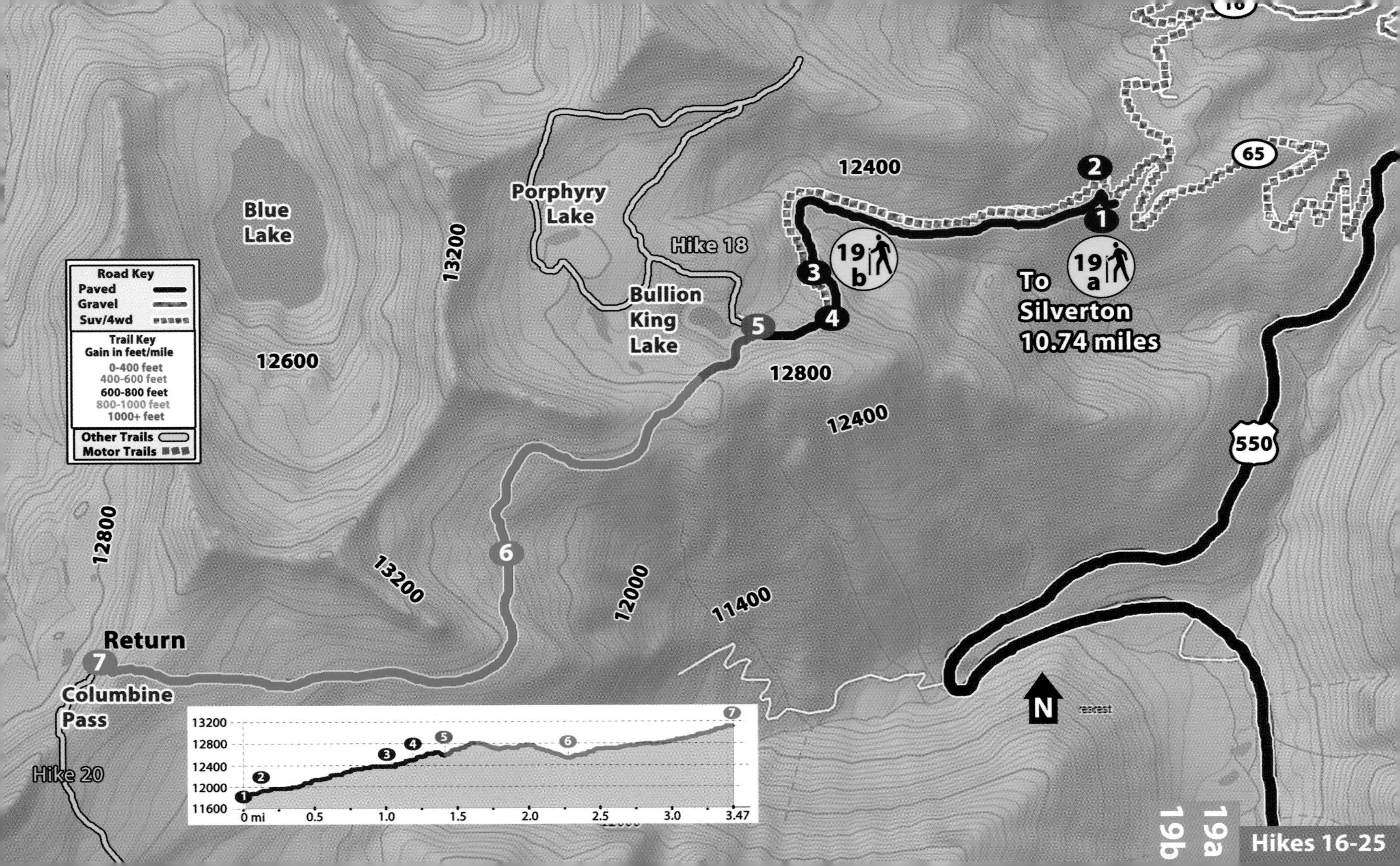
Road Key
Paved
Gravel
Suv/4wd
Trail Key
Gain in feet/mile
0-400 feet
400-600 feet
600-800 feet
800-1000 feet
1000+ feet
Other Trails
Motor Trails
Blue Lake
Porphyry Lake
Bullion King Lake
Hike 18
12400
12600
12800
13200
12000
11400
12800
13200
12400
19 a
19 b
To Silverton 10.74 miles
65
550
N
Return
Columbine Pass
Hike 20
13200
12800
12400
12000
11600
0 mi
0.5
1.0
1.5
2.0
2.5
3.0
3.47

20a
20b
20c

Columbine Lake & Pass

Star Rating
☆☆
☆☆☆☆☆

20a: To Saddle/ Return 1

Total Distance	4.12 miles RT
Difficulty Rating	Very Strenuous because of the first two miles
Surface	Mostly loose gravel that rolls underfoot; especially bad from TH to mile 2.0
Gradient	Very Steep from TH to mile 2.0
Average Time	2.5 hours
Elevations	TH: 10,325; Highest: 12,535; Gain: +2,305
Map	San Juan Mountain Maps 2010: Silverton, Telluride, Ouray

20b: To Lake/ Return 2

Total Distance	6.42 miles RT
Difficulty Rating	Very Strenuous because of the first two miles; Moderate beyond
Surface	Mostly loose gravel that rolls underfoot; especially bad from TH to mile 2.0. Packed dirt beyond.
Gradient	Very Steep from TH to mile 2.0; Moderate beyond
Average Time	5 hours
Elevations	TH: 10,325; Highest: 12,706; Gain: +2,779

Columbine Lake

	20c: To Pass/ Return 3
Total Distance	7.96 miles RT
Difficulty Rating	Very Strenuous because of the first two miles; Moderate beyond
Surface	Mostly loose gravel that rolls underfoot; especially bad from TH to mile 2.0. Packed dirt beyond.
Gradient	Very Steep from TH to mile 2.0; Moderate beyond
Average Time	6.5 hours
Elevations	TH: 10,325; Highest: 13,044; Gain: +3,233

Directions to TH	From SVC, drive 5.5 miles north on Hwy 550 and turn left onto signed Ophir Pass Road, CR 8. (Just south of milepost 76). Cross the bridge and drive about another 200 yards to a sharp right turn onto CR 100. Drive up the hill 0.7 miles to an unmarked steep path on the left side. A wide spot in the road can park 3 small cars. For more parking, drive uphill another 300 yards to the old Imogene Mine tailings.
Time & Distance to TH	25 minutes; 6.2 miles
Recommended Vehicle	SUV. Most of the route is on paved Hwy 550, but the final road CR 100 is a narrow and steep on loose rock.

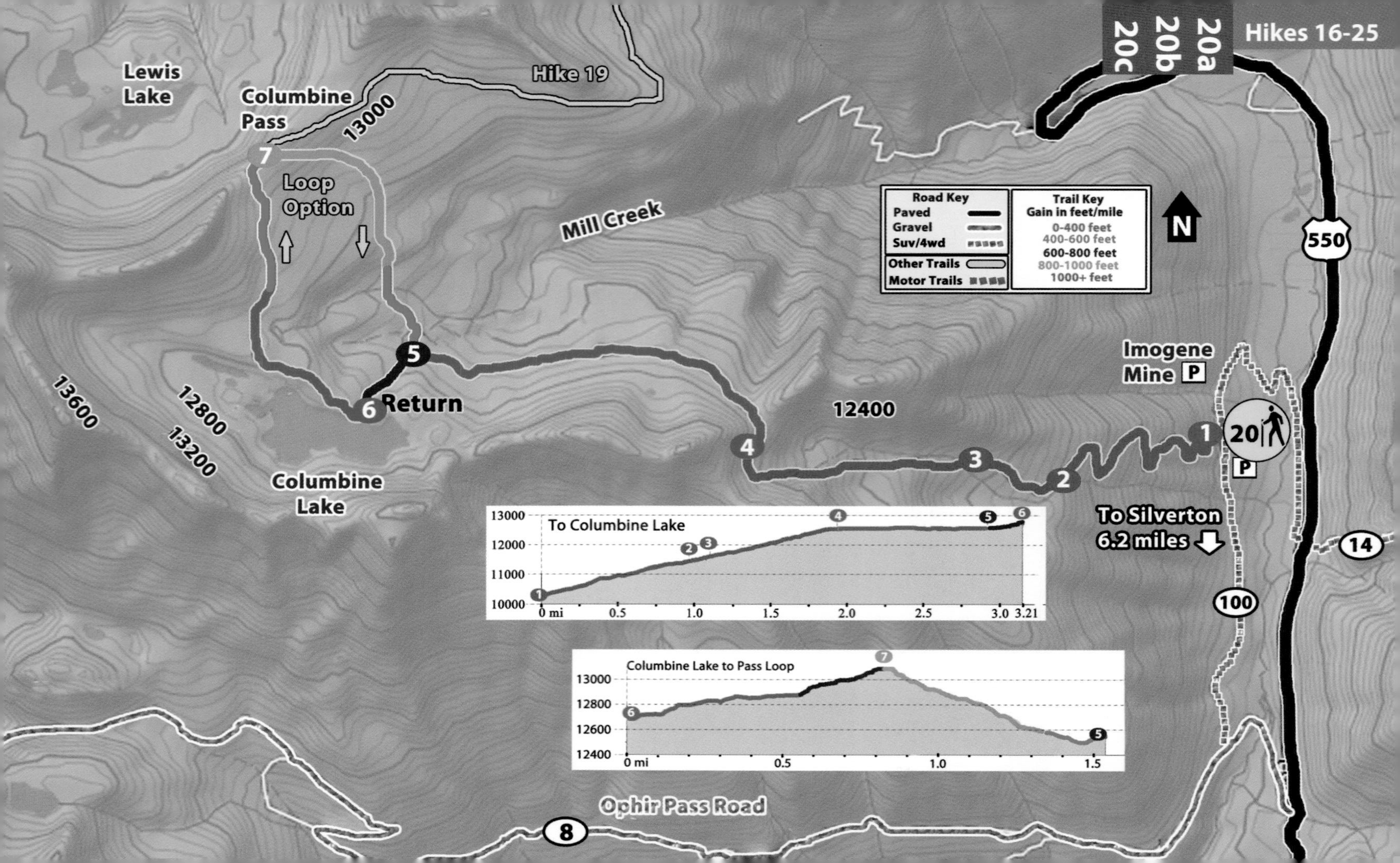
Lewis Lake
Columbine Pass
Hike 19
13000
7
Loop Option
Mill Creek
5
6
Return
13600
12800
13200
Columbine Lake
4
12400
3
2
1
20
P
Imogene Mine P
Road Key
Paved
Gravel
Suv/4wd
Other Trails
Motor Trails
Trail Key
Gain in feet/mile
0-400 feet
400-600 feet
600-800 feet
800-1000 feet
1000+ feet
N
550
To Silverton 6.2 miles
14
100
To Columbine Lake
13000
12000
11000
10000
0 mi
0.5
1.0
1.5
2.0
2.5
3.0
3.21
Columbine Lake to Pass Loop
13000
12800
12600
12400
0 mi
0.5
1.0
1.5
Ophir Pass Road
8

Summary

The first mile is in thick spruce forest with limited views. There are no wildflowers in the understory. Once you enter the open part of the drainage at mile 1.10, you can see all the way to the saddle that crosses into Mill Creek Basin. There are groups of wildflowers and the high surrounding peaks are impressive. After crossing the saddle, WOW! Mill Creek Basin is expansive. The surrounding peaks are jagged and dramatic; the three Red Mountains to the east add wonderful color. There are waterfalls and tumbling creeks. The terrain undulates; you can wander about freely. This basin is scenically rich. Add an optional loop to Columbine Pass for views to the Telluride side.

Trail Description

Ascending first basin

From the TH to ❷ the trail is very steep, climbing 1100 feet through thick spruce forest. The trail is loose rolling gravel that is particularly difficult to maintain footing during the descent. When you enter the basin and the views open up all around, the trail remains very steep and rugged because of the loose rock. There are many wildflowers in this basin. Look straight uphill and to the right. You can see your destination, the saddle that crosses into Mill Creek Basin ❹. Once you reach this point, you have done all the strenuous climbing. Crossing into Mill Creek Basin opens up astounding vistas of rugged peaks all around. The gradient undulates gently across the south side of this wide basin until it comes to the outlet creek ❺. Do not cross the creek, even though you can see a faint trail. Stay on the left bank and follow the creek to the lake ❻. If you want to ascend to Columbine Pass ❼, it is easiest to approach from the lake shore. See our map; there is no real trail. From the Pass, look down over Lewis Lake and Bridal Veil Basin on the Telluride side. You can wander about the ridge. Return the way you came, or take a steeper descent straight back to ❺.

GPS	Mile	Latitude	Longitude	Elevation	Comment
1	0.00	37,51.618N	107,43.684W	10,325′	Start Columbine Trail.
2	1.03	37,51.574N	107,44.146W	11,361′	Small meadow & view of peaks
3	1.10	37,51.590N	107,44.240W	11,471′	Enter basin. All above tree line from here
4	2.06	37,51.755N	107,44.954W	12,535′	Cross saddle into Mill Creek Basin.
5	3.01	37,51.898N	107,45.900W	12,538′	Outlet creek from Lake. Do not cross.
6	3.21	37,51.740N	107,45.999W	12,706′	Columbine Lake: return to TH or go to Pass.
7	4.04	37,52.290N	107,46.318W	13,044′	Columbine Pass: go back to lake ❻ or return steeper route to ❺.
5	4.77	37,51.898N	107,45.900W	12,538′	Cross outlet creek and return to TH.

21a
21b

US Basin & McMillan Peak Options

Star Rating

☆☆☆☆☆

San Juan Range from flower filled basin

21a: US Basin To Peak/ Return 1

Total Distance	3.86 miles RT
Difficulty Rating	Moderate
Surface	This is cross country hiking through tundra meadows. Some old tracks and animal trails
Gradient	A big variety from Easy to Steep
Average Time	4 hours
Elevations	TH: 12,059; Highest: 12,804; Gain: +1,541
Map	Latitude 40: Telluride, Silverton, Ouray

21b: US Basin To Shuttle

Total Distance	3.77 miles
Difficulty Rating	Moderate
Surface	This is cross country hiking through tundra meadows. Some old tracks and animal trails
Gradient	A big variety from Easy to Steep
Average Time	4 hours
Elevations	TH: 12,059; Highest: 12,804; Gain: +1,263

Directions to TH	From SVC, drive 9.8 miles north on Hwy 550 to Red Mountain Pass. Just before the summit on the right is the sign for CR 14 at milepost 80. Turn right on this gravel road. At the first junction, (almost immediately) turn right and drive 0.6 miles to another junction. Turn right at this junction (CR 14 sign). Continue up this steep road for an additional 2.14 miles to where the road flattens out and vistas expand. There is a wide grassy spot on the left for parking. No trailhead sign.
Time & Distance to TH	45 minutes; 12.94 miles
Recommended Vehicle	SUV. CR 14 is steep and very narrow. There may be washouts and berms. This road continues past the TH and in about 10 more miles it rejoins US 550 at Brown's Gulch. SUVs can drive the entire road. It is very scenic!
Shuttle	From SVC, drive 9.8 miles north on Hwy 550 to Red Mountain Pass. Just before the summit on the right is the sign for CR 14 at milepost 80. Turn right on this gravel road. At the first junction, (almost immediately) turn right and drive 0.6 miles to another junction. Turn right at this junction (CR 14 sign). At the next unsigned fork (mile 1.0), turn left and park in the open area. The old road climbing the hill to the east is the trail you will come out.

Summary

This is a hike of superlatives. Views of the San Juan Range from South to North require 5 photo shots to capture it all! From the ridgeline, gain additional views towards Silverton and various basins leading to the three Red Mountains. This is essentially a cross country hike. Use our photos as visual guides, or pick your own route and wander where you please; go any distance. It is open country and easy to keep track of your start point. Seasonal wildflowers display an amazing variety on the open hillsides.

View from McMillan Peak

Trail Description

From the parking area, look uphill and spot on the horizon a small, rocky knob ❷. A faint trail leaves the parking spot and heads directly for that knob. That is your first goal, and unnamed pile of rocks with a view to kill. Or just wander the beautiful flower festooned slopes in any direction and use up a card of photos on the San Juan Range. From the top of the rocky knob, descend the other side (SE) and turn NE through a very obvious notch. Once you pass through, you can see most of your route to McMillan Peak ❺ which features a massive microwave dish that looks like an outdoor movie screen on its summit. See our series of photos for guidance. Your route is to stay as high as you can and follow north along the precipice that overlooks Silverton and Cement Creek drainage ❸. Follow the ridge northeast. A rocky cliff is between you and the peak. Two trails are visible, one over the top, and one to the left. We prefer going left; the wildflowers are prolific and there is less elevation gain. After going around

Trailhead parking site

From Trailhead to knob

From top of knob

From Ridge at to McMillan Peak

Heading down the gully to creek

Final descent past house to shuttle vehicle

the cliffs, you have a choice to climb to the summit of McMillan ❺ or contour around the peak at an easy gradient on the west side ❹, Once on the northwest side of the peak, hike north down a prominent gully and cross the stream at the bottom. There is a small animal trail you can take to the right that climbs gently back up to the ridge where you can see a tiny transmitter tower on a little knob ❽. There are excellent views overlooking Prospect Gulch. From there, follow an old track that heads straight west down a grassy ridgeline; it jogs north again then straight west downhill towards a lone house ⑩. That is your next goal. Once near the house, leave the track and walk downhill through an opening in the spruce trees. Meet an old road and follow it south for a few hundred yards to your shuttle vehicle ⑪.

GPS	Mile	Latitude	Longitude	Elevation	Comment
1	0.00	37,52.542N	107,42.520W	12,059′	Start US Basin & McMillan Peak.
2	0.53	37,52.269N	107,42.183W	12,571′	Un-named knob. Top is bare rock.
3	0.89	37,52.167N	107,41.925W	12,403′	Overlook Minnesota Gulch and Silverton
4	N/A	37,52.757N	107,41.651W	12,542′	Route around McMillan Peak.
5	1.93	37,52.812N	107,41.391W	12,804′	Summit McMillan Peak. Return or continue to shuttle point.
6	2.34	37,52.962N	107,41.680W	12,537′	Top of gully with creek. Follow gully down.
7	2.62	37,53.164N	107,41.766W	12,273′	Bottom of gully with creek. Pick up animal track to right (NE).
8	2.99	37,53.463N	107,41.718W	12,284′	Overlook Prospect Gulch & Red Mt 3
9	3.12	37,53.478N	107,41.841W	12,198′	Old track turns downhill (W).
10	3.43	37,53.419N	107,42.127W	11,840′	House to west. Head downhill thru opening in spruce forest.
11	3.77	37,53.246N	107,42.387W	11,598′	Shuttle parking

Shuttle parking area. End of hike

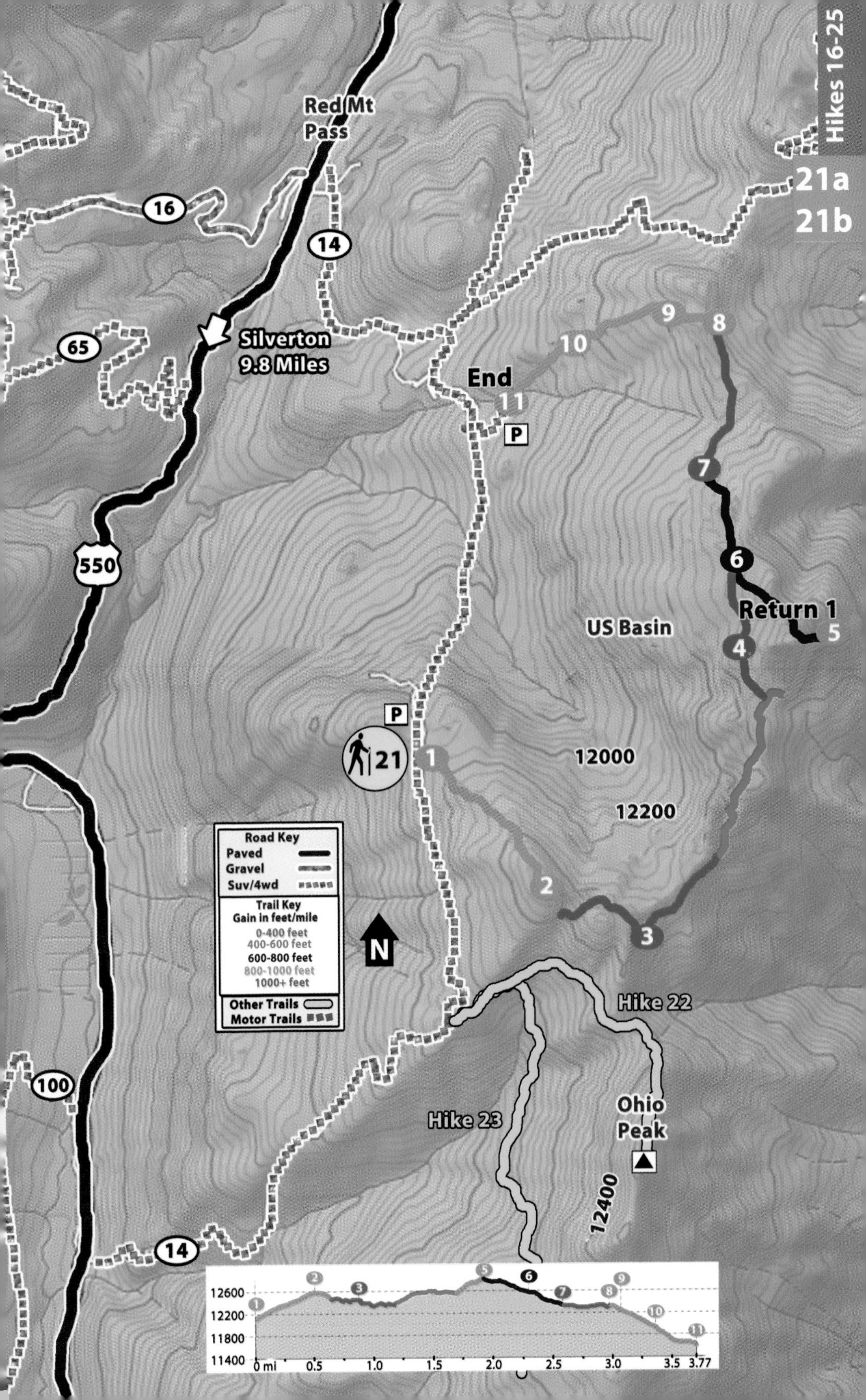
Red Mt Pass
16
14
65
Silverton 9.8 Miles
550
End
11
10
9
8
7
6
5
4
3
2
1
P
21
Return 1
US Basin
12000
12200
12400
Road Key
Paved
Gravel
Suv/4wd
Trail Key
Gain in feet/mile
0-400 feet
400-600 feet
600-800 feet
800-1000 feet
1000+ feet
Other Trails
Motor Trails
N
Hike 22
Hike 23
Ohio Peak
100
14
12600
12200
11800
11400
0 mi
0.5
1.0
1.5
2.0
2.5
3.0
3.5
3.77

Ohio Peak

Star Rating

☆☆☆☆☆

Total Distance	2.0 miles RT
Difficulty Rating	Moderate
Surface	Easy tundra and animal trails cross country
Gradient	Mostly moderate. One short steep section from saddle to peak
Average Time	2.5 hours
Elevations	TH: 12,070; Highest: 12,674; Gain: +738
Map	Latitude 40: Telluride, Silverton, Ouray. Trail not on any map

Directions to TH	From SVC, drive 5.5 miles north on Hwy 550 to mile post 76. Just 50 feet before is an unmarked dirt road to the right (E). As soon as you turn up this road, there is a CR 14 sign. Drive to mile 8.5 where you enter a wide, grassy area with a metal and wire fence protecting a reclamation area. Park across from the fence on the grass. There is no trailhead sign.
Time & Distance to TH	35 minutes; 8.5 miles
Recommended Vehicle	SUV. Although this is one of the easiest 4x4 roads in the county as the majority of it is smooth gravel and wider than a single vehicle, it still has steep switchbacks and short sections along exposed, steep cliffs.

View from Peak

Summary

Short, easy-moderate cross country route to an easy peak of 12,674 feet with great views of the San Juan Range. You can see your destination from the trailhead; pick your own route or follow our photos. Even the access road is moderate. What a winning package!

View from saddle

Route from Trailhead

Trail Description

From your parking spot look uphill due east for a tiny metal post on the horizon. Hike to that post; continue past it to the edge of the big gully. Turn left (N) and walk 100 feet ❷ where you should see a good trail heading east again as it contours around the basin. See our photos for guidance. Actually, because you can see your destination, take any route that fancies your curiosity. Once you reach the saddle ❹ you can see down Minnesota Gulch and across to all the peaks on the eastern side of the ridge as well as the magnificent westerly views that have been accompanying you all along. At the saddle are remains

Final ascent to peak

GPS	Mile	Latitude	Longitude	Elevation	Comment
1	0.00	37,51.961N	107,42.436W	12,070′	Start Ohio Peak.
2	0.13	37,52.007N	107,42.360W	12,141′	Edge of big gully where photo 2 was taken Contour around basin on animal trails.
3	0.40	37,52.039N	107,42.090W	12,163′	Cross gully that gets much deeper higher up.
4	0.63	37,51.924N	107,41.922W	12,303′	Saddle at base of Ohio Peak. Cabin remains.
5	1.00	37,51.649N	107,41.915W	12,674′	Ohio Peak summit

Route from edge of gully

of an old shelter. Now climb the steepest part of the hike to the right of the rock cliff above. Very soon you gain the ridge and it is a magnificent trek to the summit. Wow! Short and sweet!

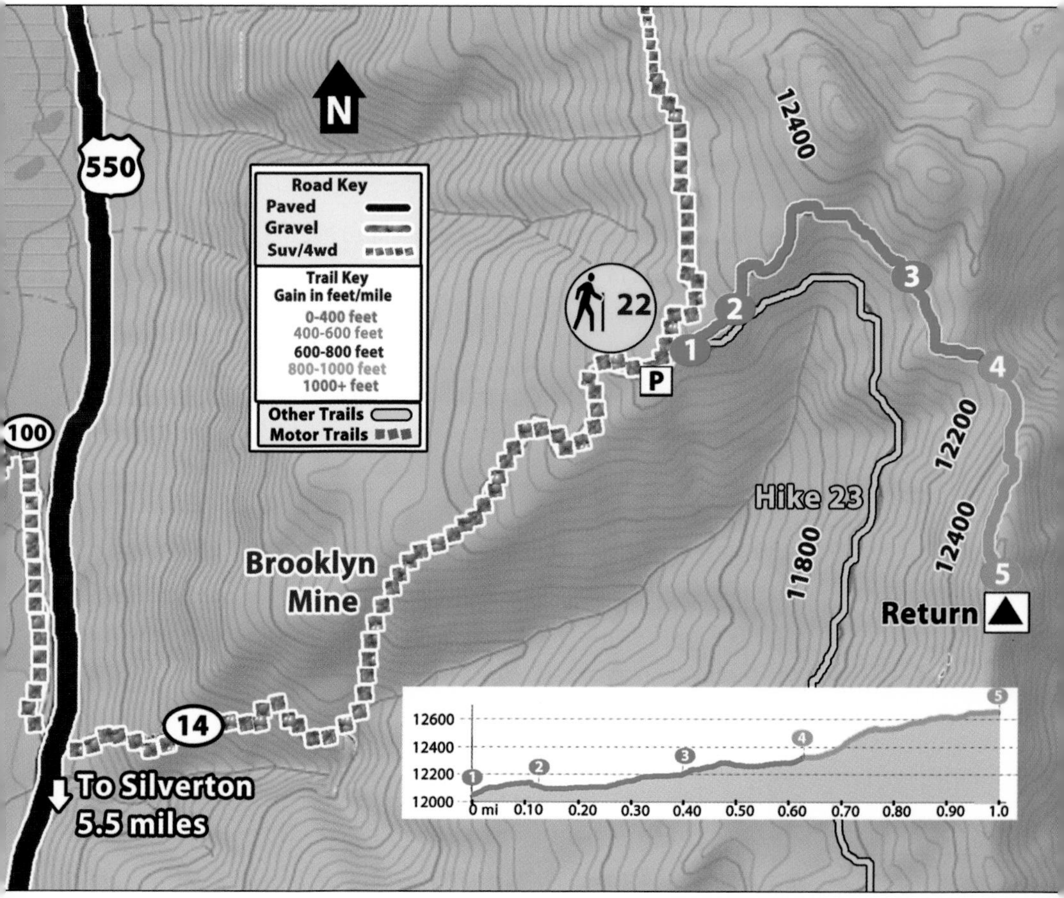

23

Nancy's Grassy Peak

Star Rating

☆☆☆☆☆

Nancy's Peak

Total Distance	4.0 miles
Difficulty Rating	Mostly Easy but with strenuous ascent to Peak
Surface	Animal trails in grassy tundra; rocky scree to summit
Gradient	Easy except for two steep, short climbs
Average Time	3 hours
Elevations	TH: 12,070; Highest: 12,296; Gain: +1,271
Map	Latitude 40: Telluride, Silverton, Ouray

Directions to TH From SVC, drive 5.5 miles north on Hwy 550 to mile post 76. Just 50 feet before is an unmarked dirt road to the right (E). As soon as you turn up this road, there is a CR 14 sign. Drive to mile 8.5 where you enter a wide, grassy area with a metal and wire fence protecting a reclamation area. Park across from the fence on the grass. There is no TH sign.

Time & Distance to TH 35 minutes; 8.5 miles

Recommended Vehicle SUV. This is a very easy 4x4 road with only a few rough spots, some sharp steep switchbacks and a short section exposed to high cliffs. Most of the road is wide; there are plenty of passing areas.

Summary

All above tree line, this is a cross country hike using animal trails. Excels in scenic value and variety of interesting terrain with numerous small basins and hills. You can see your destination from the trailhead so you don't need to worry about where you are heading. Much of the route is on an easy contour with the need to cross a few deep gullies. There are stunning views of the San Juan Range on the west side of Hwy 550. Our destination peak has no name on any map. There is a cairn at the summit and notepaper in a bottle where you can sign in. The name Nancy's Grassy Peak was given by local hiking enthusiast and author Kelvin Kent.

Stay above spruce

Route to ponds

Nancy's & Anvil Peak

Trail Description

It is possible to hike via many different animal trails; we prefer to go uphill from the parking area towards the metal stake on the horizon and contour around the big drainage on a high route rather than dropping into the drainage and climbing back up. See our photos. We stay just above the spruce clumps and below the rock talus slopes of Ohio Peak. After crossing a very deep gully, various good animal trails lead right to the summit of our peak. If you don't want to climb the steep trail up to the peak, turn around at the ponds. It has already been a superlative hike.

Ponds

GPS	Mile	Latitude	Longitude	Elevation	Comment
1	0.00	37,51,961N	107,42,436W	12,070'	Start by hiking towards metal post on horizon above parking area. At the edge of the drainage, go left and find an animal trail that contours about the same level all the way around the drainage. Aim for just above tree level.
2	1.08	37,51.429N	107,42.257W	11,957'	Ponds. Great views of Ophir Pass
3	1.56	37,51.093N	107,42.084W	12,064'	Overlook deep ravine. Great views of Nancy's Peak on other side
4	2.00	37,50.746N	107,42.173W	12,296'	Nancy's Peak. Sign into notebook in cairn. Anvil Mt across deep drainage

Final ascent to peak

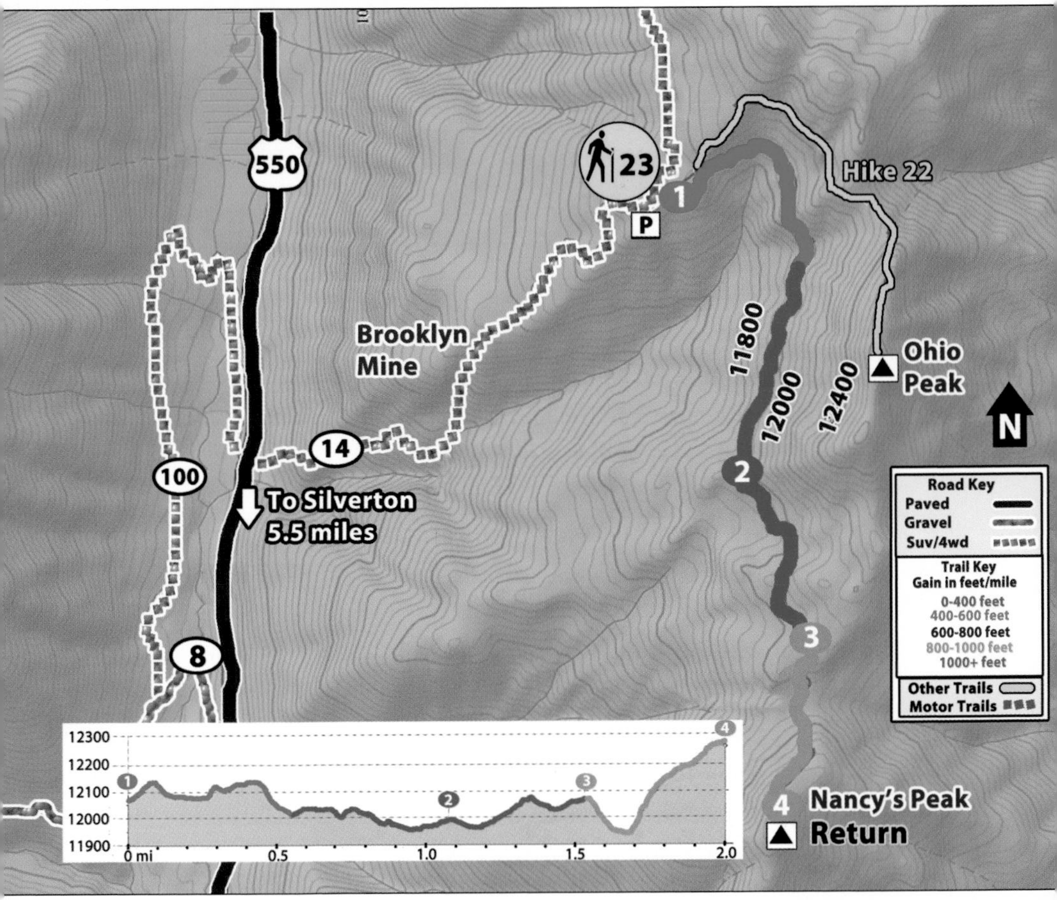

Silver Cloud Mine

Star Rating

☆☆☆

View up valley from Trailhead

Total Distance	2.34 miles RT
Difficulty Rating	Moderate
Surface	Old jeep road of mostly packed rock; last 0.30 miles is loose rock that rolls underfoot
Gradient	Moderately Steep to Steep
Average Time	2 hours
Elevations	TH: 10,503; Highest: 11,381; Gain: +995
Map	Latitude 40 Telluride, Silverton, Ouray

Directions to TH	From SVC, drive 7.4 miles north on Hwy 550. (Just south of mile post 77). In the bend of the long switchback known as Chattanooga Loop is a dirt road through some willows. Turn on this dirt road and park about 100 feet in at an obvious parking area.
Time & Distance to TH	30 minutes; 7.4 miles
Recommended Vehicle	Car. Access is via paved Hwy 550

Summary

Hike up an old mining road to two mine sites. The road is not a popular jeep route so traffic is not an issue. The road ascends a dramatic valley with sheer cliffs, rocky peaks straight above, waterfalls and tumbling streams. It is entirely in the open. There are great views across the valley to US Basin and Ohio Peak. The short distance and walking on a road makes for a good family hike even though the gradient is steep. It receives early morning sun; it can be hot as there is little shade.

Ascending lower road

View up valley from lower trail

Trail Description

The trail follows the old mining road. Enjoy the beautiful valley as you ascend. There are no structures at the first mine ❷; from there, the trail is much steeper, gaining 627 feet in just 0.67 miles. The Silver Cloud Mine is dug out of a cliff face. A road takes you to the old shaft above the tailing pile ❸.

GPS	Mile	Latitude	Longitude	Elevation	Comment
1	0.00	37,52.368N	107,44.257W	10,503′	Start Silver Cloud Mine hike.
2	0.50	37,52.291N	107,44.630W	10,785′	Silver Crown Mine site
3	1.17	37,52.412N	107,44.845W	11,381′	Silver Cloud Mine shaft

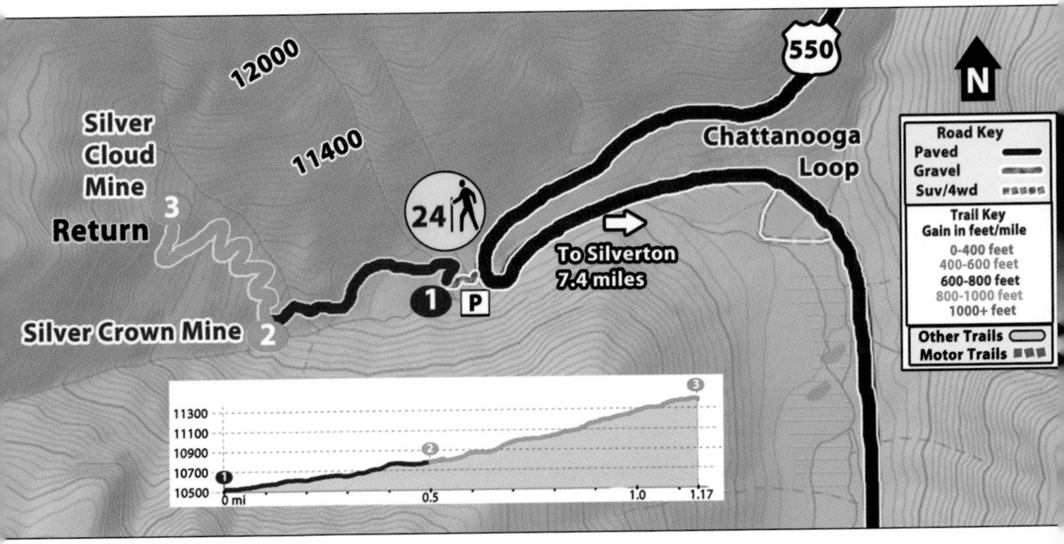

25

Paradise Basin

Star Rating

☆☆☆☆

View up valley

Total Distance	2.76 miles RT
Difficulty Rating	Moderate
Surface	Mostly animal trails and tundra
Gradient	First mile is Easy; final ascent to upper lake is Steep
Average Time	2.5 hours
Elevations	TH: 11,209; Highest: 12,025; Gain: +1,042
Map	Latitude 40: Telluride, Silverton, Ouray. No trail marked on any maps
Directions to TH	From SVC, drive 4.9 miles north on Hwy 550 to signed Ophir Pass Road, CR8. At mile 7.7, Ophir Pass road makes a switch back to the right; a lesser road goes straight ahead. A small pullout on the left has room for two vehicles. Park there. No TH sign.
Time & Distance to TH	25 minutes; 7.7 miles
Recommended Vehicle	Car. Although this is a signed 4x4 road that crosses from Silverton to Telluride, the Silverton side of the pass is mostly packed gravel and is not especially steep.

Summary

This is a relatively short hike into a picturesque basin. Massive rock walls and sheer cliffs surround the basin. Large amounts of glacial debris form one arm of the basin; wildflower meadows form another. There are two tiny lakes. A good animal trail leads from the start into the basin proper. There are many ways to climb the tundra meadows to the lakes.

Trail Description

From the parking spot, there are two trails. Take the lesser one that goes straight down the hill and crosses the creek. Do not take the easy looking flat trail. It dead ends at a steep drop to the creek. Wet shoes may be necessary through July. After crossing the creek and ascending the bank, a trail leads up the valley. It is faint, and soon gets trapped in some willow brush. Go above the brush, rather than below and meet a really good animal track that will take you all the way to ❷. See photo 1 for the approximate trail route. Just Before reaching ❷, there is a tempting avalanche chute that leads up to the right where the lakes are. But do not be fooled. Going that way will put you on a ridge smothered in willow brush. Instead, keep going into the spruce trees where the trail seems to completely disappear right in front of a straight and tall snag. This is ❷. See photo 2 on page 120. Turn right and go straight up the hill for 50 feet and you will encounter a good trail going left that contours through the trees, around the willows and quickly gets you into the open meadows above. You are heading up into the right arm of Paradise Basin. The glacial debris completely covers the left arm. Once again, the trail disappears, but you can see your direction. The lakes are completely hidden, just below the sheer rock walls of the right arm. Pick your own route up through the flowered meadows. It is possible to climb very steeply up to the obvious saddle above the upper lake. From there, you can see the other side of Ophir Pass and the town of Ophir.

Upper Lake

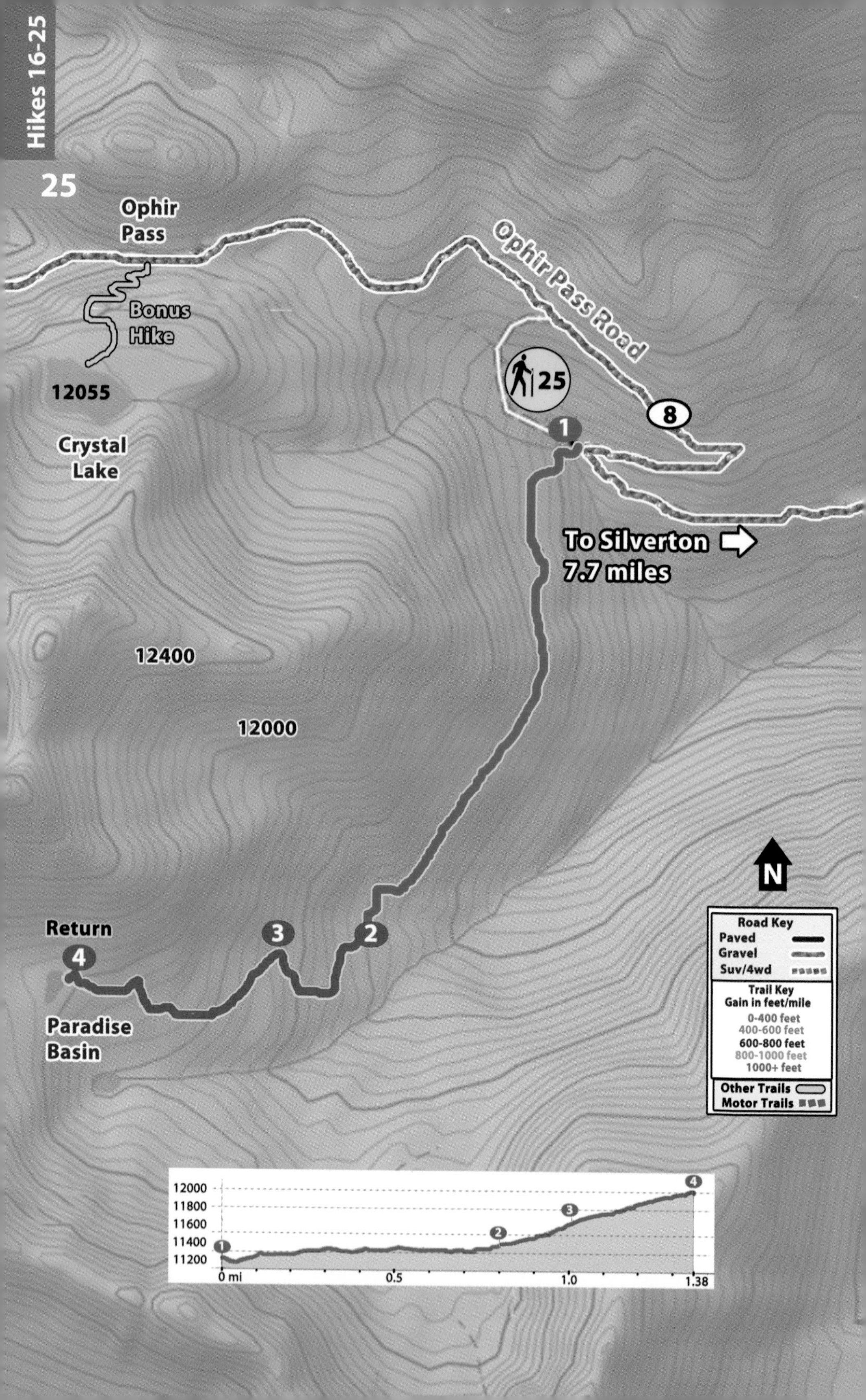
Ophir Pass
Ophir Pass Road
Bonus Hike
12055
Crystal Lake
25
1
8
To Silverton
7.7 miles
12400
12000
N
Return
4
3
2
Paradise Basin
Road Key
Paved
Gravel
Suv/4wd
Trail Key
Gain in feet/mile
0-400 feet
400-600 feet
600-800 feet
800-1000 feet
1000+ feet
Other Trails
Motor Trails
12000
11800
11600
11400
11200
0 mi
0.5
1.0
1.38

Route as seen from road

Route from snag at (2)

GPS	Mile	Latitude	Longitude	Elevation	Comment
1	0.00	37,50.830N	107,46.136W	11,209′	Start Paradise Basin. Choose trail that goes straight down to creek, not the easy flat trail.
2	0.81	37,50.251N	107,46.464W	11,332′	After crossing wide grassy avalanche area, trail disappears at dead snag in open spruce forest. Go straight uphill to find trail.
3	1.00	37,50.221N	107,46.592W	11,630′	Trail ends above tree line. Cross country up to Lake through meadows.
4	1.38	37,50.197N	107,46.916W	12,025′	Upper Lake. Return.

Crystal Lake at Ophir Pass

Star Rating

☆☆☆☆☆☆

Total Distance	0.52 miles RT
Difficulty Rating	Strenuous
Surface	Extremely rocky
Gradient	Very Steep
Average Time	1 hour
Elevations	TH: 11,789; Highest: 12,086; Gain: +319
Maps	Not on any maps

Crystal Lake

Directions to TH	From SVC, drive 4.9 miles north on Hwy 550 to signed Ophir Pass Road, CR 8. Drive approximately 10 miles to Ophir Pass. Park at the pass. There is no TH sign. The trail begins on the south side of the road.
Driving Time & Mileage	35 minutes; 10 miles
Recommended Vehicle	Cars can drive this good gravel road to the pass

Ophir Pass from the trail

Extreme rocky trail

GPS	Mile	Latitude	Longitude	Elevation	Comment
1	0.00	37,51.051N	107,46.747W	11,788′	Start Crystal Lake from Ophir Pass.
2	0.23	37,50.935N	107,46.864W	12,086′	High point
3	0.26	37,50.918N	107,46.884W	12,064′	Crystal Lake

Summary

Very short, very steep, very rocky, very beautiful! Usage: Hikers!

Trail Description

We had to give this hike a strenuous rating for all but the young in years and fleet footed. It is so short, many hikers will not mind the steepness or the extreme rocky trail, but others will find such conditions too difficult so we wanted you to know about it before you drove to the top of the pass. The beginning of the trail has collapsed and it is almost a scramble for the first 100 feet. Then the trail is obvious, though it ascends at a 33% gradient! Just keep climbing. The lake is a gem, nestled in a cirque basin. Walk east or west a bit from the lake and see down the entire Ophir Pass Road.

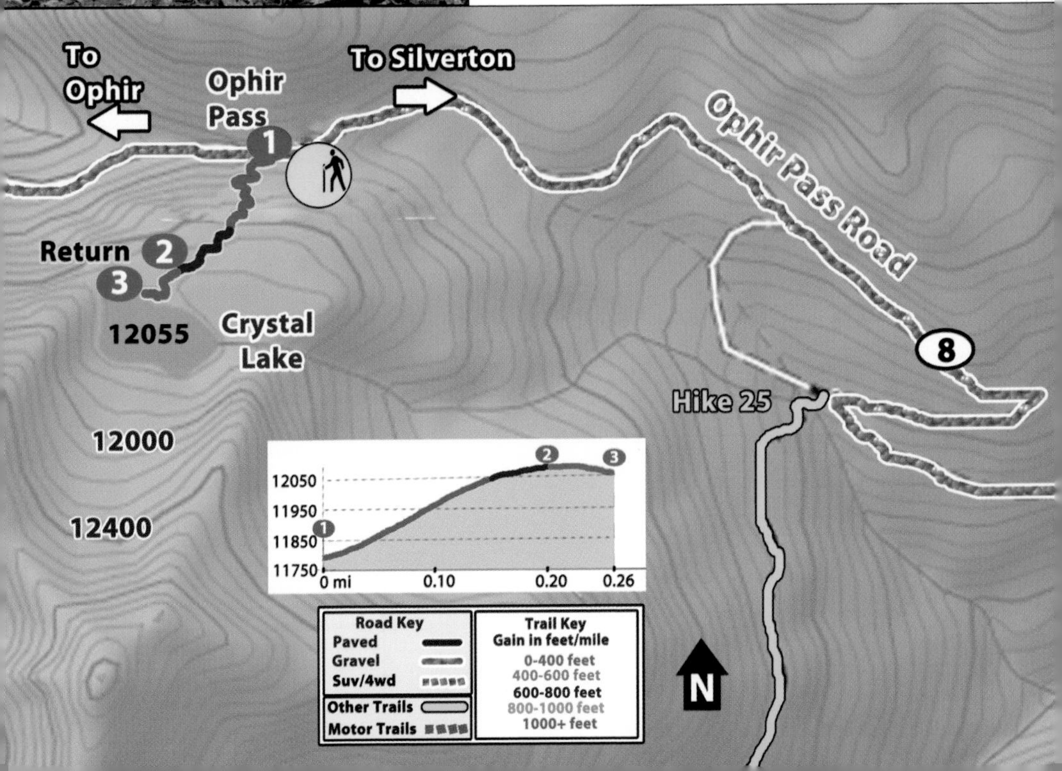

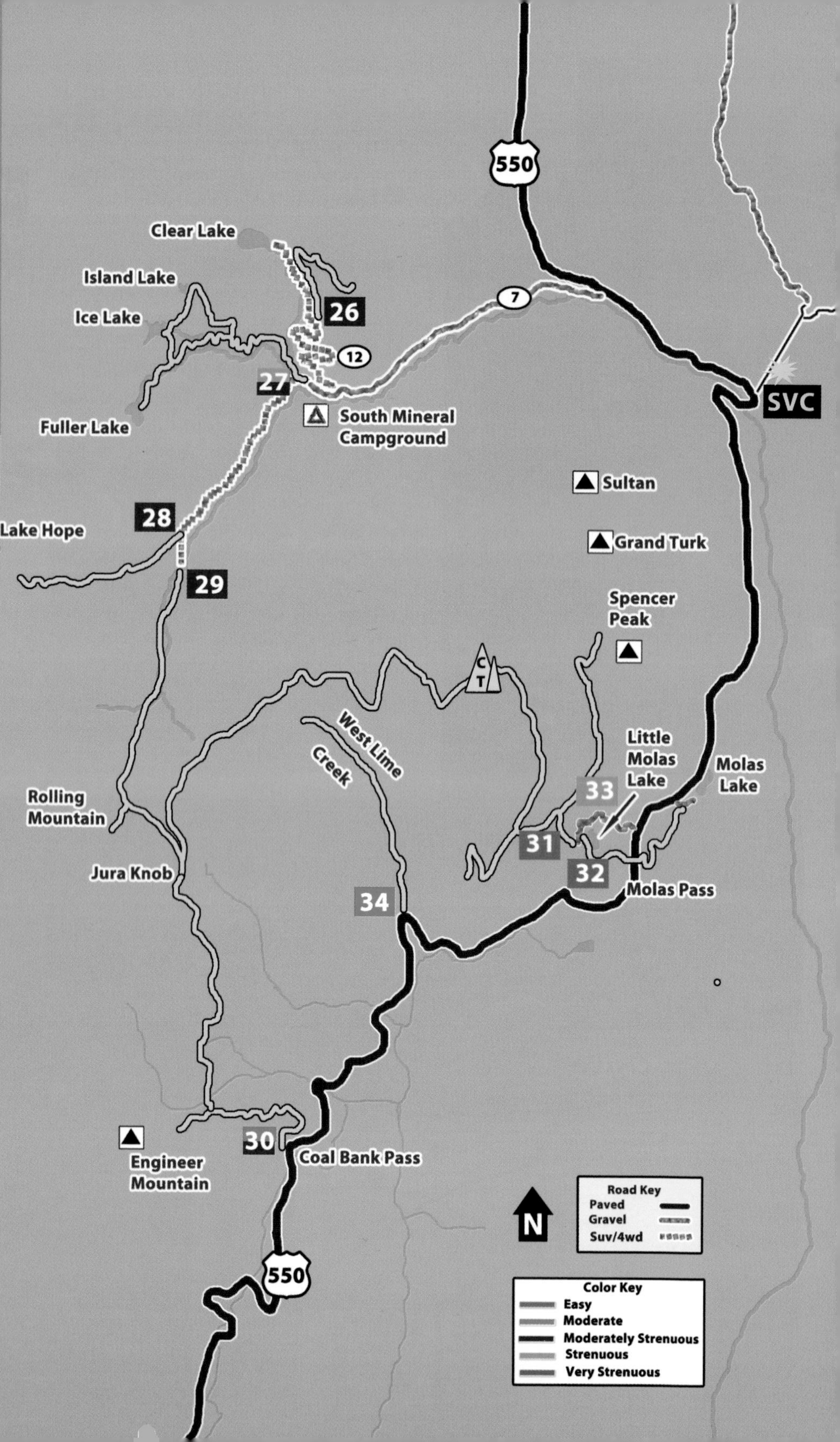
550
Clear Lake
Island Lake
Ice Lake
26
7
12
27
Fuller Lake
South Mineral Campground
SVC
Sultan
28
Lake Hope
Grand Turk
29
Spencer Peak
C T
West Lime Creek
Little Molas Lake
33
Molas Lake
Rolling Mountain
31
32
Jura Knob
Molas Pass
34
30
Engineer Mountain
Coal Bank Pass
N
Road Key
Paved
Gravel
Suv/4wd
550
Color Key
Easy
Moderate
Moderately Strenuous
Strenuous
Very Strenuous

Silverton West & South Trails Locator Map

26. Clear Lake
27. Ice Lake
28. Hope Lake Pass
29. Rico-Silo Trail
30. Pass Creek Trail
31. Little Molas CT Trail North
32. Little Molas CT Trail South
33. Spencer Saddle
34. West Lime Creek

Clear Lake

Star Rating

☆☆☆☆☆

26a
26b

View of Clear Lake

26a: Start 26a

Total Distance	3.80 miles RT. Go any distance
Difficulty Rating	Moderately Strenuous
Surface	Cantankerous, rocky, ankle twisting all the way. A brilliant hike!
Gradient	Moderate alternates with Steep
Average Time	3.5 hours
Elevations	TH: 11,516; Highest: 12,690; Gain: +1,603

26b: Start 26b

Total Distance	2.60 miles RT
Average Time	2.5 hours
Elevations	TH: 11,882; Gain: +1,166
Map	San Juan Mountain Maps 2010: Silverton, Telluride, Ouray. No trail on any map

Summary

This is a very old mining track that few hikers know about. The trail is all above tree line and has superb views of Ice Lake Basin, Clear Lake Basin, Rico-Silo Valley and South Mineral Creek Valley. Climb up past the old mine and see Silverton way down the other side. Wildflowers are some of the best. They grow in the middle of the old track and smother the hillsides. Optional peak is a very strenuous climb to 13,156 feet. There is no trail but you can see your destination clearly.

Trail Description

Views are instant. The very rocky trail climbs quickly through the massive rock slide. As you ascend, the wildflowers get thicker and thicker. They grow right in the rocky path and add to the difficulty of seeing where to place your feet, but every step is worth a photograph; you won't mind going slower. Even by late July, there could still be a snow bank blocking the trail at 3. It could be very dangerous to cross. At this point, there is a cairn that marks the optional climb to the obvious knob above. It is very steep and strenuous. If able to proceed on the trail, it contours around to an old mine shaft and ends there 4. We like to climb up the grassy hillside above the mine shaft and cross over the top to a marvelous view of Silverton 5. Worth every minute and much easier than the optional peak route.

Directions to TH From SVC, drive 2.0 miles north on Hwy 550. Turn left at CR 7 on South Mineral Road. Drive 3.6 miles on good gravel. Turn right on signed CR 12. Reset your odometer to zero. Now the road climbs and becomes rocky. Switchbacks are tight for LWB vehicles but the road is protected by trees and does not feel exposed. If driving a LWB, we recommend driving one more switchback above the waterfall switchback to mile 3.4. Park near the old conical tank in a big turnaround area. This is Start 26a. The switchback above this spot is very tight and rough for big vehicles. SUVs can drive the very rocky 0.61 more miles to the TH at Start 26b which is mile 4.01 on your odometer. Just before seeing the Lake, there are two pull off areas to the left. The TH is opposite the first pull off. Look for the remains of an old road climbing up through the rocky scree slope to your right. The entire mountainside is one massive rock slide. The trail is hard to spot. There are no signs.

Time & Distance to TH Start 26a: 9 miles; 40 minutes; Start 26b: 9.61 miles; 45 minutes

Recommended Vehicle SUV/SWB

View into Rico-Silo drainage

GPS	Mile	Latitude	Longitude	Elevation	Comment
1	0.00	37,49.162N	107,46.365W	11,516′	Start 26a: LWB vehicles park here.
2	0.61 / 0.00	37,49.459N	107,46.649W	11,882′	Start 26b: TH: No signs
3	1.43 / 0.82	37,49.387N	107,46.240W	12,534′	Dangerous Snowfield; Cairn marks route to summit knob at 13,156. Very strenuous
4	1.79 / 1.18	37,49.202N	107,45.962W	12,557′	Old Mine
5	1.90 / 1.30	37,49.198N	107,45.817W	12,690′	Silverton overlook: Return.

Silverton overlook

Start 26b Trailhead and route

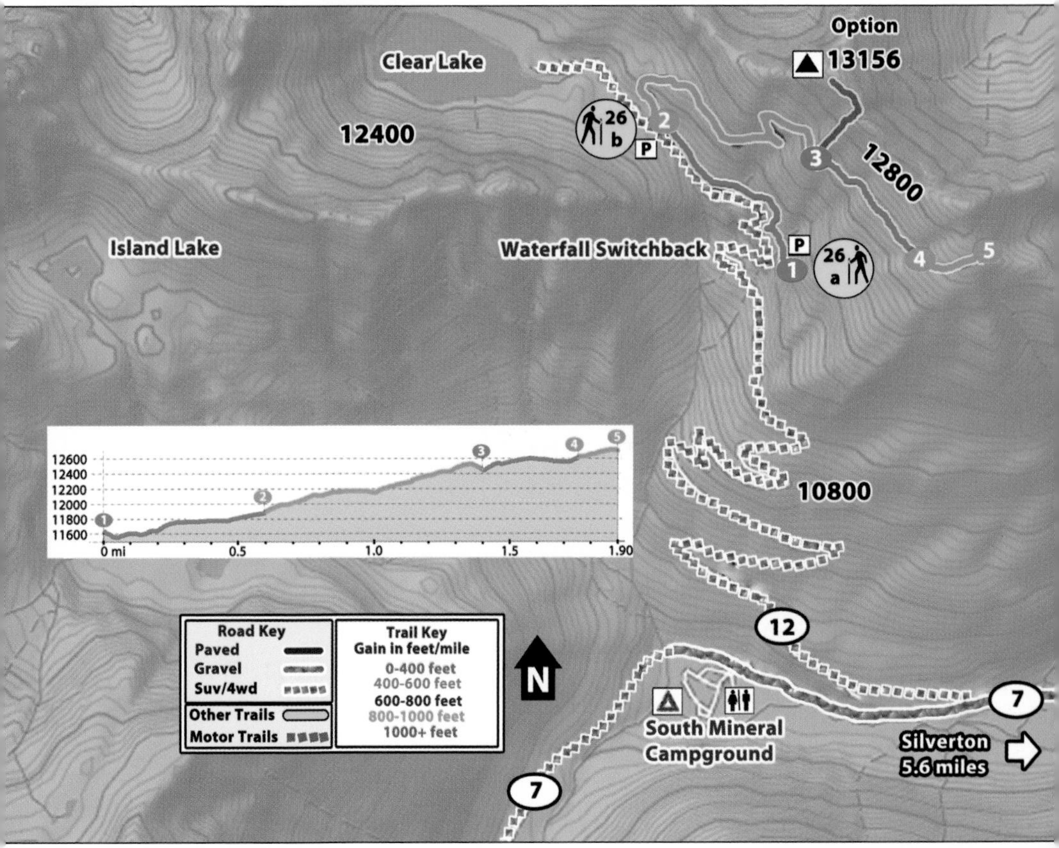

Ice Lake Options

27a
27b
27c
27d

Star Rating
☆☆☆
☆☆☆☆☆

27a: Start 27a to Ice Lake

Total Distance	6.4 miles RT
Difficulty Rating	Strenuous
Surface	Alternating easy packed dirt and loose gravel. Last 0.75 miles is very rocky
Gradient	Ranges from easy to very steep
Average Time	4 hours
Elevations	TH: 9,801; Highest: 12,275; Gain: +2,635

27b: Start 27b to Ice Lake

Total Distance	5.32 miles RT
Difficulty Rating	Moderately Strenuous
Average Time	3.5 hours
Elevations	TH: 10,311; Highest; 12,275; Gain: +2,129

Ice Lake

27c: To Fuller Lake

Total Distance	Add: 1.62 miles RT
Difficulty Rating	Easy
Gradient	Easy
Average Time	Add 1 hour
Elevations	Highest: 12,609; Gain +307

27d: To Island Lake

Total Distance	Add 1.12 miles RT
Difficulty Rating	Easy
Gradient	Easy with one short steep section
Average Time	Add 1 hour
Elevations	Highest: 12,432; Gain: +228
Maps	San Juan Mountain Maps 2010: Silverton, Telluride, Ouray

Directions to TH Start 27a: From SVC, drive 2.0 miles north on Hwy 550. Turn left (W) on South Mineral Road CR 7. Drive 4.2 miles from this junction to signed TH opposite South Mineral Campground. Ample parking.
Start 27b: From SVC, drive 2.0 miles north on Hwy 550. Turn left (W) on South Mineral Road CR 7. Drive 3.6 miles to signed junction CR 12. Go right (N) up the hill for 0.80 miles. Unsigned TH is at first switchback. Parking is minimal. DO NOT BLOCK CURVE OR ROAD!
Time & Mileage to TH Start 27a: 20 minutes; 6.2 miles; Start 27b: 30 minutes; 6.4 miles
Recommended Vehicle Car for both Start 27a and 27b

Summary

Hike through intermittent forest to ❺. Once in the lower Ice Lake Basin, views are constant. There are numerous big waterfalls and creeks. Wildflowers are tall and thick. The trail to the upper basin cuts up through a massive rock wall. Ice Lake is surrounded by sharp, jagged peaks. The rolling hills are festooned with flowers. The view is classic Colorado. Inspiring! There are two more lakes that are easy to reach and very beautiful as well. This is a very popular trail and gets high usage.

Trail Description

As you can see, there are two Start options. Start 27a is the traditional trailhead with easy access and good parking but it adds 0.81 miles and 506 feet in elevation

Climb to Fuller Lake: Photo by Sigrid Werbitsch

Descending from top to Lower Basin

Ice Lake outlet stream

Lower Ice Lake Basin

Lower Ice Lake Basin from above

gain compared to Start 27b. Very limited parking and access, however, makes Start 27b a less reliable option. Whichever you choose, the trail remains steep and you will be hiking in intermittent forest until ❺. When you enter Lower Ice Lake Basin ❻, the gradient becomes easy. The wildflowers can be 4 feet tall. See the trail climb up the rock wall. The creek at ❼ may require wet shoes to cross through July. From ❼ to ❽, the trail is very steep and rocky but the views make the effort worthwhile.

To Fuller Lake ❿. Continue on the same trail that brought you to Ice Lake. It is a good trail that passes an un-named little lake ❾ before making the moderate ascent to Fuller. Wildflowers and a spectacular look back to Ice Lake make this a great side trip.

To Island Lake: Cross the outlet stream (wet shoes) for Ice Lake ⓫ and pick up a trail contouring north up the mountainside. Island Lake ⓬ is around the saddle you can see above.

GPS	Mile	Latitude	Longitude	Elevation	Comment
1	0.00	37,48.402N	107,46.439W	9,801′	Start 27a for Ice Lake.
2	- / 0.00	37,48.630N	107,46.588W	10,311′	Start 27b for Ice Lake.
3	- / 0.13	37,48.703N	107,46.686W	10,335′	Cross waterfall creek.
4	0.81 / 0.30	37,48.752N	107,46.843W	10,439′	Junction: Start 27a and 27b meet
5	1.86 / 1.33	37,48.744N	107,47.484W	11,371′	Exit forest.
6	2.03 / 1.50	37,48.747N	107,47.651W	11,497′	Enter Lower Ice Lake Basin.
7	2.46 / 1.95	37,48.706N	107,48.104W	11,503′	Cross stream; wet shoes thru July
8	3.20 / 2.66	37,48.789N	107,48.447W	12,275′	Ice Lake

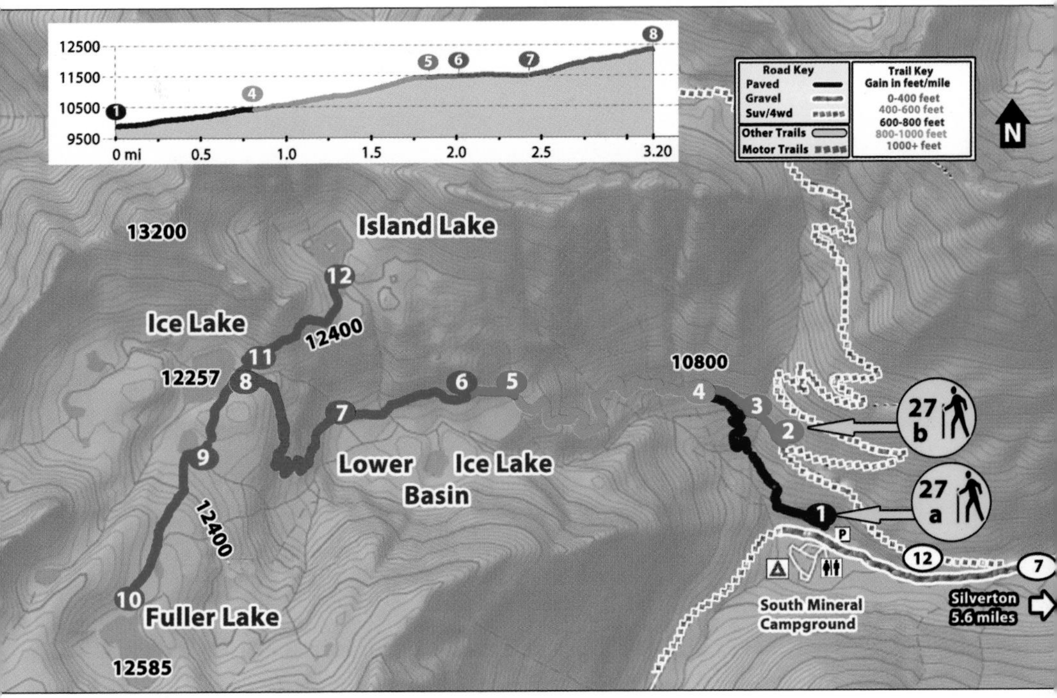

Ice Lake Basin from Island Lake Trail

28

Hope Lake Pass

Star Rating
☆☆☆
☆☆☆☆☆

Hope Lake from Pass

Total Distance	4.88 miles RT
Difficulty Rating	Moderately Strenuous
Surface	Rocky most of the way
Gradient	Moderately Steep
Average Time	3.5 hours
Elevations	TH: 10,649; Highest: 12,411; Gain: +1,866
Map	San Juan Mountain Maps 2010: Silverton, Telluride, Ouray

Directions to TH
From SVC, drive 2.0 miles north on Hwy 550. Turn left on CR 7 (South Mineral Springs Road). Drive another 7.7 miles to the old Bandora Mine site on your right. Park by the mine tailings at the base of the old buildings where the road forks. The right fork is blocked by rocks. This is the unsigned TH.

Time & Distance to TH
40 minutes; 9.7 miles

Recommended Vehicle
SUV. Although cars can easily drive the gravel road CR 7 the first 5.7 miles, the last 2.0 miles, after South Mineral Campground, are extremely rocky and rough.

Summary

The trail is an old, deteriorated mining road that climbs for one mile through spruce forest with occasional views. The remainder is above tree line as it enters a lovely basin of seasonal wildflowers and straight up granite walls. The final pitch climbs to a pass overlooking Hope Lake 500 feet below on the other side of this drainage. There are also some views up the Rico-Silo valley.

Basin wildflowers: View down valley

Trail Description

The trail follows an old mining road through intermittent spruce forest for the first mile ❷. The wildflowers in the basin can be thick as carpet. The vertical rock walls are imposing ❸. There are no water features in this basin so we give it 5 stars instead of 6. The climb to Hope Lake Pass is 681 feet in just under a mile ❹. The trail is etched in the mountain side. The views from the top of Hope Lake and its glacial basin are stunning.

GPS	Mile	Latitude	Longitude	Elevation	Comment
1	0.00	37,47.170N	107,48.085W	10,649′	Start Hope Pass at Bandora Mine site.
2	1.09	37,46.773N	107,49.006W	11,568′	Exit forest.
3	1.47	37,46.743N	107,49.409W	11,868′	Enter basin.
4	2.44	37,46.709N	107,50.378W	12,411′	Hope Lake Pass

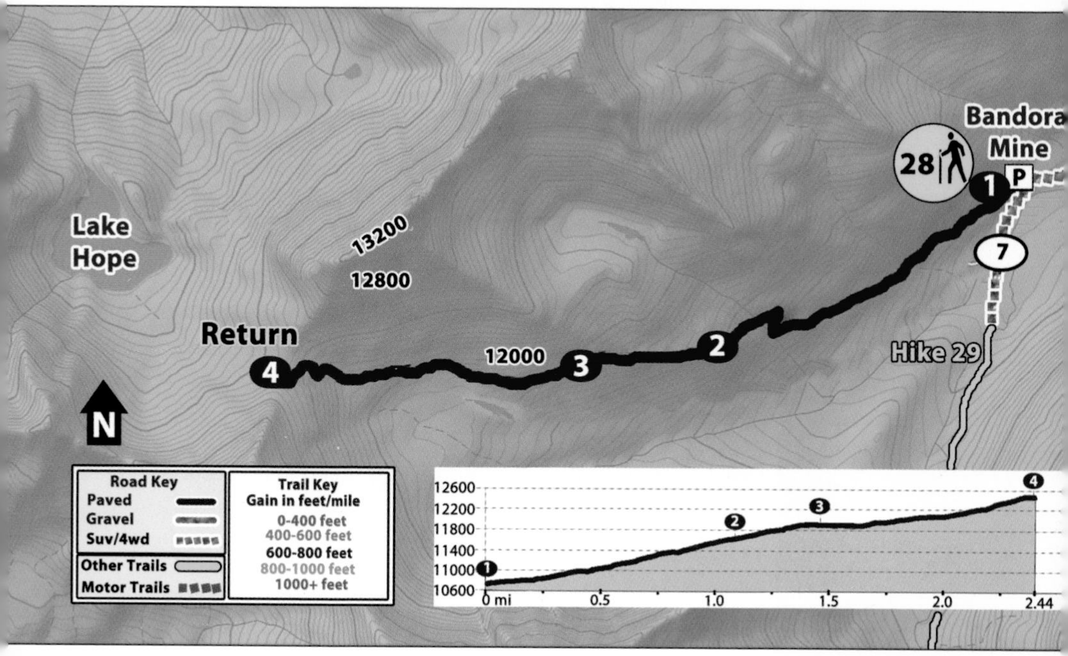

29a
29b

Rico-Silo Options

Star Rating

☆☆☆

☆☆☆☆☆☆

29a: To Rolling Pass/ Return 1

Total Distance	4.86 miles RT
Difficulty Rating	Moderately Strenuous
Surface	Lots of stream crossings requiring wet shoes in July
Gradient	Mostly Moderately Steep
Average Time	3.5 hours
Elevations	TH: 10,659; Highest: 12,589; Gain: + 1,886

27b To Jura Knob/ Return 2

Total Distance	8.12 miles RT
Gradient	Easy from Rolling Pass with Moderately Steep final ascent to Jura Knob
Average Time	4.5 hours
Elevations	12,614; Gain: +2,749
Map	San Juan Mountain Maps 2010: Silverton, Durango.
	No trail to Jura Knob

Summary

The trail begins in Spruce. After 0.80 miles, enter an incredibly beautiful valley thick with seasonal wildflowers, meadows, creeks, waterfalls and colorful mountains to Rolling Pass. Once there, you have done most of your climbing and the hike to Jura Knob is across easy tundra surrounded by spectacular peaks. An optional return route is to hike cross country through the center of the wide valley you ascended. No need for a trail until you reach the trees.

Directions to TH From SVC, drive 2.0 miles north on Hwy 550 and turn left at signed junction for CR 7 (South Mineral Road). Drive to the end of the road which is another 6.9 miles. You will have crossed at least two slow moving creeks before reaching the end of the road in a dispersed camping area. There is no trailhead sign.

Time & Mileage to TH 45 minutes; 8.9 miles

Recommended Vehicle SUV. The gravel road to South Mineral Campground is in very good condition but becomes extremely rocky after that.

Pictured: Rico-Silo valley

Trail Description

Cross a creek right at the TH. There are logs to assist in July, but be prepared with wet shoes. Hike up through spruce forest with a wonderful understory of wildflowers. At (2a) there is a major rushing creek to cross; we recommend using poles for added stability. Continue through the trees to (4a) where you will have fine views up the basin and a rich display of wildflowers. There are many rock

Trail follows along creek

outcroppings, tumbling creeks and more flowers all the way to 6a where you meet the Colorado Trail from Rolling Pass. There are wonderful views towards Bolam Pass and Hermosa Peak from Rolling Pass. 6b. Return from the Pass to 6a and continue up the trail to another junction marked by a dilapidated sign 8. This is the Colorado Trail to Little Molas Lake. Stay on the trail until you are as close as practical to the grassy knob that stands by itself. That is Jura Knob. Leave the trail 7 and pick your own route to the summit 6. The views of this impressive area extend for miles. Return from Jura Knob the way you came, or overland through the flowered meadows to the trees as you don't need a trail. Another option to consider is setting up a shuttle and returning via the Colorado Trail to Little Molas Lake. For details on this latter option, read Hike 30.

GPS	Mile	Latitude	Longitude	Elevation	Comment
1a	0.00	37,46.821N	107,48.186W	10,659'	Start Rico-Silo Cross stream. Wet shoes in July
2a	0.40	37,46.491N	107,48.311W	10,817'	Big stream crossing. Wet shoes thru July
3a	0.60	37,46.436N	107,48.407W	10,740'	Stream crossing. Wet shoes in July
4a	0.80	37,46.302N	107,48.459W	10,904'	Arrive in basin. Views
5a	0.90	37,46.217N	107,48.457W	11,108'	Out of trees. Cross stream. Find route around wet areas.
6a	2.23	37,45.119N	107,48.895W	12,257'	Junction: Colorado Trail; Right (SW) goes to Rolling Pass for additional views; left (E) for Jura Knob.
6b	2.43	37,44.803N	107,49.006W	12,589'	Rolling Pass / Return 1
6a	2.63	37,45.119N	107,48.895W	12,257'	Junction: Colorado Trail; now go right (E) for Jura Knob.
8	3.43	37,44.782N	107,48.319W	12,097'	Junction: Sign post destroyed. Go straight ahead (S) for Jura Knob. Left (N) goes to Little Molas Lake on Colorado Trail.
7	3.53	37,44.638N	107,48.303W	12,161'	Leave trail and cross country to Jura Knob.
6	4.06	37,44.278N	107,48.120W	12,614'	Top of Jura Knob / Return 2

Leave Engineer Pass Trail for Jura Knob

Lower trail enters meadows

Junction to Rolling Pass

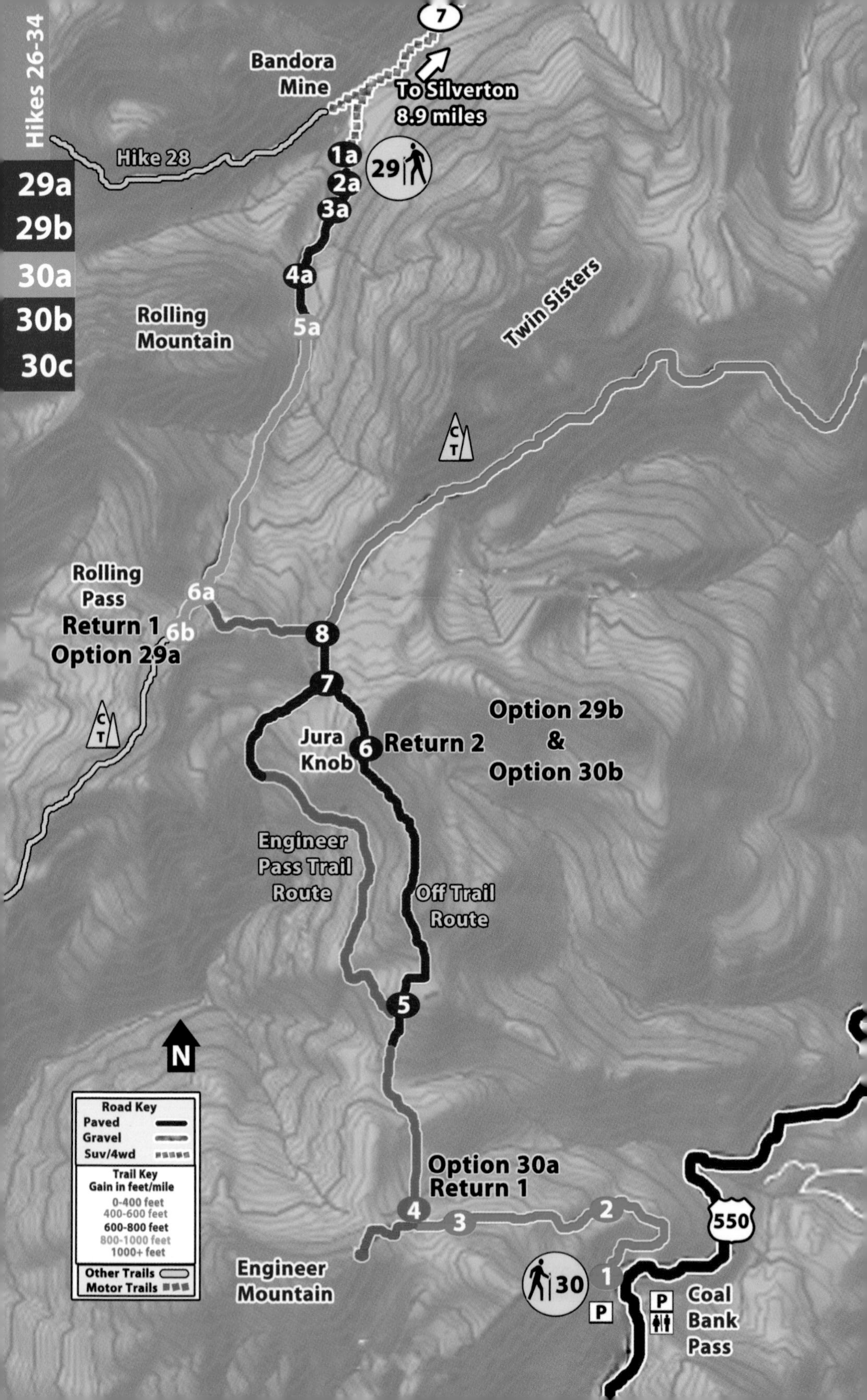

Hikes 26-34
29a
29b
30a
30b
30c
7
Bandora Mine
To Silverton 8.9 miles
Hike 28
1a
2a
3a
4a
5a
29
Rolling Mountain
Twin Sisters
C T
Rolling Pass
6a
6b
Return 1 Option 29a
8
7
C T
Jura Knob
6
Return 2
Option 29b & Option 30b
Engineer Pass Trail Route
Off Trail Route
5
N
Road Key
Paved
Gravel
Suv/4wd
Trail Key
Gain in feet/mile
0-400 feet
400-600 feet
600-800 feet
800-1000 feet
1000+ feet
Other Trails
Motor Trails
Option 30a Return 1
4
3
2
1
550
Engineer Mountain
30
P
P
Coal Bank Pass

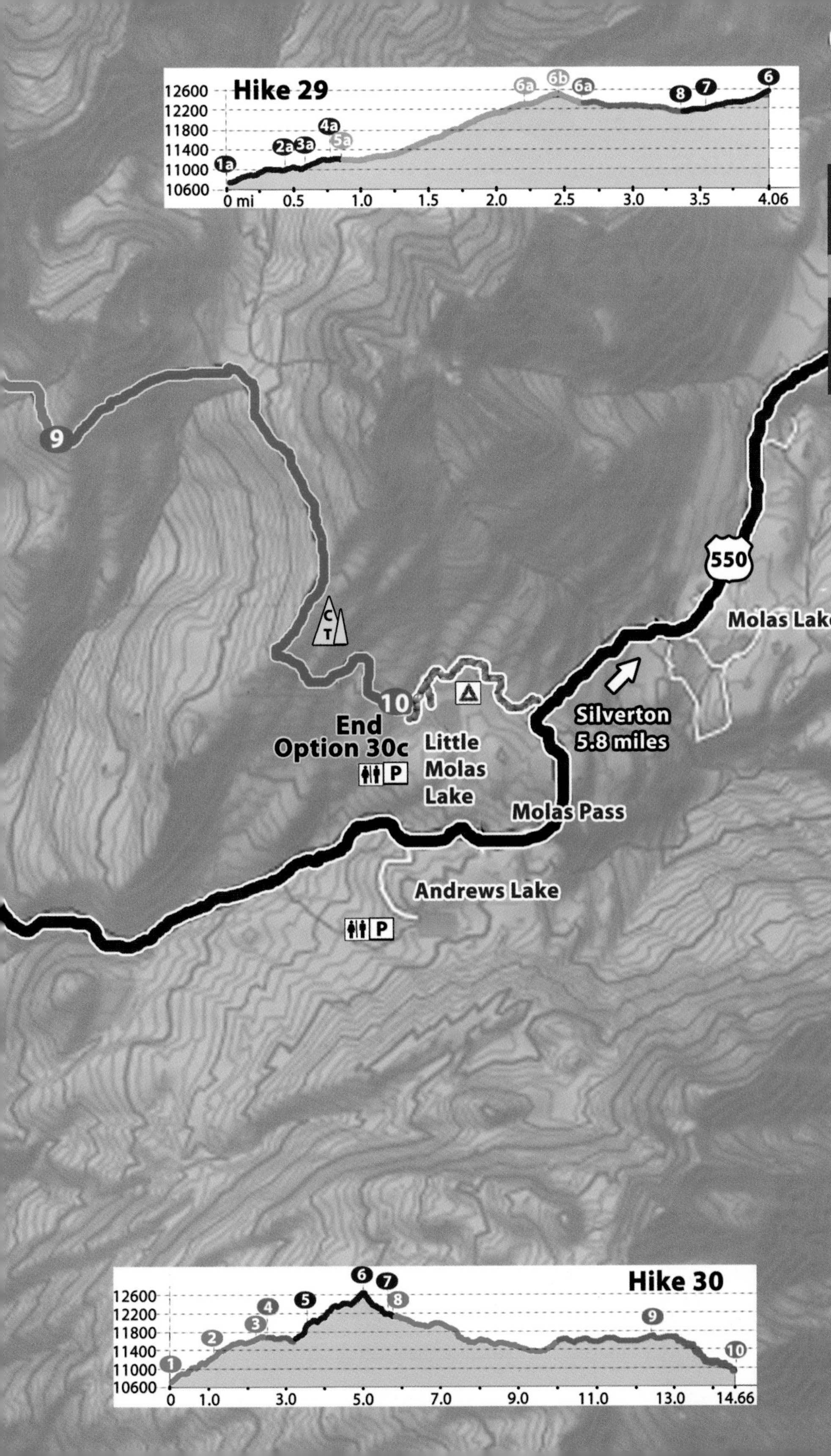
Hike 29
12600
12200
11800
11400
11000
10600
0 mi
0.5
1.0
1.5
2.0
2.5
3.0
3.5
4.06
1a
2a
3a
4a
5a
6a
6b
6a
8
7
6
9
CT
10
End
Option 30c
Little
Molas
Lake
550
Molas Lake
Silverton
5.8 miles
Molas Pass
Andrews Lake
P
Hike 30
12600
12200
11800
11400
11000
10600
0
1.0
3.0
5.0
7.0
9.0
11.0
13.0
14.66
1
2
3
4
5
6
7
8
9
10

30a
30b
30c

Pass Creek Trail Options

Star Rating
☆☆☆
☆☆☆☆☆☆

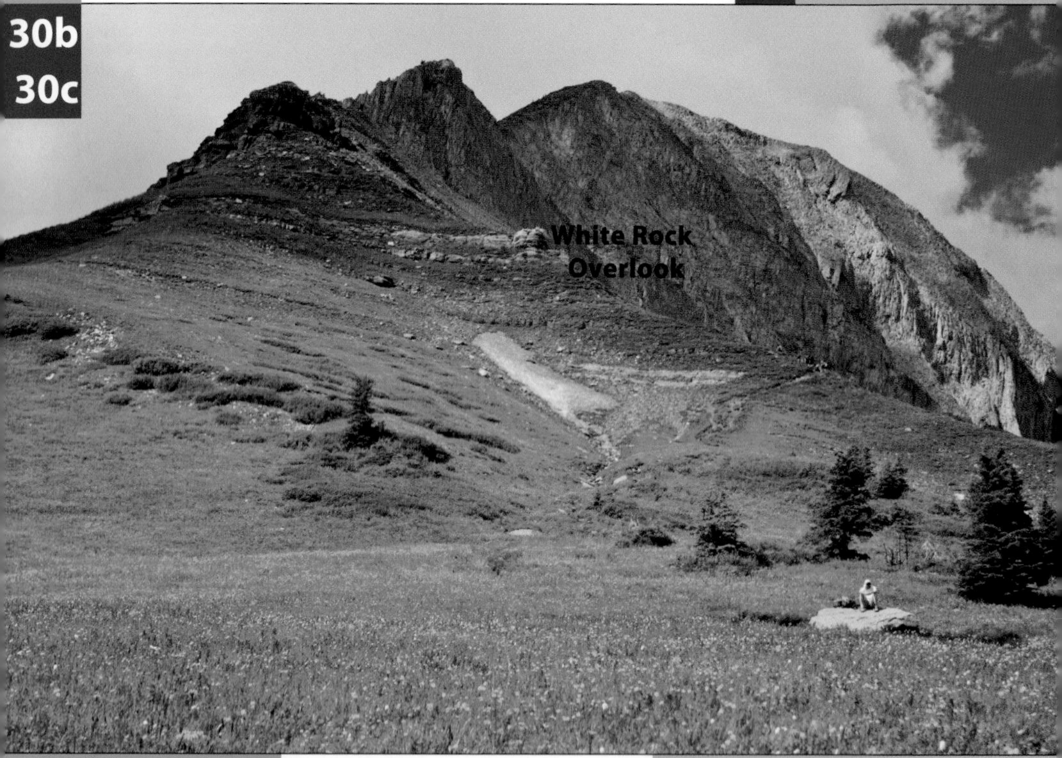

Engineer Mt from Basin

30a: To Engineer Basin/ Return 1

Total Distance	5.20 miles RT
Difficulty Rating	Moderate
Gradient	Moderate
Average Time	3 hours
Elevations	TH: 10,994; Highest: 11,661; Gain: +1,201

30b: To Jura Knob/ Return 2

Total Distance	10.08 miles RT
Difficulty Rating	Moderately Strenuous
Gradient	Moderate to Moderately steep
Average Time	6 hours
Elevations	Highest: 12,614; Gain: +2,685

Summary

Pick an option. See some of the best wildflowers from the TH to Engineer Basin; hike through high elevation tundra to Jura Knob with explosive vistas in every direction; continue on the famous Colorado Trail as it contours around the

	30c: To Little Molas Lake
Total Distance	14.66 miles to shuttle
Difficulty Rating	Moderately Strenuous because of distance
Gradient	Moderate to Moderately Steep
Average Time	8 hours
Elevations	Highest: 12,614; Gain: +3,566
Map	San Juan Mountain Maps 2010: Silverton, Durango
Directions to TH	From SVC, drive south on Hwy 550 for 13.3 miles to summit of Coal Bank Pass (milepost 57). Just north of the pass turn right (W) on a gravel road into a parking lot. Outhouse across US 550
Time & Distance to TH	25 minutes; 13.3 miles
Recommended Vehicle	Car. The TH is accessed by paved highway
Shuttle	From SVC, drive south on Hwy 550 for 5.9 miles. Turn right (W) at the signed junction for Little Molas Lake, and drive 1.0 miles through the campground to the signed TH parking lot. Outhouse
Time & Distance Shuttle	15 minutes; 6.9 miles
Recommended Vehicle	Car. Access is by paved highway and 1.0 miles of good gravel.

West Lime Creek drainage to Little Molas Lake. Although the total distance to the shuttle point is long, most of it traverses moderate terrain and offers a wonderful variety of scenery. The sections from the TH to Engineer Basin, and the last two miles to the shuttle point get heavy usage, especially on weekends. Bicycles also use these portions.

Trail Description

The trail begins in a sea of wildflowers five feet tall. Even after entering the trees, the wildflowers still grow in abundance. It is a beautiful, moderate climb through this forest that opens to many more vistas after ❷. When you enter Engineer Basin itself ❸, the wildflowers are so thick, they look like carpet. Continue into the basin to a signed junction ❹. Notice the track going up to Engineer Peak. Many hikers climb to the White Rock overlook for additional views of the San Juan Range. To continue to the summit requires bouldering and scrambling and maneuvering around a very exposed rocky ridge. To continue to Jura Knob and Little Molas Lake, stay on the main trail at ❹. According to the maps, this is now Engineer Pass Trail, not Pass Creek Trail. In about 0.9 miles on this trail, look ahead to your right and locate Jura Knob ❻. (See photos.) There is an amazing ridge line that leads right to the top. Leave the trail ❺ and hike this ridge. (If you prefer, you can continue on the trail and bypass Jura Knob. It is 2.54 miles and 683 feet gain on the trail; it is 2.10 miles and 937 feet gain via Jura Knob.) The views from Jura Knob are all encompassing; it is well worth the effort. From the summit, you can see the trail towards Little Molas. Pick your route down, join the trail and quickly you will be at the junction ❽ to Little Molas Lake. From this point to the end, the trail undulates as it contours around the lovely West Lime Creek Basin.

GPS	Mile	Latitude	Longitude	Elevation	Comment
1	0.00	37,41.967N	107,46.724W	10,994′	Start Pass Creek Trail.
2	1.10	37,42.292N	107,46.747W	11,172′	Small lake
3	2.40	37,42.244N	107,47.814W	11,611′	Enter Engineer Basin
4	2.60	37,42.244N	107,47.907W	11,661′	Return 1: Signed Colorado Trail junction. Trail goes uphill (W) for Engineer peak climb. Go straight ahead (N) for Jura Knob, or return to TH.
5	3.49	37,43.109N	107,47.971W	11,738′	Leave Engineer Pass Trail and climb the long ridge that leads to Jura Knob.
6	5.04	37,44,278N	107,48,120W	12,614′	Return 2: Top of Jura Knob; return or continue.
7	5.60	37,44.638N	107,48.303W	12,161′	Meet existing Engineer Pass Trail.
8	5.75	37,44.782N	107,48.319W	12,097′	Junction: Sign post deteriorating. Go right (NE) to Little Molas Lake on Colorado Trail. Straight (NW) joins with Rico-Silo Trail.
9	12.16	37.45.608N	107.43.332W	11,619′	Start final descent to Little Molas Lake.
10	14.66	37,44.556N	107,42.716W	10,893′	End at Little Molas Lake parking lot.

Route towards Jura Knob from Engineer Mt

Basin from White Rock Overlook

31

Little Molas Lake Colorado Trail North

Star Rating

☆☆☆☆☆

View midway along trail

Total Distance	5.0 miles RT or any distance you wish
Difficulty Rating	Easy
Surface	Easy packed dirt, easy on the feet!
Gradient	Easy
Average Time	3 hours
Elevations	TH: 10,893; Highest: 11,627; Gain: +947
Map	San Juan Mountain Maps 2010: Silverton, Telluride, Ouray

Directions to TH	From SVC, drive 5.8 miles south on Hwy 550 to the signed junction for Little Molas Lake. Turn right (W) and drive the gravel road 1.0 mile through the campground to the ample parking lot for the signed Colorado Trail. Outhouse
Time & Distance to TH	15 minutes; 6.8 miles
Recommended Vehicle	Car. Access is by paved highway and 1.0 miles of good gravel

Summary

Here is a hike all above tree line with easy road access, elevation gain, gradient and good walking surface. The views of the San Juan Range are instant. The trail winds around the top of Lime Creek drainage which is a wide flower filled basin. This is an excellent hike for children. It is also a very popular bicycle track especially on weekends.

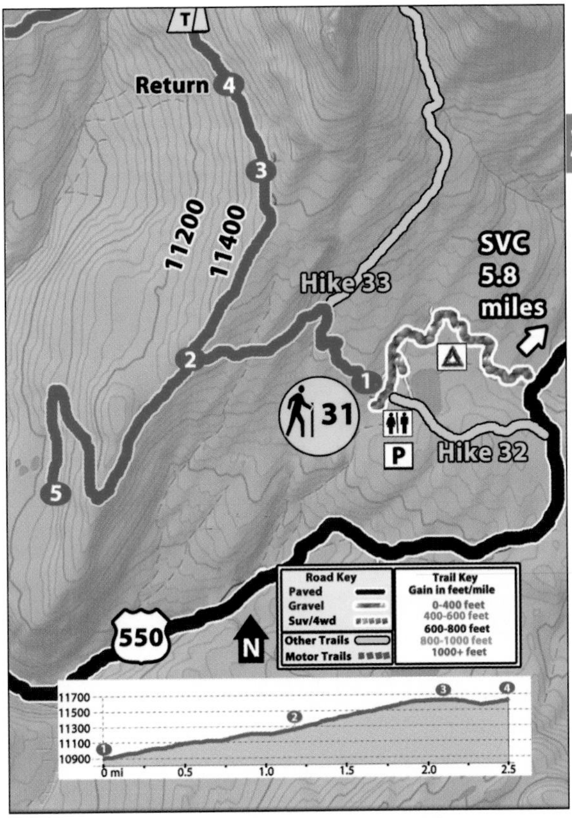

Trail Description

From the parking area, take the signed trail west and north. It is easy to follow all the way. At ❷ is an optional very easy, almost indistinct vehicle track that leads to three ponds ❺. Bicycles do not go here. It is very quiet. Otherwise, continue on the main trail up to the high point ❸ where the flowers are particularly dense. Scramble off trail up the bank and wander through amazing flower patches. After ❹ the trail enters thick brush. It makes a good return point. That's it!

GPS	Mile	Latitude	Longitude	Elevation	Comment
1	0.00	37,44.556N	107,42.716W	10,893′	Start Little Molas Colorado Trail North.
2	1.18	37,44.628N	107,43.489W	11,237′	Optional trail to pond overlook
3	2.11	37,45.294N	107,43.175W	11,627′	High point; scramble uphill for dense flower area.
4	2.50	37,45.608N	107,43.332W	11,619′	Good return point
5	2.67	37,44.266N	107,44.163W	10,849′	Optional end for hike to ponds

Little Molas Lake from trail

Wow!

32

Little Molas Lake Colorado Trail South

Star Rating

☆☆☆☆

Little Molas Lake

Total Distance	2.38 miles to shuttle point or go any distance
Difficulty Rating	Easy
Surface	Mostly packed dirt
Gradient	Easy
Average Time	2 hours
Elevations	TH:10,893; Highest: 10,983; Gain: +252; Loss: -544
Map	San Juan Mountain Maps 2010: Silverton, Telluride, Ouray

Directions to TH From SVC, drive 5.8 miles south on Hwy 550 to the signed junction for Little Molas Lake. Turn right (W) and drive the gravel road 1.0 mile through the campground to the ample parking lot for the Colorado Trail. Outhouse.

Shuttle From the SVC, drive 5.2 miles south on Hwy 550 to the signed Molas TH parking lot.

Summary

A very easy hike through meadows and open forest with dramatic peaks all around. Little Molas Lake is very pretty; there is a free campground on its shores. This trail is part of the famous Colorado Trail. A wonderful evening hike with reflections in the lake. Great for children.

View south near end of trail

Trail Description

Start the trail near the outhouse in the main parking lot for the Colorado Trail at Little Molas Lake. The trail skirts around the lake before making an easy ascent to Hwy 550 ❸ where it crosses over. After the Hwy, the trail begins an easy descent through very open forest and meadows with views of peaks all around. There are a couple of trail junctions until at ❻ a sign indicates the Colorado trail continues straight ahead to the Animas Gorge. Turn left here to get to the Molas Lake parking lot ❼.

GPS	Mile	Latitude	Longitude	Elevation	Comment
1	0.00	37,44,556N	107,42.716W	10,893'	Start Little Molas Lake Colorado Trail South.
2	0.20	37,44.501N	107,42.536W	10,931'	Trail to Little Molas beach parking lot
3	0.90	37,44.366N	107,41.874W	10,867'	Cross Hwy 550 or return to start.
4	1.80	37,44.488N	107,41.486W	10,574'	Junction with horse trail. No sign. Go straight ahead.
5	1.90	37,44.537N	107,41.489W	10,507'	Cross small stream.
6	2.20	37,44.690N	107,41.294W	10,540'	Colorado Trail sign: Go left to parking lot at Molas Lake; Straight goes to Animas River.
7	2.38	37,44.877N	107,41.288W	10,615'	Molas TH parking lot on Hwy 550

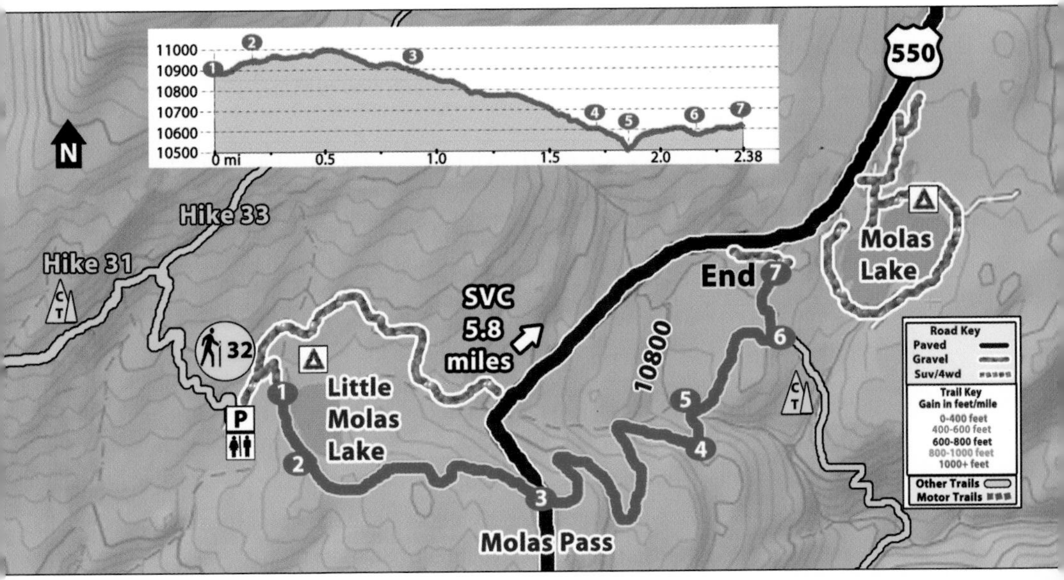

Spencer Saddle

Star Rating

☆☆☆☆☆

View from Spencer Saddle

Total Distance	5.48 miles RT; Go any distance
Difficulty Rating	Strenuous
Surface	Easy packed dirt on Colorado Trail; remainder is cross country and intermittent trails
Gradient	Easy to Moderate first 1.38 miles to creek crossing; Steep to Very Steep for remainder
Average Time	5 hours
Elevations	TH: 10,893; Highest: 12,743; Gain: +1,883
Map	San Juan Mountain Maps 2010: Silverton, Telluride, Ouray. No trail on any maps

Directions to TH From SVC, drive 5.8 miles south on Hwy 550 to the signed junction for Little Molas Lake. Turn right (W) and drive the gravel road 1.0 mile through the campground to the ample parking lot for the signed Colorado Trail. Outhouse

Summary

Three flower filled basins, wide open benches, cascading streams, dramatic crags and rock walls, views, views and more views, this is a hike of superlative variety, a true Colorado classic. Go on to climb two 13er's from the saddle. Go as far as you like. There is something wonderful to see at each stage of this hike. This is mostly off trail; follow our photo shots for easy directions; the route is very logical.

Trail Description

Most of the route and some of the destinations of this hike are clearly visible from the South side of Little Molas Lake (see photo). The trail begins by following the Colorado Trail northward (Hike 31). Walk the easy ascent about 0.55 miles to a big switchback ❷. When the Colorado Trail turns SW on this switchback, leave the trail and hike NE. Hike towards the flat area of the big drainage coming from the left in the distance. Take an easy ascent; do not try to gain too much elevation by climbing up strongly to the left. You will probably cross

Basin 1 wildflowers

View from notch down basin 2

the old Colorado Trail ❸ which is closed. Keep heading NE. Your goal is to reach the stream that comes down from the north drainage and cross it ❹ in the beautiful flat basin we call Basin 1. Wildflowers grow 4 feet tall. Now hike NW along the right bank of the stream. A steep climb gets you to basin 2 ❺. Wow! This is a magical place. Like

General route

a V shaped valley, it is formed by massive rock walls on both sides. Prolific wildflowers carpet the valley floor and curve up the sides to meet the bare rock. Wander around this basin and make it your goal. Or, continue on to the closed end of the V, and climb the steep and narrow track to the notch ❽. This short stretch is the most strenuous part of the hike. To get there, hike from ❺ up the ridge line east towards a lone clump of young spruce ❻. Once there, turn left (N) and keep as high a line as you can towards the faint trail you can see climbing to the notch. At ❼, just past a rugged gully, there is actually a trail hidden in the flowers and takes you all the way to the top. Once at

Route to Basin 1

Route ascending along creek to Basin 2

the notch, there is still a little more elevation to gain as you enter a wide, grassy couloir. Snow may still be present in August. Before climbing to the very top of the couloir, another little pass opens to the right (NE). Take this pass to reach Spencer Saddle. Once through this little pass, climb slightly up the hill to your left and start contouring around the corner. Very quickly you will enter another basin and see Spencer Saddle at the far end ⑩. Spencer Peak is the grassy knob to the right of the saddle. Keep a high traverse; there are faint trails to follow and a definite trail you can see that makes the final climb to the saddle. The wildflowers along this traverse are the thickest yet. Add new views across the Animas gorge. Hike to the saddle and sit on this craggy, jagged beauty. There are now amazing views of peaks to the north to use up the remainder of your photo card! For those with endless energy, you now have a clear view of Grand Turk and Sultan, two 13ers well within your reach. Make a whole day of it, or return from here.

Route from Basin 2 to notch

After notch, go through pass to the right

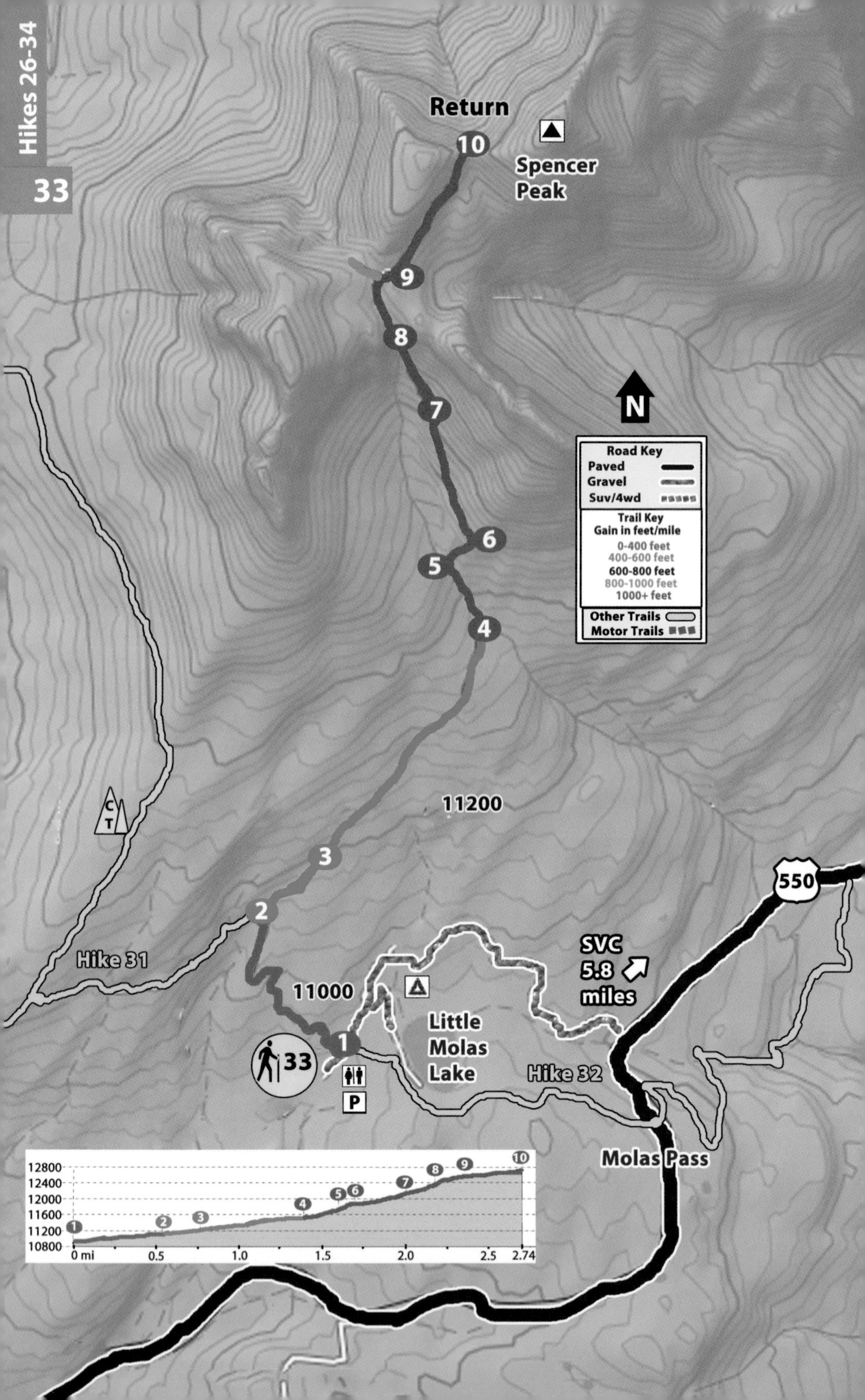
Return
10
Spencer Peak
9
8
7
N
Road Key
Paved
Gravel
Suv/4wd
Trail Key
Gain in feet/mile
0-400 feet
400-600 feet
600-800 feet
800-1000 feet
1000+ feet
Other Trails
Motor Trails
6
5
4
11200
C T
3
550
2
SVC
5.8
miles
Hike 31
11000
Little Molas Lake
1
33
P
Hike 32
Molas Pass
12800
12400
12000
11600
11200
10800
0 mi
0.5
1.0
1.5
2.0
2.5
2.74

Final ascent to saddle

GPS	Mile	Latitude	Longitude	Elevation	Comment
1	0.00	37,44,556N	107,42.716W	10.893′	Start Spencer Saddle at Colorado TH.
2	0.55	37,44.802N	107,42.906W	11,090′	Leave Colorado Trail at switchback and head NE.
3	0.75	37,44.914N	107,42.737W	11,197′	Cross old Colorado Trail. Continue NE.
4	1.38	37,45.328N	107,42.341W	11,475′	Cross stream; hike up right bank to next bench.
5	1.59	37,45.486N	107,42.427W	11,681′	Top of cascades. Enter second basin.
6	1.66	37,45.528N	107,42.374W	11,800′	Spruce clump, hike north on east side of basin.
7	1.97	37,45.790N	107,42.466W	12,098′	Deep gully; try to find trail from here to notch.
8	2.15	37,45.925N	107,42.563W	12,353′	Notch at top of 2nd basin
9	2.33	37,46.049N	107,42.577W	12,500′	At top of grassy couloir, go right through pass.
10	2.74	37,46.300N	107,42.367W	12,743′	Spencer Saddle

West Lime Creek

Star Rating

☆☆☆

Views up valley

Total Distance	5.70 miles RT
Difficulty Rating	Easy-Moderate
Surface	Mostly packed dirt
Gradient	Easy-Moderate
Average Time	3.5 hours
Elevations	TH: 9,846; Highest: 10,643; Gain: +1,273
Map	San Juan Mountain Maps 2010: Silverton, Durango

Directions to TH	From SVC, drive south on Hwy 550 towards Durango. At mile 9.7, on a very big curve, before ascending to Coal Bank Pass, is a 10,000 foot elevation sign. Park on the wide shoulder in the curve. No trailhead sign.
Time & Distance to TH	25 minutes; 9.7 miles
Recommended Vehicle	Car. Access is via paved highway 550

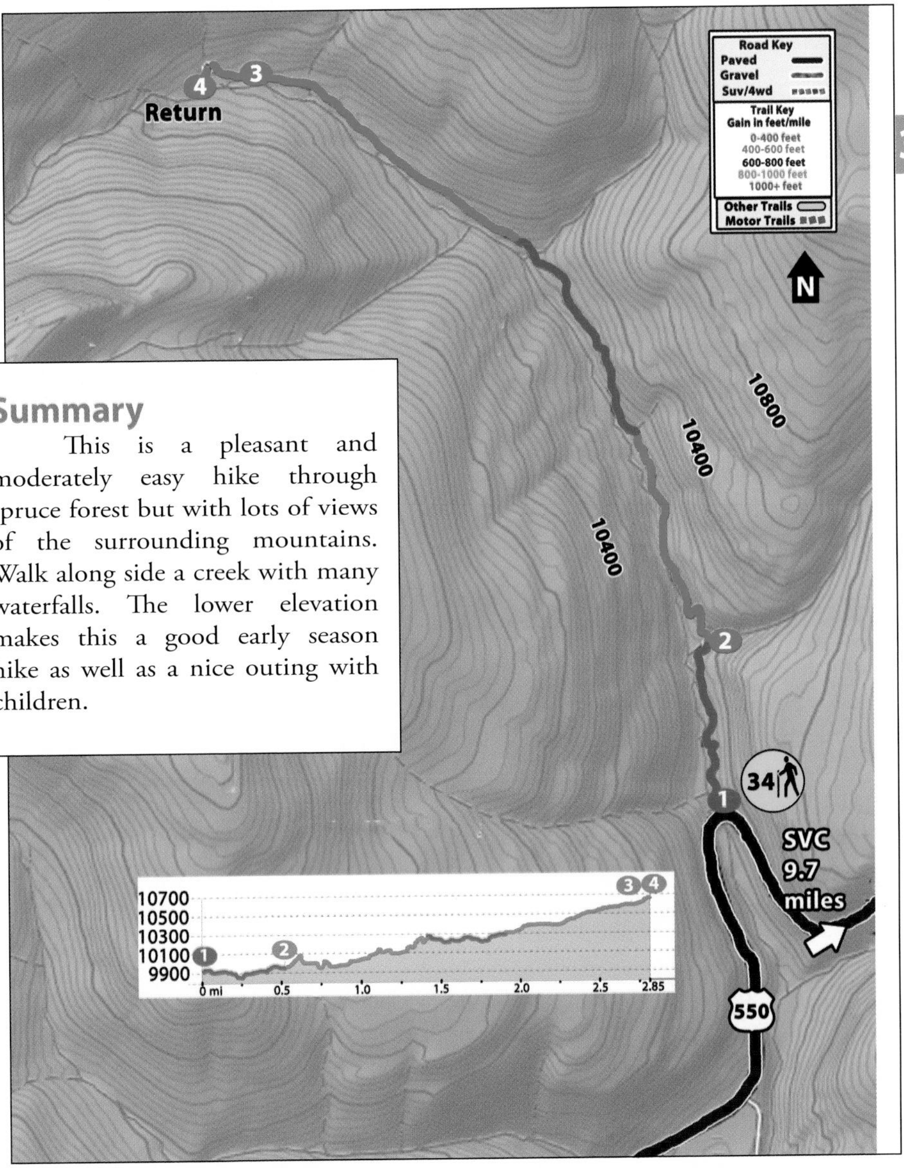

Summary

This is a pleasant and moderately easy hike through spruce forest but with lots of views of the surrounding mountains. Walk along side a creek with many waterfalls. The lower elevation makes this a good early season hike as well as a nice outing with children.

Trail Description

The trail starts on the east end of the curve on the north side; it goes down below the level of the road. It is easy to follow all the way to where an avalanche obliterated the trail at ❹.

GPS	Mile	Latitude	Longitude	Elevation	Comment
1	0.00	37,43.919N	107,45.023W	9,846′	Start West Lime Creek.
2	0.53	37,44.299N	107,45.079W	9,817′	Cross North Lime Creek.
3	2.71	37,45.575N	107,46.355W	10,551′	Avalanche
4	2.85	37,45.592N	107,46.483W	10,643′	Avalanche completely blocks trail. Return.

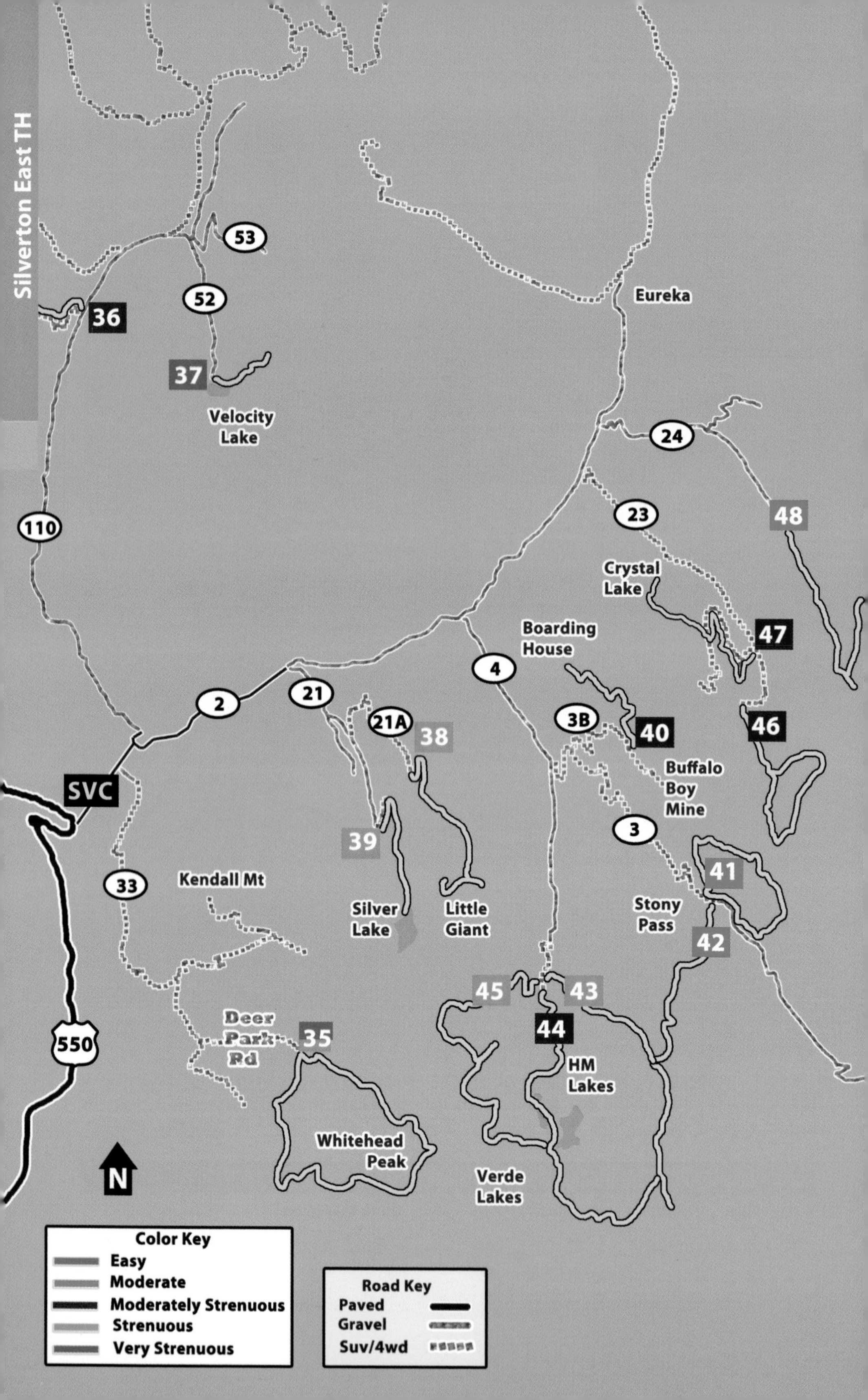
53
52
36
37
Velocity
Lake
Eureka
24
23
48
110
Crystal
Lake
Boarding
House
47
4
2
21
21A
38
3B
40
46
Buffalo
Boy
Mine
SVC
39
3
41
33
Kendall Mt
Silver
Lake
Little
Giant
Stony
Pass
42
45
43
44
Deer
Park
Rd
35
HM
Lakes
550
Whitehead
Peak
Verde
Lakes
N
Color Key
Easy
Moderate
Moderately Strenuous
Strenuous
Very Strenuous
Road Key
Paved
Gravel
Suv/4wd

Silverton East Trails Locator Map

35a
35b

Whitehead Trail Options

Star Rating

☆☆☆☆☆

35a: To Pond Overlook

Total Distance	5.02 miles RT
Difficulty Rating	Easy
Surface	Beginning is very rocky. Good packed dirt after saddle
Gradient	Mostly Easy to Moderate
Average Time	3.5 hours
Elevations	TH: 11,632; Highest: 12,350; Gain: +1,411

35b To Peak & Loop

Total Distance	6.18 miles Loop
Difficulty Rating	Strenuous
Surface	No trail to peak
Gradient	Easy to Moderate to ponds; steep to peak and down to vehicle
Average Time	5.5 hours
Elevations	TH: 11,632; Highest: 13,269; Gain: +2,241
Map	San Juan Mountain Maps 2010: Silverton, Durango

View from Whitehead Peak: Photo by Sigrid Werbitsch

Directions to TH From SVC, drive through town 0.6 miles and turn right at City Hall. No street name but sign on left side of street says Kendall Mountain. Cross the bridges and turn right on CR 33 (Kendall Mountain Road). Follow this road to an unmarked junction at mile 3.6. Turn right downhill. This road goes to Deer Park, not Kendall Mountain. Road narrows with few passing spots. Drive through alternating meadows and trees to mile 6.0 and park as soon as you enter a big meadow with views of Whitehead Peak and a cabin at the end of the valley. Look to your right (SW) for an old silver bus parked across the meadow. That is the TH.

Time & Mileage to TH 45 minutes; 6.0 miles

Recommended Vehicle SUV: Road is extremely rocky with steep sections and tight switchbacks.

Ascending from bus

View of peak and loop route from parking spot

Trailhead starts at the bus

Summary

This is an above tree line hike with views of entire mountain ranges to the west, south and east. Go as far as you wish; the views are instant. The trail maintains an easy gradient along a shelf high above various valleys. Continue on to climb a 13,000 foot peak and make a loop back to your vehicle, or return by the easy route you came. What a combination!

Trail Description

We recommend starting at the old bus ❷ and hiking counterclockwise for the loop. This is the easier climb to the peak with a steeper descent. You may also decide not to do the peak and can return on the easy trail. There are 14 wooden posts staggered along the trail to the point where you would ascend to the peak. If you count them as you proceed, we have marked 7 of them for interest and mileage.

From your parking spot, walk back 100 yards to the last small road to the SW and follow it to the bus ❷. It gets you through the wet willows. There is a good trail from the bus all the way to ❾, the last marker post. The scenic vistas are varied and beautiful. If you wish to continue from ❾, look for a narrow gully with a steep trail off to the left after passing the ponds. Use our photos to assist in finding the route to the peak ❿. The views from the summit are breathtaking. Make a loop from the peak back to your vehicle which you can see far below.

Route from pond to saddle and peak

Views along trail to pond

GPS	Mile	Latitude	Longitude	Elevation	Comment
1	0.00	37,46.314N	107,37.613W	11,632′	Parking
2	0.30	37,46.152N	107,37.624W	11,630′	Bus: TH sign
3	1.11	37,45.626N	107,37.744W	12,138′	Post #4 Saddle: Add views to south
4	1.61	37,45.199N	107,37.879W	12,308′	Post #7 Views of Whitehead Gulch
5	1.91	37,45.259N	107,37.625W	12,294′	Post # 8 Trail along edge of gulch
6	2.51	37,45.188N	107,37.183W	12,350′	Post #11 Views of pond and route to saddle/ Return 1
7	2.71	37,45.204N	107,36.966W	12,233′	Post#12 Small pond
8	3.02	37,45.203N	107,36.711W	12,226′	Post #13
9	3.12	37,45.175N	107,36.563W	12,268′	Post #14 Start ascent to peak.
10	4.33	37,45.603N	107,36.392W	13,269′	Whitehead Peak
11	4.53	37,45.791N	107,36.314W	13,136′	Saddle
1	6.18	37,46.314N	107,37.613W	11,632′	Parking

View of start of trail from saddle: photo by Sigrid Werbitsch

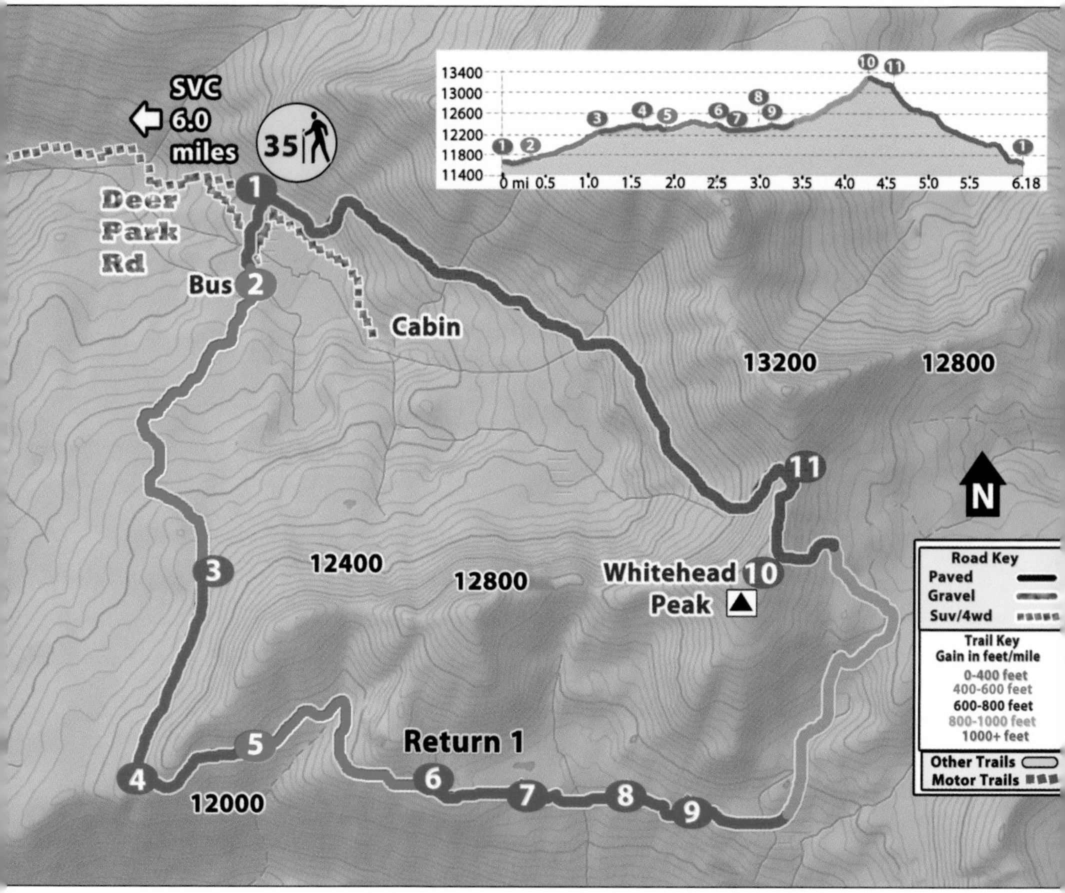

Kansas City Mine

Star Rating

☆☆☆☆

View from end of trail

Total Distance	4.0 miles RT
Difficulty Rating	Moderately Strenuous
Surface	Mostly broken rock and gravel on road
Gradient	Moderately Steep to Steep
Average Time	3 hours
Elevations	TH: 10,328; Highest: 11,731; Gain: +1,795
Map	Latitude 40: Telluride, Silverton, Ouray

Directions to TH	From SVC, drive NE through town 0.8 miles to the junction CR2 and CR110. Go straight on CR 110 following signs to Silverton Ski Area. At mile 5.8, look for CR 62 going up to the left. This is the trail. Park on the main road.
Time & Distance to TH	15 minutes; 5.8 miles
Recommended Vehicle	Car. Access is by a well maintained gravel road

Summary

Approaching the end of trail

This is a jeep track that is still driven, but you will probably not meet any vehicles on it. It goes up Georgia Gulch to an old mine in a pretty basin. Views across Cement Creek to Storm Ridge are consistent right from the start. Aspen and spruce clumps are intermittent. As you ascend, see the Red Mountains to the north. The gradient is moderately steep, but the easy walking conditions make it less difficult. It is a good early season conditioning hike as the starting elevation is low for Silverton trails. Easy driving access is another plus.

Trail Description

Walk up through open aspen and spruce with views across the valley a constant companion. The road is in good condition and makes for pleasant walking. After the 4th switchback, the gradient steepens considerably. By mile 1.05 ❷, you can see the entire basin and the road cutting up to the mine. At the first creek crossing ❸, there are wonderful views back down valley. Look up and see McMillan Peak with the large repeater station on top. It is possible to climb to the peak, or to the higher ridge line by following the drainages above the road's end ❹.

GPS	Mile	Latitude	Longitude	Elevation	Comment
1	0.00	37,52.667N	107,40.238W	10,328'	Start Kansas City Mine Hike.
2	1.05	37,52.695N	107,40.694W	10,894'	View of Basin
3	1.48	37,52.930N	107,41.001W	11,326'	Cross creek Lower level.
4	2.00	37,52.995N	107,41.148W	11,731'	Cross creek upper level. Road ends just ahead.

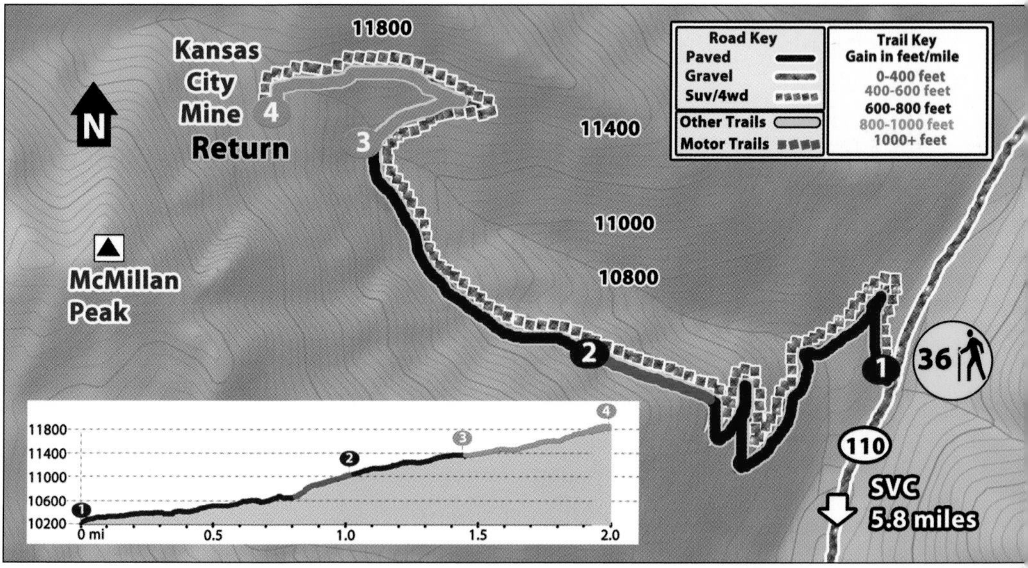

Velocity Basin Options

Star Rating

☆☆☆☆☆

37a: To Saddle

Total Distance	1.94 miles RT
Difficulty Rating	Very Strenuous
Surface	Mostly cross country on bumpy tundra; intermittent trails
Gradient	Very steep
Average Time	2.5 hours
Elevations	TH: 11,327; Highest: 12,563; Gain: +1,330
Map	Latitude 40: Telluride, Silverton, Ouray

37b: To Peak

Total Distance	2.74 miles RT
Difficulty Rating	Very Strenuous
Surface	Mostly cross country on bumpy tundra; intermittent trails
Gradient	Very steep
Average Time	3.5 hours
Elevations	TH: 11,327; Highest: 13,060; Gain: +1,910

Summary

Velocity Basin is an exceptionally dramatic cirque basin with a small turquoise lake at its base. An easy road gets you right to the lake. The hike is climbing a steep grassy route to a ridgeline and peaks that surround the lake. The views of the cirque and the very colorful 3 Red Mountains and deep gorges across the valley are superb. Hike at least to the second bench where an easier route from there on an old, intermittent pack trail is said to exist. We did not research it, but marked it on our map.

Trail Description

The noticeable but unmarked trail takes off due east from the parking area. In just a few feet, you can see the beautiful turquoise lake. Hike to almost the end of the clump of spruce trees. Keep your eyes open for a very faint, unmarked trail that goes left (N) through the grass towards another clump of spruce. An "artsy" snag marks the spot ❷. (See photo). If you find this, by the time you reach the spruce trees to the north, you will be on a very good trail that takes you all the way to the

General route from basin 1 to ridge

Directions to TH	From SVC, drive through town 0.8 miles and take the left fork CR 110 past the city park. At mile 7.2, take the right fork at a signed junction. (Left goes to Hurricane Pass). Drive into the old mining complex and look for a prominent CR 53 sign after a switch back to the left. The road opposite is CR 52 (the sign is further up the road). Follow CR 52 to the end and park at the obvious turnaround.
Time & Distance to TH	30 minutes; 9.1 miles
Recommended Vehicle	Car. This is a good gravel road all the way to the remains of the Gladstone Mine at mile 7.2. From there, it is a little rockier but still a good road for cars.

General route as seen from parking area

first bench ❸. If you miss it, the main trail ends at the little drainage you see ahead. Do not cross the drainage, but climb up the grassy slope towards the obvious bench. You may intersect the good trail at some higher point.

From ❸ there is no trail across the bench. Wildflowers are prolific here! Cross the bench heading for the next level and either of the rock outcroppings. There are numerous intermittent trails to both. The best defined trail goes to the higher rock outcropping. Cross the obvious gully before it gets steep and hike up its left bank to the traverse trail that goes to the higher rock. Once there ❹, the views across the valley and the colorful Red Mountains are excellent.

From this point, hike up the ridgeline, which gets much steeper as you ascend, and traverse towards the saddle ❺. This is very steep and difficult hiking as the tundra is bumpy and finding good flat spots for footing gets harder. An old pack trail heads north from ❹ and goes at a moderate contour all the way around the other side of the mountain, following a stream before climbing steeply to ❻ (See map). We did not research this. Try it if you prefer. It adds 1.66 miles one way and 963 feet gain.

From ❺, you can now see intermittent trails up the ridge to the two peaks ❻ & ❼. Go as far as you wish. It has been a steep climb, but the views are worth the effort.

GPS	Mile	Latitude	Longitude	Elevation	Comment
1	0.00	37,52.155N	107,38.665W	11,327′	Start
2	0.10	37,52.134N	107,38.560W	11,263′	"Artsy" snag. Go left through grass to next group of spruce trees to meet good trail.
3	0.42	37,52.136N	107,38.347W	11,777′	First bench. Wildflowers! No trail. Head for rock outcroppings.
4	0.67	37,52.263N	107,38.189W	12,046′	Top of higher rock outcropping
5	0.97	37,52.386N	107,38.021W	12,563′	Saddle / Return 1
6	1.18	37,52.255N	107,37.874W	12,931′	1st Peak 12,931 feet
7	1.37	37,52.048N	107,37.854W	13,060′	2nd peak 13,060 feet / Return 2

Turn left at "artsy" snag

Route from saddle to peaks

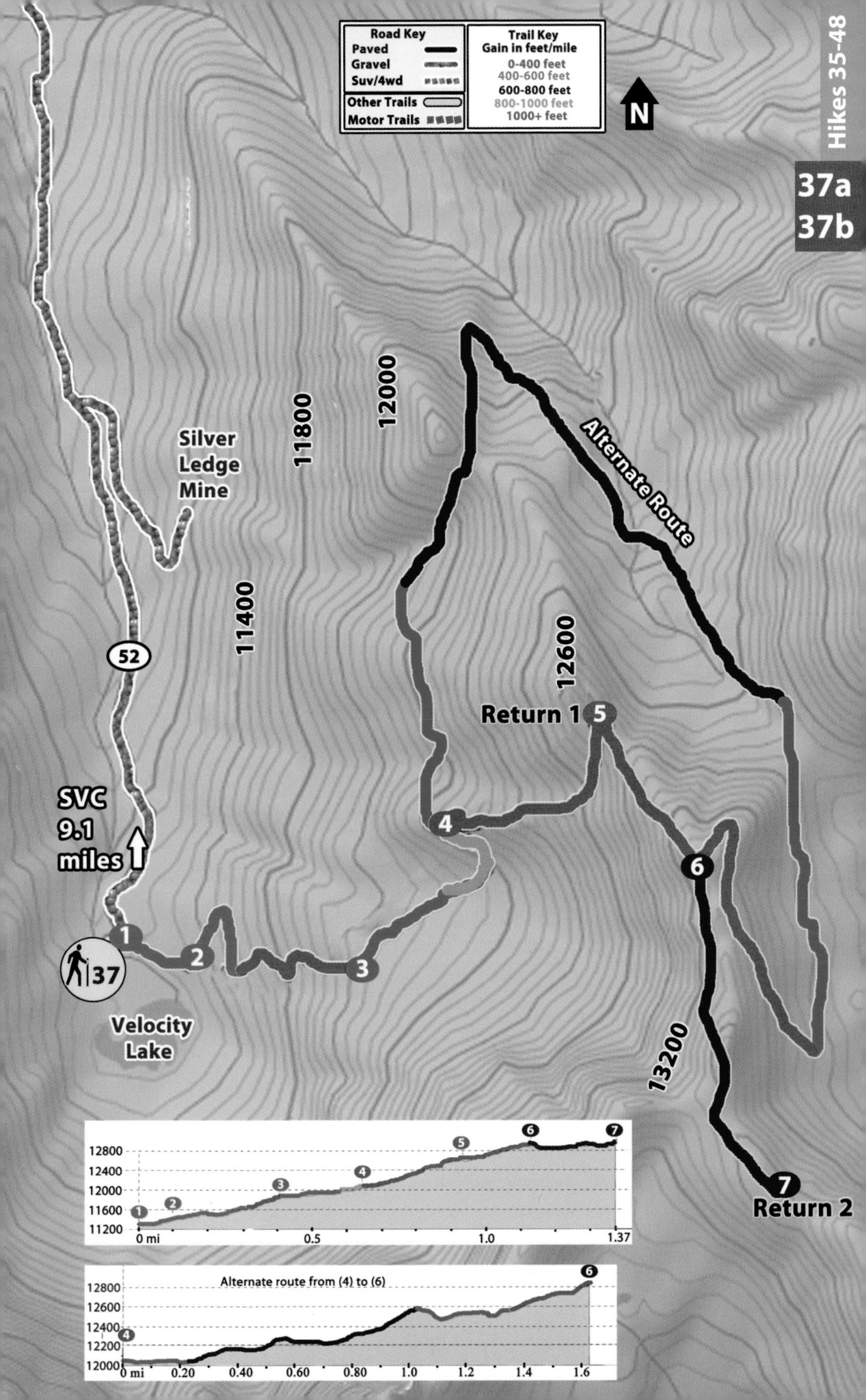
Road Key
Paved
Gravel
Suv/4wd
Other Trails
Motor Trails
Trail Key
Gain in feet/mile
0-400 feet
400-600 feet
600-800 feet
800-1000 feet
1000+ feet
N
Silver Ledge Mine
11800
12000
11400
12600
13200
Alternate Route
52
Return 1
SVC 9.1 miles
1
2
3
4
5
6
7
37
Velocity Lake
Return 2
12800
12400
12000
11600
11200
0 mi
0.5
1.0
1.37
Alternate route from (4) to (6)
12800
12600
12400
12200
12000
0 mi
0.20
0.40
0.60
0.80
1.0
1.2
1.4
1.6

Little Giant Basin Options

38a
38b
38c
38d

Star Rating

☆☆☆☆☆

	38a: Start 38a to Ridge
Total Distance	3.44 miles RT
Difficulty Rating	Strenuous
Surface	Mostly loose rock
Gradient	Very steep
Average Time	3 hours
Elevations	TH: 11,408; Highest:13,000; Gain: +1,740

	38b: Start 38b to Ridge
Total Distance	1.94 miles RT
Difficulty Rating	Strenuous
Average Time	2 hours
Elevations	TH: 12,012; Gain: +1,081

View from peak: Photo by Rozanne Evans

38c: Add To Promontory

Total Distance	Add: 0.36 miles RT
Difficulty Rating	Moderate
Average Time	Add 30 minutes
Elevations	Add +218 gain

38d: Add To Peak

Total Distance	Add 1.0 mile RT
Difficulty Rating	Very Strenuous
Average Time	Add 1.5 hours
Elevations	Add +492 gain
Maps	San Juan Mountain Maps: Silverton, Telluride, Ouray & Silverton, Durango

Directions to TH From SVC, drive 0.80 mile east through town. Turn right (NE) on Hwy 2 and drive to mile 2.8. Zero odometer here. Turn right (S) on CR 21, Arrastra Gulch Road; go down gravel road and cross Animas River bridge; drive to mile 0.9; signed junction says Silver Lake & CR 55. Go left to Silver Lake and drive to mile 1.2. Road forks; take hard left and see small sign for CR 21A. Drive to mile 3.1. This section of road is very narrow, steep and with no passing spots. Arrive in open area of the old Big Giant Mine site. This is Start 38a. It is a very scenic walk up the road from here to Start 38b and not as steep as the actual trail. Or, continue driving to Start 38b. There is one very tight switchback (SWB recommended); it is a narrow road with unguarded cliffs. Park across from the outlet stream for the small lake. Look for a cairn on the north side of the road just below the parking space. No trailhead signs.

Time & Mileage to TH 25 minutes; To Start 38a is 5.9 miles; To Start 38b is 6.65 miles

Recommended Vehicle SUV. Road has narrow sections with exposed cliffs.

Summary

This hike is all above tree line and includes an optional peak ascent to 13,416 feet. The basin is thick with seasonal wildflowers, is enclosed by jagged peaks, and overlooks a lovely lake as you ascend. At the top is a narrow ridgeline that affords amazing views off both sides. This spot is special. Cross the ridge and climb to the peak, or take the route out a promontory and see Highland Mary Lakes in the distance.

Ascending Little Giant Basin

Ascending Little Giant Basin

Trail Description

From Start 38a, hike the steep road (wonderful views) 0.75 miles to the lake outlet and look for a faint trail climbing the left bank; this is Start 38b. Once on the trail ❷, hike through hillsides thick with wildflowers. It climbs steadily all the way to the amazing narrow ridge where vistas off both sides are dramatic ❹. This is a good return point, but there is so much more. Hike across the grassy ridge and up to another level ❺ where the views of Cunningham Creek drainage far below and mountain ranges to the horizon are even more spectacular. This is also where you can decide to go out the wide promontory to the east ❻, or hike west and make a long steady uphill traverse before the final steep ascent to Little Giant Peak ❼. Trails to these destinations are intermittent. Use our photos for guidance.

Cross the grassy ridge to promontory and peak

Promontory

General route to peak

GPS	Mile	Latitude	Longitude	Elevation	Comment
1	0.00	37,48.779N	107,36.338W	11,408′	Start 38a for Little Giant Basin at old mill site. Good views from road. Or continue driving up narrow cliff road to Start 38b.
2	0.75 / 0.00	37,48.451N	107,36.046W	12,012′	Start 38b. Parking spots opposite lake outlet. Small cairn marks a faint trail ascending left bank.
3	1.62 / 0.87	37,48.042N	107,35.653W	13,000′	Top of climb to ridge
4	1.72 / 0.97	37,47.957N	107,35.682W	12,904′	Center of grassy ridge. Return 1
5	1.87 / 1.12	37,47.839N	107,35.666W	12,948′	Unmarked junction: Go left (E) out promontory for views of Highland Mary Lakes; go right (W) to climb Little Giant Peak.
6	2.05 / 1.30	37,47.801N	107,35.519W	12,854′	Promontory: Highland Mary Lakes in distance
7	2.87 / 2.12	37,47.821N	107,35.912W	13,416′	Little Giant Peak

Silver Lake from Peak: Photo by Rozanne Evans

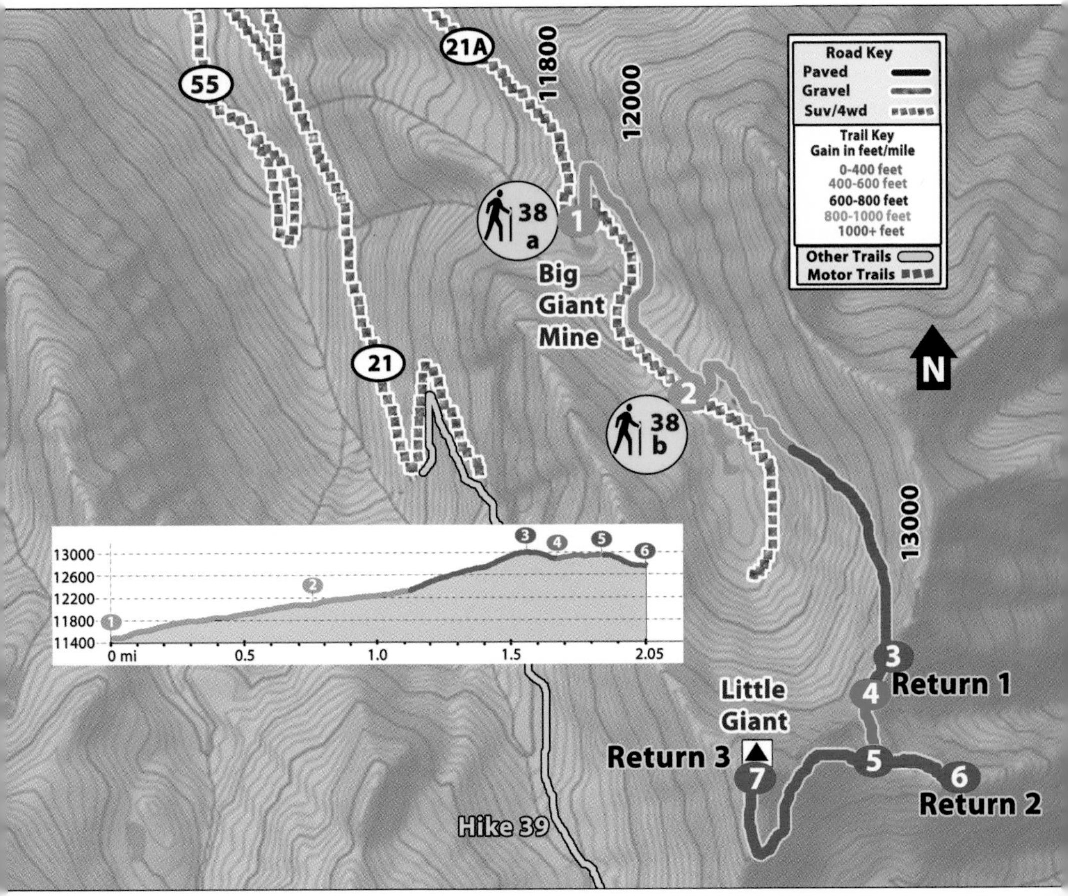

39a
39b

Silver Lake via Arrastra Gulch

Star Rating

☆☆☆☆☆

Arrastra Gulch from the trail

39a: Start 39a to Lake

Total Distance	3.22 miles RT
Difficulty Rating	Strenuous with rock climbing necessary across landslide
Surface	Extreme broken rock that slides underfoot on steep descents
Gradient	Very Steep for first mile
Average Time	2.5 hours
Elevations	TH: 10,574; Highest: 12,192; Gain: +1,708

39b: Start 39b to Lake

Total Distance	2.22 miles RT
Average Time	3.5 hours
Elevations	TH: 11,268; Gain: +1.102
Map	Latitude 40: Telluride, Silverton, Ouray

Directions to TH

From SVC, drive 0.80 mile east through town. Turn right (NE) on Hwy 2 and drive to mile 2.8. Zero odometer here. Turn right (S) on CR 21, Arrastra Gulch Road; go down gravel road and cross Animas River bridge; drive to mile 0.9; signed junction says Silver Lake & CR 55. Go left to Silver Lake and drive to mile 1.2. Road forks again; go straight ahead (hard left goes to hike 38). Road becomes narrow with exposed cliffs. Park at mile 2.1 where the road makes a strong switchback to the left. This is Start 39a. DO NOT CONTINUE DRIVING UNLESS YOU HAVE A JEEP TYPE VEHICLE AND ARE AN EXPERIENCED 4X4 DRIVER.

Time & Mileage to TH

30 minutes; 4.9 miles

Recommended Vehicle

Cars can drive to Start 39a. The road is rocky in parts and there are exposed cliffs with one lane. DO NOT ATTEMPT TO DRIVE TO START 39b unless you are an experienced 4x4 driver and have a SWB vehicle with low gearing and lockable differentials. One very tight switchback on steep loose rock requires back & fill along a steep cliff.

Bouldering through crevice

Top of steep ascent

Remains of mine structures at Silver Lake

Summary

This is an amazing trail heading straight up through a massive headwall that looks impenetrable. If you do not like narrow trails along steep cliffs, this trail is not for you! Parts of the trail have eroded away; there is a section that requires rock climbing with the aid of a cable. Once above the headwall, the trail follows a pretty stream. Summer wildflowers are abundant. The entire Arrastra Valley is full of mining remains. Explore remnants of an entire town around the lake itself. Intermittent trails go completely around the lake to many mine shafts. There are trails to various saddles and peaks. If you get an early start, there are many options to explore.

Use cable for assistance

Trail Description

From Start 39a, walk up the steep, rocky road 0.50 miles to the Old Mayflower Mine site which is Start 39b ❷. All around are mining remains and steep trails to various shafts in the hillsides. The head of the valley is a steep headwall. From the Mayflower Mine, the trail hugs the cliff, climbing very steeply up the very rocky trail. At ❸ is a massive landslide that destroyed the trail. It is necessary to rock climb along a narrow ledge using the aid of a cable. Once above this obstacle, the trail climbs one more switchback to more open meadowlands. It is a moderate ascent from here to the lake. The old mining town at the lake looks as if a tornado destroyed it. There are still intact buildings to explore and a variety of trails leading to old mine sites and the peaks that surround this fascinating site.

GPS	Mile	Latitude	Longitude	Elevation	Comment
1	0.00	37,48.320N	107,36.733W	10,574′	Start 39a. Do not proceed up road with vehicle unless experienced jeep driver.
2	0.50 / 0.00	37,48.346N	107,36.548W	11,268′	Start 39b at Mayflower Mine.
3	0.90 / 0.40	37,48.081N	107,36.515W	11,675′	Landslide: use cable to climb up.
4	1.48 / 0.98	37,47.649N	107,36.355W	12,188′	Silver Lake
5	1.61 / 1.11	37,47.548N	107,36.381W	12,192′	Mine buildings and remains

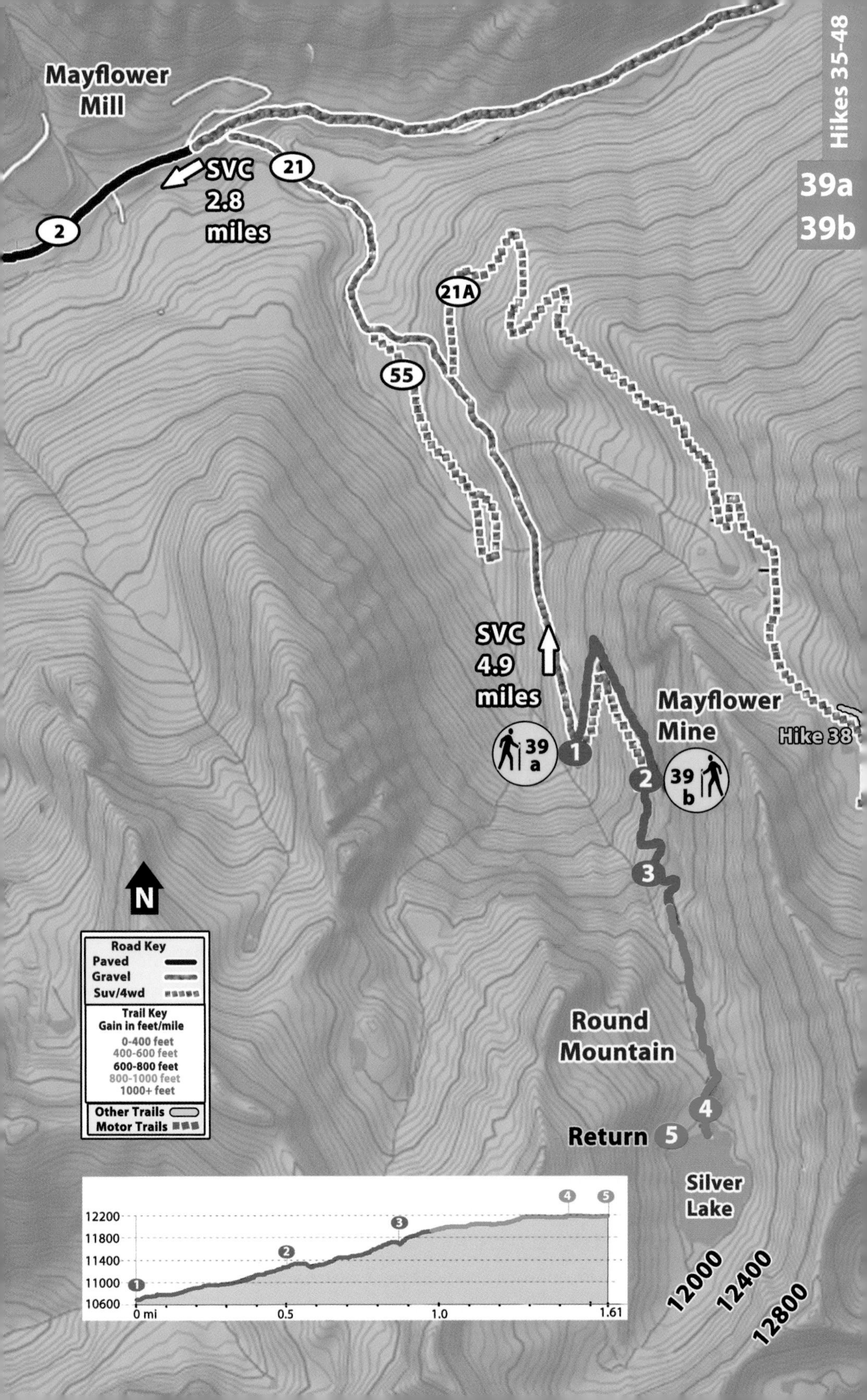
Mayflower Mill
SVC 2.8 miles
21
2
21A
55
SVC 4.9 miles
Mayflower Mine
Hike 38
39 a
39 b
1
2
3
N
Road Key
Paved
Gravel
Suv/4wd
Trail Key
Gain in feet/mile
0-400 feet
400-600 feet
600-800 feet
800-1000 feet
1000+ feet
Other Trails
Motor Trails
Round Mountain
4
Return 5
Silver Lake
12200
11800
11400
11000
10600
0 mi
0.5
1.0
1.61
12000
12400
12800

40

Boarding House Trail

Star Rating ☆☆☆☆☆☆

Total Distance	3.50 miles RT
Difficulty Rating	Moderately Strenuous
Surface	Packed dirt and rocky with sections of loose rock that moves underfoot on steep
Gradient	Easy-moderate sections alternate with steep and very steep
Average Time	3.5 hours
Elevations	TH: 11,773; Highest: 12,628; Gain: +1,824
Map	San Juan Mountain Maps 2010: Telluride, Silverton, Ouray

Directions to TH

From the SVC, drive 0.8 miles NE through town. Take the right fork at the signed Junction CR 2. At mile 2.8, the pavement turns to good gravel road. At mile 4.8, turn right (S) on CR 4, Cunningham Gulch Road. At mile 6.6, turn left up the steep hill at signed junction CR 3, Creed via Stony Pass. At mile 7.86, there is a very sharp switchback

Looking down on the Boarding House

Directions to TH cont.	to the left. This is CR 3B. Turn up CR 3B. This road is rougher and steeper. Take a hard right up the very next switchback. Do not go straight ahead towards the creek. As soon as you come out of the trees, look for a tiny parking spot on the right (mile 8.46) just before crossing the creek at the curve. The road continues up to Buffalo Boy Mine. It is a beautiful valley and worth the drive up to the mine if you have time.
Time & Distance to TH	30 minutes; 8.46 miles
Recommended Vehicle	Jeep. Switchbacks are extremely tight and steep on CR 3B which goes the final 0.15 miles to the parking spot. Low gearing and SWB vehicle highly suggested. Regular SUV can make it up the Stony Pass Road which is also steep and rocky and has narrow sections with steep, exposed drop offs.

Summary

The second half of this trail is thrilling. It follows a very narrow path along steep cliffs and drop offs. If you have fear of heights, this hike may not be for you. Having said that, the trail is spectacular. It hugs sheer cliff faces as it climbs up and down and around various drainages and exposed rock outcrops to arrive high above the old boarding house for miners who worked the Old Hundred Mine. There are a variety of splendid vistas as the trail winds around: See up Cunningham Gulch, Stony Pass and Buffalo Boy Gulch. The Grenadiers stand tall in the distance; see down on Silverton, across to Ice Lake's jagged peaks, and the Red Mountains. The trail is in good condition except for one extremely steep 0.10 mile where you need to sharpen your toenails!

Trail Description

The trail starts at the curve on the right bank of the creek. You can see it for a long way as it contours up the grassy hillside. One photo shows most of the route as seen from the trailhead. It's amazing! There is a short section of overgrown willow crowding the trail before you get to Sterling Gulch. Because the trail winds so deeply into Sterling gulch, there are many varied and beautiful vistas along the way. After the gulch ❷ is where the cliffs begin. Sharp, jagged peaks rise straight above. Look for the trail high above as it cuts around another basin and outcrop. There is a fascinating mine shaft going deep into the hillside. Wow! A herd of goats must have made the trail from ❸ to ❹ as it goes straight up with barely a place for a toehold. That is the most difficult section.

Beginning of cliffs

Beginning of trail is not along cliffs

A good, although exposed trail continues from there to a fabulous viewpoint high above the boarding house ❺. If you continue to the end of the trail ❻ it is possible to scramble down a very steep slope to the buildings. We did not go there but several hikers did. Remember the climb back up!

High traverse

GPS	Mile	Latitude	Longitude	Elevation	Comment
1	0.00	37,48.999N	107,33.743W	11,773′	Start boarding house trail on right bank of creek.
2	0.89	37,49.435N	107,33.974W	12,153′	Narrow trail along steep cliffs
3	1.20	37,49.567N	107,34.196W	12,240′	Start extremely steep and slippery section.
4	1.31	37,49.637N	107,34.259W	12,508′	Dramatic cliffs. End extreme steep.
5	1.67	37,49.690N	107,34.475W	12,556′	View of boarding house below
6	1.75	37,49.787N	107,34.531W	12,628′	Trail ends. Possible to descend to buildings

General route as seen from Trailhead

Trailhead on road to Buffalo Boy Mine

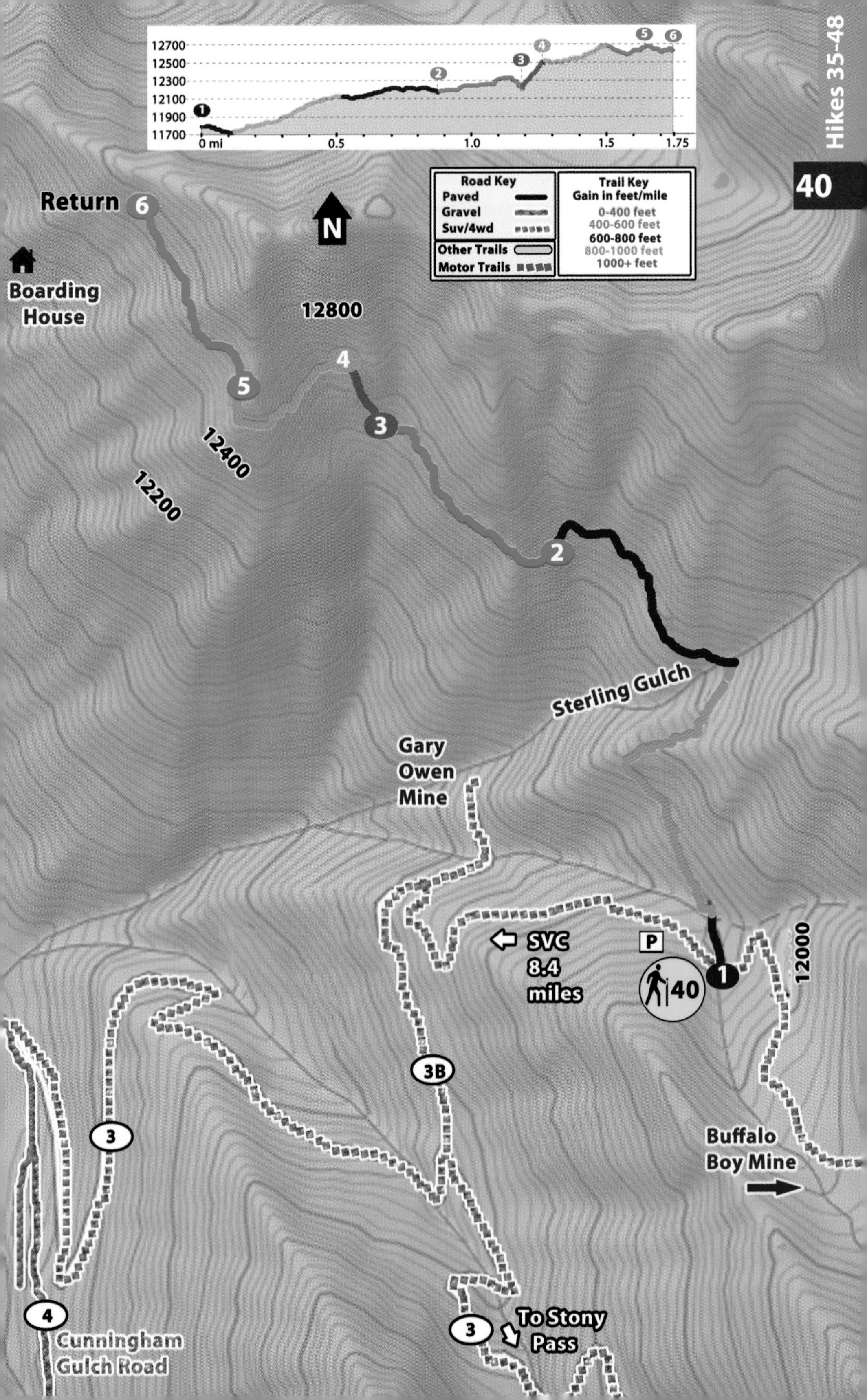
12700
12500
12300
12100
11900
11700
0 mi
0.5
1.0
1.5
1.75
1
2
3
4
5
6
Road Key
Paved
Gravel
Suv/4wd
Other Trails
Motor Trails
Trail Key
Gain in feet/mile
0-400 feet
400-600 feet
600-800 feet
800-1000 feet
1000+ feet
N
Return
Boarding House
12800
12400
12200
Sterling Gulch
Gary Owen Mine
SVC 8.4 miles
P
40
12000
3B
3
4
Buffalo Boy Mine
To Stony Pass
Cunningham Gulch Road

41

Stony Pass: Continental Divide Trail South

Star Rating

☆☆☆☆☆

The Grenadiers from CDT trail

Total Distance	8.20 miles RT. Go any distance
Difficulty Rating	Moderate
Surface	Mostly packed dirt but rocky climbing south side out of drainage
Gradient	Easy-moderate sections alternate with steep and very steep
Average Time	6 hours
Elevations	TH: 12,514; Highest: 12,649; Gain: +2007
Map	Latitude 40: Telluride, Silverton, Ouray

Directions to TH	From the SVC, drive 0.8 miles NE through town. Turn right at the signed Junction CR 2. At mile 2.8, the pavement turns to good gravel road. At mile 4.8, turn right (S) on CR 4, Cunningham Gulch Rd. At mile 6.6, turn left up the steep hill at signed junction CR 3, Creed via Stony Pass. At mile 7.86 continue straight ahead. (Hard left goes to Buffalo Boy Mine.) Stony Pass is mile 10.8. Drive over the pass a few hundred feet to an interpretive sign on the right. Trail begins from there.
Time & Distance to TH	40 minutes; 10.9 miles
Recommended Vehicle	SUV. This is a rocky, steep 4x4 road with one very narrow section along steep, exposed drop offs.

Summary

This is Colorado. All above tree line, the famous trail undulates through flower filled meadows with 180 degree vistas of various mountain ranges, including our favorite, the Grenadiers and two of the three spiked peaks called the Needles. Start early. This trail is exposed to afternoon thunder storms.

Trail Description

The trail starts with an easy descent past the remains of an old cabin and crosses a creek. Seasonal wildflowers are already thick and views are far reaching. From this tiny creek, it is a 432 foot climb to the highest point ❷ on the north side of a large drainage basin which is the start of the Rio Grande River. The gently undulating slopes burst with wildflowers. Now it is just over a mile 557 foot descent to the basin itself ❹. Every step produces a variety of stunning views. Once in the basin, there are two junctions, ❸ & ❹, both of which converge to the east and lead to Cunningham Road. Now the trail climbs 489 feet up a rocky trail. There is a tough, but short, section through some very muddy overgrown brush. Once the steep climb is over ❺ you are beside a small lake. Hike another 200 feet above the Lake and look due east to a rounded peak. You can climb 320 feet straight up to the summit for grand views of Highland Mary Lakes and more. Staying on the trail, soon ❻ you will see the Grenadier Peaks as you peer down a deep gully leading to Verde Lakes. Wow! If you continue out the CDT, the gradient remains easy for another 1.5 miles before descending 368 feet. Go as far as you wish.

Flowers and peaks: Photo by Rozanne Evans

SVC 10.9 miles 3
41
Stony Pass
P
12600
Hike 4
12700
12600
12500
12400
12300
12200
12100
0 mi
0.5
1.0
1.5
2.0
2.5
3.0
3.5
4.10
1
2
3
4
5
6
7
12600
Hike 43
12200
Cunningham Gulch
CT
CD
HM Lakes
12600
12905
N
Hike 44
Verde Lakes
Return
Road Key
Paved
Gravel
Suv/4wd
Trail Key
Gain in feet/mile
0-400 feet
400-600 feet
600-800 feet
800-1000 feet
1000+ feet
Other Trails
Motor Trails

Small lake near high point

Panoramic vistas

GPS	Mile	Latitude	Longitude	Elevation	Comment
1	0.00	37,47.660N	107,32.765W	12,514′	Start CDT Trail south from Stony Pass.
2	1.41	37,46.790N	107,33.323W	12,635′	Highest point north of drainage
3	2.22	37,46.414N	107,33.342W	12,180′	Almost to bottom of descent. Take faint trail to left (S) No sign. Straight ahead goes to Cunningham Gulch Road.
4	2.47	37,46.288N	107,33.499W	12,168′	Junction: CDT sign. Go left (S) and climb up through rocky hillside. Straight ahead goes to Cunningham Gulch also.
5	3.55	37,45.493N	107,33.434W	12,605′	Top of steepest part of climb. Scramble up 12,905' peak to east for views of Highland Mary Lakes.
6	3.90	37,45.195N	107,33.376W	12,609′	Small Cairn: Great view of Gully to Verde Lakes and Grenadier Peaks.
7	4.10	37,45.038N	107,33.297W	12,649′	Approx 4 miles out. Good return point

42

Canby Mountain Loop & Options

Star Rating

☆☆☆☆☆

Total Distance	3.20 mile loop
Difficulty Rating	Moderately-Easy
Surface	Combination of tundra and good trail
Gradient	Easy to Moderate with one short steep section at the start
Average Time	3 hours
Elevations	TH: 12,546; Highest: 13,082; Gain: +1,021
Map	San Juan Mountain Maps 2010: Silverton, Durango

Stony Pass from trail

Directions to TH From the SVC, drive 0.8 miles NE through town. Turn right at the signed Junction CR 2. At mile 2.8, the pavement turns to good gravel road. At mile 4.8, turn right (S) on CR 4, Cunningham Gulch Road. At mile 6.6, turn left up the steep hill at signed junction CR 3, Creed via Stony Pass. At mile 7.86 continue straight ahead. (Hard left goes to Buffalo Boy Mine.) Stony Pass is mile 10.8. Drive over the pass a few hundred feet to an interpretive marker on the right. Park there.

Time & Distance to TH 40 minutes; 10.9 miles

Recommended Vehicle SUV. This is a rocky, steep 4x4 road with one very narrow section along steep, exposed drop offs.

Summary

This is another all above timberline trail with a tremendous variety of vistas that encompass expansive views across four different drainages. Optional walk up opportunity to "bag" Canby Peak (13,478') as well. There is a trail to follow much of the way; including a section of the famous Continental Divide Trail; the route is easy to see for the remaining cross country sections. Another optional ridge walk adds moderate, but spectacular mileage. The wildflowers in Maggie Gulch are rich and fabulous. This is a superb route.

Parking and start of hike

Trail Description

Walk up the road from the parking spot to a wide area on the right where a small drainage ascends straight up the grassy slope. Walk up this drainage. Very

Climb up steep from parking area

Maggie Gulch from Saddle

soon, there is a steep right fork in the drainage. Climb it and meet a very good trail that goes to 2 and 3. This is splendid scenery right away. At 3 overlook beautiful Maggie Gulch. A trail goes left & right offering three options: hike left out a long up and down ridgeline to 3a & 3b. The views off both sides of the ridge are panoramic.. Walk right up the grassy ridgeline to Canby Peak 3c. There is a steep but easy, safe route all the way out the sharp appearing rocks. You can see forever. To continue the loop, look out over Maggie Gulch from the saddle 3 and spot the conspicuous saddle to the southeast 4 (See photos). That is your goal. Contour across the expansive meadows, finding various animal trails and always staying above the level of the saddle. It's a beautiful and basically easy route to follow. At

Route up peak is easy to see from saddle

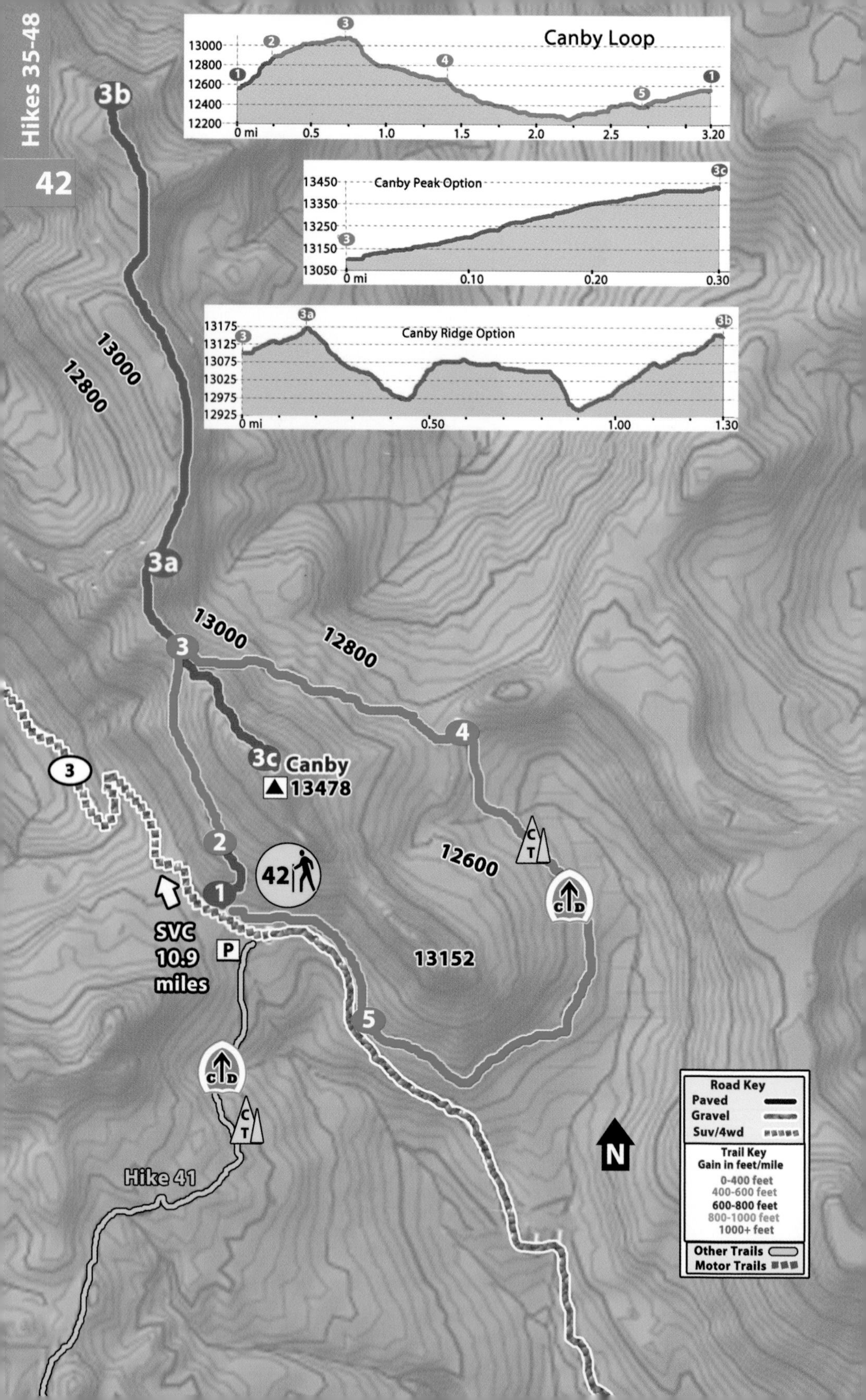
Canby Loop
13000
12800
12600
12400
12200
0 mi
0.5
1.0
1.5
2.0
2.5
3.20
Canby Peak Option
13450
13350
13250
13150
13050
0 mi
0.10
0.20
0.30
Canby Ridge Option
13175
13125
13075
13025
12975
12925
0 mi
0.50
1.00
1.30
3b
3a
3
3c
1
2
4
5
13000
12800
12600
Canby
13478
13152
42
SVC
10.9
miles
P
C T
C D
Hike 41
N
Road Key
Paved
Gravel
Suv/4wd
Trail Key
Gain in feet/mile
0-400 feet
400-600 feet
600-800 feet
800-1000 feet
1000+ feet
Other Trails
Motor Trails

View from Canby Peak

❹ is a CDT sign. Continue south on a good trail down a splendid valley. Note the flat ridgeline above to your left. That is Sheep Ridge leading to Sheep Mountain which is another marvelous ridge walk. It's a moderate and wonderful hike from here back to your car.

GPS	Mile	Latitude	Longitude	Elevation	Comment
1	0.00	37,47.685N	107,32.857W	12,546′	Start just south of Stony Pass Walk up drainage. Find trail off to right.
2	0.26	37,47.839N	107,32.891W	12,847′	1st bench. Good trail continues north.
3	0.71	37,48.211N	107,32.990W	13,082′	Saddle. Go right for loop & peak. Go left for ridge walking.
3a	Add 0.40	37,48.348N	107,33.107W	13,214′	First high point on ridge walk; add 83 feet gain
3b	Add 2.60	37,49.239N	107,33.165W	13,174′	Second high point on ridge walk; add 703 feet gain
3c	Add 0.60	37,47.988N	107,32.765W	13,444′	Canby Peak. Add 328 feet gain
4	1.42	37,48.067N	107,32.297W	12,619′	Meet CDT trail at saddle. Go south.
5	2.78	37,47.499N	107,32.555W	12,347′	Trail meets Stony Pass road south of pass. Walk back to start.
1	3.20	37,47.685N	107,32.857W	12,546′	Finish loop.

43

Cunningham Gulch to Continental Divide Trail

Star Rating

☆☆☆☆☆

View from top of steep climb

Total Distance	3.7 miles RT
Difficulty Rating	Strenuous
Surface	Loose gravel and rocks that slide underfoot on the steep descents
Gradient	Steep to Moderately Steep
Average Time	3 hours
Elevations	TH: 10,818; Highest: 12,146; Gain: + 1,490
Map	Latitude 40: Telluride, Silverton, Ouray

Directions to TH From SVC, drive NE through town 0.8 miles. Turn right on CR 2. At mile 4.8, turn right on CR4 which is Cunningham Gulch Road. At mile 6.5, stay right. Stony Pass is signed to the left. At mile 8.4, go right downhill and cross over the creek. This is where the road narrows and becomes rocky. At mile 9.2, park on the hilltop, or go left downhill and drive through the steep creek. The trailhead sign is immediately after crossing the creek. There is no parking there. You must continue 200 yards to the Highland Mary parking lot and walk back.
Time & Mileage to TH 35 minutes; 9.2 miles
Recommended Vehicle SUV; The first 8 miles are suitable for car but the last section is rough, steep and rocky. Possible stream crossing.

Summary

Here is an opportunity to hike to the Continental Divide Trail in a very short distance from an easy access road. This hike has views across the valley into Spencer Basin right from the start all the way to the return point. Dramatic views expand up Highland Mary drainage and down Cunningham Gulch as you ascend. The open forest turns to grassy tundra. While Highland Mary Trail will have many hikers, you will see very few on this scenic route. The trail is steep and elevation is gained quickly.

Trail Description

From the TH sign, which is very small and easy to miss, go north through the willows along the right bank of the creek. In a hundred yards you will come to the sign in box.

Lower portions of trail is through open forest

Once on top, wildflowers flourish

Instantly, the gradient becomes steep with some short, flatter sections for respite for about a mile before breaking completely above tree line ❸. Remember to look behind you through this section as the views across the valley into Spencer Basin are wonderful. Then the gradient eases from very steep to moderately steep as you hike between two grassy knobs. Wildflowers are not thick, but are very pretty. See up the Highland Mary drainage and down Cunningham Gulch. Cross a tiny creek ❹ and make the final ascent to the CDT trail sign. This is the return point for this hike. For more information on this part of the CDT trail, read hikes 41 and 44.

Spencer Basin

GPS	Mile	Latitude	Longitude	Elevation	Comment
1	0.00	37,46.938N	107,34.754W	10,818′	Start Cunningham Gulch to Continental Divide Trail.
2	0.64	37,46.802N	107,34.441W	11,339′	Signed junction: Go straight to CDT. Right to Highland Mary Lakes
3	0.92	37,46.711N	107,34.228W	11,666′	View of grassy knobs; trail goes between them.
4	1.55	37,46.516N	107,33.655W	12,008′	Cross tiny creek and make final climb to CDT.
5	1.85	37,46.289N	107,33.501W	12,146′	CDT signed junction. Return point for this hike

Cunningham Gulch from trail

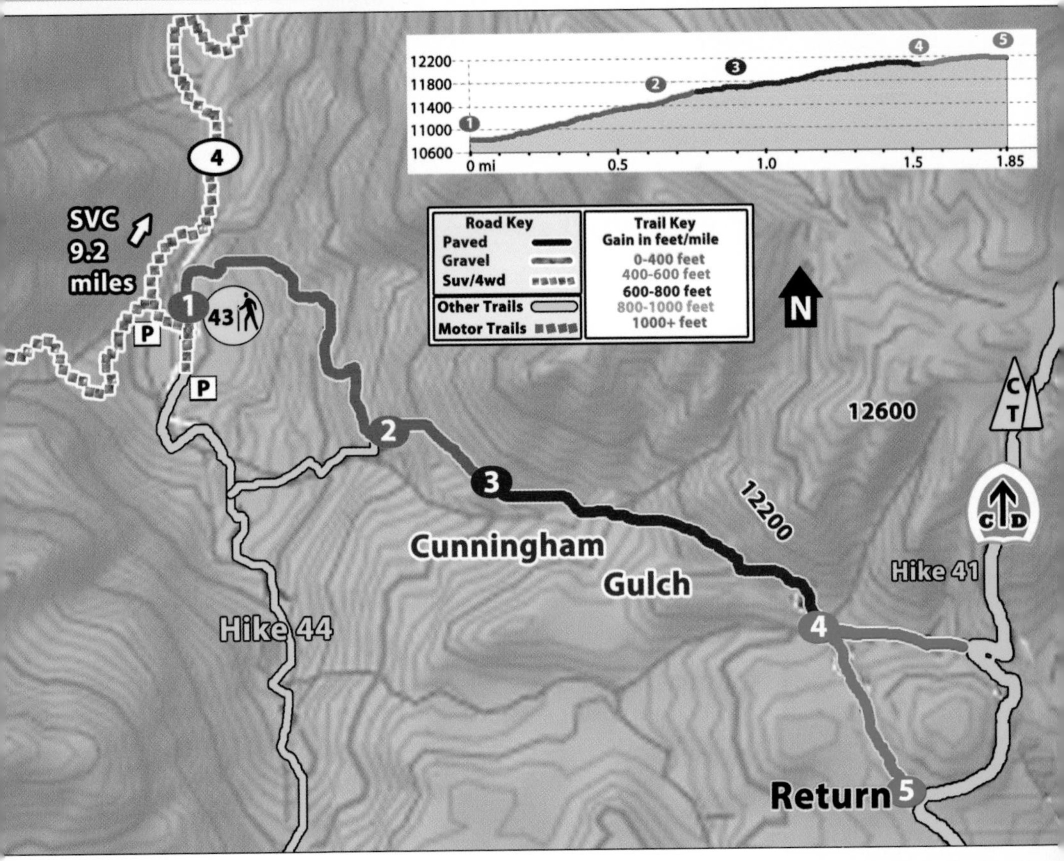

Highland Mary Lake Options

44a
44b
44c

Star Rating

☆☆☆☆☆

Highland Mary Lakes: Photo by Sigrid Werbitsch

44a: To Highland Mary Lakes/ Return 1

Total Distance	3.50 miles RT
Difficulty Rating	Moderately Strenuous
Surface	Rocky high steps and loose rock trail
Gradient	Moderately Steep
Average Time	2.5 hours
Elevations	TH: 10.790; Highest: 12,126′; Gain: +1,393
Map	Latitude 40: Telluride, Silverton, Ouray

44b: To Verde Lakes/ Return 2

Total Distance	6.0 miles RT
Average Time	4 hours
Elevations	TH: 10,790; Highest: 12,309′; Gain: +1,806

	44c: Continental Divide Loop
Total Distance	7.36 mile loop
Difficulty Rating	Moderately Strenuous
Surface	There is quite a mixture from big rocky, high step ups to Highland Mary Lakes, to packed dirt on the CDT, to loose, slippery gravel on the steep descent in Cunningham Gulch
Gradient	Sections vary from Easy to Steep
Average Time	6 to 7 hours
Elevations	TH: 10,790; Highest: 12,606; Gain: + 2,341

Directions to TH	From SVC, drive NE through town 0.8 miles. Turn right on CR 2. At mile 4.8, turn right on CR4 which is Cunningham Gulch Road. At mile 6.5, stay right. Stony Pass is signed to the left. At mile 8.4, go right downhill and cross the creek. This is where the road narrows and becomes rocky. At mile 9.2, go left downhill and cross the steep creek. Continue 200 yards to the Highland Mary parking lot.
Time & Distance to TH	35 minutes; 9.2 miles
Recommended Vehicle	SUV: The first 8 miles are suitable for car but the last section is rough, steep and rocky.

Lower trail is through forest and meadow

First Highland Mary Lake

Summary

This hike has all the ingredients of a scenic Colorado Classic: Forest trail along a rushing creek, waterfalls, wildflowers, meadows, lakes, rugged rocky peaks, soft rounded tundra knobs, and expansive views of whole mountain ranges from the famous CDT Trail. The entire loop follows a variety of trails. Weekends are very crowded to Highland Mary Lakes.

Trail Description

We prefer to hike up the less steep gradient and hike down the more difficult. That's why we hike this loop counterclockwise, starting up the Highland Mary Lake drainage and coming down Cunningham Gulch. Just reverse our notes if you prefer otherwise. The trail begins in dense spruce forest up a steep, very rocky route. A tumbling creek keeps you company most of the way to Highland Mary Lakes. There are many wonderful waterfalls. As the forest opens up ❸ you can see up valley to the dramatic, rocky walls that enclose the drainage. The trail turns constantly, providing new and interesting views. At ❺, the valley narrows and the trail comes close to the creek. Pay attention here as the original route leaves the creek and turns right uphill into a very rocky area that soon crosses very difficult talus. It is better to follow up along the creek on a lesser trail. There is a small cairn marking the unsigned junction. Rejoin the original trail as it goes left up through a notch for the final ascent to the lakes. Reach the first lake which is very small and has an island in it. Go around it to the right. The second lake is only a few hundred feet further ❻. Most of the hard climbing is now accomplished. Enjoy the ease and openness of hiking around the lake on the left side, past the third lake to the posts on the horizon due south. The second post ⑨ is the junction with the CDT Trail and Verde Lakes. Go left on the CDT Trail (or right to Verde Lakes for a RT option). The trail cuts through an amazing gorge to ⑩ where another unmarked junction connects with the portion of trail from Stony Pass. Go left and hike a little more than a mile along this spectacular trail with expansive vistas of entire mountain ranges. Seasonal wildflowers are thick and colorful. Pass a small lake and start descending down a rocky bluff to a grassy meadow and a junction marked with a post ⑫. Go NW to continue loop. Right goes to Stony Pass. Now the trail begins the long descent down Cunningham Gulch trail to your starting point.

Verde Lake: Photo by Sigrid Werbitsch

Along the CDT: Photo by Sigrid Werbitsch

Start descent into Cunningham Gulch

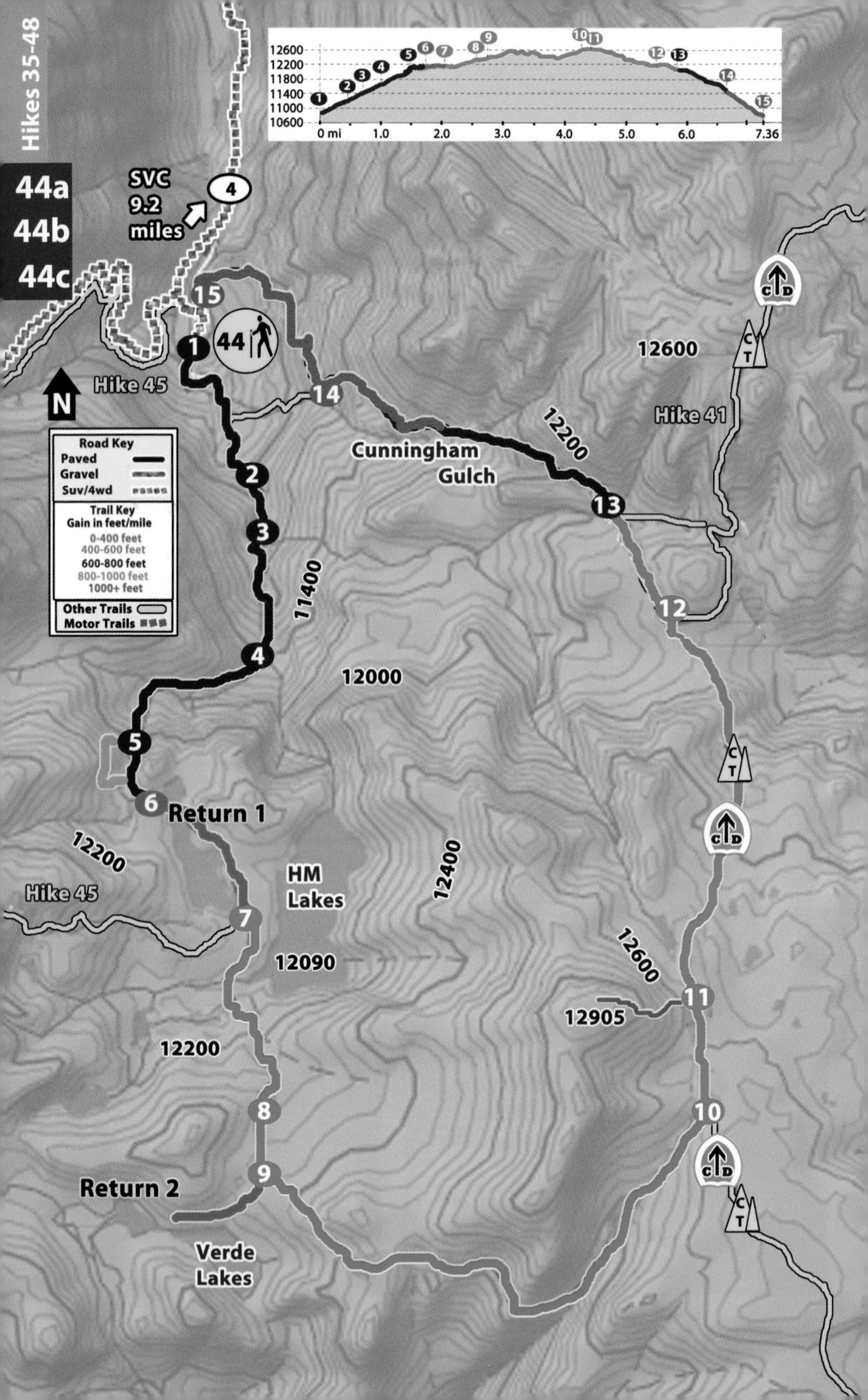

Hikes 35-48
44a
44b
44c
12600
12200
11800
11400
11000
10600
0 mi
1.0
2.0
3.0
4.0
5.0
6.0
7.36
SVC
9.2
miles
4
15
44
1
Hike 45
14
N
Road Key
Paved
Gravel
Suv/4wd
Trail Key
Gain in feet/mile
0-400 feet
400-600 feet
600-800 feet
800-1000 feet
1000+ feet
Other Trails
Motor Trails
2
3
4
5
6
Return 1
Cunningham
Gulch
12600
12200
Hike 41
13
12
11400
12000
12400
12200
Hike 45
HM
Lakes
7
12090
12600
11
12905
12200
8
10
9
Return 2
Verde
Lakes
CT
CD

Follow the creek above 5

GPS	Mile	Latitude	Longitude	Elevation	Comment
1	0.00	37,46.853N	107,34.784W	10,790′	Start Highland Mary Lakes, CDT Loop.
2	0.46	37,46.615N	107,34.630W	11,045′	Small waterfall. Bigger falls 100 yards upstream
3	0.71	37,46.445N	107,34.596W	11,378′	Cross creek. Wet shoes in July. Views up valley and another big waterfall
4	1.04	37,46.213N	107,34.571W	11,639′	Cross creek over logs. Immediately go right and cross creek again. Wet shoes in July. Now climb steep up.
5	1.47	37,46.042N	107,34.930W	11,963′	Trail goes right up steep hill through broken rock. Follow stream instead. Easier route
6	1.75	37,45.888N	107,34.814W	12,101′	Return 1: Second Highland Mary Lake
7	2.16	37,45.681N	107,34.616W	12,126′	End second Highland Mary Lake. Continue on trail and climb to markers on the horizon.
8	2.60	37,45.298N	107,34.596W	12,303′	Right hand post on the horizon
9	2.78	37,45.137N	107,34.601W	12,309′	Junction: Post, no sign; Go right to Verde Lakes and Return 2 or go left on CDT Trail.
10	4.37	37,45.359N	107,33.404W	12,606′	Unsigned junction: CDT trail. Go left for loop.
11	4.52	37,45.493N	107,33.434W	12,605′	Scramble up 12,905' peak to east for views of Highland Mary Lakes.
12	5.55	37,46.288N	107,33.499W	12,168′	CDT sign. Go straight ahead (NW) for loop.
13	5.85	37,46.516N	107,33.655W	12,008′	Cross tiny creek.
14	6.74	37,46.802N	107,34.441W	11,339′	Signed junction: Go straight. Left to Highland Mary Lakes TH through forest
15	7.36	37,46.938N	107,34.754W	10,818′	Finish loop.

Spencer Basin Options

Star Rating

☆☆☆☆☆

Spencer Basin: Photo by Sigrid Werbitsch

45a: To Spencer Basin/ Return 1

Total Distance	3.52 miles RT
Difficulty Rating	Strenuous
Surface	Mostly old road bed
Gradient	Steep
Average Time	2.5 hours
Elevations	TH:10,799'; Highest: 12,218'; Gain: +1,526
Map	Latitude 40: Telluride, Silverton, Ouray

Directions to TH From SVC, drive NE through town 0.8 miles. Turn right on CR 2. At mile 4.8, turn right on CR4 which is Cunningham Gulch Road. At mile 6.5, stay right. Stony Pass is signed to the left. At mile 8.4, go right downhill and cross the creek. This is where the road narrows and becomes rocky. At mile 9.2, there is a wide spot in the road for parking. There is no trailhead sign. The trail is the road due west of the parking spot. The small road that goes east and crosses the creek goes to Highland Mary Lakes Trailhead which is where you would come out if you hiked the loop option.

Time & Mileage to TH
35 minutes; 9.2 miles

Recommended Vehicle SUV: The first 8 miles are suitable for car but the last section is rough, steep and rocky

45b: To Sugarloaf Peak/ Return 2

Total Distance	5.8 miles RT
Surface	Cross country and intermittent trails
Gradient	Steep
Average Time	4 hours
Elevations	TH:10,799'; Highest:12,754'; Gain: +2,316

45c: Highland Mary Lakes Loop

Total Distance	6.56 mile loop
Surface	Old road, cross country, rock steps
Gradient	Sections vary from Easy to Steep
Average Time	6 hours
Elevations	TH:10,799; Highest: 12,658'; Gain: + 2,388

From basin to peak: Photo by Sigrid Werbitsch

Summary

Hike up an old road to a flower filled basin with spectacular views across the valley. Sugarloaf Peak is a fabulous addition to the hike with views of the Grenadiers, Highland Mary Lakes and so much more. Return from there or continue on cross country and make a loop into Highland Mary Lakes. Pick your route. It is all visible from Sugarloaf saddle.

Trail Description

Although steep, the road is wide and leads to the mine (2a). From the junction to the mine (2), look for a post on the horizon to guide you to Sugarloaf saddle. Our photos will also help. Trails are intermittent to the saddle. Once there, the ridgeline leads right to the peak, which is an additional 0.60 miles RT and 242 feet gain (4a). Return from here or go back down to the saddle and pick your route to the south end of Highland Mary's second lake (5) where you meet the HM trail. It is possible, but very steep to hike to the north end of the lake. Read the description for hike 44 for this trail. It returns you to your parking spot.

Peak to HM Lake: Photo by Sigrid Werbitsch

General route

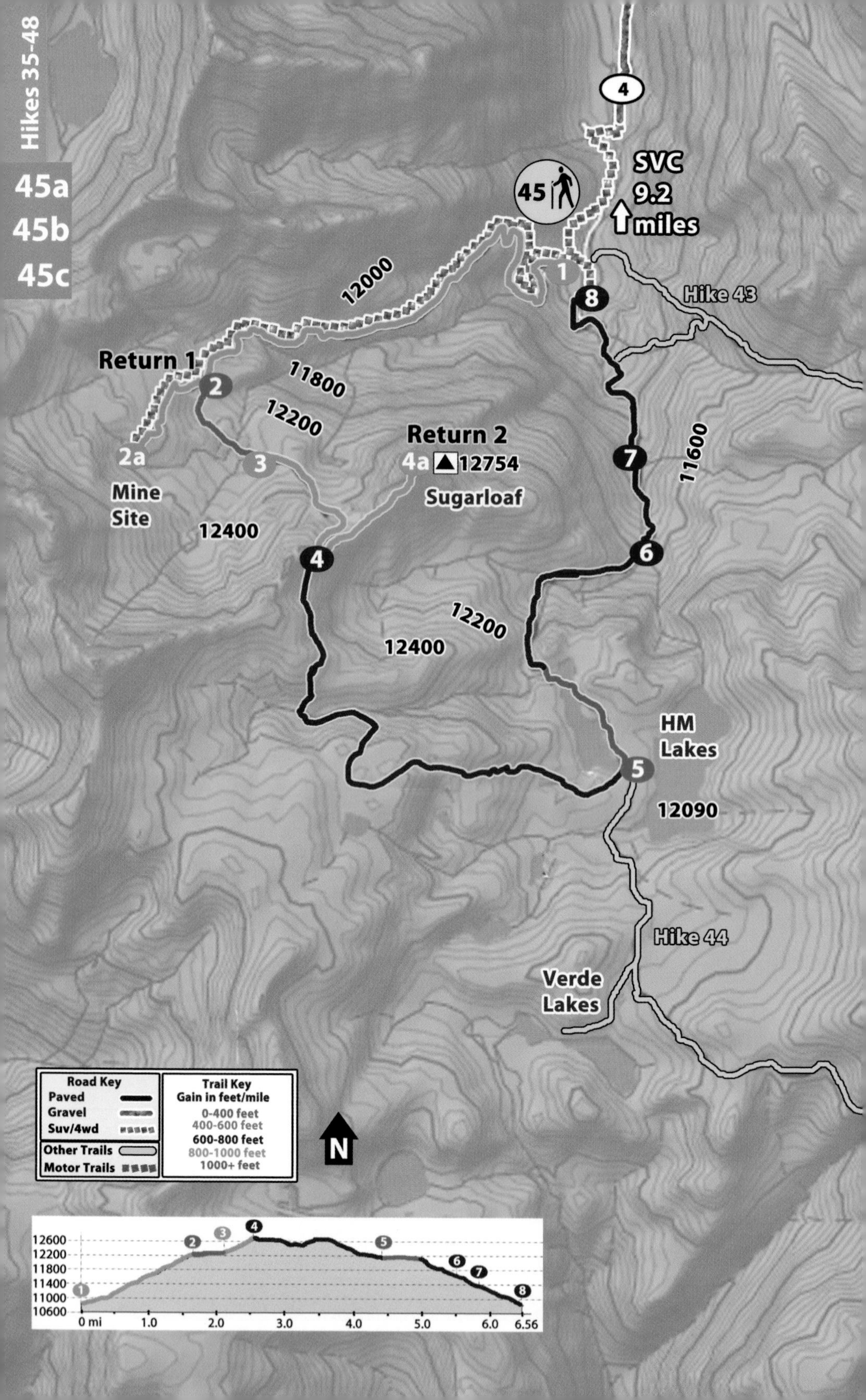
4
45
SVC
9.2
miles
1
8
Hike 43
12000
Return 1
2
11800
12200
2a
Mine
Site
3
Return 2
4a
12754
Sugarloaf
12400
7
11600
6
4
12200
12400
HM
Lakes
5
12090
Hike 44
Verde
Lakes
Road Key
Paved
Gravel
Suv/4wd
Other Trails
Motor Trails
Trail Key
Gain in feet/mile
0-400 feet
400-600 feet
600-800 feet
800-1000 feet
1000+ feet
N
12600
12200
11800
11400
11000
10600
0 mi
1.0
2.0
3.0
4.0
5.0
6.0
6.56

GPS	Mile	Latitude	Longitude	Elevation	Comment
1	0.00	37,46.971N	107,34.844W	10,799′	Start Spencer Basin Trail on old road.
2	1.76	37,46.654N	107,35.981W	12,218′	Unsigned Junction: Cairn straight ahead to mine, Smaller trail to left thru willows goes to Sugarloaf / Return 1.
2a	+.60	37,46.479N	107,36.195W	12,365′	Mine; add 246 feet gain
3	2.11	37,46.459N	107,35.809W	12,226′	Marker post is 100 yards to the left of trail.
4	2.60	37,46.213N	107,35.634W	12,658′	Saddle: go left to Sugarloaf Summit along ridge; go right to HM Lakes / Return 2.
4a	+.60	37,46.433N	107,35.301W	12,754′	Sugarloaf summit; add 242 feet gain
5	4.50	37,45.681N	107,34.616W	12,126'	South end of second HM lake. Meet trail.
6	5.58	37,46.213N	107,34.571W	11,639'	Cross creek twice. Wet shoes in July
7	5.90	37,46.445N	107,34.596W	11,378′	Cross creek. Wet shoes in July
8	6.56	37,46.853N	107,34.784W	10,790'	Highland Mary Lakes TH

Sugarloaf Peak: Photo by Sigrid Werbitsch

46 Maggie Gulch to CDT Loop

Star Rating ☆☆☆☆☆

Maggie Gulch

Total Distance	3.32 miles
Difficulty Rating	Moderately Strenuous
Surface	Combination of dirt packed trail and cross country tundra
Gradient	Ranges from Easy to Steep
Average Time	3.5 hours
Elevations	TH: 11,850; Highest: 12,822; Gain: +1,145
Map	40: Telluride, Silverton, Ouray. Not shown completely or correctly on any map

Directions to TH	From SVC, drive NE through town 0.8 miles and turn right on CR 2. At mile 6.6, turn right (SE) on signed Maggie Gulch Rd. Immediately go left past outhouse and CR 23 sign. At mile 7.8, stay left uphill. (Right goes to Ruby Mine). At mile 9.5 go straight ahead. At mile 10.3, continue straight ahead. (The unsigned road to the right goes to Empire Mine and Crystal Lake hike.) The road ends at mile 10.8. Park in the turnaround. The trailhead is unmarked. It is a small dirt trail taking off from the eastern side of the turnaround area.
Time & Mileage to TH	40 minutes; 10.8 miles
Recommended Vehicle	SUV. This is an easy 4x4 road with mostly good surface. However, there are very narrow sections with steep, exposed cliffs.

Summary

This loop incorporates another incredibly scenic stretch of the famous Continental Divide Trail. It is all above tree line in a beautiful basin surrounded by grassy slopes and dramatic peaks. The route follows intermittent trails through thick wildflower tundra that remain vibrant into late August. After connecting with the well marked CDT route, follow ridge lines and basins from near Canby Mountain to West Pole Creek with expansive views all around.

CDT Trail

Trail Description

The trail is not well marked, nor consistent. Use our photos to help you find our route to the CDT trail. Your goal is to hike to saddle ⑥ in the photos where you will meet the CDT. From there the trail is easy to follow all the way to ❽ along the spectacular Continental Divide Trail. You will see it is also possible to hike directly to saddle ❼, but we prefer the slightly longer route so we can spend more time on the Divide.

View from saddle

GPS	Mile	Latitude	Longitude	Elevation	Comment
1	0.00	37,48.796N	107,32.171W	11,850′	Start Maggie Gulch loop hike.
2	0.05	37,48.785N	107,32.122W	11,880′	Small cairn marks junction: go left and follow lesser trail to next uphill cairn with stick.
3	0.18	37,48.785N	107,31.978W	12,094′	Meet good trail and turn right (S) at base of cliff.
4	0.61	37,48.461N	107,32.173W	12,232′	Flat area above cliff. Trail fades completely. Make your own switchbacks toward ❺.
5	0.75	37,48.343N	107,32.116W	12,460′	Go towards saddle ❻ to right of big dark cliffs. Intermittent trail to follow
6	1.22	37,48.077N	107,32.303W	12,652′	First Saddle. Meet CDT trail and turn left (E) for loop.
7	1.52	37,48.147N	107,32.034W	12,706′	Second Saddle. Continue on CDT trail.
8	2.55	37,48.840N	107,31.471W	12,530′	Cairn & sign. Go left on lesser trail for this loop hike. Right follows West Fork Pole Creek. Straight ahead follows CDT to Minnie Gulch.
9	2.73	37,48.942N	107,31.626W	12,359′	Unmarked junction: Do not cross gully. Stay on lesser trail that goes straight ahead and hike on left bank of gully.
3	3.14	37,48.785N	107,31.978W	12,094′	Small cairn; Leave good trail; turn right downhill on lesser trail to vehicle.
1	3.32	37,48.796N	107,32.171W	11,850′	Finish loop hike.

This is a wild flower basin

General route to saddle

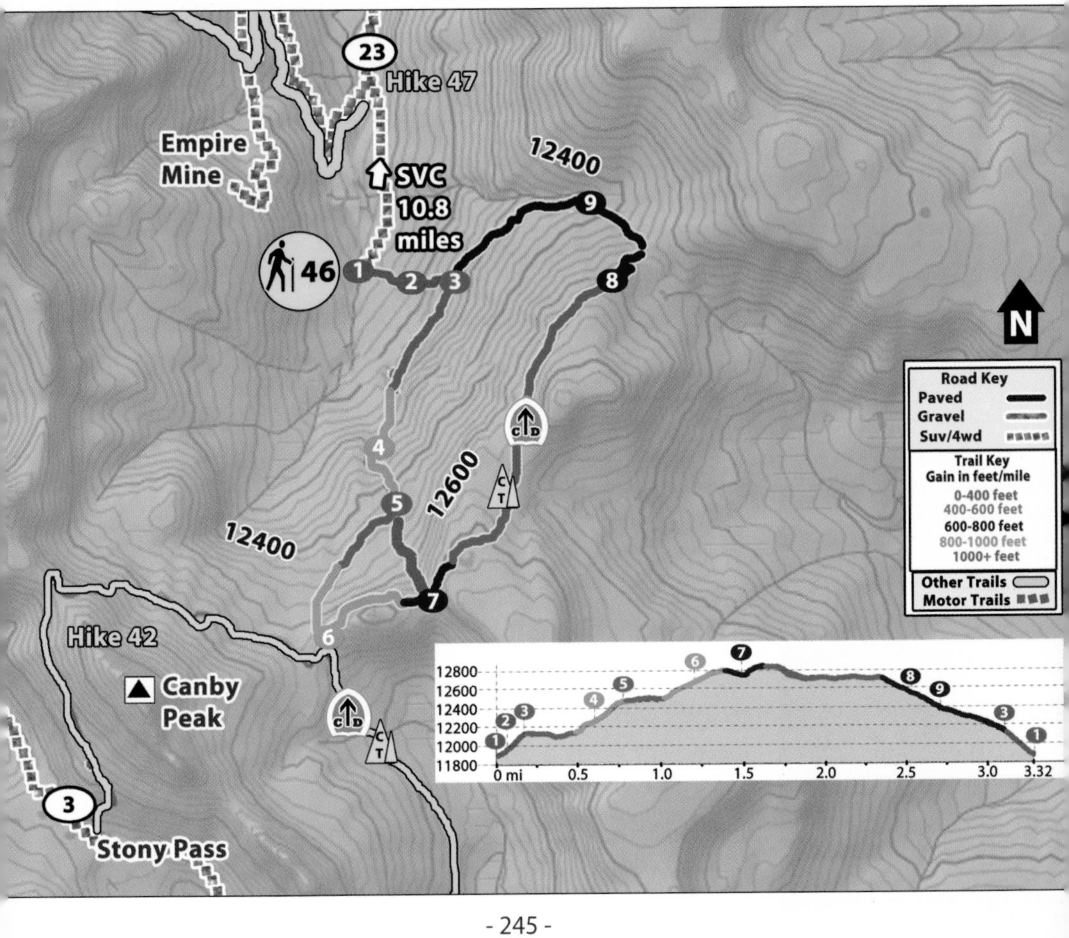

47a
47b

Maggie Gulch to Crystal Lake

Star Rating

☆☆☆☆

47a: Start 47a

Total Distance	3.2 miles RT
Difficulty Rating	Moderately Strenuous
Surface	Half on old mining road; half on intermittent trail on tundra
Gradient	Easy up road; Steep on tundra
Average Time	2.5 hours
Elevations	TH: 11,708; Highest: 12,389; Gain: +1,407

47b: Start 47b

Total Distance	1.64 miles RT
Average Time	1.5 hours
Elevations	TH: 11,955; Gain: +736
Map	Latitude 40: Telluride, Silverton, Ouray. No map shows trail accurately

Crystal Lake

Directions to TH From SVC, drive NE through town 0.8 miles and turn right on CR 2. At mile 6.6, turn right (SE) on signed Maggie Gulch Rd. Immediately go left past outhouse and CR 23 sign. At mile 7.8, stay left uphill. (Right goes to Ruby Mine). At mile 9.5 go straight ahead. At mile 10.3, the unsigned road to the right to Empire Mine is the start of this hike. Park at the junction for Start 47a. It is possible to drive up the mining road all the way to the mine building but, for this hike, if you prefer to drive, stop and park where the old Chalmers Cat is parked for Start 47b. The road is narrow and very rough but passable for SUVs.

Time & Mileage to TH 35 minutes; 10.3 miles

Recommended Vehicle SUV. This is an easy 4x4 road with mostly good surface. However, there are very narrow sections with steep, exposed cliffs.

Summary

Maggie Gulch is a wide, beautiful basin with grassy mountains framing the sides, and Canby Mountain towering above at the end. The area is rich with wildflowers even into late August. Crystal Lake is completely hidden high above the valley floor and tucked against steep mountain walls. A large marshy area supports a wealth of wildflowers. The hike is entirely above tree line which offers expansive views of Maggie Gulch Basin as you ascend.

Trail Description

Hiking up the road from the junction offers great views of the Maggie Basin as you ascend. Above the Chalmers Cat at ❸, there is a very old grassy road starting up to the right. Follow it just a hundred feet to the first switchback and climb up the bank to the right. Your goal is to hike straight up the ridgeline on the right bank of the very prominent gorge now in front of you. Follow this route all the way to the viewpoint ❹ on a grassy saddle. It is a steep descent to the lake, and very marshy, but the wildflowers in this area are especially thick.

GPS	Mile	Latitude	Longitude	Elevation	Comment
1	0.00	37,49.152N	107,32.173W	11,708′	Start 47a: junction of Empire Mine Road and Maggie Gulch Road
2	0.78 / 0.00	37,49.356N	107,32.466W	11,955′	Start 47b: Switchback with rusted old Chalmers Cat. Minimal parking and turnaround space
3	0.91 / 0.13	37,49.239N	107,32.458W	12,019′	Leave main mining road and turn right up very old road grown over with grass.
4	1.49 / 0.71	37,49.454N	107,32.914W	12,389′	Viewpoint of Crystal Lake 160 feet below
5	1.60 / 0.82	37,49.547N	107,32.855W	12,236′	Crystal Lake shore

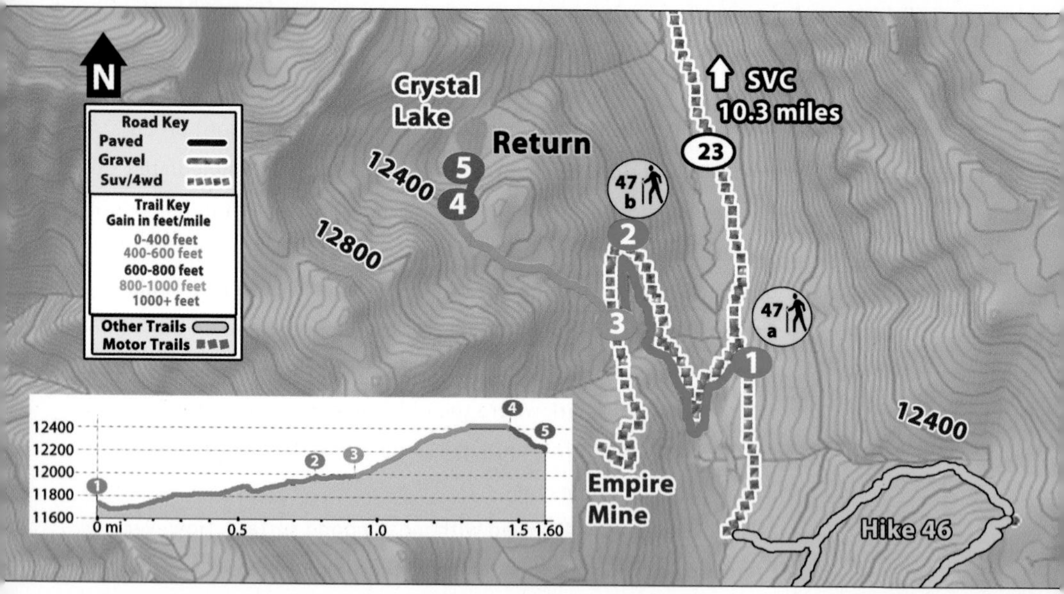

Wow!

Leave road and hike up this gully

48

Minnie Gulch to CDT Trail & Ridge

Star Rating

☆☆☆☆☆☆

Total Distance	9.50 miles RT. Go any distance
Difficulty Rating	Easy-Moderate
Surface	Mostly broken rock trail through grassy tundra to CDT. Packed surface along CDT
Gradient	Easy-Moderate
Average Time	4 to 6 hours depending on distance
Elevations	TH: 11,576; Highest: 13,182; Gain: +2,332
Map	Latitude 40: Telluride, Silverton, Ouray

Ascending the gulch

Directions to TH	From SVC, drive NE through town and turn right on CR 2 at 0.8 miles. At mile 7.2, turn right (E) on CR 24, Minnie Gulch Road which is signed. At mile 8.7, the only junction, go straight. (Left goes to Kitti Mack Mine.) At mile 10.0 is a sharp switchback to the left. A signs on the curve says, "Closed. No motorized vehicles." Park here. There is room for 3 vehicles. A well defined trail leads directly up the center of the valley from here.
Time & Mileage to TH	45 minutes; 10 miles
Recommended Vehicle	Car. The access road is one of the easiest of all the 4x4 roads in the county. There are no steep drop-offs; most of the road has passing areas; there are few rough sections.

Summary

This is by far the easiest hiking route to gain the high ridges of the Continental Divide. It is all above tree line. Minnie Gulch is rarely visited; rounded, grassy hillsides with rocky outcrops and dramatic cliffs punctuate the softness of this peaceful valley. There is a good display of wildflowers although not as lasting as in Maggie Gulch. From the CDT trail, there are stunning views down Pole Creek, and Cuba Gulch. Walk out the nearly level ridgeline that heads due north for easy walking and expansive vistas. This should not be missed! We did not hike the optional, steep return route to Kitti Mack Mine (1.52 miles.) The trail is said to be intermittent and very steep. Arrange a shuttle vehicle.

Trail Description

This is a well defined trail that is easy to follow all the way to the CDT trail. From the junction with the CDT ❷, you can hike right (S) and cross the steep hill over to Maggie Gulch, or hike straight ahead (E) and wander down the route for Middle Fork of Pole Creek just far enough to get a great view. For this hike, go left (N) and follow the CDT to the ridgeline for spectacular views of the peaks that make up the famous Alpine Loop (N). Just beyond sight of a small pond, the CDT trail goes right into Cuba Gulch ❸. You can see a faint trail going left. This follows the ridgeline north. Go as far as you wish. It is spectacular scenery and the walk is very easy.

Minnie Gulch

Minnie Gulch from CDT

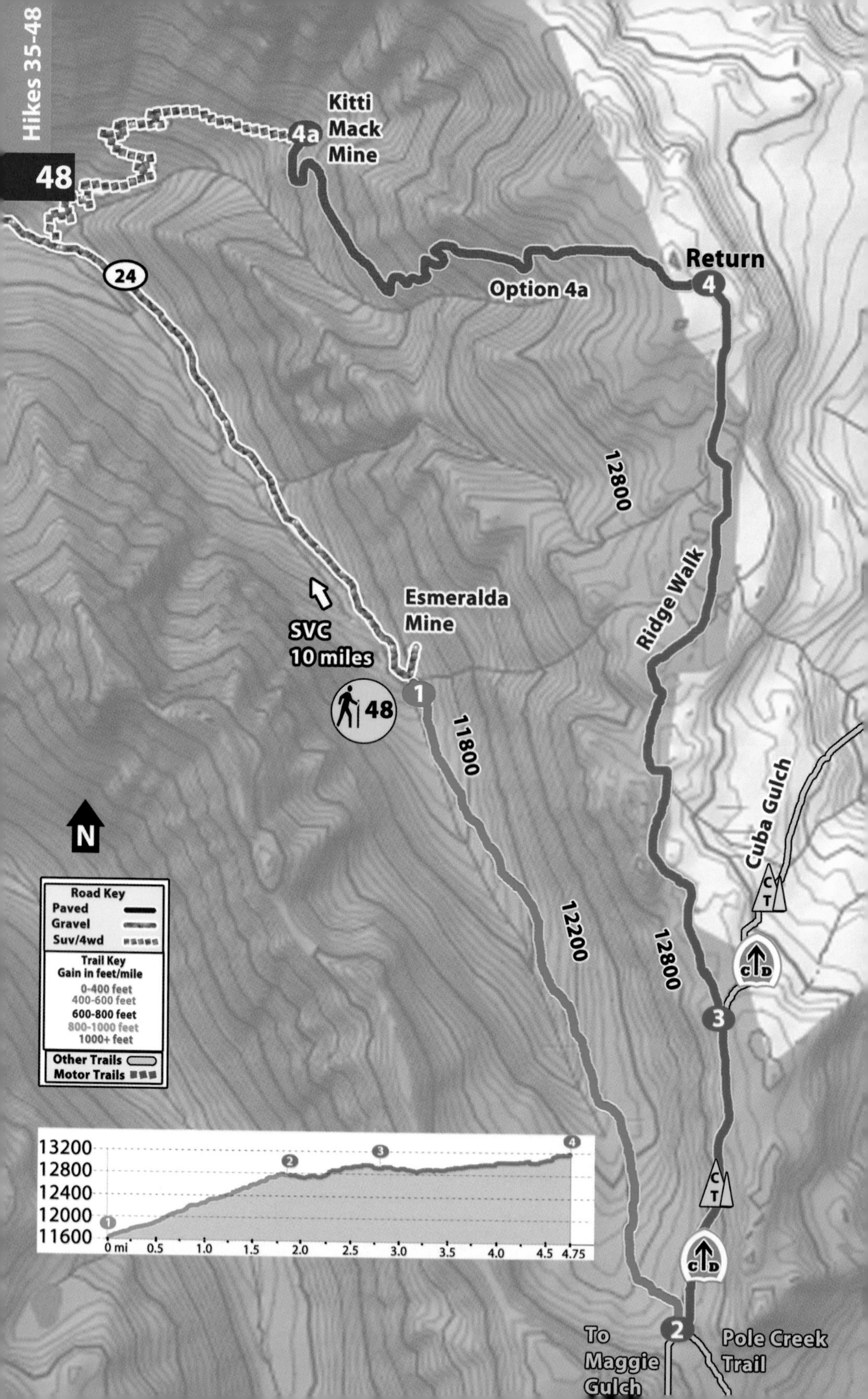
Kitti
Mack
Mine
4a
Return
4
Option 4a
24
12800
Ridge Walk
Esmeralda
Mine
SVC
10 miles
1
48
11800
N
Cuba Gulch
C
T
C D
12200
12800
3
Road Key
Paved
Gravel
Suv/4wd
Trail Key
Gain in feet/mile
0-400 feet
400-600 feet
600-800 feet
800-1000 feet
1000+ feet
Other Trails
Motor Trails
13200
12800
12400
12000
11600
0 mi
0.5
1.0
1.5
2.0
2.5
3.0
3.5
4.0
4.5
4.75
2
To
Maggie
Gulch
Pole Creek
Trail

GPS	Mile	Latitude	Longitude	Elevation	Comment
1	0.00	37,50.852N	107,31.927W	11,576′	Start Minnie Gulch to CDT.
2	1.77	37,49.568N	107,31.207W	12,728′	CDT sign. Go straight ahead 300 yards to overlook Middle Fork Pole Creek. Return to sign and hike north on CDT.
3	2.86	37,50.235N	107,31.092W	12,919′	Unsigned junction: CDT trail goes right down Cuba Gulch Take the lesser trail to the left for ridge walking.
4	4.75	37,51.637N	107,31.234W	13,182′	Ridge drops off to Kitti Mack Mine way below.

Hiking the CDT

Lake City: A Peak Experience

Lake City's book store

Peak Baggers go to Lake City. There are five famous 14ers easily accessible from Lake City, not to mention over twenty 13,000 peaks that attract high country hikers. The peaks are challenging, yet there are also many superb trails around Lake City for hikers looking for a scenic punch without going to 14,000 feet. Some of the best sections of the famous Colorado Trail/Continental Divide Trail pass right through the stunning San Juan Mountains that surround Lake City. Five of our routes are selections along these magnificent trails that you can do as day hikes.

With 96 percent public land around Lake City, there is an amazing amount of wildlife in the area including large elk herds, deer, even with newborn spotted fawns, and moose browsing many of the willow areas. Opportunities abound to see them in the wild as well as in Lake City proper where the animals graze all summer long.

Lake City itself is a National Historic District with over 200 historic structures. It is a tiny town, reminiscent of Alaska in the 60's, with one main commercial street that incorporated in 1875 as a hub for silver and gold mining. It maintains its authentic pioneer atmosphere with its lodges, cabins, campgrounds, and eateries. You won't see any box stores here. The grocery store is privately owned and operated like most businesses in Lake City.

Visitors come to Lake City to hike, fish, camp, horse ride, boat, bike, and jeep tour. The famous, scenic Alpine Loop is a network of 4WD roads connecting Lake City, Silverton and Ouray. Drive your own vehicle around the circuit, rent a jeep from one of the many lodges and businesses in the surrounding towns, or hire a guided jeep tour. The loop climbs to 12,800 feet and features many historic mining sites, and ghost towns. The Alpine Loop provides access to many of the hikes near Lake City.

The easier, paved route to Lake City is via Hwy 149. It is 55 miles south of Gunnison and about a two hour drive from Montrose. Lake City is remote. It is unique. It defines high country hiking.

Lake San Cristobal

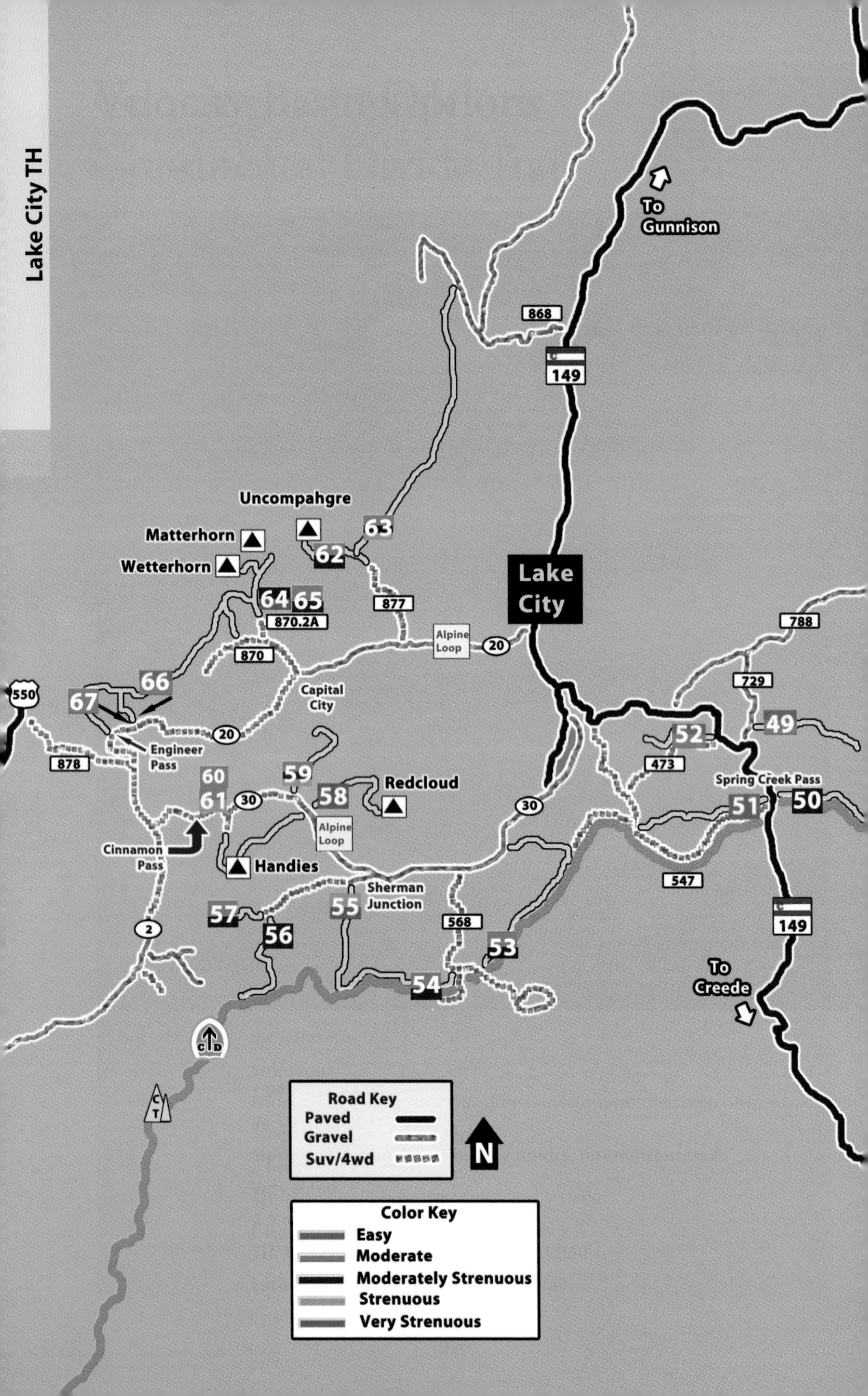
To Gunnison
868
149
Uncompahgre
63
Matterhorn
Wetterhorn
62
Lake City
64 65
870.2A
877
788
Alpine Loop
20
870
729
550
66
67
Capital City
49
52
20
Engineer Pass
878
473
59
60
Redcloud
Spring Creek Pass
61
30
58
30
51
50
Alpine Loop
Cinnamon Pass
Handies
547
Sherman Junction
57
55
149
568
56
2
53
To Creede
54
C D
C T
Road Key
Paved
Gravel
Suv/4wd
N
Color Key
Easy
Moderate
Moderately Strenuous
Strenuous
Very Strenuous

Lake City Trails Locator Map

49. Tumble Creek
50. CT East from Spring Creek Pass
51. CT West from Spring Creek Pass
52. 473 Road
53. CT East from Wager Gulch
54. CT West from Wager Gulch
55. Cataract Gulch
56. Cuba Gulch
57. Snare Basin
58. Red Cloud & Sunshine Peaks
59. Cooper Lake
60. Handies Peak & Grizzly Gulch
61. Uncompahgre Peak
62. Ridge Stock Driveway
63. Matterhorn Basin to Peaks
64. Matterhorn Cutoff to Alice Creek
65. High Country Traverse
66. American Flats to Engineer Pass

Tumble Creek Options

49a
49b
49c

Star Rating
☆☆☆
☆☆☆☆☆

49a: To Creek Crossing/ Return 1

Total Distance	3.96 miles RT
Difficulty Rating	Easy
Surface	Mostly packed dirt
Gradient	Easy
Average Time	2 hours
Elevations	TH: 10,290; Highest: 10,878; Gain: +785
Map	Trails Illustrated: Telluride, Silverton, Ouray, Lake City

49b: To View Meadows/ Return 2

Total Distance	6.44 miles RT
Difficulty Rating	Moderate
Surface	Mostly packed dirt with some rocky sections
Gradient	Ranges from Easy to Moderately Steep
Average Time	4 hours
Elevations	TH: 10,290; Highest: 11,689; Gain: +1,590

View from the high saddle/ Return 3

49c: To Saddle/ Return 3

Total Distance	8.40 miles RT
Difficulty Rating	Moderate
Surface	Mostly packed dirt with some rocky sections
Gradient	Ranges from Easy to Moderately Steep
Average Time	5.5 hours
Elevations	TH: 10,290; Highest: 12,111; Gain: +2,007

Directions to TH	From LCVC, drive 15.9 miles south on Hwy 149. Just south of milepost 57, turn left (N) at the Oleo Ranch junction (729). Drive approximately 2 miles to the signed Tumble Creek Trailhead. There is a sign in box. Trail signs say Skyline and Cebolla Creek.
Time & Mileage to TH	35 minutes; 17.9 miles
Recommended Vehicle	Car. This is paved road and good gravel road the last 2 miles.

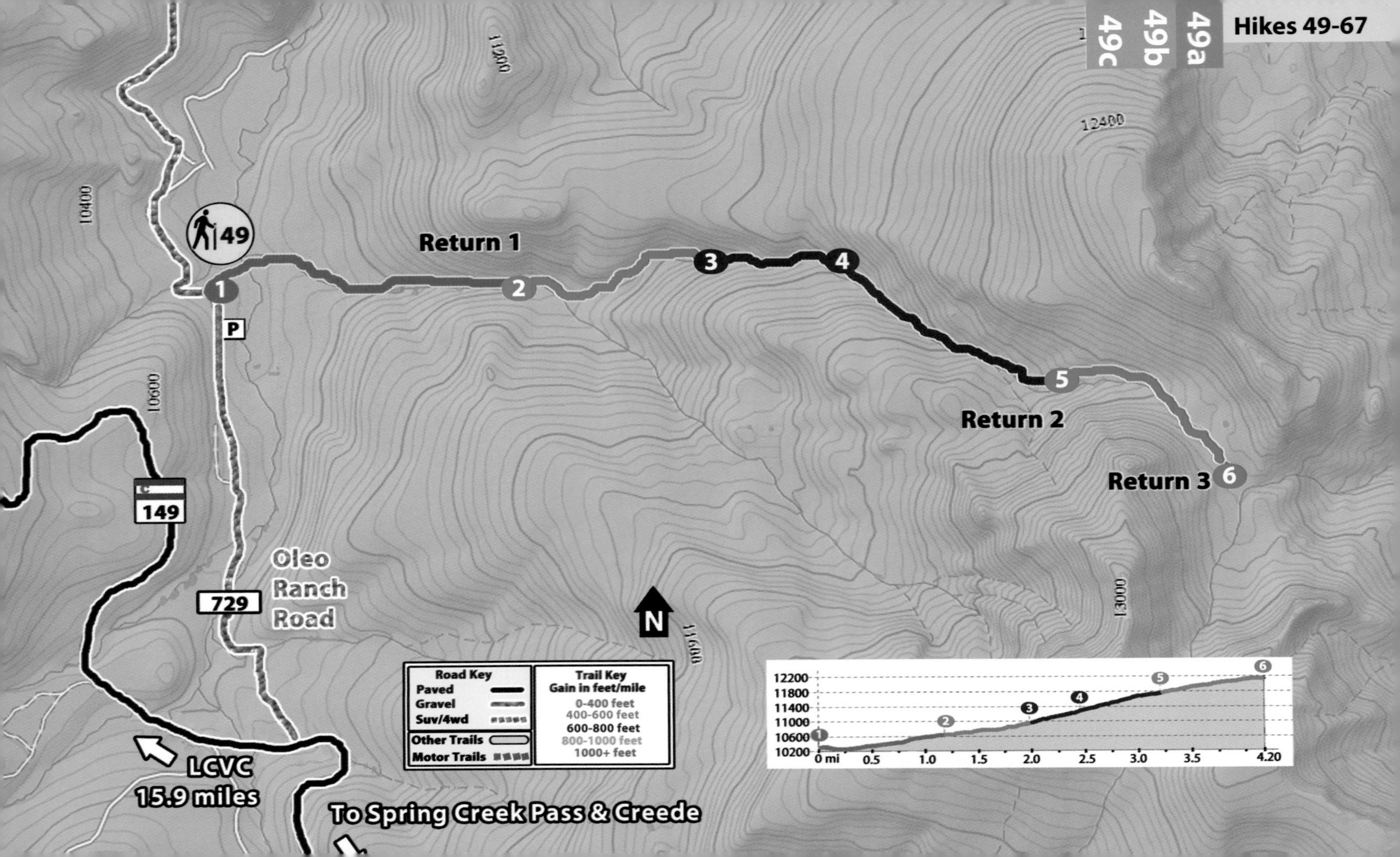
49
Return 1
Return 2
Return 3
1
2
3
4
5
6
P
149
729
Oleo Ranch Road
N
LCVC 15.9 miles
To Spring Creek Pass & Creede
10400
10600
11200
11600
12400
13000
Road Key
Paved
Gravel
Suv/4wd
Other Trails
Motor Trails
Trail Key
Gain in feet/mile
0-400 feet
400-600 feet
600-800 feet
800-1000 feet
1000+ feet
12200
11800
11400
11000
10600
10200
0 mi
0.5
1.0
1.5
2.0
2.5
3.0
3.5
4.20

Beaver ponds and willows in the lower trail

Summary

This is a delightful, moderate hike up a drainage to impressive vistas of a wide basin surrounded by peaks. Tumble Creek is mostly in view or ear shot throughout the hike. We saw Elk and Moose browsing in the willows.

Trail Description

Hike gently downhill from the sign in box, pass through a gate and cross Tumble Creek. You may want wet shoes even into mid-August. Pass through another gate and cross the creek again. You can usually hop across this section a little upstream. Climb gently through open ranchland. Cattle graze here; this is also a favorite horse trail and backpacking route. The valley remains picturesque and open for about 2 miles where you come to a pretty section of Beaver Ponds ❷. After the ponds, the trail turns up the narrower valley to the east. At ❸, cross Tumble Creek again. Now the trail begins a steeper ascent up through spruce forest. This is Return 1, which makes for a very nice short hike. Views are more restricted by intermittent forest and the narrower drainage, and the trail is a little steeper from here to ❺ But, if you go at least to Return 2 at ❺, you will see into the wide meadowlands that lead to the upper basin. It is very picturesque. At ❻ you can see down the other side into this lovely high basin surrounded by peaks.

GPS	Mile	Latitude	Longitude	Elevation	Comment
1	0.00	37,58.728N	107,10.206W	10,290′	Start Tumble Creek at Skyline TH sign.
2	1.18	37,58.759N	107,09.062W	10,539′	Lovely area of beaver ponds
3	1.98	37,58.843N	107,08.270W	10,878′	Return 1: Cross Tumble Creek; enter forest.
4	2.44	37,58.829N	107,07.818W	11,112′	Cross Tumble Creek again.
5	3.22	37,58.487N	107,07.131W	11,689′	Return 2: Leave forest and enter view meadows. Views of Baldy Cinco
6	4.20	37,58.162N	107,06.264W	12,111′	Return 3: High point with views into beautiful valley

View of meadows approaching the high saddle

Colorado Trail East from Spring Creek Pass

Star Rating

☆☆☆

☆☆☆☆☆

Hiking Snow Mesa

50a: To Mesa/ Return 1

Total Distance	3.80 miles RT
Difficulty Rating	Moderately Strenuous
Surface	Mostly packed dirt except for climb through the notch
Gradient	Moderately steep
Average Time	3 hours
Elevations	TH: 10,898; Highest: 12,251; Gain: +1,370
Map	Latitude 40: Southwest Colorado Trails

50b: To Ponds/ Return 2

Total Distance	9.6 miles RT
Difficulty Rating	Moderately Strenuous & Easy
Surface	Mostly packed dirt except for climb through the notch
Gradient	Moderately Steep first 1.9 miles; Easy after that
Average Time	6 hours 45 min
Elevations	TH: 10,898; Highest: 12,370; Gain: +1,978

	50c: To Miner's Creek/ Return 3
Total Distance	11.8 miles RT
Difficulty Rating	Moderately Strenuous due to distance and gain
Surface	Mostly packed dirt except for climb through the notch
Gradient	Moderately Steep first 1.9 miles; Easy until trail drops 480 feet to junction
Average Time	8 hours
Elevations	TH: 10,898; Highest: 12,370; Gain: +2,752

	50d: To Baldy Cinco Summit
Total Distance	5.83 miles RT
Difficulty Rating	Moderately Strenuous
Surface	Mostly packed dirt except for climb through the notch; Tundra to Peak
Gradient	Moderately Steep
Average Time	4.5 hours
Elevations	TH: 10,898; Highest: 13,383; Gain: +2,510

Directions to TH	From LCVC, drive south through town on Hwy 149 towards Creede for 17.3 miles to signed Spring Creek Pass. Parking on the west side; the trailhead is on the east side of the highway.
Time & Mileage to TH	35 minutes; 17.3 miles
Recommended Vehicle	Car

Summary

Hike uphill moderately steeply for 2 miles through open conifer forest with occasional views towards the south. Arrive at Snow Mesa, a huge expanse of grassland with see forever views of the San Juan Mountains in the distance. Hike the Mesa any distance you choose. It is an easy, undulating, dirt packed trail, or return at any of our specific return points. Make the optional ascent to 13,383 foot Baldy Cinco Peak.

Ascending to the mesa through the rocky gulch

Trail Description

The trail climbs moderately steeply up through mixed conifer forest to a small meadow marked by the first giant stone cairn ❷. Ascend again through forest a short distance before coming to a very rocky gully. Watch and listen for pikas and marmots. At the top of this gully is the expansive Snow Mesa ❸ marked by a cairn with numerous orange plastic poles. This is Return 1 for a short hike. You can see across most of the Mesa. Look behind for magnificent views of the San Juan Range. Continuing on, the views do not change much across the entire Mesa until you have gone 4.8 miles from the trailhead and arrive at a collection of small, pretty ponds with wildflowers flourishing in season ❼. Of course, you can return at any point

Route to Baldy Cinco

sooner. If you are still energetic, descend 480 feet to a trail junction where you have wonderful views east down Miner's Creek drainage ❽.

A final option is to leave the trail back at ❹ and climb the ridge to Baldy Cinco Peak. If the cairn with the orange plastic poles at the top of the gully is counted as number one cairn, the 5th cairn (also with many orange poles) is the spot to turn off the trail ❹. Head up the obvious ridge for the rocky escarpment near what looks like the top. There is actually an easy route around this ledge once you get there. But this is a false summit. The real summit is another 0.3 miles up and is easily seen from this new vantage point.

GPS	Mile	Latitude	Longitude	Elevation	Comment
1	0.00	37,56.389N	107,09.527W	10,898'	Start Colorado Trail at Spring Creek Trailhead.
2	1.00	37,56.275N	107,08.601W	11,632'	First giant rock cairn marks trail; view of 2 rocky knobs. Trail climbs through notch between them.
3	1.90	37,56.091N	107,07.829W	12,251'	End of climbing. Enter Mesa. Return 1
4	2.95	37,56.194N	107,06.668W	12,336'	Cairn #5 from start of mesa. Many orange poles. Good place to leave trail and hike up ridgeline to Baldy Cinco Peak.
5	3.47	37,56.283N	107,06.100W	12,307'	Trail drops down and climbs back up wide gully.
6	3.95	37,56.298N	107,05.599W	12,320'	Trail drops again into wide gully.
7	4.80	37,56.300N	107,04.685W	12,290'	Ponds; Return 2
8	5.90	37,56.876N	107,03.885W	11,897'	Trail junction at pass; Return 3

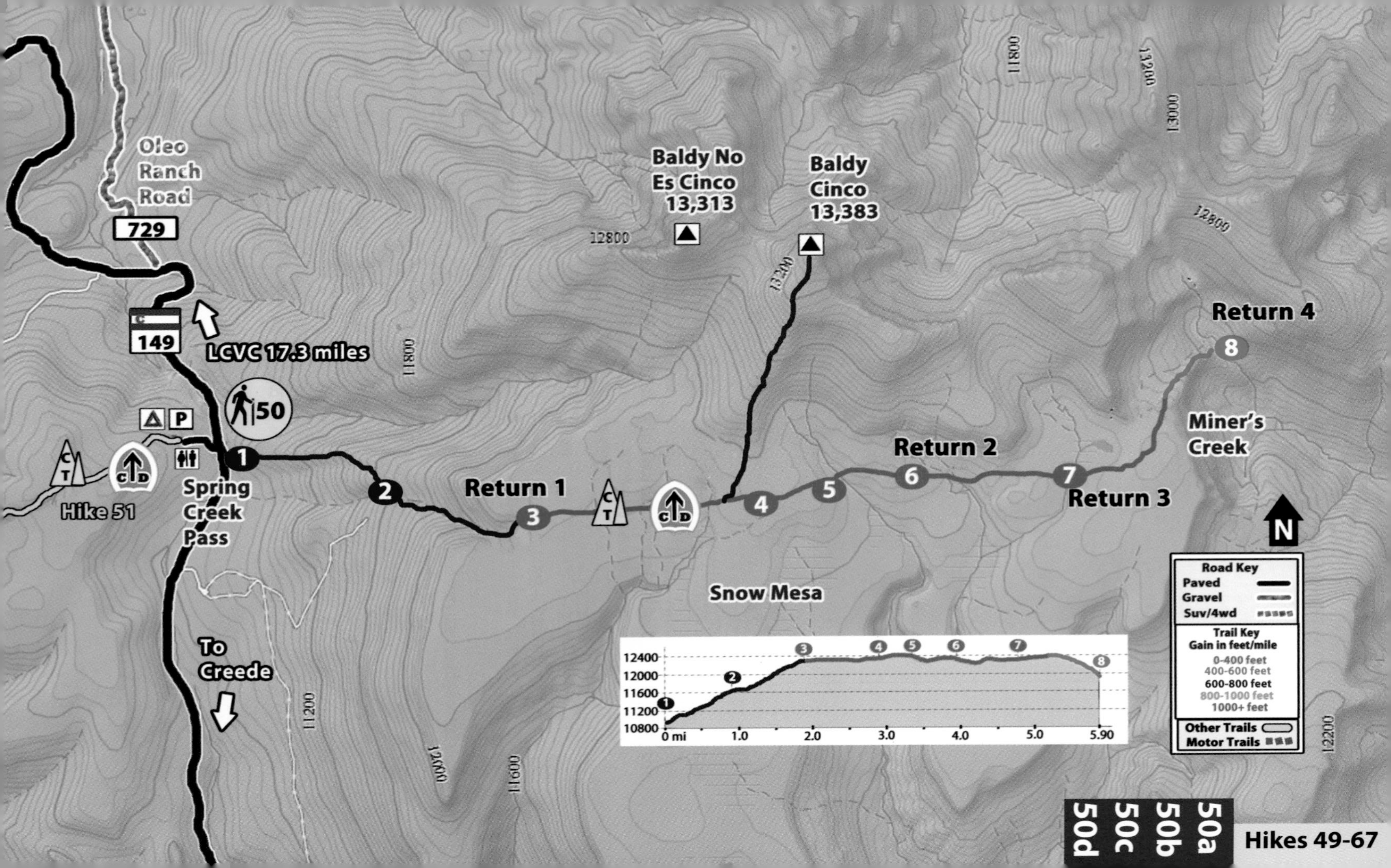

Oleo Ranch Road
729
149
LCVC 17.3 miles
50
Hike 51
Spring Creek Pass
To Creede
Baldy No Es Cinco 13,313
Baldy Cinco 13,383
12800
13200
11800
13000
12800
Return 1
Return 2
Return 3
Return 4
Miner's Creek
Snow Mesa
11200
12000
11600
12200
Road Key
Paved
Gravel
Suv/4wd
Trail Key
Gain in feet/mile
0-400 feet
400-600 feet
600-800 feet
800-1000 feet
1000+ feet
Other Trails
Motor Trails
12400
12000
11600
11200
10800
0 mi
1.0
2.0
3.0
4.0
5.0
5.90

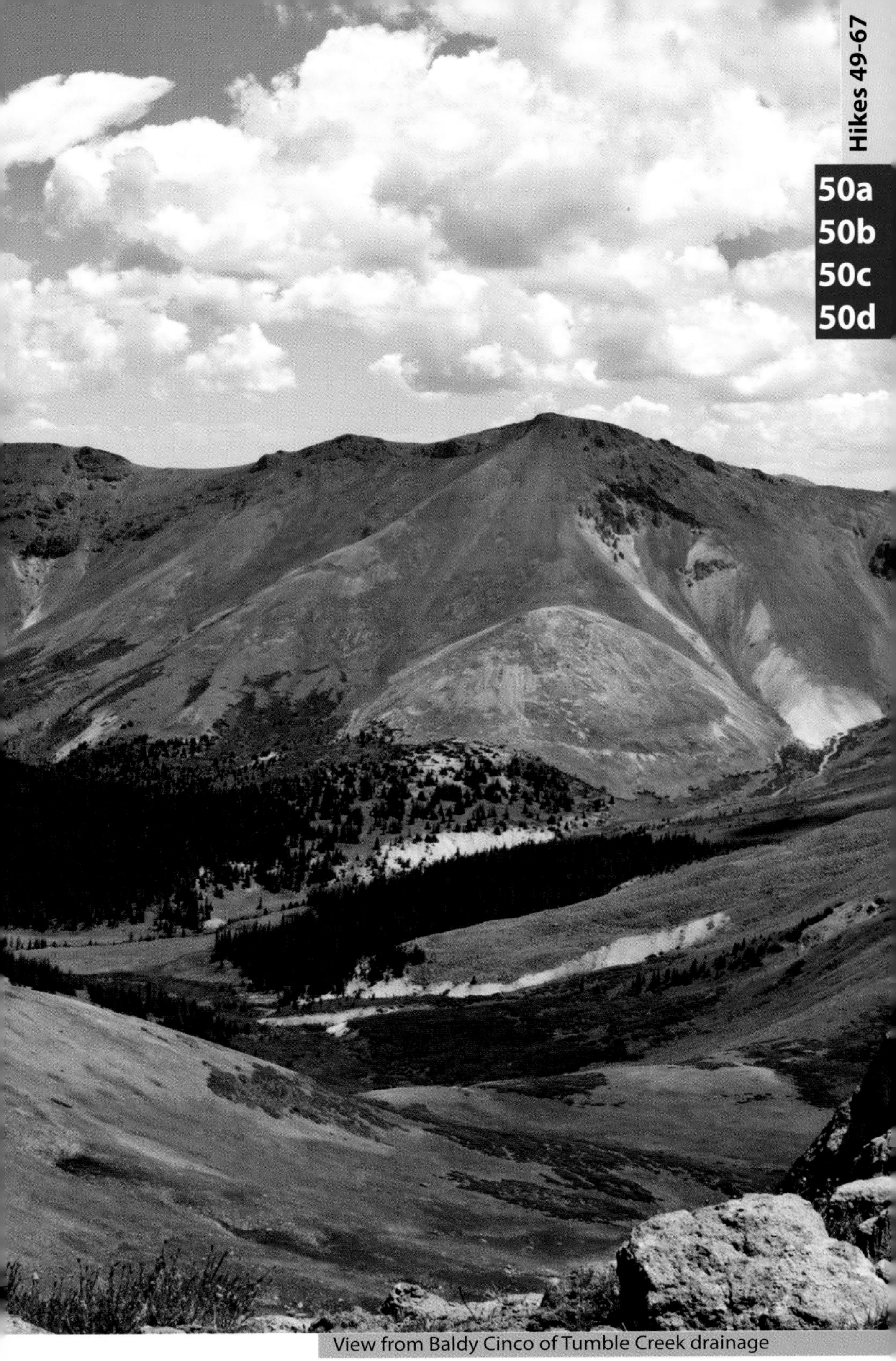

View from Baldy Cinco of Tumble Creek drainage

Colorado Trail West from Spring Creek TH

Star Rating

☆☆☆☆

☆☆☆☆☆

View of peaks from Jarosa Mesa

Total Distance	8.80 miles RT or go any distance
Difficulty Rating	Easy
Surface	Good packed dirt on wide road first 2.56 miles; intermittent single track over rocky tundra after that
Gradient	Mostly Easy with Moderate section
Average Time	5 hours
Elevations	TH: 10,891; Highest: 12,014; Gain: +1,424
Map	Latitude 40: Southwest Colorado Trails_Durango, Lake City, Ouray, Pagosa Springs, Silverton, Telluride
Directions to TH	From LCVC, drive south through town on Hwy 149 towards Creede for 17.3 miles to signed Spring Creek Pass. Parking and pit toilet. Tiny TH sign marks a jeep road that climbs west just north of the outhouse.
Time & Mileage to TH	35 minutes; 17.3 miles
Recommended Vehicle	Car

Summary

Wow! Easy road access on an easy trail that gets you views of Uncompahgre Peak and the San Juan Range. This is one of the easiest sections of the famous Colorado Trail.

Trail Description

The first 2.56 miles follow a good dirt road that allows motorized vehicles. We encountered only two motorcycles the entire day. The road is part of the famous Colorado Trail and you will probably meet more hikers than vehicles along this section. Begin in open spruce forest that by ❷ enters big meadows with far reaching vistas of very distant valleys and peaks. Always look behind you on the ascent for good views of Baldy Cinco and Baldy No Es Cinco. This is mellow terrain through rolling grassy fields that ascend gently to the Continental Divide. Leave the road at ❸ and follow the rock and stick markers on intermittent trails through more rocky tundra all the way to Jarosa Mesa. At ❹ you will get your first view of Uncompahgre Peak. Matterhorn is also visible, but Wetterhorn is hiding behind the red mountain. Walk across the Mesa as far as you wish. By ❺, you can even see Canby Mountain.

Trail follows road from the beginning

View of Baldy Cinco on the return trip

GPS	Mile	Latitude	Longitude	Elevation	Comment
1	0.00	37,56.456N	107,09.611W	10,891'	Start Colorado Trail west from Spring Creek TH.
2	0.80	37,56.256N	107,10.356W	11,134′	Leave spruce forest and enter big meadows.
3	2.56	37,55.724N	107,11.970W	11,381′	Trail leaves road at first cairn marker with post.
4	4.00	37,55.753N	107,13.389W	12,014′	First views of Uncompahgre Peak and San Juan Range
5	4.40	37,55.677N	107,13.817W	12,012′	Good return point as trail begins gentle descent

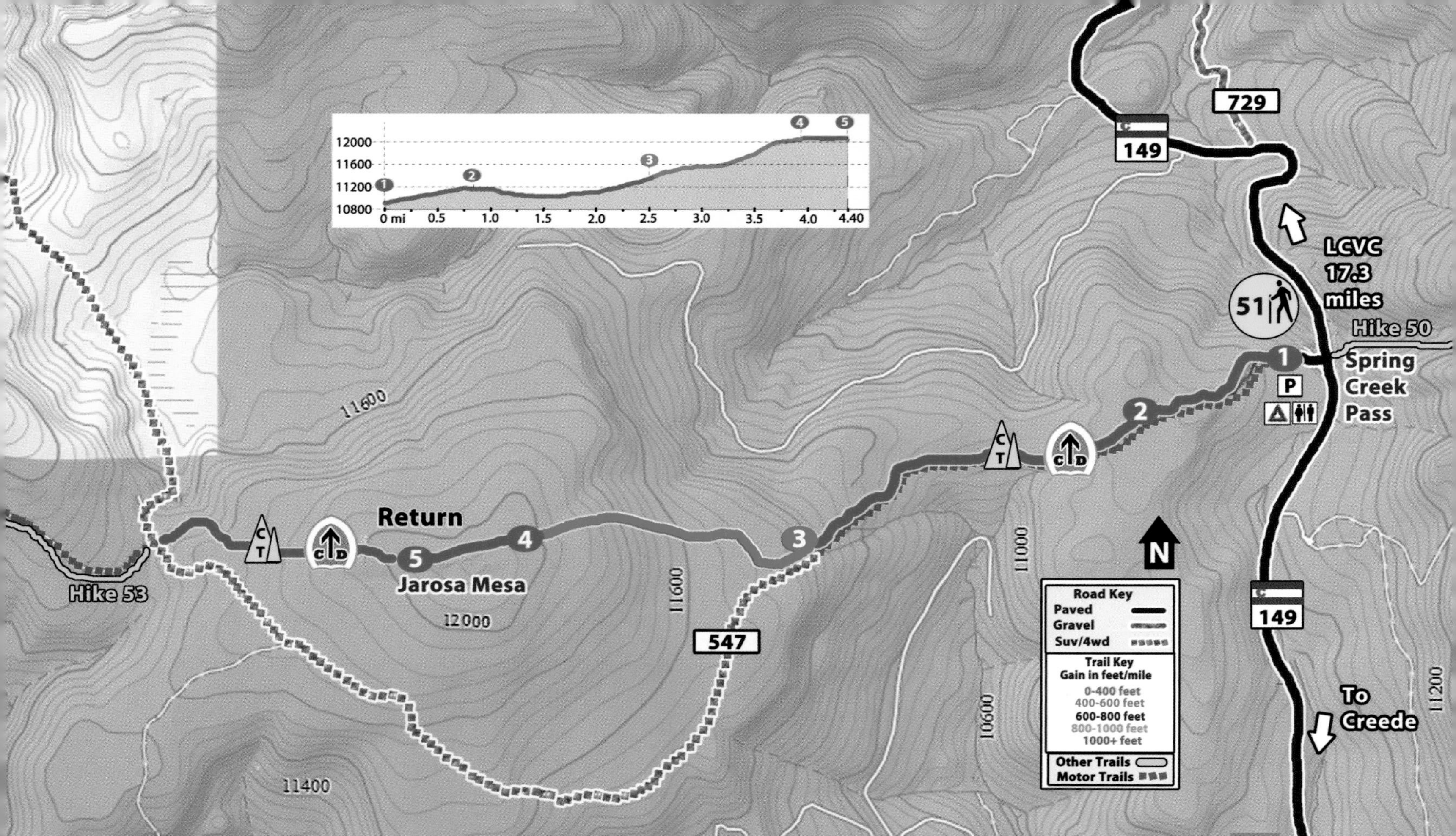
12000
11600
11200
10800
0 mi
0.5
1.0
1.5
2.0
2.5
3.0
3.5
4.0
4.40
729
149
LCVC
17.3
miles
51
Hike 50
Spring
Creek
Pass
P
C T
C D
Return
Jarosa Mesa
Hike 53
11600
12000
547
11000
10600
N
Road Key
Paved
Gravel
Suv/4wd
Trail Key
Gain in feet/mile
0-400 feet
400-600 feet
600-800 feet
800-1000 feet
1000+ feet
Other Trails
Motor Trails
To
Creede
11200
11400

473 Road Options

Star Rating
☆☆☆☆☆
☆☆☆☆☆

52a
52b

View hiking along Slumgullion ridge

52a: To Rambouillet Park/ Return 1

Total Distance	8.92 miles RT or any distance you like
Difficulty Rating	Easy
Surface	Mostly packed dirt
Gradient	Mostly Easy
Average Time	5 hours if going 8.92 miles
Elevations	TH: 11,205; Highest: 11,922; Gain: +1,106
Map	Latitude 40: Southwest Colorado Trails_Durango, Lake City, Pagosa Springs, Silverton, Telluride

52b: To Slumgullion Peak/ Return 2

Total Distance	7.0 miles RT
Difficulty Rating	Easy to Moderate
Surface	Mostly packed dirt and tundra
Gradient	Mostly Moderate
Average Time	4 hours
Elevations	TH: 11,205; Highest: 12,210; Gain: +1,374

Directions to TH

From LCVC, drive south through town on Hwy 149 towards Creede for 9.9 miles. Just south of mile marker 60 is an old jeep trail taking off up to the right (W) side of the road. A metal post marks 473. Park along side the highway and hike up this road

Time & Mileage to TH

25 minutes; 9.9 miles

Recommended Vehicle

Car

Summary

This is a motorized road. Why hike a road with vehicles? Because you probably won't see any. This is not high on the list of jeep routes. It is a wonderful hiking trail into a fabulous wide open valley with great views of Baldy Cinco and Tumble Creek drainage. Make the optional climb to the Slumgullion ridge and gain stunning views of Uncompahgre, Matterhorn and Wetterhorn Peaks. Easy car access, Easy to Moderate gradient. We saw about 75 elk in the meadows. Go any distance.

Leave main road and hike up to ridge for option 52b

Trail Description

The trail begins in very healthy spruce forest and alternates with small meadows for about the first mile. At ❷ is a metal sign post with a white arrow. Continue

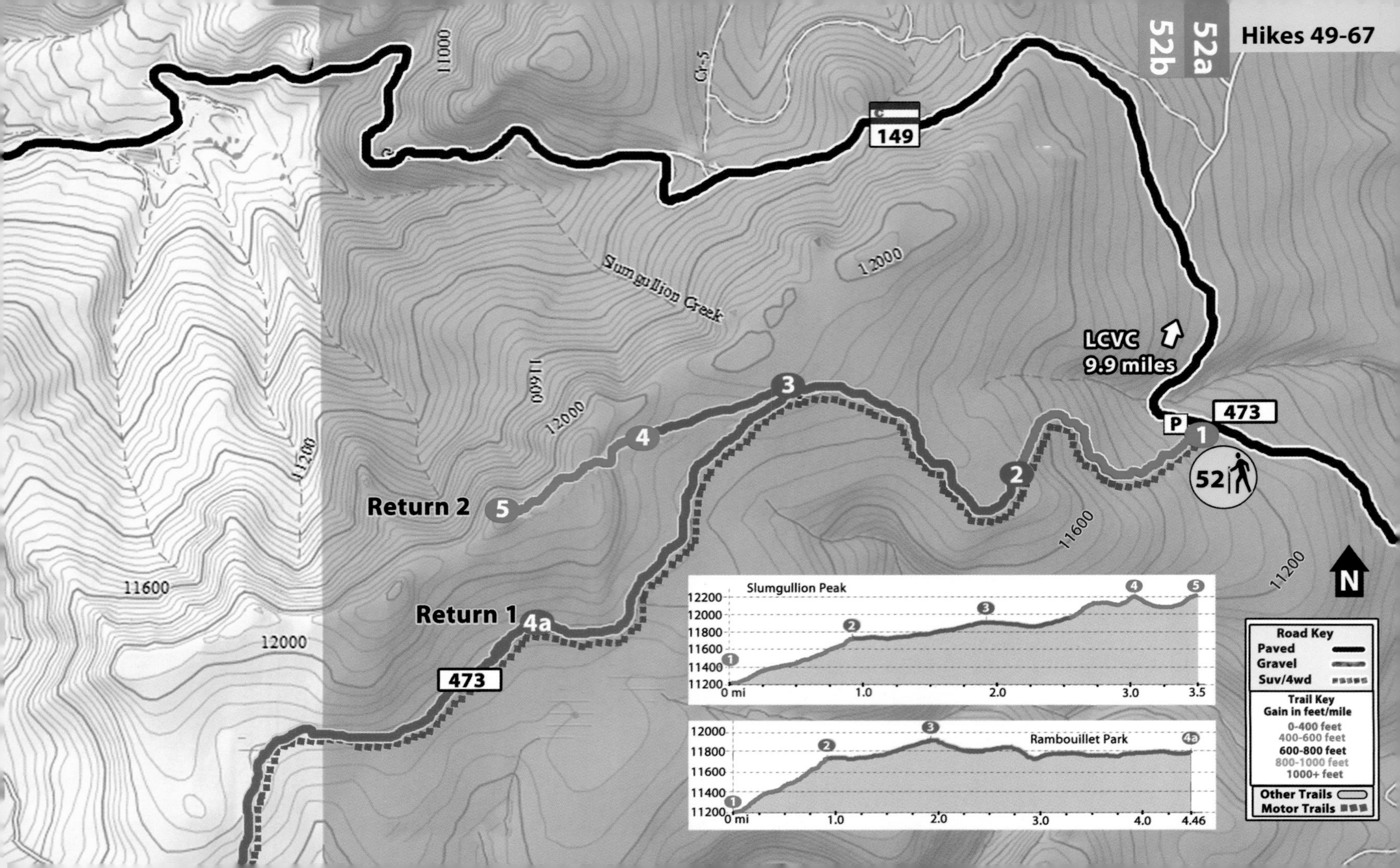
149
Gr-5
11000
Slumgullion Creek
12000
11600
11200
LCVC
9.9 miles
473
P
1
2
3
4
5
4a
52
Return 1
Return 2
N
Slumgullion Peak
12200
12000
11800
11600
11400
11200
0 mi
1.0
2.0
3.0
3.5
Rambouillet Park
4.0
4.46
Road Key
Paved
Gravel
Suv/4wd
Trail Key
Gain in feet/mile
0-400 feet
400-600 feet
600-800 feet
800-1000 feet
1000+ feet
Other Trails
Motor Trails

following the main track and shortly after this post, you will arrive at the edge of the grand opening. The track winds around low willow brush; look behind for great views of Baldy Cinco. Climbing gently to the high point in the road ❸, you can now see a long distance into Rambouillet Park. As you begin the easy descent, either continue following the road as far as you wish, perhaps to 4a, or leave the road and hike towards the prominent ridge to the west. As you approach the bottom of the ridge, many animal tracks wind through the thick willows. Follow trails that gain elevation gradually, always heading for the ridge top. See our photos for guidance. Once on the ridge, it is another 200 feet climb to the first unnamed peak ❹ and another 0.50 miles to Slumgullion Peak ❺. There are splendid vistas of the 14er peaks all along this route so go as far as you wish.

GPS	Mile	Latitude	Longitude	Elevation	Comment
1	0.00	37,58.388N	107,11.752W	11,205′	Start 473 road.
2	0.93	37,58.234N	107,12.325W	11,743′	Metal post with white arrow; stay on main road; leave forest shortly after and enter open terrain.
3	1.91	37,58.469N	107,13.071W	11,922′	High point on road. Begin easy descent and either stay on road to Rambouillet Park or leave road and contour towards higher ridgeline and Slumgullion Peak.
4	3.04	37,58.155N	107,14.119W	12,213′	Reach 1st un-named peak. Fantastic views
5	3.50	37,57.919N	107,14.479W	12,210'	Slumgullion Peak; more great views along entire ridge walk
4a	4.46	37,57.307N	107,14.998W	11,793′	If you stayed on road, return at any time you wish.

Option 52a through Rambouillet Park

Colorado Trail East from Wager Road Options

Star Rating

☆☆☆☆☆

53a
53b
53c
53d
53e

53a: To Return 1

Total Distance	5.44 miles RT
Difficulty Rating	Moderate
Surface	Mostly dirt packed to high point; more rocky sections after that
Gradient	Ranges from Steep to Easy
Average Time	4 hours
Elevations	TH: 12,285; Highest: 13,264; Gain: +1,446
Map	Trails Illustrated: Telluride, Silverton, Ouray, Lake City & La Garita Cochetopa Hills

53b: To Return 2

Total Distance	7.40 miles RT
Difficulty Rating	Moderate
Surface	Mostly dirt packed to high point; more rocky sections after that
Gradient	Ranges from Steep to Easy
Average Time	5.5 hours
Elevations	TH: 12,285; Highest: 13,264; Gain: + 1,740

Approaching Return 1

53c: To Shuttle 1/ Friendship Yurt

Total Distance	8.25 miles to shuttle
Difficulty Rating	Moderate
Surface	Mostly dirt packed with some rocky sections
Gradient	Mostly Easy and Moderate with one short steep downhill
Average Time	5.5 hours
Elevations	TH: 12,285; Highest: 13,264; Gain: +1,610; Loss: -2,198

53d: To Shuttle 2/ Sawmill Park Road

Total Distance	11.3 miles to shuttle
Difficulty Rating	Moderately Strenuous due to distance
Surface	Mostly dirt packed with some rocky sections
Gradient	Mostly Easy to Moderate with two short steep downhill sections
Average Time	7 hours
Elevations	TH: 12,285; Highest: 13,264; Gain: +2,158; Loss: -2,732

53e: To Shuttle 3/ Camp Trail TH

Total Distance	12.23 miles to shuttle
Difficulty Rating	Moderately Strenuous due to distance
Surface	Mostly dirt packed with some rocky sections
Gradient	Ranges from Easy to Moderately Strenuous
Average Time	7.5 hours
Elevations	TH: 12,285; Highest: 13,264; Gain: +1,660; Loss: -4,862

Directions to TH	From LCVC, drive west through town 2.7 miles to the signed junction to Creede and Cinnamon Pass. Turn right towards Cinnamon Pass on CR 30. From here drive 8.9 miles to signed CR 36 (568 on map). From this point it is 4.88 miles on a slow 4x4 road to the Continental Divide. There is one unsigned fork in the road about halfway up; both forks are equally used. Take the right fork uphill. Once at the Divide, there are many forks. Keep taking the left forks going a little downhill. Park where the road starts to climb back up again, in sight of some ruined cabins.
Time & Mileage to TH	1.5 hour; 16.48 miles
Recommended Vehicle	SUV with high clearance and 4-wheel drive to ascend CR 36. It is possible to drive to ❸ if you have low gearing. It is very steep with side hill and can be very slippery after rain. This short section is a very popular ATV route.

Directions to Shuttle 1&2 From LCVC drive south 5.84 miles on Hwy 149 to a signed turnoff for Rd 3322. This is just beyond the pull off area for the Lake San Cristobal viewpoint. Drive this road 4.60 miles to the Continental Divide and shuttle 2. You will see signs marking the Colorado Trail at this point. It is possible to drive the Colorado Trail (which is a grassy road at this point) another 3.8 miles to shuttle 1 which is the end of the road just below Friendship Yurt.

Time & Mileage To Shuttle 1: 1.5 hours; 14.24 miles
To Shuttle 2: 1 hour 15 minutes; 10.44 miles

Recommended Vehicle SUV with high clearance and 4x4. The beginning of road 3322 is excellent but after the first mile, it becomes very steep and very rocky. Sections of the route from shuttle 2 to shuttle 1 are also extremely rocky.

Directions to Shuttle 3 (Camp Trail) From LCVC, drive south on Gunnison Ave 2.7 miles to the signed junction to Creede and Cinnamon Pass (Lake San Cristobal). Turn right on Cinnamon Pass Road CR 30. Drive 7.1 miles to the signed parking area for Camp Trail TH. Cars can drive to this shuttle. Allow 20 minutes.

On route to Return 2

Summary

This part of the Colorado Trail hugs the Continental Divide quite closely. It is all above tree line across alpine tundra. You can see five 14ers, Red Mountain and Lake San Cristobal from various parts along the trail. Go as far as you wish for a round trip, or hike all the way through for a shuttle or key exchange.

Trail Description

Hike up the steep road for about 0.60 miles where a sign shows the Colorado Trail leaves the road ❷ After a little more climbing, look north for splendid views of Sunshine and Red Cloud Peaks. At ❸, the trail crosses the road again twice. This is

On route to Friendship Yurt. Photo by Rozanne Evans

Lake San Cristobal. Photo by Rozanne Evans

Approaching shuttle 2

the parking spot if you have driven a vehicle with low gearing. Continue following the trail. At the high point ❹, you cannot see any 14ers to the north although the views south are see forever. Be sure to look west as well and see up the beautiful valley where the Colorado Trail goes towards Cataract Gulch. Continue on an easy downhill gradient around a long corner. In about another half mile, you can see Handies, Sunshine, Red Cloud, Wetterhorn, and even the top of Uncompahgre. Wow! Return from ❺ for a shorter out and back or continue another mile to ❻ where you can also see Lake San Cristobal. From this point, return or continue to one of the shuttle points. The trail continues to offer wonderful vistas of the peaks to the west as well as expansive views of the rolling grasslands to the east and south. This is a delicious section of the Colorado Trail.

GPS	Mile	Latitude	Longitude	Elevation	Comment
1	0.00	37,51.312N	107,21.939W	12,285′	Wager Gulch Road East on Colorado Trail
2	0.60	37,51.467N	107,21.380W	12,755′	Leave road at CT sign and follow single track.
3	1.06 0.00	37,51.304N	107,21.034W	13,118′	Trail crosses road twice. Park here if you drove and follow trail, not the road.
4	1.52 0.46	37,51.407N	107,20.742W	13,264′	High point. No views of 14ers here. Continue around corner for grand views.
5	2.72 1.06	37,52.150N	107,20.450W	12,856′	Return 1: Low point with great views. Good return if you don't want to climb again.
6	3.70 2.64	37,52.625N	107,19.944W	12,862′	Return 2: Views of Lake San Cristobal
7	5.74 4.68	37,53.591N	107,18.467W	12,473′	Fantastic View of Lake San Cristobal
8	8.25 7.15	37,54.762N	107,17.218W	11,715′	Signed junction: Trail meets jeep road below Friendship Yurt. This is shuttle 1, or follow Colorado Trail straight ahead (N) through trees to shuttle 2, or hike left (W) up grassy road .05 miles to ridge for Camp Trail and shuttle 3.
9	9.03 7.97	37,55.311N	107,16.893W	12,036′	Colorado Trail meets road again. Follow road uphill (N).
10	9.60 8.54	37,55.702N	107,16.499W	12,214′	High point on road
11	9.96 8.90	37,55.963N	107,16.312W	12,044′	Great views of Red Mountain with Uncompahgre behind
12	11.30 10.24	37,55.719N	107,15.005W	11,731′	Colorado Trail/road meets Sawmill Park Road. This is shuttle 2.
Camp Trail route to shuttle 3 begins 0.50 miles uphill (W) from junction at (8).					
13	8.30 7.24	37,54.820N	107,17.455W	11,783′	Signed junction: to Camp Trail at top of ridge near the old foundation for Friendship Yurt
14	8.45 7.39	37,54.936N	107,17.507W	11,737′	Pole marking trail; excellent trail from here down to Cinnamon Pass Rd
15	12.23 11.17	37,55.018N	107,19.947W	9,279′	Camp Creek TH sign on Cinnamon Pass Rd; This is shuttle 3.

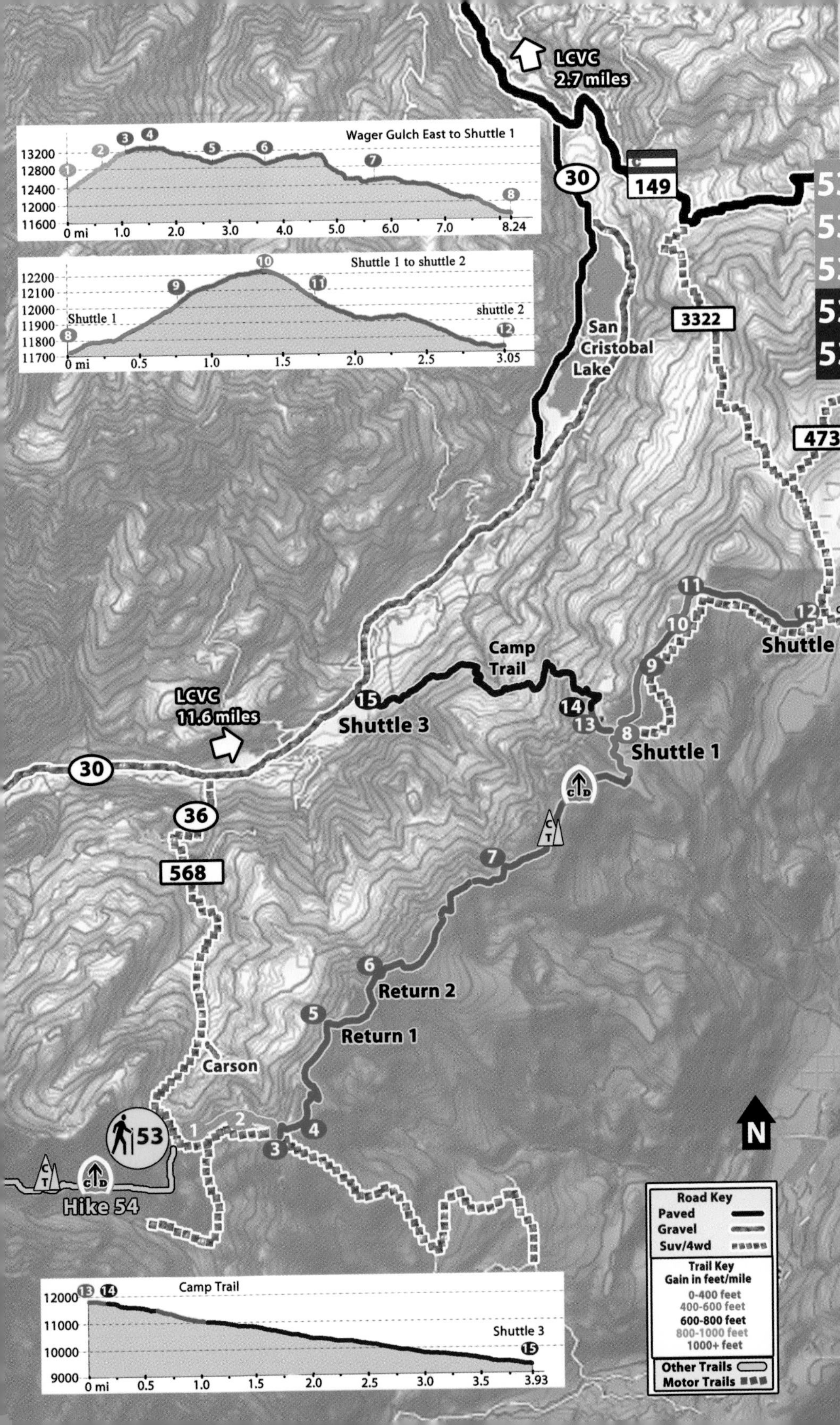
LCVC
2.7 miles
Wager Gulch East to Shuttle 1
13200
12800
12400
12000
11600
0 mi
1.0
2.0
3.0
4.0
5.0
6.0
7.0
8.24
Shuttle 1 to shuttle 2
12200
12100
12000
11900
11800
11700
Shuttle 1
shuttle 2
0 mi
0.5
1.0
1.5
2.0
2.5
3.05
30
149
3322
San Cristobal Lake
473
Shuttle 2
Camp Trail
Shuttle 3
Shuttle 1
LCVC
11.6 miles
30
36
568
Return 2
Return 1
Carson
53
Hike 54
N
Camp Trail
12000
11000
10000
9000
Shuttle 3
0 mi
0.5
1.0
1.5
2.0
2.5
3.0
3.5
3.93
Road Key
Paved
Gravel
Suv/4wd
Trail Key
Gain in feet/mile
0-400 feet
400-600 feet
600-800 feet
800-1000 feet
1000+ feet
Other Trails
Motor Trails

54a
54b

Colorado Trail West from Wager Road/ Options

Star Rating
☆☆☆☆☆
☆☆☆

Trail climbs through Lost Trail Valley to high point

54a: To Saddle/ Return 1

Total Distance	7.56 miles RT
Difficulty Rating	Moderate
Surface	Mostly packed dirt
Gradient	Easy to Moderate
Average Time	4.5 hours
Elevations	TH: 12,352; Highest: 12,943; Gain: +1,461
Map	Trails Illustrated: Telluride, Silverton, Ouray, Lake City

54b: To Cataract TH

Total Distance	10.57 miles to shuttle
Difficulty Rating	Moderately Strenuous due to distance and steep descent last 3 miles
Surface	Easy packed dirt on Colorado Trail; Much more rock and brushy trail on Cataract Gulch side
Gradient	Ranges from Easy to Steep
Average Time	8 hours
Elevations	TH: 12,352; Highest: 12,943; Gain: +2,047; Loss: -4,773

Directions to TH	From LCVC, drive west through town 2.7 miles to the signed junction to Creede and Cinnamon Pass CR 30. Turn right towards Cinnamon Pass. From here drive 8.9 miles to signed CR 36 (568 on map). From this point it is 4.88 miles on a slow 4x4 road to the Continental Divide. There is one unsigned fork in the road about halfway up; both forks are equally used. Take the right fork uphill. Once at the Divide, there are many forks. Keep taking the left forks going a little downhill. Park at the small metal sign that says Trail 518 Colorado Trail.
Time & Mileage to TH	1.5 hour; 16.48 miles
Recommended Vehicle	SUV with high clearance and 4-wheel drive to ascend CR 36. If you wish to hike through to Cataract Gulch TH, a suggestion is to hire a shuttle to drop you off at the top of CR 36 while leaving your own vehicle at Cataract Gulch TH. Contact The Sportsman Outdoors & Fly Shop for information on shuttle services.
Directions to Shuttle	From the junction of CR 36 and Cinnamon Pass Road, drive west another 3.7 miles to the signed Cataract Gulch TH just past Sherman Junction (Take the left fork at Sherman Junction).
Time & Mileage	Add 10 minutes; add 3.7 miles
Recommended Vehicle	Car; this is good gravel road.

High point/ Return 1

One of many waterfalls in Cataract Gulch

Summary

This is a very scenic section of the Colorado Trail. The route along the top is moderate and filled with a variety of scenic vistas including much of the San Juan Range between Silverton and Lake City. The view down Cataract Gulch and of Cataract Lake is superb. The toughest part of this hike is the descent through the lower half of Cataract Gulch which is steep and rocky.

Trail Description

Upper Cataract Gulch

The trail begins on the Continental Divide and at the Colorado Trail sign 518. Follow the dirt packed road downhill for just half a mile. Another trail sign marks the point where you leave this road on a single track off to the right ❷. Very soon, the trail rounds a corner for outstanding views of the beautiful Lost Trail Creek drainage. Descend easily and ascend moderately to the prominent saddle in the distance, all the while enjoying the solitude and beauty of this picturesque valley. At the saddle, ❸ gain inspiring views of the San Juan Range, Pole Creek drainage, the head of Cataract Gulch, and the Colorado Trail as it continues west. What a spot! Add seasonal wildflowers and it's hard to limit the photo shots. This makes a great return point if you drove your own vehicle to the Divide and don't want to shuttle. If continuing, cruise down the moderate trail to the head of Cataract Gulch where trails signs ❹ & ❺ give adequate directions. Stay on the trail west around the left side of the sharp cliff to find where the Colorado Trail descends towards Cataract Lake. From ❻ which is another beautiful photograph overlooking Cataract Lake, the trail shortly after disappears in the grassy tundra. New rock cairns and a marker post lead you across this nebulous section, not following Cataract Creek down the drainage to the left as it shows on the maps, but heading around to the right hand drainage. This is also why the distance is not 4.1 miles as the sign says but 4.9

30
LCVC
15.3
miles
P
9 End
To
hike 56
Sherman
Junction
10000
LCVC
1.6
miles
36
568
11200
8 Waterfall
Beaver
Ponds
7
Carson
12200
13000
13600
12800
54
1
Hike 5
3
Return 1
C
T
C
D
12200
11800
2
Cataract
Lake
6
4
5
N
787
822
12500
11500
10500
9500
0 mi
1.0
2.0
3.0
4.0
5.0
6.0
7.0
8.0
9.0
10.57
Road Key
Paved
Gravel
Suv/4wd
Trail Key
Gain in feet/mile
0-400 feet
400-600 feet
600-800 feet
800-1000 feet
1000+ feet
Other Trails
Motor Trails

View of Cataract Lake from CDT

miles to the TH. The trail undulates through this section to a point where the trail drops through this right hand drainage, twisting and turning through a very rocky section. Eventually, you come to ❼ which looks over the beaver ponds that show on the map. Shortly after, the trail crosses Cataract Creek for the first of 4 times in about .90 miles. There is a pretty waterfall at ❽. After this point, it is a 2 mile downhill trek through mostly dense spruce forest to the TH.

GPS	Mile	Latitude	Longitude	Elevation	Comment
1	0.00	37,51.343N	107,22.027W	12,352′	Start CDT trail at top of Wager Road.
2	0.53	37,50.956N	107,22.147W	12,216′	Marked junction: Leave road and begin Colorado Trail.
3	3.78	37,51.199N	107,25.194W	12,943′	High point: Views of Canby Mt and Handies Peak
4	4.86	37,50.800N	107,26.147W	12,466′	Marked junction: Go straight ahead on 787 Lost Creek Trail (non-motorized). Left is West Lost Creek Trail 822 which is motorized.
5	5.07	37,50.712N	107,26.301W	12,383′	Marked junction: Go straight ahead climbing a bit around left side of cliff. Left fork of trail is Pole Creek motorized trail.
6	5.67	37,50.828N	107,26.749W	12,216′	Marked junction: 2 signs: Go right following Cataract Trail 475. Sign says 4.1 miles to TH but it is really 4.9 miles as trail has been re-routed.
7	7.68	37,52.278N	107,26.297W	11,731′	Overlook beaver ponds
8	8.57	37,52.811N	107,26.201W	11,152′	Bottom of big waterfall
9	10.57	37,54.029N	107,25.987W	9,546′	Finish by crossing creek two more times; last time on new bridge.

Cataract Gulch Options

55a
55b
55c

Star Rating

☆☆☆

☆☆☆☆☆☆

Above the waterfall, Cataract Gulch opens to wildflower meadows.

55a: To Waterfall/ Return 1

Total Distance	4.0 miles RT
Difficulty Rating	Strenuous
Surface	Dirt packed about 1st mile; rocky after that
Gradient	Steep to Moderately Steep
Average Time	3.5 hours
Elevations	TH: 9,546; Highest: 11,152; Gain: +2,184
Map	Trails Illustrated: Telluride, Silverton, Ouray, Lake City

55b: To Lake Viewpoint/ Return 2

Total Distance	9.8 miles RT
Difficulty Rating	Very Strenuous due to distance and elevation gain
Surface	Dirt packed 1st mile; rocky next 2.5 miles
Gradient	Ranges from Steep to a little bit of Easy
Average Time	7 hours
Elevations	TH: 9,546; Highest: 12,216; Gain: +3,731

55c: To Continental Divide/ Return 3

Total Distance	11.0 miles RT
Difficulty Rating	Very Strenuous due to distance and elevation gain
Surface	Dirt packed 1st mile; rocky next 2.5 miles
Gradient	Ranges from Steep to a little bit of Easy
Average Time	8 hours
Elevations	TH: 9,546; Highest: 12,383; Gain: +4,073

Directions to TH	From LCVC, drive 2.7 miles south on Hwy 149 to the signed junction to Creede, Cinnamon Pass and San Cristobal Lake. Turn right on CR 30. From this point, drive 11.5 miles to signed Sherman Junction. Take the left fork and drive another 1.1 miles to the Cataract TH sign where there is an outhouse and ample parking.
Time & Mileage to TH	40 minutes; 15.3 miles
Recommended Car	Car. After passing Lake San Cristobal, it is good gravel road to the TH.

Cataract Lake from below

Main Cataract Gulch waterfall

Summary

Climb steeply through dense spruce forest to a pretty waterfall. It is still another 0.89 miles up before the forest opens to views both down and up valley. The upper basin is stunning but is very strenuous to get to. Check out our route Colorado Trail: Wager Road to Cataract TH for an easier way to see the upper basin and so much more of the Colorado Trail.

Trail Description

Hike through dense spruce forest most of the way to the waterfall ❷. There are good in season wildflowers in the understory as you ascend. The trail becomes steeper and more rocky the higher you go. After crossing the creek three more times above the waterfall, the trail leaves the dense forest behind and begins an ascent through a very rocky gulch. Part way up are some viewpoints of beaver ponds and the lush green valley in which they lie ❸. It is still another 0.50 miles before the trail reaches the upper basin with good views to the Continental Divide. Now the trail undulates across variable terrain; parts of the trail disappear so follow the marker posts and cairns. Cataract Lake is hidden from view, below the sharp cliffs. You cannot see it until you start to climb above it. There is a marker post ❹ at mile 4.9. You will have some good lake views shortly before that point. If you want to continue to the Continental Divide ❺, it is another steep climb but the views down valley and across the divide are stunning. This is one magnificent basin. If you

View behind approaching upper Cataract Gulch

want to enjoy a lot more of this part of the Colorado Trail, see the details for our route "Colorado Trail: Wager Road to Cataract TH. That total route is 10.57 miles with only 2047 feet elevation gain and over seven splendidly scenic miles to boot. A much easier route than this one!

GPS	Mile	Latitude	Longitude	Elevation	Comment
1	0.00	37,54.029N	107,25.987W	9,546′	Start Cataract Gulch.
2	2.00	37,52.811N	107,26.201W	11,152′	Return 1: Bottom of big waterfall
3	2.89	37,52.278N	107,26.297W	11,731′	Overlook beaver ponds
4	4.90	37,50.828N	107,26.749W	12,216′	Return 2: Great view of Cataract Lake. Marked junction: 2 signs: Go left uphill to Continental Divide and stunning lake view.
5	5.50	37,50.712N	107,26.301W	12,383′	Return 3: Colorado Trail on the Continental Divide. Marker post says Pole Creek Motorized Trail 787.

Upper Cataract Gulch

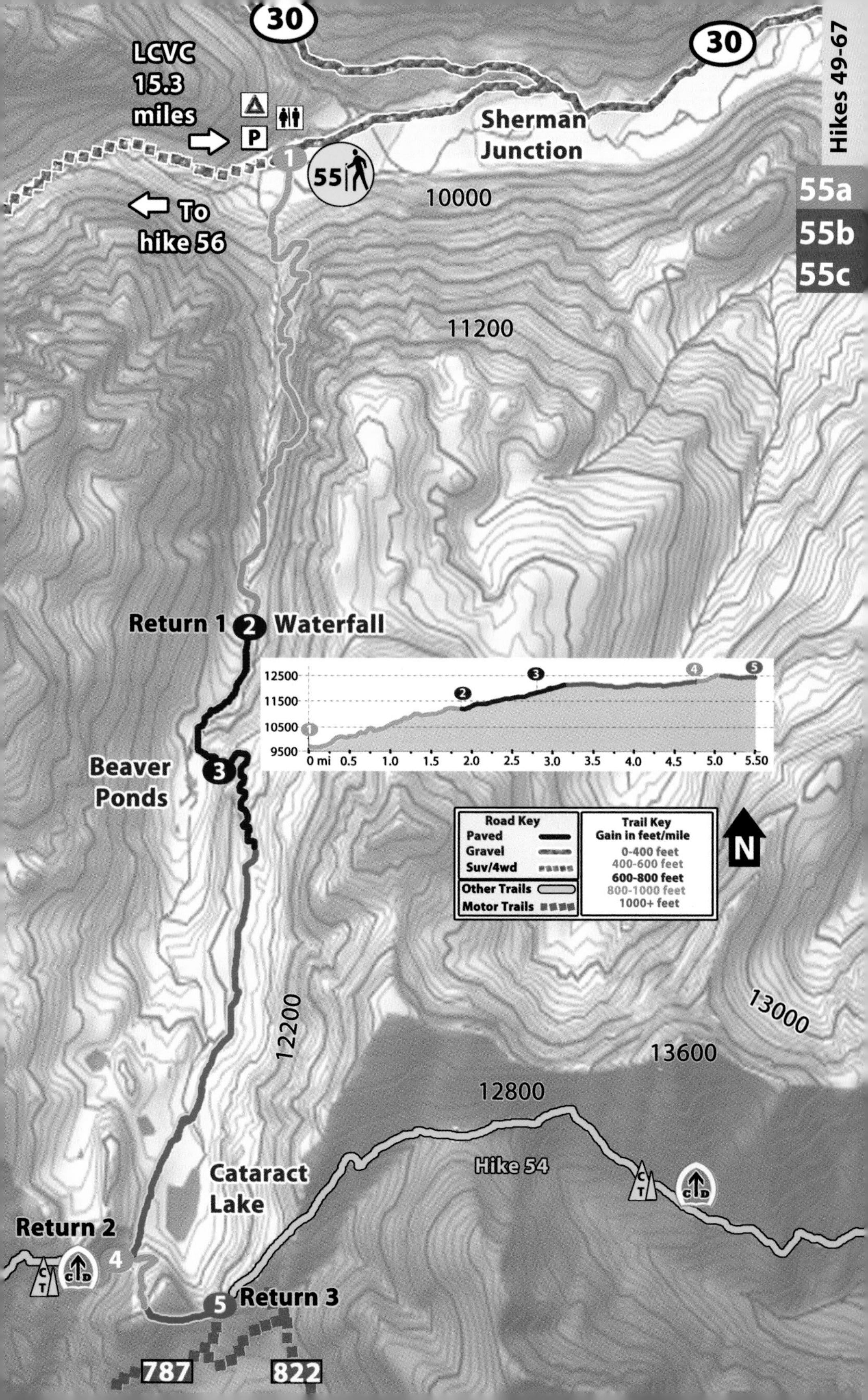
30
30
LCVC
15.3
miles
P
Sherman
Junction
1
55
10000
To
hike 56
11200
Return 1
2
Waterfall
12500
11500
10500
9500
0 mi
0.5
1.0
1.5
2.0
2.5
3.0
3.5
4.0
4.5
5.0
5.50
3
4
5
Beaver
Ponds
Road Key
Paved
Gravel
Suv/4wd
Other Trails
Motor Trails
Trail Key
Gain in feet/mile
0-400 feet
400-600 feet
600-800 feet
800-1000 feet
1000+ feet
N
12200
13000
13600
12800
Hike 54
Cataract
Lake
Return 2
Return 3
787
822

Cuba Gulch to Colorado Trail Options

Star Rating

☆☆☆

☆☆☆☆☆☆

Colorado Trail near end of this section

56a: To Colorado Trail/ Return 1

Total Distance	6.16 miles RT
Difficulty Rating	Moderately Strenuous
Surface	Mostly dirt packed with a few rocky sections; tundra
Gradient	Ranges from Very Steep to Easy
Average Time	4.25 hours
Elevations	TH: 10,681; Highest: 12,346; Gain: +1,889
Map	Trails Illustrated: Telluride, Silverton, Ouray, Lake City

56b: To High Point West on Colorado Trail/ Return 2

Total Distance	7.72 miles RT
Difficulty Rating	Moderately Strenuous
Surface	Easy packed dirt
Gradient	Ranges from Very Steep to Moderate
Average Time	5.25 hours
Elevations	Highest: 12,725; Gain: +2,308

	56c: To Cuba Gulch Sign West on Colorado Trail/ Return 3
Total Distance	8.96 miles RT
Difficulty Rating	Moderately Strenuous
Surface	Easy packed dirt
Gradient	Very Steep to Moderate
Average Time	6.5 hours
Elevations	Highest: 12,725; Gain: +2,547
Directions to TH	From LCVC, drive 2.7 miles south on Hwy 149 to the signed junction to Creede, Cinnamon Pass and San Cristobal Lake. Turn right on CR 30. From this point, drive 11.5 miles to signed Sherman Junction. Take the left fork. Drive another 4.4 miles to the trailhead on a rough 4x4 road.
Time & Mileage to TH	1 hour; 18.6 miles
Recommended Vehicle	SUV. High clearance is a must for the 4.4 mile section to the TH. The road is one lane with passing spots. Steep rocky ledges to drive over. Road is not exposed to cliffs.

Summary

Hike about two miles through intermittent spruce forest with a section following the deep Cuba Gulch gorge. The last mile is in open tundra in a wide, pretty valley. There is a confusion of trails as you near the open valley that may cause delay.

View back from high meadows

Trail Description

We wanted to make a circular trip, ascending Cuba Gulch East branch of the trail and returning down Cuba Gulch West branch of the trail as it shows on the Trails Illustrated Map and several more maps we researched. We hiked to ⑨ where a good sign said Cuba Gulch and pointed the way with an arrow. An obvious trail descended from there, but quickly disappeared. We only encountered scattered animal trails from there. The entire route down consisted of bashing through endless willow brush. The lower we went, the worse the willows. We do not recommend this route! A delightful alternative to our folly is to hike the Cuba Gulch East branch to the Colorado Trail as we have detailed. From there, hike out east or west on the Colorado trail as far as you wish; return the way you came. It is all above tree line and mostly moderate hiking. The views are wonderful.

There is a new sign at the trailhead on the south side of the parking area. Descend immediately and cross the creek on a log bridge. Quickly begin a moderately

It's a puzzle to get through a section of forest.

strenuous ascent. A massive blow down demonstrates the power of Mother Nature. At ❷ cross a wood bridge over Cuba Gulch Gorge. You will follow this very deep gorge for about a half mile. The trail winds through spruce forest with views of the surrounding canyon. At ❸, cross a small tributary creek. Just ahead is a fine camping spot. The trail continues SW up steeply between two creeks. At ❹ is an unsigned fork in the trail. Continue uphill. The trail to the right was to be our return route which never materialized. This is very steep climbing from here through thick forest. When you reach a place where you can see the open valley ascending to

Once clear of the willows, hike towards the V notch.

the saddle, animal and people trails get all mixed up and head in many confusing directions. The best advice we can offer is to stay in the trees. The best route is to keep the steep hillside close on your right shoulder rather than heading out into the open towards the stream. The willow brush is thick, tall and will lead you on animal trails in frustrating circles! Keep heading south. With luck, you will reach the grassy tundra at ❻. The trail is intermittent from there, but the destination, the low saddle to your right, is obvious.

Meet the Colorado Trail at ❼. Return from here, or hike east or west on this marvelous trail for as far as you wish. It is all above tree line and the vistas are wonderful.

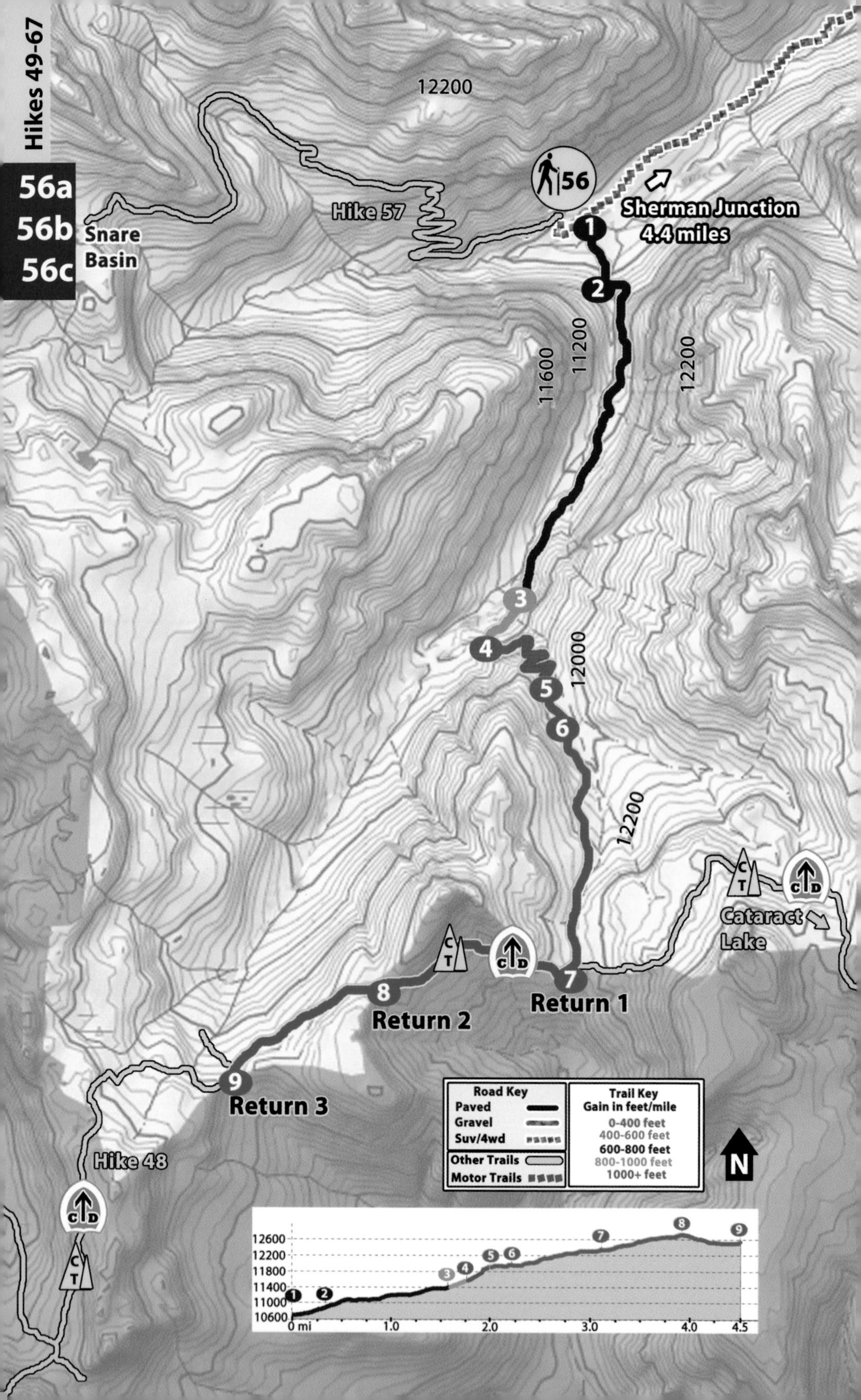
12200
56
Hike 57
Snare
Basin
Sherman Junction
4.4 miles
11600
11200
12200
12000
12200
Cataract
Lake
Return 1
Return 2
Return 3
Hike 48
Road Key
Paved
Gravel
Suv/4wd
Other Trails
Motor Trails
Trail Key
Gain in feet/mile
0-400 feet
400-600 feet
600-800 feet
800-1000 feet
1000+ feet
N
12600
12200
11800
11400
11000
10600
0 mi
1.0
2.0
3.0
4.0
4.5

Cuba Gulch Trail meets the Colorado Trail

GPS	Mile	Latitude	Longitude	Elevation	Comment
1	0.00	37,53.015N	107,29.144W	10,681′	Start Cuba Gulch Trail up the east branch.
2	0.30	37,52.821N	107,29.038W	10,842′	Cross deep gorge on wood bridge.
3	1.60	37,51.878N	107,29.435W	11,273′	Cross tributary creek; nice campsite. Continue SW on trail climbing between two streams.. Cross right hand stream.
4	1.77	37,51.746N	107,29.500W	11,499′	Trail forks; no signs. Go left uphill, not right on the flat. Begin very steep climb.
5	1.96	37,51.695N	107,29.347W	11,867′	Trail becomes very confusing. Best advice is to stay in trees. Do not go out into clearing yet as willows are too thick.
6	2.21	37,51.493N	107,29.243W	11,986′	Finally out of the willows hiking on grassy tundra. Head for the right hand saddle.
7	3.08	37,50.749N	107,29.195W	12,346′	Return 1: Meet the Colorado Trail. Hike in either direction for wonderful vistas. Must climb from saddle either way you go. Hike as far as you wish.
8	3.86	37,50.705N	107,29.982W	12,725′	High point on Colorado Trail west from Cuba Gulch
9	4.48	37,50.444N	107,30.512W	12,530′	Signed junction: Cuba Gulch. This good trail quits very quickly. There is no good trail down this gulch. Severe willow bashing. Return 3

Snare Basin

Star Rating

☆☆☆☆☆

57a

57b

57a: To Lower basin/ Return 1

Total Distance	5.1 miles RT
Difficulty Rating	Moderate
Surface	Switchbacks are through broken spree from a massive landslide
Gradient	Average is moderate with some easier and some steeper sections
Average Time	4 hours
Elevations	TH: 10,669; Highest: 11,965; Gain: +1,674
Map	Trails Illustrated #141: Telluride, Silverton, Ouray, Lake City

Snare Creek drainage from switchback section

57b: To Snare Basin/ Return 2

Total Distance	8.00 miles RT
Difficulty Rating	Moderately Strenuous
Surface	Switchbacks are through broken spree from a massive landslide; remainder is on packed rock
Gradient	Average is moderate with some easier and some steeper sections
Average Time	5 hours
Elevations	TH: 10,669; Highest: 12,450; Gain: +2,500

Directions to TH	From LCVC, drive 2.7 miles south on Hwy 149 to the signed junction to Creede, Cinnamon Pass and San Cristobal Lake. Turn right on CR 30. From this point, drive 11.5 miles to signed Sherman Junction. Take the left fork. Drive another 4.4 miles to the trailhead on a rough 4x4 road.
Time & Mileage to TH	1.5 hour; 18.6 miles
Recommended Vehicle	SUV. High clearance is a must for the 4.4 mile section to the TH. The road is one lane with passing spots. Steep rocky ledges to drive over. Road is not exposed to cliffs.

Snare Basin is on other side of the peak

Summary

This is a most beautiful hike to a high basin surrounded by dramatic peaks. Once in the basin, wander around the various lakes or find your own route to the high ridge. The trail is particularly pretty in the fall; the basin is lush and green in the summer.

Trail Description

From the parking area, hike up the wide gravel road where the sign says, "Road Closed". You can start up the very steep direct route uphill, or take the easier switchback to the same point. The route follows this road all the way to Snare Basin. Once above the first long switchback, you begin to have wonderful views up and down valley. The switchbacks have been cut through a massive rock slide

Great fall color along the switchbacks

Cabin just before entering lower basin

The long traverse before Snare Basin. Photo by Rozanne Evans

and this section is particularly rocky. There are beautiful aspens to photograph in every direction. Climb just a bit more above the cabin at ❷ and you will be in a big, barren basin. You can see the trail climbing around the mountain to your left. This is a good return point for a shorter hike ❸. The views have been excellent. To continue onward, there are some mining roads to confuse the issue at ❹ and ❺, but once you know where the trail climbs around the mountain to your left, you can determine easily how to get there. After rounding that mountain, there is still a little headwall to climb before reaching the first lake. Snare Basin is huge and quite beautiful. Worthy of exploration.

GPS	Mile	Latitude	Longitude	Elevation	Comment
1	0.00	37,53.015N	107,29.134W	10,669′	Start Snare Basin at end of Cuba Gulch Rd.
2	2.38	37,53.187N	107,30.231W	11,818′	Cabin
3	2.55	37,53.247N	107,30.291W	11,965′	Enter lower basin/ Return 1.
4	2.71	37,53.317N	107,30.420W	12,000′	Cairn marks intersection.
5	2.90	37,53.388N	107,30.601W	12,101′	Unmarked intersection
6	4.00	37,53.011N	107,31.083W	12,450′	First of the Snare Basin Lakes/ Return 2

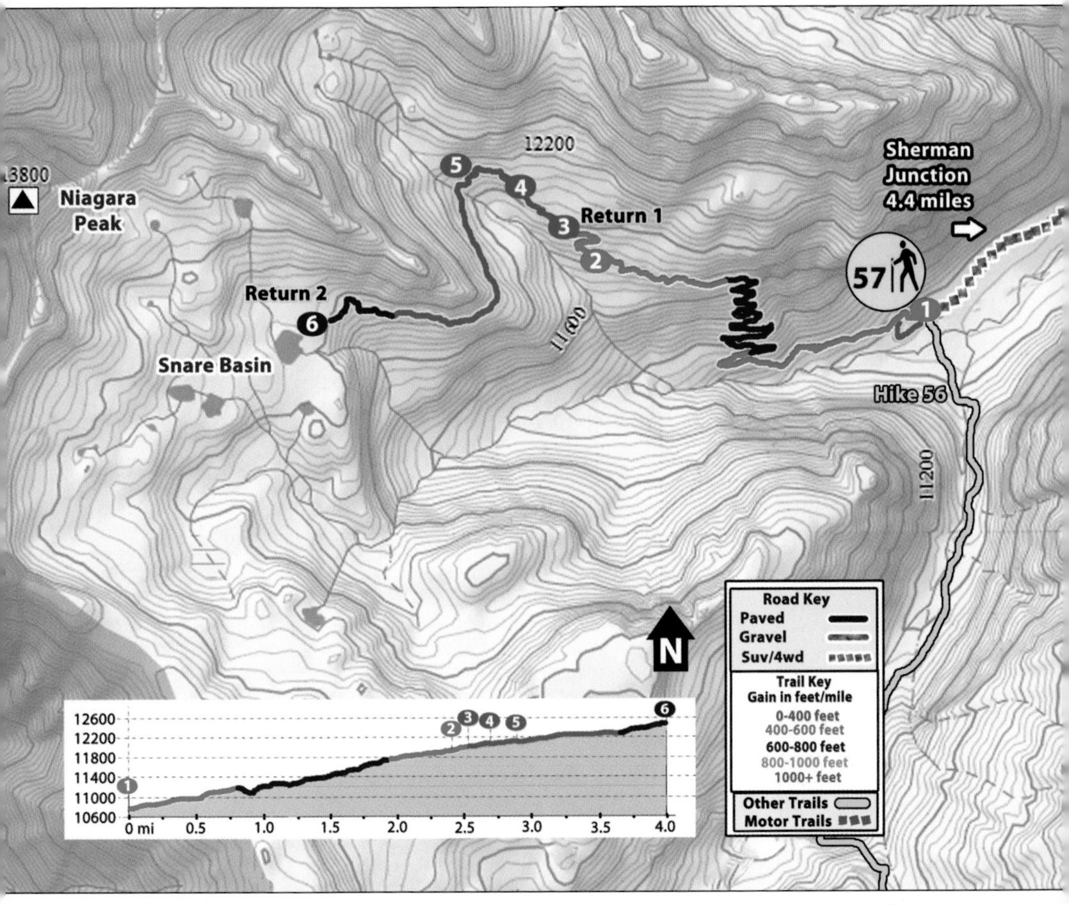

Silver Creek Trail to Redcloud & Sunshine Peaks

Star Rating

☆☆☆☆☆

58a: To Redcloud Peak/ Return 1

Total Distance	9.26 miles RT
Difficulty Rating	Very Strenuous
Surface	Varies from packed dirt to large broken rock
Gradient	Moderately Steep to Very Steep
Average Time	6.25 hours
Elevations	TH: 10,392; Highest: 14,034; Gain: +3,994
Map	Trails Illustrated Telluride, Silverton, Ouray, Lake City

58b: To Sunshine Peak/ Return 2

Total Distance	12.0 miles RT
Difficulty Rating	Very Strenuous
Surface	Mostly broken rock from Redcloud to Sunshine
Gradient	Varies from Easy to Very Steep from Redcloud to Sunshine
Average Time	8.25 hours
Elevations	TH: 14,034; Highest: 14,034; Gain: 5,287

View from Redcloud to Sunshine

Directions to TH	From LCVC, drive south 2.7 miles on Hwy 149 towards Creede. At the Cinnamon Pass & Creede junction, take the right fork to Cinnamon Pass on CR 30 and drive 11.5 miles to the signed Sherman Junction. Take the right fork and drive another 3.8 miles to the signed Silver Creek TH.
Time & Mileage to TH	50 minutes; 18 miles
Recommended Vehicle	SUV. High clearance is important. 4x4 not necessary

Summary

Redcloud and Sunshine are two famous 14er's that are often hiked together. These two peaks together are about 12 miles RT and over 5000 feet total elevation gain. This is no simply undertaking! Plan an early start.

Trail Description

Hike for almost 1 mile through mixed conifer forest on a good packed dirt trail. Leaving the forest, the trail cuts through high brush before coming to a 1 mile

Lower section of trail follows Silver Creek

section of rock slides along side the stream. The big broken rock makes for more difficult walking in our opinion. When you reach the bench area at ❷, the canyon really opens up and the trail is easy walking again. This is a beautiful meadow surrounded by soaring rock walls. At the saddle ❸, you can see a trail going up due east (left). This is a route around the ridges of several 13ers that we did not hike.

View of 13ers from Redcloud flank

See my observations about this trail on the Cooper Creek description. Redcloud trail is due west (right) from the saddle and now begins a very steep and somewhat slippery ascent to the peak. This is the most difficult section of the entire route. Once on the summit, it is easy to see the trail to Sunshine. Remember that there is about a 325 foot elevation drop between Redcloud and Sunshine that you must hike back up to return to the trailhead.

GPS	Mile	Latitude	Longitude	Elevation	Comment
1	0.00	37,56.214N	107,27.649W	10,392′	Start Redcloud at Silver Creek TH.
2	2.43	37,57.209N	107,25.609W	12,036′	Bench
3	3.73	37,56.769N	107,24.881W	13,043′	Saddle
4	4.63	37,56.482N	107,25.315W	14,034′	Redcloud Peak/ Return 1
5	6.00	37,55.364N	107,25.531W	14,001′	Sunshine Peak/ Return 2

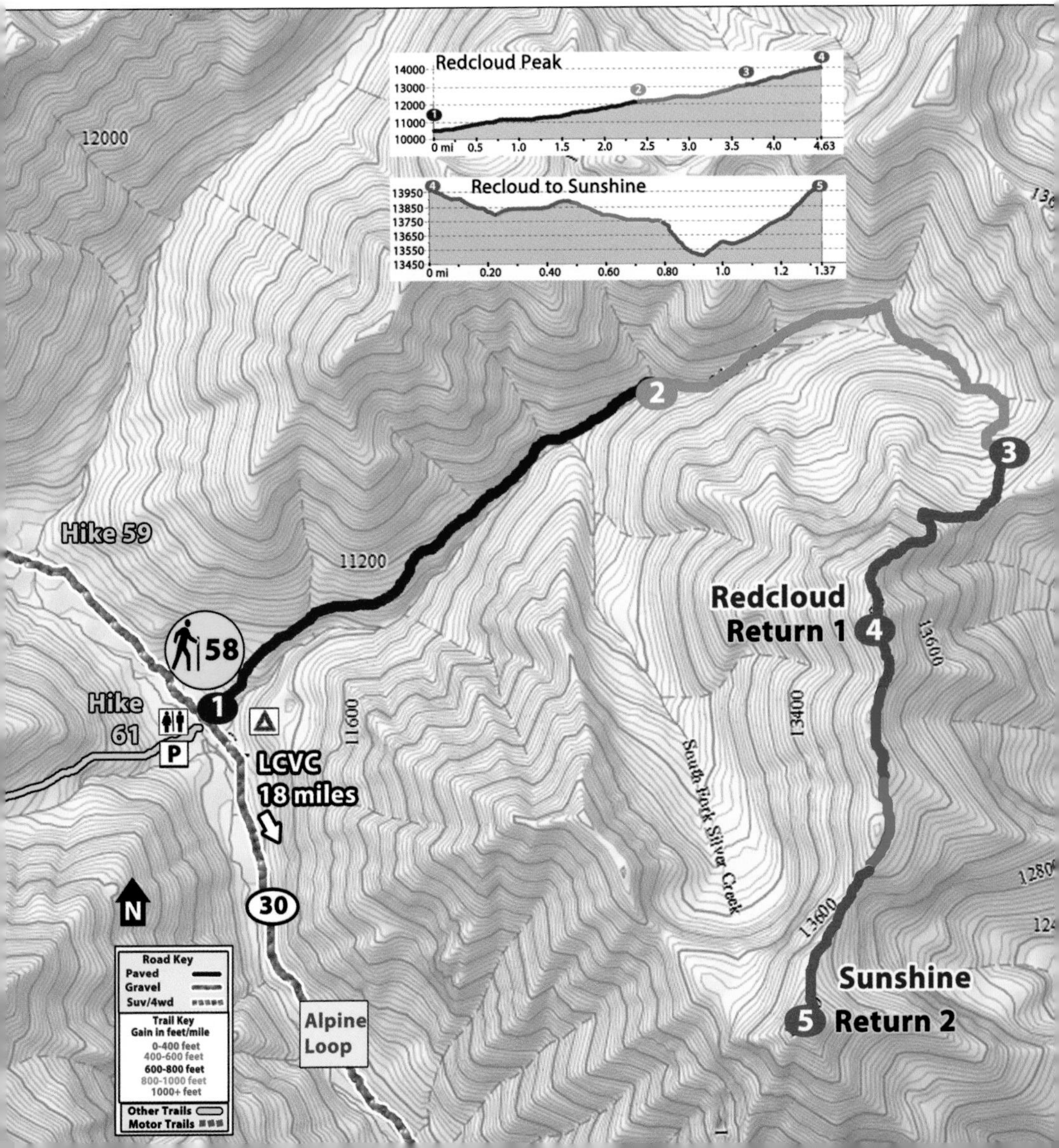

Cooper Creek Trail Options

59a
59b
59c

Star Rating
☆☆☆☆☆

Cooper Lake

59a: To 2nd Creek Crossing/ Return 1

Total Distance	4.94 miles RT
Difficulty Rating	Moderate
Surface	Mostly packed dirt with small rocks
Gradient	Moderately Steep to Easy
Average Time	3.5 hours
Elevations	TH: 10,596; Highest: 11,576; Gain: +1,407
Map	Trails Illustrated: Telluride, Silverton, Ouray, Lake City

59b: To High Basin/ Return 2

Total Distance	6.52 miles RT
Difficulty Rating	Moderately Strenuous
Surface	Mostly packed dirt with small rocks to Return 1; more rocky to basin
Gradient	Ranges from Easy to Steep
Average Time	4.5 hours
Elevations	TH: 10,596; Highest: 12,295; Gain: +2,104

59c: To Lake

Total Distance	7.58
Difficulty Rating	Strenuous
Surface	The climb from Basin to Lake is extremely difficult hard packed dirt. We do not recommend following the trail. See our comments below.
Gradient	From Basin to Lake is Extremely Steep
Average Time	6 hours
Elevations	TH: 10,596; Highest: 12,731; Gain: +2,648
Directions to TH	From LCVC, drive south 2.7 miles on Hwy 149 towards Creede. At the Cinnamon Pass & Creede junction, take the right fork to Cinnamon Pass CR 30 and drive 11.5 miles to the signed Sherman Junction. Take the right fork and drive another 4.7 miles to the signed Cooper Creek TH.
Time & Mileage to TH	1 hour; 18.9 miles
Recommended Vehicle	SUV. High clearance is important. 4x4 not necessary

View up valley from lower meadows

Summary

What a beautiful valley! Most folks climb the 14ers so you may have this trail to yourself. I did! Hike about 1 mile in beautiful spruce forest with many vistas of soaring peaks all around. Enter a wide green valley and hike an easy contour. Look frequently behind for in your face views of Handies and Whitecross Mountain. Climb to a picturesque basin with sheer walls to frame it. The Lake is stunning, but the trail is exceptionally difficult this last stretch.

Trail Description

Cooper Creek Trail starts right out with splendid views of Redcloud, Whitecross Mountain and numerous unnamed peaks. Hike across the flats before turning up the drainage. It ascends moderately steeply for the first mile through lovely spruce forest with many young trees. Constantly look around as various peaks seem to be in view most of the time, especially Whitecross Mountain which looms behind you as you hike. When you reach ❷, the valley opens and from here there are constant views up and down valley. The trail mellows into an easy saunter across green meadows; Cooper Creek is always nearby. If you want an easy hike for the day, turn around at ❸, before the trail begins a steep climb to the high basin. You will have enjoyed wonderful views of Handies, Whitecross Mountain, the high 13ers and so much more by this point. The climb up to the high basin ❹ opens up more splendid views of the continuing valley below and the peaks above. The basin itself is captured by straight up walls of rock. Most impressive. (Note the steep trails to the north. We have read it is possible to climb to the high 13er peaks via these trails and hike the ridges to Redcloud Peak. My observation? These trails look far too steep and dangerous to negotiate safely.) To get to Cooper Lake is difficult enough. The visible trail is extremely steep and too slippery to get any footholds. The hard packed dirt covered with small rocks is like climbing on ball bearings. We do not recommend following this trail. Instead, look to the drainage to the right of the trail. There is a grassy strip between the rock sections. The foot holds are easier to find and more stable if you climb up through the grass and stay off the rocky packed sections. Looking up, there is an obvious notch ❺ near the top of the stream drainage. Again, the visible trail is slick, narrow and on a sidehill. We crossed to the notch below the existing trail in softer gravel.

Approaching the high basin and Return 2 before climbing to Lake

Once above the notch, the battle is won. Footing is now stable again. It is a short jaunt to the lake ❻ which is most impressive.

Whitecross Mt with Handies Peak off to the left

View down valley from Return 1

GPS	Mile	Latitude	Longitude	Elevation	Comment
1	0.00	37,56.625N	107,28.305W	10,596′	Start Cooper Creek.
2	1.26	37,57.391N	107,27.782W	11,153′	Cross Cooper Creek for 1st time. Wet shoes maybe in high runoff
3	2.47	37,58.084N	107,26.960W	11,576′	Return 1: Cross Cooper Creek 2nd time.
4	3.26	37,58.655N	107,26.819W	12,295′	Return 2: Basin 1
5	3.54	37,58.606N	107,27.090W	12,645′	The notch below Cooper Lake
6	3.79	37,58.646N	107,27.325W	12,731′	Cooper Lake

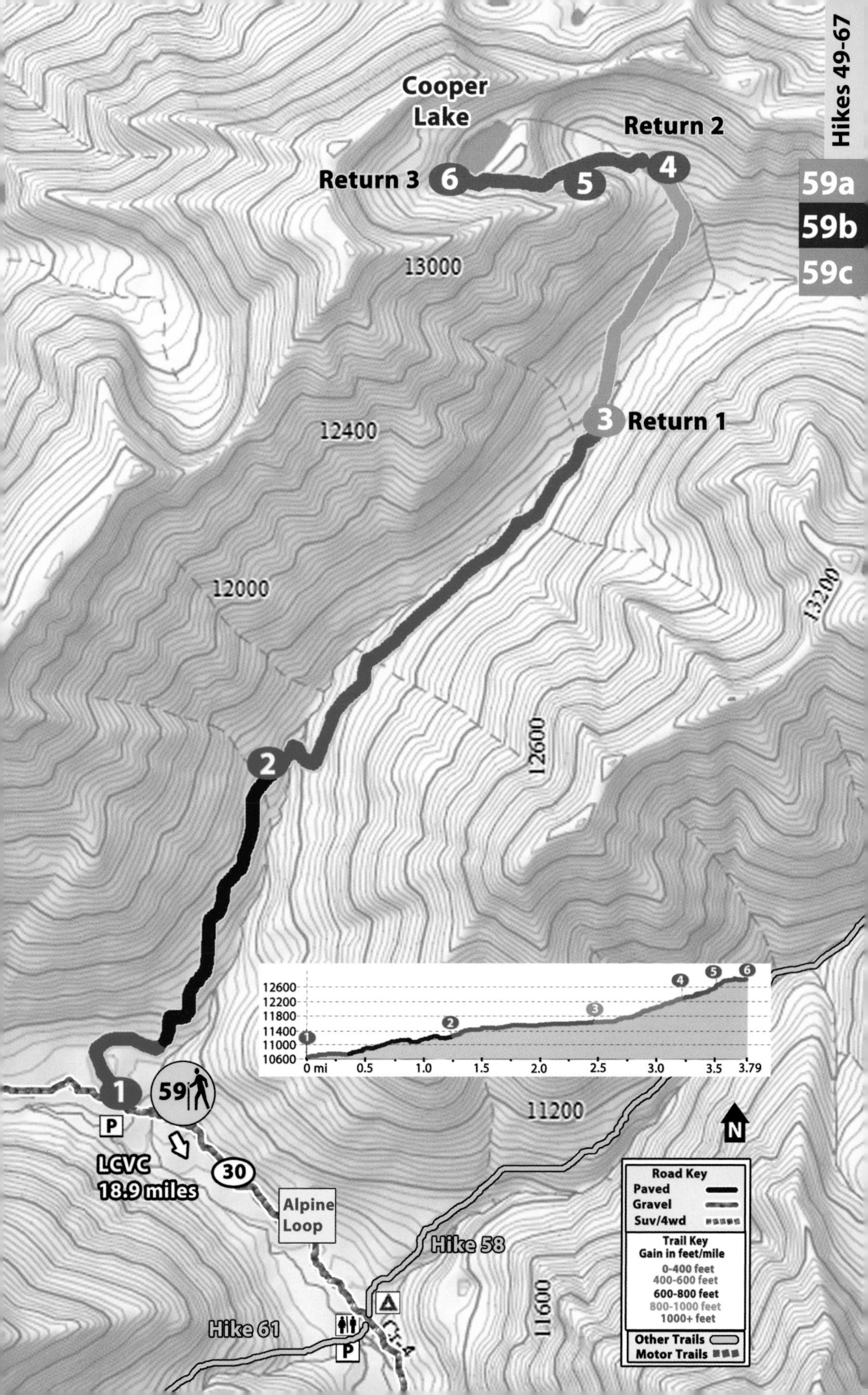
Cooper Lake
Return 2
Return 3
Return 1
13000
12400
12000
13200
12600
11200
11600
12600
12200
11800
11400
11000
10600
0 mi
0.5
1.0
1.5
2.0
2.5
3.0
3.5
3.79
59
LCVC
18.9 miles
30
Alpine Loop
Hike 58
Hike 61
CT-4
N
Road Key
Paved
Gravel
Suv/4wd
Trail Key
Gain in feet/mile
0-400 feet
400-600 feet
600-800 feet
800-1000 feet
1000+ feet
Other Trails
Motor Trails

American Basin

Star Rating

☆☆☆☆☆☆

Sunrise in American Basin. Photos by Rozanne Evans

Total Distance	1.80 miles RT
Difficulty Rating	Moderate
Surface	4x4 rocky road
Gradient	Moderate
Average Time	1.5 hours plus photo time!
Elevations	TH: 11,241; Highest: 11,647; Gain: +424
Directions to TH	From LCVC, drive south 2.7 miles on Hwy 149 towards Creede. At the Cinnamon Pass & Creede junction, take the right fork to Cinnamon Pass on CR 30 and drive 11.5 miles to the signed Sherman Junction. Take the right fork and drive another 7.5 miles to the signed turnoff to American Basin. There is limited parking near the intersection as well as a little ways up the road. This description follows the road to the trailhead for Handies Peak.
Time & Mileage to TH	1 hour 15 minutes; 21.5 miles
Recommended Vehicle	SUV. High clearance is the issue here. After Sherman Junction, the road steadily increases in rocky conditions. More rocky ledges to negotiate after Grizzly Gulch TH.

Summary

Hike the most famous wildflower trail in Lake City area. This 4x4 road provides a moderate trail through a spectacular basin thick with splendid displays of seasonal flowers, tumbling creeks and rocky peaks.

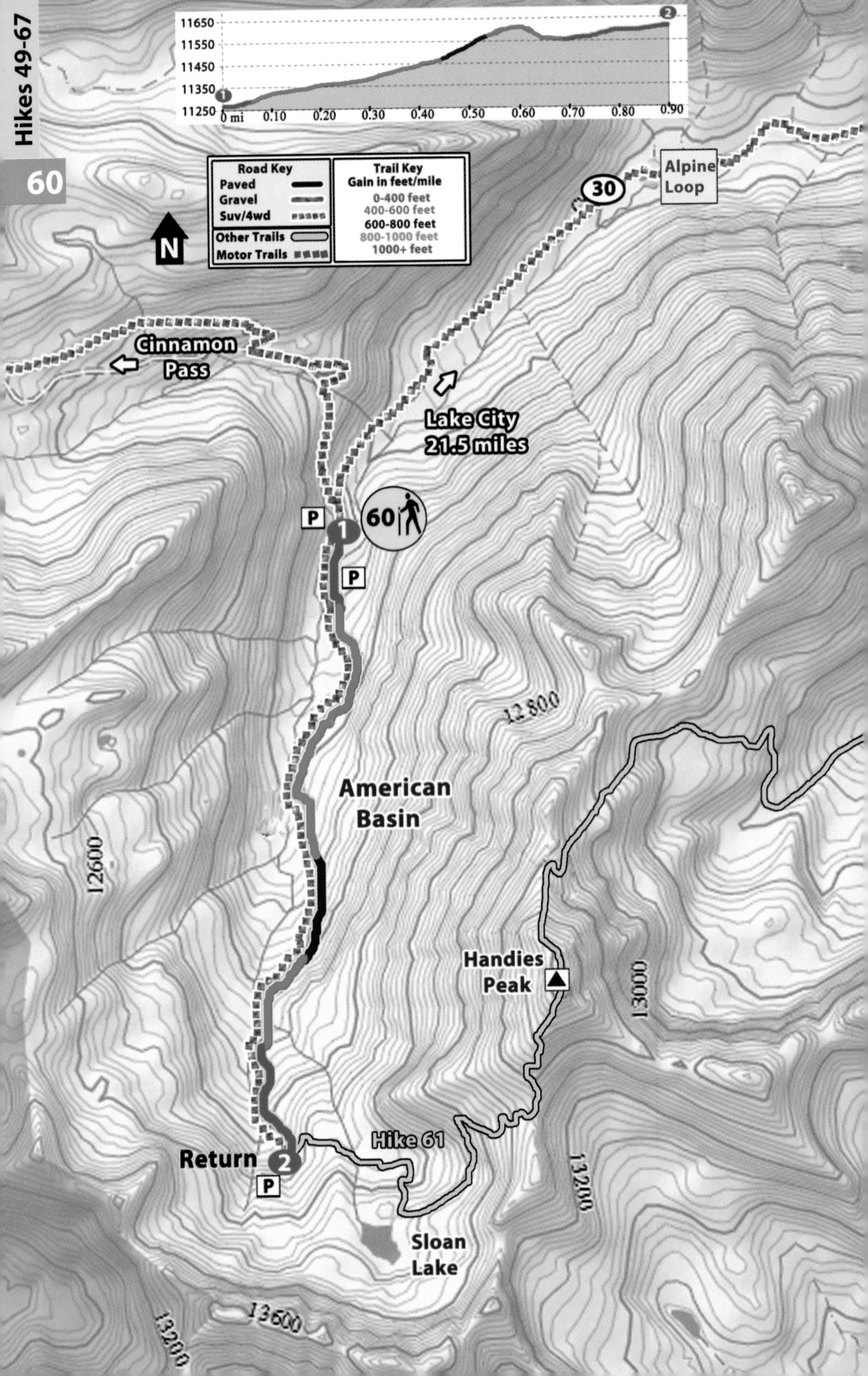
11650
11550
11450
11350
11250
0 mi
0.10
0.20
0.30
0.40
0.50
0.60
0.70
0.80
0.90
Road Key
Paved
Gravel
Suv/4wd
Other Trails
Motor Trails
Trail Key
Gain in feet/mile
0-400 feet
400-600 feet
600-800 feet
800-1000 feet
1000+ feet
N
30
Alpine Loop
Cinnamon Pass
Lake City 21.5 miles
60
American Basin
12800
12600
Handies Peak
13000
Hike 61
Return
Sloan Lake
13200
13600
13200

Lower American Basin. Starting on the trail to Handies Peak.

Trail Description

This is the most visited hike in the area. American Basin is renowned for its prolific wildflower display. There are many photographic opportunities as the basin is flanked by dramatic peaks. Be aware that in early morning light, the basin itself is in shade and photos of the peaks point into the rising sun. Afternoon shots are best. Hike as far as you wish. It is 0.90 miles from the intersection to Handies TH.

GPS	Mile	Latitude	Longitude	Elevation	Comment
1	0.00	37,55.876N	107,30.861W	11,241′	Start at junction of Cinnamon Pass Road and American Basin Road.
2	0.90	37,55.203N	107,30.992W	11,647′	Return at TH parking lot for Handies Peak.

Handies Peak TH to Grizzly Gulch TH Options

Star Rating

☆☆☆☆☆☆

View of American Basin from Handies Peak

61a: Grouse Gulch Saddle

Total Distance	3.54 miles RT
Difficulty Rating	Moderately Strenuous
Surface	Small broken rock
Gradient	Ranges from Easy to Very Steep
Average Time	2.5 hours
Elevations	TH: 11,647; Highest: 13,023; Gain: +1,935
Map	Trails Illustrated: Telluride, Silverton, Ouray, Lake City

Directions to TH

From LCVC, drive south 2.7 miles on Hwy 149 towards Creede. At the Cinnamon Pass & Creede junction, take the right fork to Cinnamon Pass on CR 30 and drive 11.5 miles to the signed Sherman Junction. Take the right fork and drive another 3.8 miles to the signed Grizzly Gulch TH and leave a shuttle vehicle if hiking through. Continue on yet another 3.5 miles to the signed turnoff to American Basin. Drive American Basin Road 0.90 miles to the signed TH for Handies Peak.

Time & Mileage to TH

1 hour 15 minutes; 22.4 miles

Recommended Vehicle

SUV. High clearance is the issue here. After Sherman Junction, the road steadily increases in rocky conditions. More rocky ledges to negotiate after Grizzly Gulch TH. At the turnoff to American Basin, a sign recommends 4x4 capability, but if you had an easy time to this point, the drive to the Handies TH is not really much worse.

61b: to Sloan Lake/ Return 1

Total Distance	3.06 miles RT
Difficulty Rating	Moderately Strenuous
Surface	Mostly small broken rock
Gradient	Ranges from Moderately Steep to Steep
Average Time	2.25 hours
Elevations	TH: 11,647; Highest: 12,918; Gain: +1,334

View north of Grizzly Gulch from Handies Peak

61c: to Handies Peak/ Return 2

Total Distance	5.40 miles RT
Difficulty Rating	Strenuous
Surface	Mostly small broken rock
Gradient	Ranges from Moderately Steep to Very Steep
Average Time	4 hours
Elevations	TH: 11,647; Highest: 14,048; Gain: +2,498

61d: to Grizzly Gulch TH

Total Distance	6.62 miles to shuttle
Difficulty Rating	Strenuous
Surface	Mostly small broken rock. Very rocky on Grizzly Gulch side
Gradient	Ranges from Moderately Steep to Very Steep
Average Time	6 hours
Elevations	TH: 11,647; Highest: 14,048; Gain: + 2,498; Loss: -3,689

Summary

This trail offers many options, from a moderate short hike through magnificent wildflowers, to a climb to a saddle overlooking the Silverton side, to a stunning high alpine Lake, a 14,048 foot peak, an amazing ridge walk, a 13,542 foot peak, a gulch rich in greenery surrounded by towering peaks and a side trip to another alpine lake. Choose your destination based on desire and fitness. Go out & back or hike all the way through for a shuttle. Reverse our directions for the ultimate challenge.

Trail Description

From the TH sign, the trail climbs moderately steeply. At an unmarked junction about 0.94 miles up, just before the trail climbs steeply up a set of switchbacks, notice a faint trail and some small cairns off to your right ❷. This is the Grouse Gulch Trail that comes from the Silverton side. It is a steep climb to the saddle (2a) that you can easily spot, but much easier than the climb to Handies Peak. If you are looking for a less strenuous and shorter outing, try this option. Continuing on the trail to Handies, ascend the switchbacks above ❷; the trail levels for a while through a beautiful flower filled basin and a meandering creek. Great photo ops. It is one more series of steep switchbacks to reach Sloan Lake ❸. This is Return 1. Towering cliffs of naked rock are everywhere. Now look north and see the formidable task ahead. Handies Peak is almost hidden by the flanking rock walls. First the trail drops through a landslide, then climbs relentlessly to Handies Saddle ❹. Now you can see down the Grizzly Gulch side. What a view! It is 0.51 more miles to the peak ❺. The surface is loose rock on hard packed dirt. The gradient is 29%, over 1000 feet per mile. With my emphysema, it took me 1 hour to reach the top from the saddle. Never have I stood in such a magnificent spot. Colorado high country at its best!

Return from here or start the amazing descent into Grizzly Gulch if you provided for a shuttle. From the peak, spot the trail continuing due north along the ridge. Quickly it drops, heading directly towards Whitecross Mountain. For those with extraordinary energy, cross the saddle and climb Whitecross to 13,542 before continuing the descent into Grizzly Gulch. How green and verdant this valley is compared to the stark rock walls of the American Basin side. Be sure to look back at Handies as you descend. From this viewpoint, Handies appears formidable. As you descend, just after you spot Grizzly Lake in the distance, keep a sharp lookout for a trail heading off to your right ❻. We did not hike this but presumed it leads to the lake. It is a long, rocky, steep descent all the way to Grizzly TH (4.2 miles and minus 3689 feet from Handies Peak). If you prefer hiking steeply up, rather than down, reverse our notes and hike this beautiful drainage all the way through or as far as you wish.

GPS	Mile	Latitude	Longitude	Elevation	Comment
1	0.00	37,55.203N	107,30.992W	11,647′	TH parking lot for Handies Peak
2	0.94	37,54.488N	107,31.074W	12,415′	Unmarked junction; notice trail to Grouse Gulch Saddle at 2a.
3	1.53	37,54.294N	107,30.709W	12,918′	Return 1; Sloan Lake
4	2.21	37,54.523N	107,30.339W	13,457′	Handies Saddle
5	2.70	37,54.781N	107,30.268W	14,048′	Handies Peak
6	4.92	37,55.478N	107,29.034W	11,793′	Enter forest to end of trail/optional route to Grizzly Lake; 1.0 miles RT additional.
7	6.62	37,56.217N	107,27.659W	10,376′	End at Grizzly Gulch TH

Optional route to Grouse Saddle as seen from Handies Trail

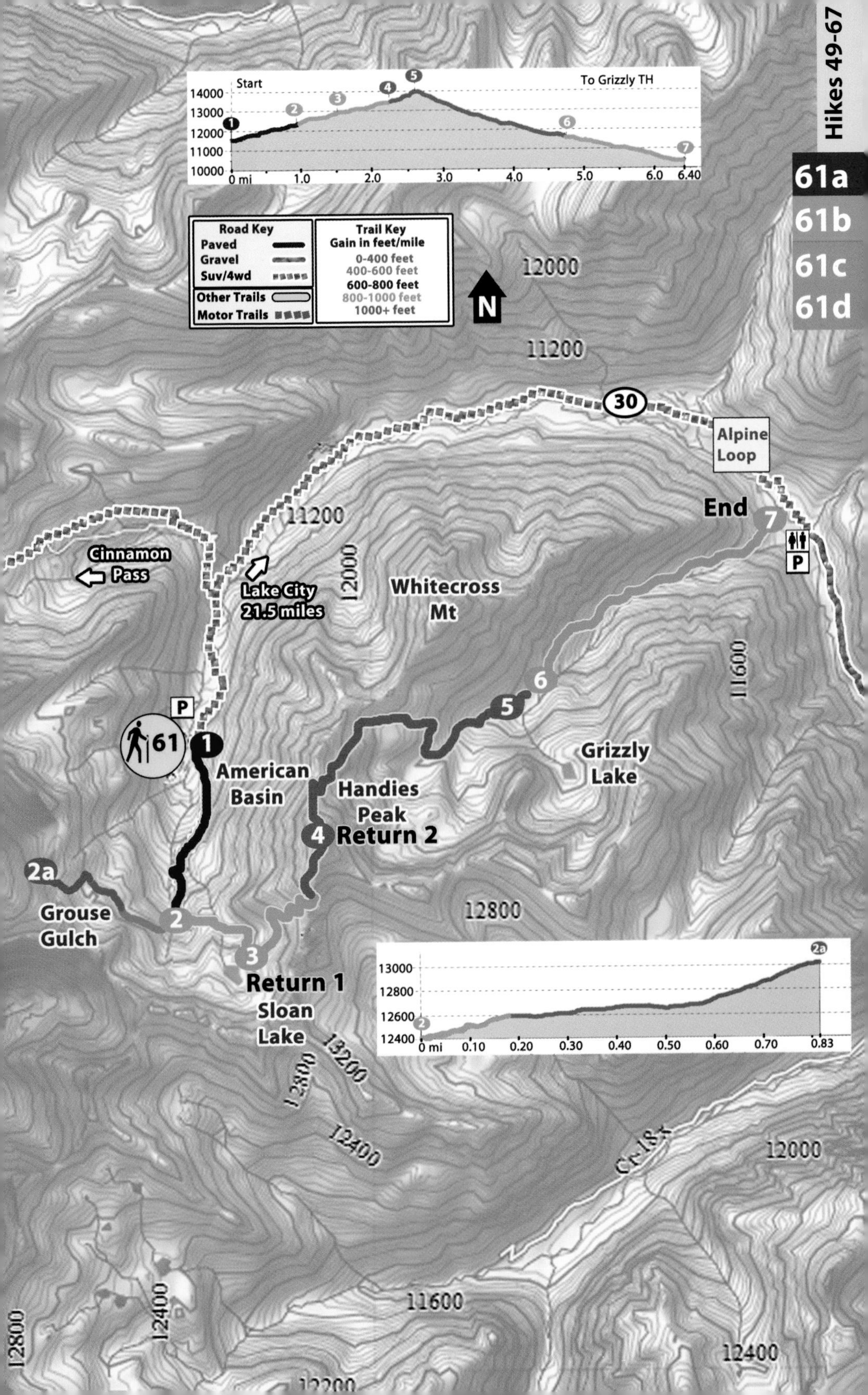
Start
To Grizzly TH
14000
13000
12000
11000
10000
0 mi
1.0
2.0
3.0
4.0
5.0
6.0
6.40
Road Key
Paved
Gravel
Suv/4wd
Other Trails
Motor Trails
Trail Key
Gain in feet/mile
0-400 feet
400-600 feet
600-800 feet
800-1000 feet
1000+ feet
N
12000
11200
30
Alpine Loop
End
Cinnamon Pass
Lake City 21.5 miles
11200
12000
Whitecross Mt
11600
61
American Basin
Handies Peak
Return 2
Grizzly Lake
2a
Grouse Gulch
12800
Return 1
Sloan Lake
13000
12800
12600
12400
0 mi
0.10
0.20
0.30
0.40
0.50
0.60
0.70
0.83
13200
12800
12400
12000
11600
12400
12800
12400

Uncompahgre Peak Options

Star Rating

☆☆☆☆☆

Standing on the peak. Photo by Rozanne Evans

62a:To Viewpoint/ Return 1

Total Distance	4.74 miles RT
Difficulty Rating	Moderate
Surface	Mostly packed dirt with some rocky sections
Gradient	Moderate to Moderately Steep
Average Time	3 hours
Elevations	TH: 11,425; Highest: 12,939; Gain: +1,545
Map	Trails Illustrated: Telluride, Silverton, Ouray, Lake City

62b:To Rock Climb/ Return 2

Total Distance	6.60 miles RT
Difficulty Rating	Moderately Strenuous
Surface	Becomes more rocky after Viewpoint
Gradient	Changes to Steep after Viewpoint
Average Time	4.5 hours
Elevations	TH: 11,425; Highest: 13,771; Gain: +2,378

62c:To Peak/ Return 3

Total Distance	7.30 miles RT
Difficulty Rating	Strenuous
Surface	Very difficult rock debris near the top
Gradient	Becomes very steep last 0.35 miles
Average Time	6 hours
Elevations	TH: 11,425; Highest: 14,309; Gain: +2,988

Directions to TH	From the middle of Lake City on Hwy 149, turn north on 2nd St. Signs say to Engineer Pass. Drive 5.2 miles to the signed Nellie Creek turnoff. From this point, drive another 4.1 miles to the signed TH.
Time & Mileage to TH	1 hour; 9.3 miles
Recommended Vehicle	SUV with high clearance and 4x4. This is a very rocky, bumpy, one lane road with few passing spots.

Stunning views of the peak from lower trail

Summary

This is our favorite peak for scenic beauty all around; even if you do not want to climb to the summit, hike this trail to one of our suggested return points. The trail begins moderately and climbs steeper as you progress. At Return 1, you will have gained wonderful views into Matterhorn Basin; by Return 2 you will see several dramatic views through the cliffs of Uncompahgre's flank to Wetterhorn and Matterhorn Peaks.

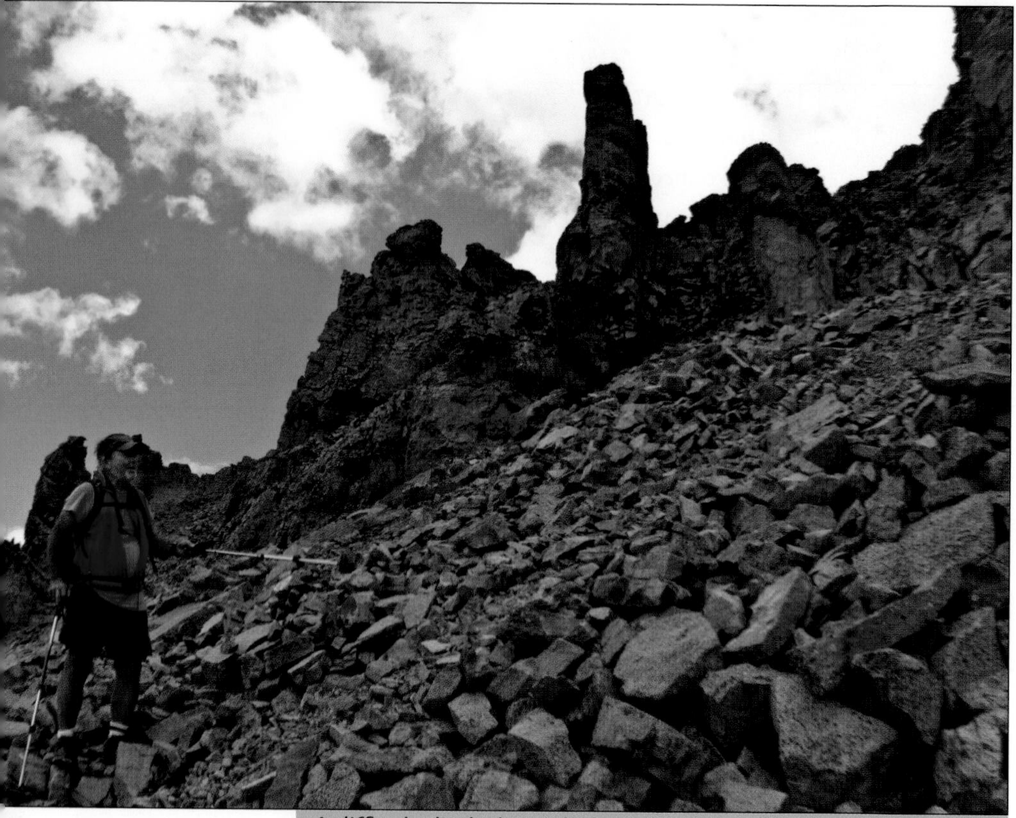

A difficult climb through the rocks. Photo by Rozanne Evans

Trail Description

The trail begins in spruce forest but within half a mile, you are in the open with stunning views of Uncompahgre Peak to accompany you for the rest of the hike. On the east side of the peak, the cliffs drop over 1000 feet straight down. The trail meanders along Nellie Creek through some fascinating rocks before climbing switchbacks to the high meadow and the junction to Big Blue Trail ❷. It's a beautiful, pleasant walk through the undulating, green meadow; you can see your destination all along as you climb. When you reach ❸, the junction to Matterhorn Creek, an un-named peak looms off your left shoulder and you can see the trail to Matterhorn as it descends a picturesque valley. The trail steepens as it climbs the ridge; there are amazing views through the rock cliffs towards Matterhorn and Wetterhorn. Look ahead; it is easy to

Views from the high ridge. Photo by Rozanne Evans

View into Matterhorn Basin and trail across high ridge. Photo by Rozanne Evans

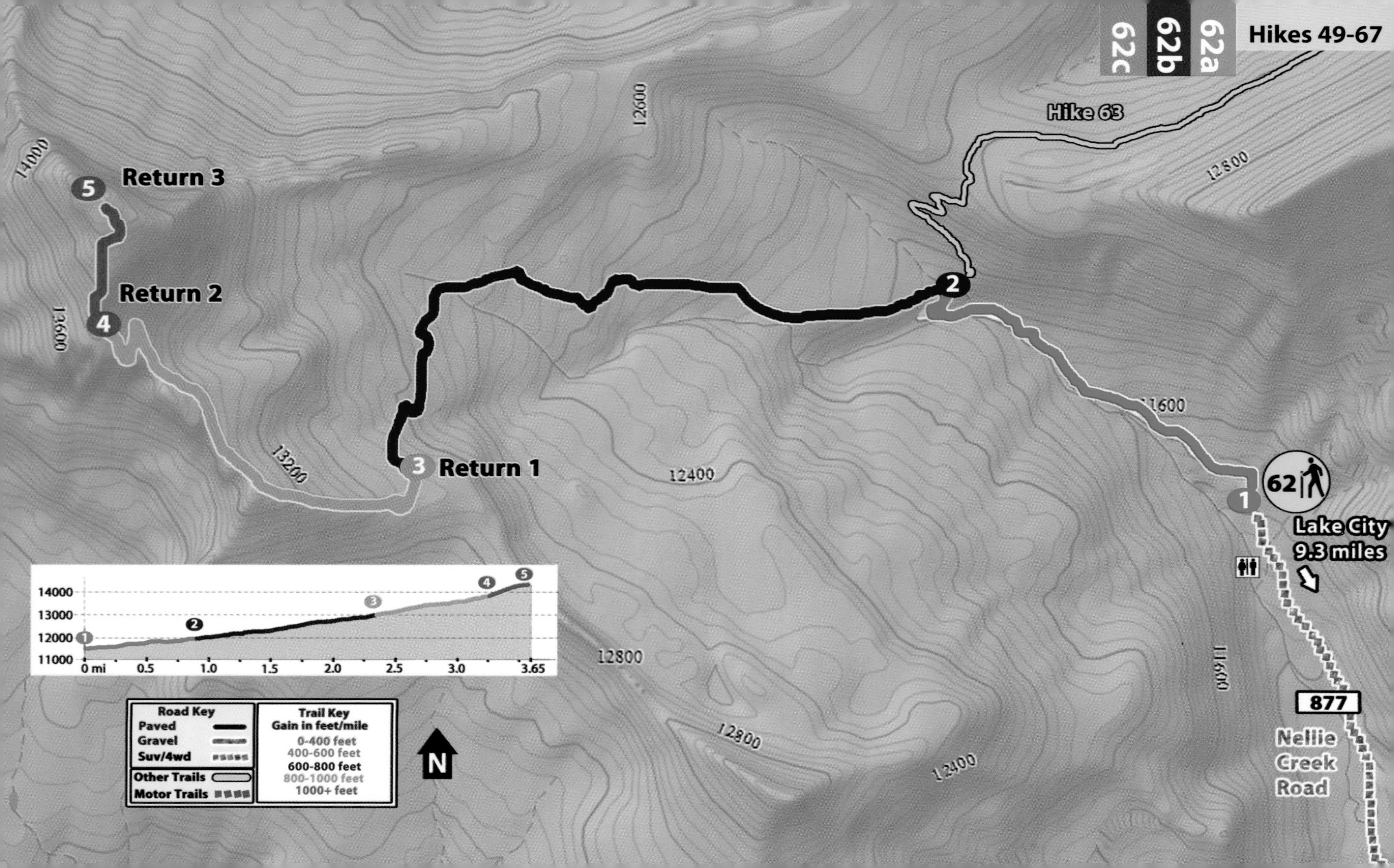
Hike 63
Return 3
Return 2
Return 1
Lake City
9.3 miles
877
Nellie
Creek
Road
14000
13600
13200
12800
12600
12400
11600
0 mi
0.5
1.0
1.5
2.0
2.5
3.0
3.65
11000
12000
13000
Road Key
Paved
Gravel
Suv/4wd
Other Trails
Motor Trails
Trail Key
Gain in feet/mile
0-400 feet
400-600 feet
600-800 feet
800-1000 feet
1000+ feet
N

see the trail switchback steeply up to the base of steep cliffs ❹. Now you can see most of Matterhorn Basin and the trails leading down the Cimarron River drainage. From this point, the trail goes over the ridge to the south side of the peak. The trail becomes entangled in giant rock debris. The climb from here to the top is 570 feet gain in only 0.35 miles! A very steep gully off your right shoulder has a few cairns to point the way up, but this is not the best route because the rocks are loose and footing is most difficult. Continue straight ahead across the rock debris to the next gully. A little better trail ascends here although also very steep and difficult. If you do not like such places, return to ❹. It has already been a marvelous day with many stunning vistas to take home with you. Or continue to the peak by climbing up through the rock. The trail improves considerably on the last leg to the summit. What a spot. There are too many peaks and valleys to name. Bring out your map and see how many you can identify. Congratulations!

GPS	Mile	Latitude	Longitude	Elevation	Comment
1	0.00	38,03.759N	107,25.318W	11,425′	Start
2	0.91	38,04.112N	107,25.947W	11,943′	Signed junction: Go straight ahead (W) for Peak; right goes to Big Blue.
3	2.37	38,03.814N	107,27.064W	12,939′	Return 1: Signed junction: Go right (SW) uphill; Left goes to Matterhorn Creek drainage.
4	3.30	38,04.064N	107,27.710W	13,771′	Return 2: Cross ridge. Begin very difficult section climbing up steeply through rocks.
5	3.65	38,04.300N	107,27.727W	14,309′	Uncompahgre Peak

A peak experience!

Ridge Stock Driveway Options

Star Rating

☆☆☆☆☆☆

☆☆☆

63a: To Ridge/ Return 1

Total Distance	5.70 miles RT
Difficulty Rating	Moderate
Surface	Mostly packed dirt with just a few rocky sections
Gradient	Ranges from Moderate to Steep
Average Time	4 hours
Elevations	TH: 11,425; Highest: 12,730; Gain: +1,472
Map	Trails Illustrated: Telluride, Silverton, Ouray, Lake City

63b: To Un-named Peak/ Return 2

Total Distance	6.70 miles RT
Difficulty Rating	Moderate
Surface	Packed dirt and grassy slopes
Gradient	Mostly Moderate
Average Time	4.5 hours
Elevations	TH: 11,425; Highest: 13,072; Gain: +1,806

Big Blue Valley from saddle

63c: Ridge Walk/ Return 3

Total Distance	11.76 miles RT
Difficulty Rating	Moderately Strenuous
Surface	Good dirt packed and several rocky sections
Gradient	Climb Moderately Steep first 3 miles; remainder is Easy
Average Time	8 hours
Elevations	TH: 11,425; Highest: 12,730; Gain: +2,171

63d: To Alpine Road Shuttle

Total Distance	13.0 miles to shuttle point
Difficulty Rating	Strenuous due to distance and 4 miles of rocky surface
Surface	About 4 miles of the ridge is hiking across ankle twisting rock
Gradient	Climb Moderately Steep first 3 miles; remainder is Easy
Average Time	9 hours
Elevations	TH: 11,425; Highest: 12,730; Gain: +1,836; Loss: -3,210

Directions to TH	From the middle of Lake City on Hwy 149, turn north on 2nd St. Signs say to Engineer Pass. Drive 5.2 miles to the signed Nellie Creek turnoff. From this point, drive another 4.1 miles to the signed TH.
Time & Mileage to TH	1 hour; 9.3 miles
Recommended Vehicle	SUV with high clearance and 4x4. This is a very rocky, bumpy, one lane road with few passing spots.
Directions to Shuttle	From LCVC, drive north 10.2 miles on 149 to Alpine Road 868. Sign says Big Blue. Drive 7.7 miles on this good gravel road. There is no trailhead sign. Park in the meadow opposite an old sheep corral and spot the trail coming across the meadow from the south.
Time & Mileage	40 minutes; 17.9 miles
Recommended Vehicle	Car. This is a reasonably good gravel road most of the way with a few narrow places.

Splendid views of Uncompahgre early on trail

Summary

Spectacular views of Uncompahgre Peak, Big Blue Valley, Wetterhorn, Cockscomb and Redcliff in the distance, and Lake Fork of the Gunnison Valley. Take your pick: hike out and back or hike an epic 13 miles out a ridge averaging over 12,000 feet elevation.

Trail Description

The trail begins in spruce forest but within half a mile, you are in the open with stunning views of Uncompahgre Peak. On the east side of the peak, the cliffs

Big Blue Valley is far below

drop over 1000 feet straight down. The trail meanders along Nellie Creek through some fascinating rocks before climbing switchbacks to the high meadow and the junction to Big Blue Trail ❷. Go right at this junction and begin climbing the steep switchbacks. All the while, views of Uncompahgre are outstanding. The trail fades at the top of the switchbacks. Walk over the crest of the hill and you will see a sign post ❸. From this sign, which points to the Big Blue Trail, hike due east towards the long ridge. In 100 yards you will meet a good trail that cuts upward and across that ridge to the top at ❹. A reminder: if you get an early morning start, much of the trail to ❹ is in the cold shade of the morning. Be prepared. This is a good return point if you don't want to shuttle. The views of Uncompahgre are simply marvelous. You can see down most of Big Blue Valley. Another short option is to climb the un-named peak (4a) to the southwest. A moderate grassy slope leads to the summit about 13,000 feet in approximately 1 mile RT. You could also continue out the ridge itself for as far as you wish. Views of Big Blue Valley along

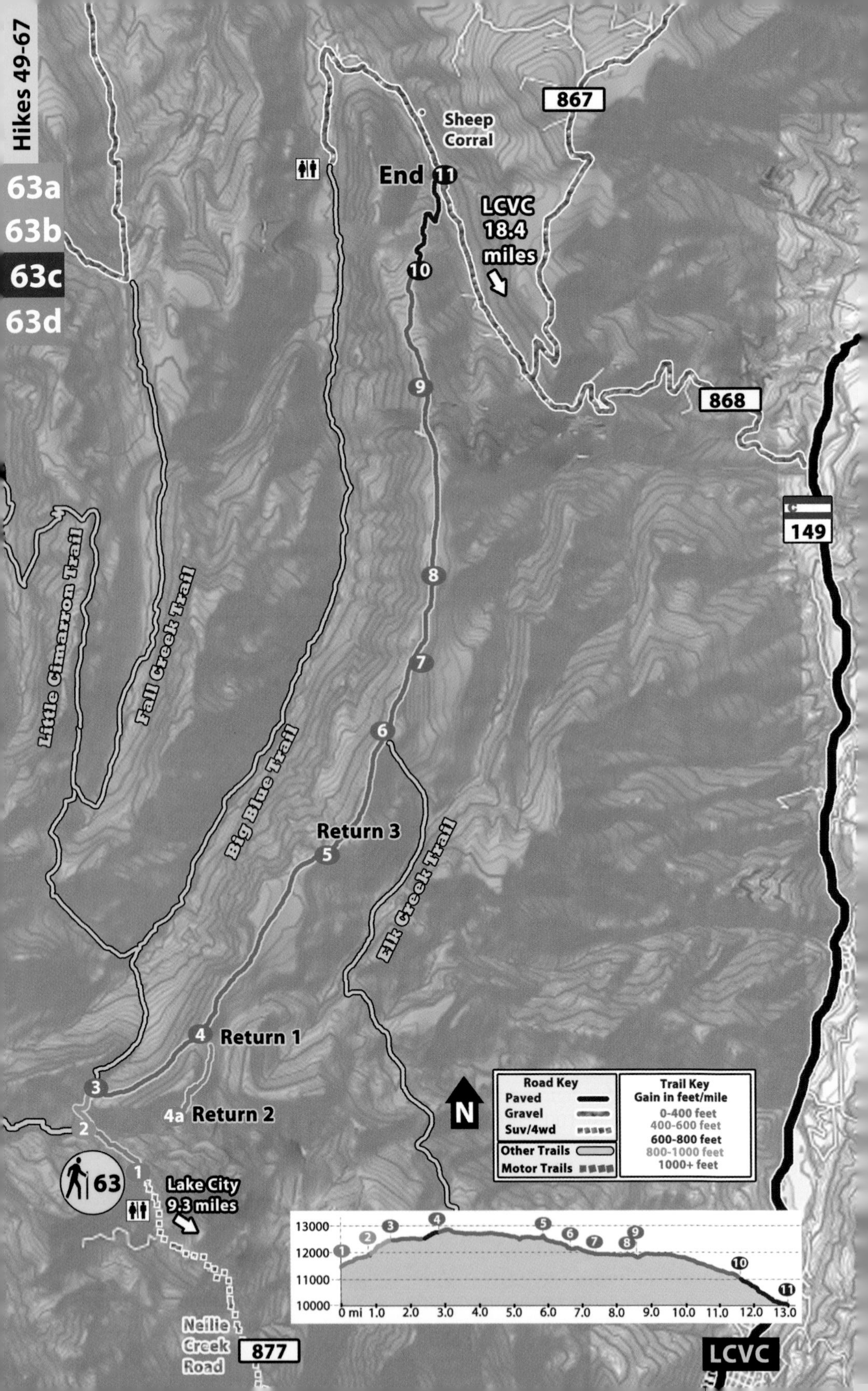
867
Sheep Corral
End 11
LCVC 18.4 miles
10
9
868
149
8
7
6
Little Cimarron Trail
Fall Creek Trail
Big Blue Trail
Elk Creek Trail
Return 3
5
4 Return 1
3
2
4a Return 2
1
63
Lake City 9.3 miles
N
Road Key
Paved
Gravel
Suv/4wd
Other Trails
Motor Trails
Trail Key
Gain in feet/mile
0-400 feet
400-600 feet
600-800 feet
800-1000 feet
1000+ feet
13000
12000
11000
10000
0 mi 1.0 2.0 3.0 4.0 5.0 6.0 7.0 8.0 9.0 10.0 11.0 12.0 13.0
Nellie Creek Road
877
LCVC

About midway through the hike

the rocky cliffs and across the valley to Silver peak are beautiful. Soon Wetterhorn Peak appears. The trail is intermittent; just follow the ridge. By ❺, you will be on top of a knob about 12,500 feet. Here the ridge turns exceptionally rocky and makes walking more difficult. There is no real trail. We recommend good map reading skills or use of a GPS as there are numerous confusing points beyond here. The GPS chart describes these points.

GPS	Mile	Latitude	Longitude	Elevation	Comment
1	0.00	38,03.759N	107,25.318W	11,425′	Start Ridge Stock Trail at Uncompahgre Peak TH.
2	0.91	38,04.115N	107,25.942W	11,919′	Signed junction: Go right (N) for Stock Trail & Big Blue; straight ahead (W) is Uncompahgre Peak.
3	1.50	38,04.389N	107,25.870W	12,352′	Just over crest of hill is signpost that says Big Blue & Stock Driveway; go right (E) towards the long ridge. Pick up trail in 100 yards.
4	2.85	38,04.899N	107,24.683W	12,730′	Return 1: Reach the ridge.
4a		38,04.426N	107,24.896W	13,072′	Summit of un-named peak
5	5.88	38,06.925N	107,22.771W	12,496′	Route becomes very rocky for next 4 miles. Intermittent trail. Follow ridge.
6	6.66	38,07.571N	107,22.549W	12,179′	See two sign posts downhill to your right (E). They mark the trail to Crystal Lake.
7	7.40	38,08.145N	107,22.253W	11,971′	Multiple animal trails confusing. Instead of climbing the ridge ahead (N), drop downhill to the right (E) about 50 feet and meet a good trail.
8	8.40	38,08.942N	107,22.029W	11,857′	Two tall cairns to the left (W) of the trail mark a wonderful view up Big Blue Valley.
9	8.71	38,09.247N	107,21.989W	11,825′	Climb up last, rocky knob using the left hand trail. After this knob, it is downhill all the way to the end. Soon enter spruce forest.
10	11.60	38,11.598N	107,22.165W	10,987′	Start switchbacks to end of trail.
11	13.00	38,12.397N	107,21.956W	10,049′	End hike on Alpine Road.

Matterhorn Basin to Saddle & Peaks

Star Rating

☆☆☆☆☆

	64a: To Matterhorn Basin High Saddle
Total Distance	4.96 miles RT
Difficulty Rating	Moderately Strenuous
Surface	Somewhat rocky much of the way
Gradient	Moderately Steep
Average Time	3.5 hours
Elevations	TH: 10,770; Highest: 12,469; Gain: +1,723
Maps	Trails Illustrated: Telluride, Silverton, Ouray, Lake City

	64b: To Matterhorn Peak
Total Distance	6.40 miles RT
Difficulty Rating	Very Strenuous
Surface	Tundra
Gradient	Very Steep
Average Time	5 hours
Elevations	TH: 10,770; Highest: 13,590; Gain: +2,844

Entering Matterhorn Basin

	64c: To Wetterhorn Peak
Total Distance	7.20 miles RT
Difficulty Rating	Very Strenuous
Surface	Rocky and dirt packed; Class 3 exposed section near summit
Gradient	Very Steep
Average Time	6 hours
Elevations	TH: 10,770; Highest: 14,015; Gain: +2,836

Summary

No matter how far you go, this is a wonderful hike into a gorgeous basin surrounded by soaring peaks. Wetterhorn and Matterhorn connect via a sharp dramatic ridge line; wildflowers flourish in the wide basin; hike to the saddle and get a close up view of massive Uncompahgre Peak. This is a thrilling scenic hike on all accounts!

Wetterhorn Peak from main trail

Directions to TH	From the middle of Lake City on Hwy 149, turn right (N) on 2nd Ave. Signs say to Engineer Pass. Drive 9.0 miles to the Capital City signed intersection. Turn right (NW) uphill on North Henson Creek Road. Drive 2 miles to the road signed Wetterhorn. Drive another 0.70 miles up this steep road to the end.
Time & Mileage to TH	50 minutes; 11.7 miles
Recommended Vehicle	4X4. The good gravel road to Capital City is passable for cars but the 2 miles beyond needs a high clearance vehicle. The Wetterhorn Road is very steep, very rocky and narrow. Any 4x4 with high clearance can drive this section. Just before the end, the road forks. Drive the left fork rather than straight ahead. A boulder and tree make the route straight ahead very narrow; that route is exceptionally rocky, and steep. If you do not have 4WD, park at the bottom and hike Wetterhorn Road. Add 1.40 miles RT and +471 feet elevation gain.

Trail Description

The trail starts out rocky for a short while through healthy, intermittent spruce forest. From ❷, views expand: first is a wonderful vista up Matterhorn cutoff trail; Matterhorn Peak and soon Wetterhorn Peak come into view. Enter Matterhorn Basin proper at ❸, shortly after the wilderness sign. Ascend into the basin for stunning views

Uncompahgre Peak from saddle

Matterhorn Peak from saddle

View back down Matterhorn Basin

of Matterhorn and Wetterhorn and the sharp connecting ridge. Wetterhorn trail departs at ❹. The climb to Wetterhorn Peak 4a is a class 3 near the top, but the lower section of trail is a wonderful hike through the surrounding basin meadows. Meanwhile, the main basin trail splits above ❹ into a left and right fork. The right fork is easier walking. Gain views of Uncompahgre Peak from the high saddle at ❺. This is a good place to ascend Matterhorn's grassy slopes. There is no trail to the summit of Matterhorn Peak ❻. It is very steep and rocky near the top and requires some negotiating around ledges.

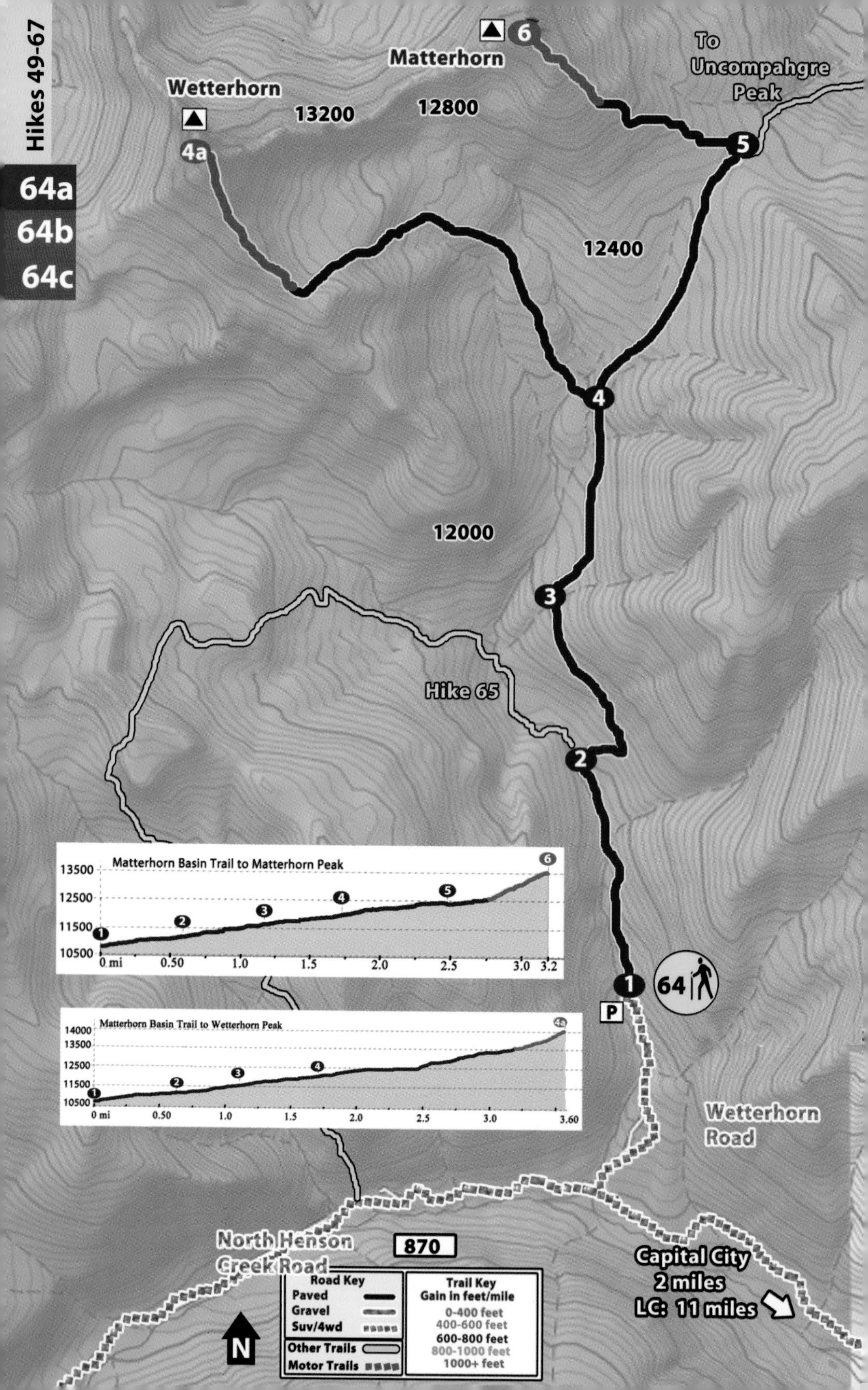
Matterhorn
6
To
Uncompahgre
Peak
Wetterhorn
13200
12800
4a
5
12400
4
12000
3
Hike 65
2
Matterhorn Basin Trail to Matterhorn Peak
13500
12500
11500
10500
0 mi
0.50
1.0
1.5
2.0
2.5
3.0
3.2
1
64
P
Matterhorn Basin Trail to Wetterhorn Peak
14000
13500
12500
11500
10500
0 mi
0.50
1.0
1.5
2.0
2.5
3.0
3.60
Wetterhorn
Road
North Henson
Creek Road
870
Capital City
2 miles
LC: 11 miles
Road Key
Paved
Gravel
Suv/4wd
Other Trails
Motor Trails
Trail Key
Gain in feet/mile
0-400 feet
400-600 feet
600-800 feet
800-1000 feet
1000+ feet
N

Final ascent to Wetterhorn Peak is a class 3. Photo by Rozanne Evans

View from Wetterhorn Peak. Photo by Rozanne Evans

GPS	Mile	Latitude	Longitude	Elevation	Comment
1	0.00	38,01.842N	107,29.471W	10,770′	Parking and trailhead sign
2	0.60	38,02.324N	107,29.608W	10,949′	Signed Junction: Go right for Matterhorn Basin and peaks; left is Matterhorn Cutoff trail.
3	1.17	38,02.693N	107,29.691W	11,658′	Enter Matterhorn Basin just after wilderness sign.
4	1.73	38,03.106N	107,29.576W	12,008′	Signed junction: Left to climb Wetterhorn; straight to Matterhorn saddle and peak access.
4a	3.60	38,03.649N	107,30.680W	14,015′	Wetterhorn Peak
5	2.48	38,03.643N	107,29.190W	12,469′	Signed junction at saddle. Go left to climb to Matterhorn Peak; straight is Ridge Stock Driveway. Return 2
6	3.20	38,03.914N	107,29.781W	13,590′	Matterhorn Peak

Matterhorn Cutoff Options

Star Rating

☆☆☆☆☆☆

☆☆☆

65a: Matterhorn Cutoff to Alice Creek Loop

Total Distance	6.07 miles back to vehicle at bottom of Wetterhorn Road
Difficulty Rating	Moderately Strenuous
Surface	Mostly dirt packed with some rocky sections
Gradient	Ranges from Easy to Very Steep
Average Time	5 hours
Elevations	TH: 10,380; Highest: 12,444; Gain: +2,119
Map	Trails Illustrated: Telluride, Silverton, Ouray, Lake City

65b: Matterhorn Cutoff to Waterfall/ Return 1

Total Distance	3.0 miles RT from upper Wetterhorn Road
Difficulty Rating	Moderate
Surface	Mostly dirt packed
Gradient	Ranges from Easy to Steep
Average Time	2.5 hours
Elevations	TH: 10,770; Highest: 11,701; Gain: +1,315

View from saddle looking back at Wetterhorn Peak/Return 2

View of Matterhorn Cutoff Basin from below

Directions to TH From the middle of Lake City on Hwy 149, turn right (N) on 2nd St. Signs say to Engineer Pass. Drive 9.0 miles to the Capital City signed intersection. Turn right (NW) uphill on North Henson Creek Road. Drive 2 miles to the road signed Wetterhorn. Park here if you are planning to do the loop hike. Drive another 0.70 miles up Wetterhorn Road if you plan to hike out and back.

Time & Mileage to TH 40 minutes; 11.0 miles to Wetterhorn Road

Recommended Vehicle SUV/4x4. The good gravel road to capital City is passable for cars but the 2 miles beyond needs a high clearance vehicle. Wetterhorn Road is very steep, very rocky and narrow. Any 4x4 with high clearance can drive this section. Just before the end, the road forks. Drive the left fork rather than straight ahead. A boulder and tree make the route straight ahead very narrow. That route is exceptionally rocky, and steep.

Directions to Shuttle Drive another .62 miles up North Henson Creek Rd and park just before crossing Mary Alice Creek if you have a shuttle vehicle and don't want to walk North Henson Creek Road. The trail is the old roadbed heading uphill on the west side of the creek.

Entering Matterhorn Cutoff Basin

Summary

Make a loop trip by hiking through a rarely visited, picturesque basin to a dramatic high point and descending down steep Alice Creek back to your vehicle. Or, make a shorter day by hiking to a waterfall in the basin and return. Some route finding through the basin as trails are intermittent.

Trail Description

This description begins from the bottom of Wetterhorn Road which is where you would park if hiking the entire loop. Wetterhorn Road is rocky and steep but views of the valley open up after only 0.30 miles where there is a grassy campsite After the trailhead sign at ❷, the trail continues rocky for a short while through healthy, intermittent spruce forest. At ❸ is the signed junction to Matterhorn Cutoff Trail. From here the trail is intermittent in sections. Hike through meadows and forest up this very beautiful basin lined by dramatic peaks. Choose to wander freely about this basin and return, or hike to the pass separating you from Alice Creek drainage for the loop option. Wet shoes are recommended at the first stream crossing in early season ❹. The creek crossing at ❺ could be impassable during high runoff. At ❻ is a sign stating the old trail is closed. Continue on to the next stream crossing and small waterfall ❼ which is our Return 1. Cross the stream here; do not continue up the NE bank on another trail. It leads to a sheep camp. After this crossing, the trail is very confusing. Hike SW through sparse spruce forest until coming to the upper basin area that is open to the top. Sheep trails confuse the issue so continue ascending to a saddle to the left of the impressive rock walls at the end of the basin. The views of the basin and peaks from the high point ❽ are most impressive. There are numerous forest service signs to various stock trails in the area. Start heading south downhill, towards the main drainage The upper section of Alice Creek is open meadows thick with seasonal wildflowers. We saw about 50 elk browsing. Another Forest Service sign at ❾. The trail you see in the distance heading due south is our hike 66 trail. At ❿, the creek narrows through a tight rocky gorge. Stay on the east (left) side of the creek. The intermittent trail meets the old mining road at ⓫. Follow old roads to ⓭ and cross

Waterfall/ Return 1

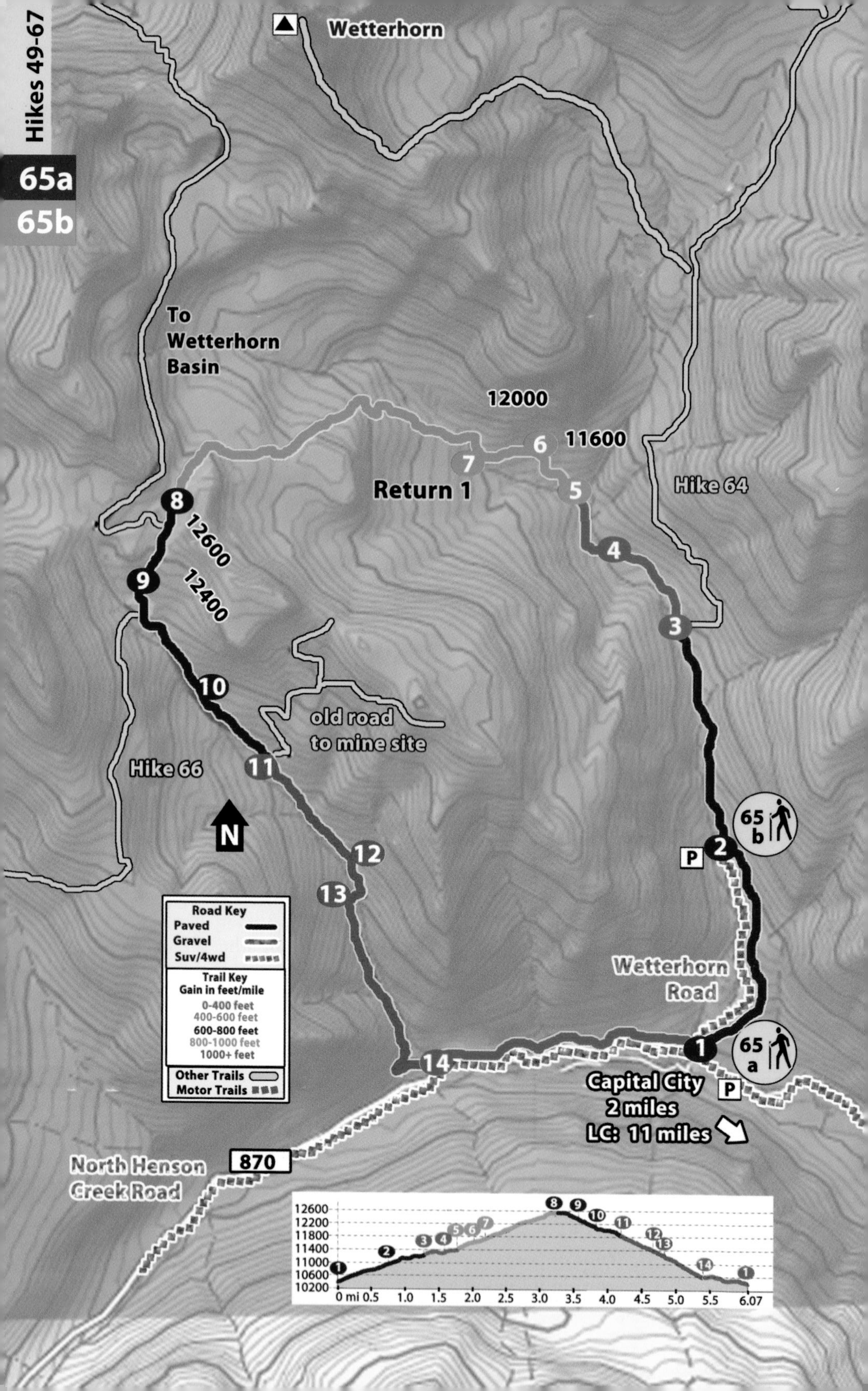
Wetterhorn
To
Wetterhorn
Basin
12000
11600
Return 1
Hike 64
12600
12400
old road
to mine site
Hike 66
N
65 b
P
Wetterhorn
Road
65 a
Capital City
2 miles
LC: 11 miles
P
North Henson
Creek Road
870
Road Key
Paved
Gravel
Suv/4wd
Trail Key
Gain in feet/mile
0-400 feet
400-600 feet
600-800 feet
800-1000 feet
1000+ feet
Other Trails
Motor Trails
12600
12200
11800
11400
11000
10600
10200
0 mi 0.5 1.0 1.5 2.0 2.5 3.0 3.5 4.0 4.5 5.0 5.5 6.07

Alice Creek. From here the trail is especially narrow and steep. Hike back to your vehicle on North Henson Creek Road for 0.62 miles.

After crossing waterfall, hike towards left hand saddle.

GPS	Mile	Latitude	Longitude	Elevation	Comment
1	0.00	38,01.370N	107,29.548W	10,380′	Signed junction for Wetterhorn Road and North Henson Creek Road
2	0.70 0.00	38,01.842N	107,29.471W	10,770′	Parking and trailhead sign for RT option
3	1.30 0.60	38,02.324N	107,29.608W	10,949′	Signed Junction: Go left for Matterhorn Cutoff Trail; right is Matterhorn Basin Trail.
4	1.60 0.90	38,02.483N	107,29.805W	11,272′	Stream crossing; need shoes in high runoff.
5	1.80 1.10	38,02.596N	107,29.879W	11,312′	Stream crossing. Could be impassable in high runoff.
6	2.02 1.32	38,02.700N	107,30.010W	11,592′	Sign where old trail is closed
7	2.20 1.50	38,02.729N	107,30.186W	11,701′	Cross stream left below waterfall. Unmarked junction. Return 1 for short out & back hike.
8	3.26	38,02.607N	107,31.020W	12,444′	High point. Two FS signs mark directions to Cross Cut, Wetterhorn Basin and Middle Canyon trails. Trails are very faint.
9	3.62	38,02.384N	107,31.132W	12,237′	FS sign marks route. Trail intermittent
10	3.87	38,02.203N	107,30.999W	12,031′	Cairn with no stick along east edge of Alice Creek. Stay on east bank above creek.
11	4.22	38,02.022N	107,30.681W	11,742′	Unmarked fork in road. Go right downhill.
12	4.73	38,01.774N	107,30.487W	11,364′	Unmarked fork in the road; do not follow road to the east.
13	4.89	38,01.715N	107,30.517W	11,160′	Cross Alice Creek
14	5.45	38,01.335N	107,30.255W	10,586′	Alice Creek TH. Shuttle car here or walk down road 0.62 miles to Wetterhorn Road.
1	6.07	38,01.370N	107,29.548W	10,380′	Signed junction for Wetterhorn Road and North Henson Creek Road

High Country Traverse

Star Rating

☆☆☆☆☆

66a
66b
66c
66d
66e

American Lake/ Return 1

66a: To American Lake/ Return 1

Total Distance	6.46 miles RT
Difficulty Rating	Easy
Surface	Mixture of tundra, dirt packed and some rocky sections
Gradient	Easy
Average Time	3.5 hours
Elevations	TH: 12,399; Highest: 12,487; Gain: +815
Map	Trails Illustrated: Telluride, Silverton, Ouray, Lake City

66b: To Boundary Line/ Return 2

Total Distance	10.12 miles RT
Difficulty Rating	Moderate
Surface	Mixture of tundra, dirt packed and some rocky sections
Gradient	Easy
Average Time	6 hours
Elevations	TH: 12,399; Highest: 12,487; Gain: +1,397

66c: To N Henson Road/ Option 3

Total Distance	7.44 miles to shuttle
Difficulty Rating	Easy
Surface	Mixture of tundra, dirt packed and some rocky sections
Gradient	Easy to Moderate
Average Time	4.5 hours
Elevations	TH: 12,399; Highest: 12,487; Gain: +479; Loss: -2,080

66d: To Mary Alice TH/ Option 4

Total Distance	9.48 miles to shuttle
Difficulty Rating	Moderate
Surface	Mixture of tundra, dirt packed and some rocky sections
Gradient	Mostly Easy with two steep climbs; Very steep descent to Mary Alice TH
Average Time	6 hours
Elevations	TH: 12,399; Highest: 12,289; Gain: +1,314; Loss: -3,156

66e: To Matterhorn TH/ Option 5

Total Distance	10.39 if driving 4x4 to upper parking; 11.09 if parked at bottom of Wetterhorn Road
Difficulty Rating	Moderate
Surface	Mixture of tundra, dirt packed and some rocky sections
Gradient	Mostly Easy with two short steep climbs and a steep descent into Cutoff Basin
Average Time	7 hours
Elevations	TH: 12,399; Highest: 12,444; Gain: +1,615; Loss: -3,642

Summary

This is our favorite hike. Stay high for almost 9 miles; hike through 5 different basins with a wonderful variety of stunning mountain scenery. This is high country hiking at its best! The gradient is mostly easy with a couple of short steep climbs. Two of the options have steep descents. Take your choice. We think going out all the way to Matterhorn TH offers the most magnificent scenic experience for the effort but there are also much shorter routes with a scenic punch. Enjoy!

Trail Description

Start on Engineer Pass Road at the signed TH for Horsethief Trail. Climb the short, easy hill to American Flats. Immediately there are superb views of the major 14er peaks that make Lake City famous: Uncompahgre, Matterhorn, and

Cow Creek drainage

Directions to TH	From the middle of Lake City on Hwy 149, turn north on 2nd St. Signs say to Engineer Pass. Drive 9.0 miles to the Capital City signed intersection. Go left at this intersection and drive 8.7 miles on Engineer Pass Road to the signed Horsethief TH. There is ample parking.
Time & Mileage to TH	1 hour, 30 minutes; 17.7 miles
Recommended Vehicle	SUV with high clearance and 4x4. A car can drive the first 14.4 miles to an outhouse. After that, high clearance is necessary and 4x4 recommended. After Thoreau Cabin, the road is very steep and rocky with exposed cliffs.
Directions to Shuttle	At the Capital City signed intersection, turn right (NW) uphill on North Henson Creek Road. Drive 2 miles to the road signed Wetterhorn. This is the lower parking area and the end for option 5. (or drive another 0.70 miles up the steep 4x4 road to the upper parking). For option 4 end, drive another 0.62 miles up this road and park just this side of Mary Alice Creek. The trail is an old road bed heading uphill on the west side of the creek. For option 3, drive still another 0.72 miles to the end of North Henson Creek Rd and park at the switchback. The trail is an old road marked by a No Motorized Vehicle sign. It heads west from the switchback below the gate to private property.
Recommended Vehicle	It is possible to drive a car on North Henson Creek Road, but we still recommend any higher clearance vehicle. 4x4 is not necessary unless driving to the upper parking area for option 5.

Wetterhorn. Hike through the flower filled mesa following intermittent tracks and cairns with wood posts. A little confusion arises at ❷ where two faint tracks diverge and it is difficult to see a post marker because they are often quite far apart. One track goes uphill to the west (left) and makes a noticeable switchback on a rocky ridge. The track you want to follow goes due north towards the dramatic Wildhorse Peak, downhill to the right. This is magnificent, wide open country. At ❸ is a signed junction to Bear Creek Trail and Ridge Stock Driveway. Go east on the Ridge Stock Driveway and soon you will be at tiny American Lake ❹. This is a Return 1 for an easy roundtrip hike with beautiful scenery and no shuttle. Continuing on, however, the trail contours around into the dramatic Cow Creek drainage. Excellent views of Coxcomb and the sharp

imb up gully just after Exit to N Henson Road (66c)

Uncompahgre Peak before Return 2

Second big climb on route to Mary Alice Creek

Approaching high point above Mary Alice Creek

pinnacle rocks of Cow Creek come into view. Uncompahgre, Matterhorn and Wetterhorn can be seen from many different vantage points as well as Wildhorse Peak which is now behind. A wilderness sign 5 marks the county line and makes a good spot for lunch and Return 2 for a longer but superb out and back hike, again with no shuttle. Now the trail descends gently to still another pretty basin. A sign 6 marks the end of Ridge Stock Driveway and the start of Saddle Trail. This is where you can hike down the drainage to the end of Henson Creek Road and your shuttle vehicle 6a (Option 3). The trail is intermittent, but the direction is not hard to determine. Go downhill! This is a very easy way to exit the hike, especially if the weather has changed to threatening. To continue, the trail climbs steeply through a gully. Once at the top,

Uncompahgre Peak before descending to Alice Creek

View into Alice Creek

you are in another un-named drainage with un-named peaks bordering the north side. Descend and cross a tiny creek. The trail heads due north then completely disappears. Continue north, but do not climb the knoll in front of you; stay about level along the right hand side of the knoll. You are heading for the deep drainage ahead and will cross 2 creeks. 7. If you look carefully, you can see the trail climbing a steep traverse up the far bank. This is the steepest climb on the entire trail. Reach a precipice at 8 with a most impressive view of Mary Alice drainage. Wetterhorn and Uncompahgre tower dramatically above the head of the basin. Still climbing a bit along the edge, the trail then begins an easy although rocky descent to upper Mary Alice Creek. Cross the creek and meet up with a stake and cairn with no sign 9. Make a choice here to go down Mary Alice drainage to your shuttle vehicle (option 4) or continue uphill towards another post, this time with a sign 10. (The trail down Mary Alice is also intermittent. Do not follow down the creek but head more easterly to pick up the old road. When the road splits, keep going downhill. Eventually you will cross Mary Alice Creek 9a where the trail becomes very narrow and steep to the finish 10a.

Continuing on to Option 5, the trail climbs for the last time to the prominent saddle. Wow; what a view! The peaks are all lined up on the other side of the gorgeous Matterhorn Cutoff Basin. A sign 11 at the top points the way, but there is no obvious trail. Your first goal is to descend into the basin towards the stream and cross just below a small waterfall 12. You may pick up the trail there. Eventually, by following the general direction of the stream, you will come to the signed junction to Wetterhorn Peak 16. Continue downhill to the upper 17 or lower 18 parking. Now you know why this is our favorite hike!

GPS	Mile	Latitude	Longitude	Elevation	Comment
1	0.00	37,58.651N	107,34.628W	12,399′	Start at Horsethief TH.
2	1.25	37,59.355N	107,35.075W	12,487′	Trails diverge. Go right (due north) downhill.
3	2.15	38,00.054N	107,34.826W	12,327′	Marked junction: go right (E) on the flat.
4	3.23	38,00.178N	107,33.725W	12,243′	American Lake: Return 1
5	5.06	38,00.841N	107,32.308W	11,910′	Wilderness sign at county line: Return 2
6	5.49	38,01.015N	107,32.046W	11,769′	Signed junction: Go up steep hill on Wetterhorn Trail or go down drainage for option 3 exit to North Henson Creek Rd (option 3).
6a	7.44	38,01.004N	107,30.933W	10,805′	North Fork Henson Creek Rd; end option 3
7	6.55	38,01.781N	107,31.568W	11,804′	Cross two creeks and begin steep ascent.
8	6.96	38,01.775N	107,31.146W	12,183′	Overlook Mary Alice Creek
9	7.66	38,02.342N	107,31.112W	12,273′	Meet Alice Creek trail at post with no sign. Go downhill for option 4 or continue uphill to visible saddle and Matterhorn Cutoff Trail.
9a	8.88	38,01.715N	107,30.517W	11,160′	Cross Alice Creek on descent to Option 4 End.
10a	9.48	38,01.360N	107,30.255W	10,667′	Alice Creek TH; option 4 End
10	7.71	38,02.384N	107,31.132W	12,237′	FS sign marks route. Trail intermittent to saddle
11	7.83	38,02.607N	107,31.020W	12,444′	Two FS signs mark directions to CrossCut, Wetterhorn Basin and Middle Canyon trails. Trails are very faint. High point with magnificent views of peaks and Crosscut Basin
12	8.89	38,02.729N	107,30.186W	11,701′	Cross stream below waterfall.
13	9.07	38,02.700N	107,30.010W	11,592′	Signed junction; continue downhill.
14	9.29	38,02.596N	107,29.879W	11,312′	Stream crossing. Could be impassable in high runoff.
15	9.45	38,02.483N	107,29.805W	11,272′	Stream crossing; need shoes in high runoff
16	9.75	38,02.324N	107,29.608W	10,949′	Signed Junction: Go straight (S); left is Matterhorn Basin Trail to the peaks.
17	10.39	38,01.842N	107,29.471W	10,770′	Upper parking and trailhead sign
18	11.09	38,01.370N	107,29.548W	10,380′	End at signed junction for Wetterhorn Road and North Henson Creek Road.

View into Matterhorn Cutoff Basin from high saddle

12400
12600
6
Return 2
5
12000
12800
Wildhorse Peak
Return 1
4
Hike 67
3
12400
2
66
1
P
Lake City 17.7 miles
Alpine Loop
20
Engineer Pass

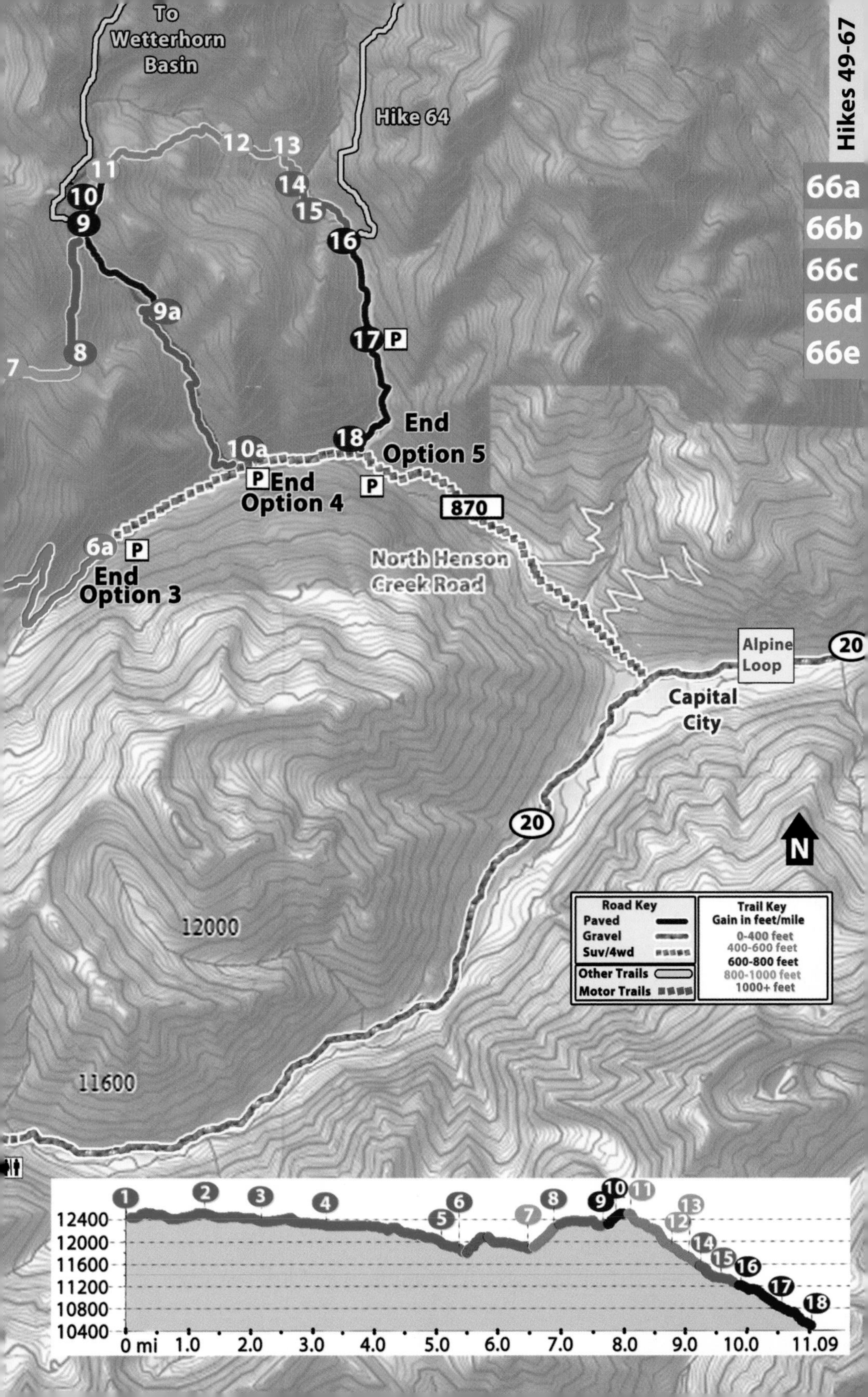
To Wetterhorn Basin
Hike 64
End Option 5
End Option 4
End Option 3
870
North Henson Creek Road
Alpine Loop
Capital City
20
12000
11600
N
Road Key
Paved
Gravel
Suv/4wd
Other Trails
Motor Trails
Trail Key
Gain in feet/mile
0-400 feet
400-600 feet
600-800 feet
800-1000 feet
1000+ feet
12400
12000
11600
11200
10800
10400
0 mi
1.0
2.0
3.0
4.0
5.0
6.0
7.0
8.0
9.0
10.0
11.09

67

American Flats to Engineer Pass

Star Rating

☆☆☆☆☆

Total Distance	6.93 miles to shuttle
Difficulty Rating	Moderate
Surface	Alternating large broken rock and packed dirt
Gradient	Ranges from Easy to Moderately Strenuous
Average Time	5 hours
Elevations	TH: 12,399; Highest: 12,809; Gain: +2,163; Loss: -1,773
Map	Trails Illustrated: Telluride, Silverton, Ouray, Lake City

Directions to TH

From the middle of Lake City on Hwy 149, turn north on 2nd St. Signs say to Engineer Pass. Drive 9.0 miles to the Capital City signed intersection. Go left at this intersection and drive 8.7 miles on Engineer Pass Road to the signed Horsethief TH. There is ample parking.

Time & Mileage to TH

1 hour 30 minutes; 17.7 miles

Recommended Vehicle

SUV with high clearance and 4x4. A car can drive the first 14.4 miles to an outhouse. After that, high clearance is necessary and 4x4 recommended. After Thoreau Cabin, the road is very steep and rocky with exposed cliffs.

Directions to Shuttle

Engineer Pass is 0.90 miles farther uphill from the trailhead.

American Flats. From left to right is Wildhorse Peak, Wetterhorn, Matterhorn, Uncompahgre Peaks

Summary

This hike provides a variety of scenery and terrain. It starts on a high mesa with wonderful vistas of Uncompahgre, Matterhorn, Wetterhorn, Wildhorse and even Coxcomb peaks. In season wildflowers thrive in the expansive meadows. Hike downhill, then back uphill through beautiful green valleys bordered by dramatic rocks and walls. The scenery is constantly changing.

Trail Description

Climb the short, easy hill to American Flats. Immediately there are superb views of the major 14er peaks that make Lake City famous: Uncompahgre, Matterhorn, and Wetterhorn. Hike through the flower filled mesa following intermittent tracks and cairns with wood posts. A little confusion arises at ❷ where two faint tracks diverge and it is difficult to see a post marker because they are often quite far apart. One track goes uphill (left) to the west and makes a noticeable switchback on a rocky ridge. The track you want to follow goes due north, towards the dramatic Wildhorse Peak, downhill to the right. This is magnificent, wide open country. At ❸ is a signed junction. Go left to Bear Creek Trail (SW) uphill following the post markers to the top. After the Wilderness sign ❹, once again the trail becomes vague. Keep heading east. You may notice a post far distant to the south but do not go that way. Heading east, soon you will see another post and the trail again. Large prominent rock outcrops and peaks dominate this section as the trail descends Bear Creek drainage. The trail gets lost again at ❺ but now you can see it as it ascends the Engineer Pass drainage. Cross the creek and you will meet that ascending trail. The Engineer Pass trail is lush and green with healthy trees, tumbling creeks and varied views. It is a delight.

Bear Creek

Descending Bear Creek drainage

GPS	Mile	Latitude	Longitude	Elevation	Comment
1	0.00	37,58.651N	107,34.628W	12,399′	Start at Horsethief TH.
2	1.25	37,59.355N	107,35.075W	12,487′	Trails diverge. Go right (due north) downhill.
3	2.15	38,00.054N	107,34.826W	12,327′	Marked junction: go left (SW) uphill.
4	2.61	37,59.840N	107,35.203W	12,627′	Wilderness sign. Trail is faint. Continue east.
5	4.20	37,59.799N	107,36.482W	11,449′	Trail gets lost in weeds. Cross stream. Can see the trail on the other side.
6	4.46	37,59.596N	107,36.564W	11,035′	Marked junction: Go left to Engineer Pass; Right goes to Bear Creek TH.
7	6.93	37,58.439N	107,35.125W	12,809′	End of trail at Engineer Pass. Meet shuttle or walk down road to vehicle.

Meet the Authors

Anne and Mike Poe have been adventuring together since their marriage in 1970.From whitewater kayaking to glacier skiing, to bicycling for six months at a time, their adventures began to expand more and more. In the 1980's Anne started writing and photographing all their trips so the memories would always stay fresh. She published numerous articles in various outdoor magazines.

In 1984, they bicycled from Costa Rica to Peru. In successive years, they bicycled from Alaska to Idaho; six months through New Zealand; six months around Australia; and finally, in 1997, a six month odyssey from Bali, Indonesia to Hong Kong, China. Anne wrote her first book, ***On Our Own: A Bicycling Adventure in Southeast Asia***, about that amazing journey. It is currently for sale on Amazon.com in print as well as in Kindle format.

From 1984 to 1990, they instructed downhill skiing in Vail, Colorado. During the summer months, they instructed Outward Bound Courses in the Boundary Waters Wilderness area of northern Minnesota. By 1990, backpacking Canada's wilderness trails became the new focus. For six summers, they returned to explore new areas, photograph, and write.

In 2004, they started hiking Colorado's more than 4,000 miles of trails. When they went to Crested Butte, they knew they had found a hiker's paradise. For four summers, they researched, hiked, photographed and mapped this marvelous area, and produced their first guidebook: ***Crested Butte Colorado: 60 Scenic Day Hikes***. When that sold out the first summer, before just printing another edition, they made revisions suggested by their followers and came out with the second edition: ***Crested Butte Colorado: 65 Scenic Day Hikes***. The book is a hot item in local stores as well as in REI and on Amazon.com.

Summer 2011, they hiked trails in Silverton & Ouray, Colorado with the intention of producing another book. They knew the area's potential from having hiked many of the area trails over the years. In spring of 2012, they introduced: ***Southwest Colorado: High Country Day Hikes***. You will find it in many stores in Silverton & Ouray as well as in REI and on Amazon.com.

Telluride is perhaps the most well-known historic mining town in the southwest region of Colorado. The Poe's knew the area well from past years so they spent the summer of 2012 putting together this selection of hikes.

All those years in Colorado, they spent the off seasons of April, May, and October in Moab, Utah hiking trails for another new book: ***Utah National Parks, Arches and Canyonlands Day Hikes***.

Hikers from all over continue to be enthusiastic about this new style of hiking guides that the Poe's are producing. So, put your boots on and go take a hike! The information you need is in your hands.

Become our fan on facebook: **facebook.com/takeahikeguidebooks**.
Get updated trail information, and leave feedback or comments.

Anne is an Alpha. Alpha-1 is a lung emphysema that is inherited. It is progressive and life-long. She had lost 30% of her lung capacity before the disorder was discovered and abated through augmentation therapy. There are only 10,000 Americans currently diagnosed correctly, with a potential 100,000 possible cases. An estimated 20 million Americans are carriers of the abnormal genes. At risk groups include chronic COPD, irreversible asthma, and emphysema sufferers. Her goal is to bring awareness of the disorder to a public place. For more information, go to www.alpha-1foundation.org.

Utah National Parks: Arches & Canyonlands Day Hikes

by Anne and Mike Poe

Published Spring 2013

Hiking Guide for the world famous Utah Parks of Arches and Canyonlands. A full color guide in the popular new style created by Anne & Mike Poe. Available for purchase in local Moab stores, local and park visitor centers. Also in west and southwest Colorado stores, REI and Amazon.com.

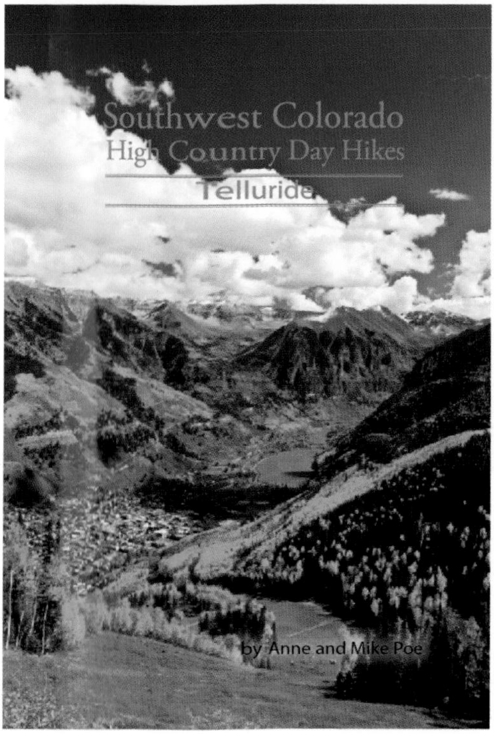

Southwest Colorado High Country Day Hikes Telluride

by Anne and Mike Poe

Published Spring 2013

We chose 35 routes especially for the visitor to world famous Telluride Colorado. Includes hikes for all ability levels. Purchase in local stores and surrounding towns, REI, and on Amazon.com.

Crested Butte Colorado 65 Scenic Day Hikes

by Anne and Mike Poe

2nd Edition Published Spring 2012

One book devoted just to the incredibly scenic trails in Crested Butte. Available for purchase in many Crested Butte stores, in Gunnison, Ouray, Silverton, Durango, Ridgway, Montrose and Telluride. Also available at REI and on Amazon.com.

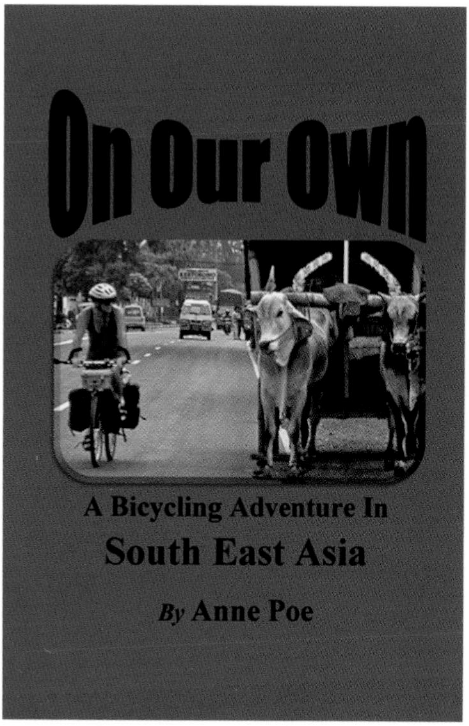

On Our Own: A Bicycling Adventure in Southeast Asia

by Anne and Mike Poe

Published Spring 2011

An 8,000-mile journey by bicycle through the heart of Southeast Asia. Available on Amazon.com in paperback and kindle formats.